DATE DUE

DEMCO 38-297

Sixth Edition

PURCHASING:
Principles
and Applications

Stuart F. Heinritz

Paul V. Farrell, C.P.M.

Managing Editor of *Purchasing World*

PRENTICE-HALL, INC., Englewood Cliffs, N.J. 07632

Library of Congress Cataloging in Publication Data

HEINRITZ, STUART F.(DATE)
   Purchasing: principles and applications.

   Bibliography: p. 475
   Includes index.
   1. Purchasing. I. Farrell, Paul V., joint
author. II. Title.
HF5437.H4 1981   658.7'2   80-22411
ISBN 0-13-742163-X

Editorial/ production supervision and interior
   design by Richard C. Laveglia
Cover design by Carol Zawislak
Manufacturing buyer: Gordon Osbourne

Printed in the United States of America

10 9 8 7 6 5 4 3

Prentice-Hall International, Inc., *London*
Prentice-Hall of Australia Pty. Limited, *Sydney*
Prentice-Hall of Canada, Ltd., *Toronto*
Prentice-Hall of India Private Limited, *New Delhi*
Prentice-Hall of Japan, Inc., *Tokyo*
Prentice-Hall of Southeast Asia Pte. Ltd., *Singapore*
Whitehall Books Limited, *Wellington, New Zealand*

Contents

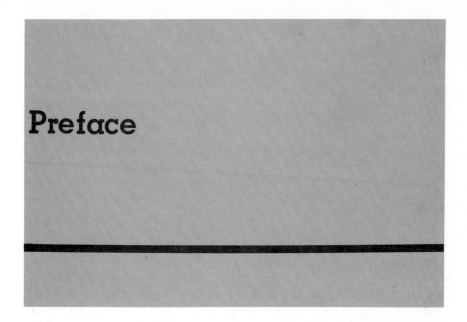

Preface

The steady upward growth in the scope and status of the purchasing function—in industry, in government, and in institutions—that can be charted from previous editions of this book has accelerated considerably in recent years. The gradual shift of purchasing from being a rather passive service to being active and participatory is complete; the managerial-type purchasing organization has become the rule rather than the exception.

This greater importance of the purchasing function may be attributed to a number of things: the determination and superior performance of progressive purchasing executives, the relatively sudden awakening of management to the importance of materials in the operation of an enterprise, or simply the course of events. In any case, modern purchasing managers now find themselves shouldering greater and more complex responsibilities than ever before. Top management today judges the performance of purchasing personnel and departments by the same criteria that are applied to other functions—the impact of their operations on the "bottom line," whether or not that line represents profit in business, or more efficiency at lower cost in governments and institutions.

One major cause of purchasing's leap into the foreground of modern management was the 1973–1974 economic crunch triggered by the oil embargo. In the face of soaring prices and shortages of critical materials worldwide at that time, purchasing managers in general performed minor and major prodigies in helping their organizations to keep operating. They and their managements learned many lessons from their experiences in those difficult years: the need for more and better purchasing and planning in a turbulent world; the uncertainty of a long-range supply of some critical materials; the necessity for intensive search of substitutes and alternatives; the awareness that the purchasing manager's real market for materials, components, and equipment is the entire world, regardless of geographical and political boundaries; and the importance of cultivating suppliers who have the ability to help with materials problems. The list could go on. According to David K. Barnes, vice president and general manager of DuPont's Energy and Materials Department (the recent creation of which emphasizes the developments in the realm of purchasing practices):

> In this suddenly mad world, corporate management quickly redis-
> covered the purchasing function and came to the conclusion that planning
> to achieve future supply needs and executing those plans well was going to
> be a major factor in determing future earnings.[1]

Mr. Barnes's use of the word "rediscovered" is significant. None of the ideas or techniques just noted are actually new; various professional purchasing executives have been using them for decades. What is new, however, is the intensity and sophistication with which they began to be applied and the interest in them displayed by managements that heretofore had been indifferent to the potential inherent in scientific purchasing.

The economic turmoil of the 1970s was not, however, the only factor producing changes in the purchasing environment. For some time now, a number of far-reaching developments have been affecting all businesses, and their impact has been felt in the purchasing function. Efforts by government and the private sector to bring minority businesses into the mainstream, for example, placed new and serious responsibilities on purchasing. Consumerism in its various forms, occupational safety and health legislation, and environmental regulations all required new responses by purchasing managers.

This revised edition deals with basic principles and procedures that have been adapted by purchasing and materials managers to meet the challenges and responsibilities of an era of rapid change. In addition, it has new chapters on such significant developments as materials management, the purchase of transportation services, purchasing in international markets, and purchasing in nonprofit organizations.

The book is designed as a text that business students at all levels can use, whether they have a particular interest in purchasing as a career or

---

[1]"The Purchasing Agent Gains More Clout," *Business Week*, January 13, 1975.

require knowledge of the function as a part of their overall education. It will serve equally well in training programs for practicing personnel. Finally, it will continue to be a current general reference on purchasing and materials management operations.

Textbook authors must necessarily be somewhat arbitrary in the presentation of their material. Users, on the other hand, may have varying ideas on the order in which different phases of the subject should be considered. Some instructors, for example, believe that students of purchasing should be introduced early to some of the more dramatic aspects of purchasing, such as negotiation and value analysis; others think that a grounding in fundamental principles and systems should come first. To aid those teachers and students who prefer a flexible approach to the study of purchasing concepts, we have grouped the twenty-three chapters of the book under six major section headings that deal, respectively, with (1) the purchasing department's overall position and responsibility, (2) the administrative organization and functioning of purchasing, (3) basic purchasing activities, (4) specialized purchasing operations that have evolved in recent years, (5) legal and ethical responsibilites in purchasing, and (6) the evaluation of purchasing performance. It need hardly be said that the sections and chapters are not presented in order of importance.

Case studies have been grouped together in the appendix rather than placed singly at the end of individual chapters. This has been done to make it easier for instructors to make maximum use of those cases that involve principles covered in more than one chapter.

Space does not permit acknowledging with thanks the information and guidance that literally scores of purchasing executives have given us in the preparation of various editions. In thanking the following purchasing professionals, who assisted generously in the current revision, we wish to express our gratitude to the many others who have been so helpful in the past.

Thomas F. X. Dillon, *Purchasing;* George E. Howlett and George Weyhrich, Hyster Company; Caleb L. Johnson, Kohler Company; Harry Johnson, consultant, formerly with Westinghouse Electric Corporation; Neil Markee, National Association of Educational Buyers; Anne Repko, Howmedica, Inc.; Clifton L. Smith, International Harvester Company; Claude J. Trafas, Wilmington Medical Center.

Also, the authors would like to express their gratitude to Professors Charles Hoitash, Robert D. Miller, and Russell Sloan for their help in reviewing the manuscript.

Section I

PURCHASING: A MODERN MANAGEMENT FUNCTION

Role
And Scope
Of Purchasing

1

Every manufacturing process requires materials, supplies, and services. Before men or machines can start turning out products, the materials must be on hand, and there must be assurance of a continuing supply to meet production needs and schedules. The quality of materials must be adequate for the intended purpose and suitable for the process and the equipment used. If the material fails on any of these points, the results can be costly: expensive delays (with the cost of the delay often greatly exceeding the value of the materials themselves), inefficient production, inferior products, broken delivery promises, and unhappy customers.

If a company wants to stay competitive and earn satisfactory profits, it must procure materials at the lowest cost consistent with quality and service requirements. At the same time, it must keep the administrative cost of buying and the cost of material inventories at an economic level. These elementary considerations are the basis of the whole function and science of industrial purchasing.

These concerns relate, as well, to purchasing in nonprofit organizations, such as governmental agencies and various types of institutions. Pressed by shortages of funds and rising costs, these service entities are seeking to maximize operational efficiency with minimum expenditure. Good purchasing is a critical element in their efforts to achieve this objective. (Purchasing for nonprofit organizations is discussed more fully in Chapter 19.)

PURCHASING'S SHARE OF THE SALES DOLLAR

On the average, in the manufacturing industry more than half of every dollar taken in as income from sales of products is expended in the purchase of materials, supplies, and equipment needed to produce the goods. The First National City Bank of New York (Citibank) annually analyzes the disposition of receipts by the one hundred largest manufacturers in the United States. Invariably, these studies show that the costs of goods and services purchased from others amounted to more than 50 percent of the sales dollar. Perhaps the most significant indicators of the scope and importance of purchasing in relation to sales, however, are the actual annual reports of companies (see Figure 1-1).

Examples of the percentages of income spent on purchased goods and services in a representative group of companies reported in their annual reports of the past few years are as follows:

Air Reduction Company, 59.9 percent
Ford Motor Company, 63.0 percent
A.B. Dick Company, 55.0 percent
Robertshaw Controls Company, 33.3 percent

In the majority of manufacturing companies, materials costs are found to be reasonably close to the average, from 40 percent to 60 percent of total product cost. But, in special cases, purchases may range widely beyond these limits, according to the type of business and the kinds of materials used. Purchase expenditure in nonprofit organizations generally represent a lower percentage of income (see Chapter 19).

In the basic processing of a single raw material that in the processed state makes up the bulk of the finished product, the purchase cost of material is generally a high proportion of finished product cost—up to 85 percent or more. Examples of this are found in those industries producing fabrics, shoes, food, and similar products. A high degree of mechanization, which reduces labor cost per unit of product, also tends to make materials cost a higher percentage of the total, even though the materials themselves may be relatively low in terms of unit cost. Most mass-production industries are in this category. The same is true of assembly operations, in which product components are purchased in more highly fabricated form and have thus acquired additional costs in the earlier stages of fabrication, prior to purchase.

On the other hand, in extractive industries such as mining or oil production, in which the product is manufactured from purchased materials but comes from natural deposits, the purchase ratio is relatively low. Purchased materials and services in such industries generally account for about 25 percent of the sales dollar.

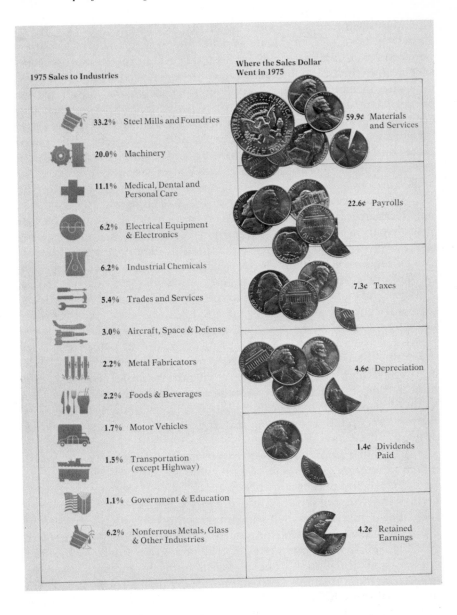

1975 Sales to Industries

Where the Sales Dollar Went in 1975

33.2% Steel Mills and Foundries

20.0% Machinery

11.1% Medical, Dental and Personal Care

6.2% Electrical Equipment & Electronics

6.2% Industrial Chemicals

5.4% Trades and Services

3.0% Aircraft, Space & Defense

2.2% Metal Fabricators

2.2% Foods & Beverages

1.7% Motor Vehicles

1.5% Transportation (except Highway)

1.1% Government & Education

6.2% Nonferrous Metals, Glass & Other Industries

59.9¢ Materials and Services

22.6¢ Payrolls

7.3¢ Taxes

4.6¢ Depreciation

1.4¢ Dividends Paid

4.2¢ Retained Earnings

Figure 1-1. Air Reduction Company's purchases of materials and services accounted for almost 60 percent of the sales dollar as shown in the Airco annual report for that year.

Manufacturing operations that involve highly skilled workmanship and a large labor factor applied to smaller quantities of material also show purchases as a smaller percentage of total cost. In service industries in which, after the original facilities have been installed, supplies are the somewhat incidental means of implementing the service, purchases are likely to be relatively low in proportion to the total cost of doing business. For example, a typical railroad operating statement shows expenditures for equipment, materials, and supplies, including fuel, as slightly less than 25 percent of the total cost of providing and maintaining the railroad service. Even so, this item has represented an expenditure of nearly $65 million annually.

In some manufacturing industries, despite rising wages, the ratio of purchased materials cost to total product cost is generally rising. This fact is due in part to increasing mechanization. It is also due, in great measure, to the growing trend toward specialization in manufacturing. The automobile industry, for example, buys batteries and tires, wheels and axles, carburetors, springs, bumpers, grilles, completely wired dashboard assemblies, and many other parts from specialized makers of such products, to be incorporated into the finished car. Thus, the prices paid for these items by the automobile manufacturer include the supplier's labor and indirect charges and the supplier's profits. Yet, for the automobile manufacturer, these prices represent true "purchased materials costs." Several decades ago, when more of the actual parts manufacturing was being done in the automobile plants, average materials cost in the industry was about 52 percent of total product cost. Today, when many components are procured in fabricated form, materials costs have risen to an average of about 60 percent.

The dollar amounts involved in purchasing, even in organizations of moderate size, are substantial. They demand prudent, skillful administration. Efficiency in purchasing affords opportunities for making important savings and avoiding serious waste and loss. The effect on product cost is such that it may easily spell the difference between leadership in an industry and an untenable competitive position. Management properly gives close and continuous attention to labor costs, production efficiency, and costs of distribution. The materials item is sometimes taken for granted, as if it were a fixed cost and nothing could be done about it. Yet, in terms of the value received in return for purchase expenditures, this factor also reflects good and poor management and performance. It is, in fact, of equal importance with other functions of industrial activity and the other elements of product cost in attaining successful, profitable company operation.

The simple mathematics of the situation dramatizes the powerful effect that good purchasing can have on company profits. Using a hypothetical case, a national publication showed that there is as much profit in a 1.5 percent purchasing saving in an average manufacturing company as there is in a 10 percent sales increase.

The publication assumed a sales volume of $60 million in the XYZ Company, of which 53.7 percent, or $32.2 million, went for purchased material, supplies, and services. The average profit margin in the manufacturing industries at the time was 8.2 percent before taxes. Therefore, it would have taken $6 million in additional sales—or a 10 percent increase—to make an additional $492,000 profit. But a reduction of only 1.5 percent in purchasing costs would mean an identical $492,000 that could be added to profit.[1]

A prominent management consultant has suggested another way to estimate purchasing's potential economic impact.[2] He recommended that management set a reasonable improvement goal for each broad parameter of company profitability (e.g., sales volume, gross profit margins, labor costs, etc.) and then set one for purchasing—a reduction of 5 percent in materials cost, for example. A profit sensitivity analysis, such as that shown in Figure 1-2, may reveal that the profit potential in improved purchasing easily outstrips the potential for gains in those other areas that normally are more closely scrutinized by top management. It should be noted that the impact of purchasing in nonprofit organizations must be judged against other standards (see Chapter 19).

EFFECT OF PURCHASING ON OTHER COSTS

Direct expenditure for materials and components is by no means the only way in which purchasing affects end-product costs. The effect of delays due to lack of materials has already been noted. Shutdowns and waiting time at machines may be charged to production costs, but the end result is the same. More insidious is the situation in which purchased materials are on hand as needed but are not uniform in quality or dimension, or are otherwise of inferior workability. Improper materials impair manufacturing efficiency and add to the "hidden" costs of production. In addition, they may entail extra costs for closer inspection and result in excessive waste and rejections that sacrifice not only the spoiled material itself but also the time and labor expended on it.

[1] *Purchasing Magazine* advertisement, *Harvard Business Review* Vol. 41 (March–April 1963): 181.
[2] Frank L. Bauer, "Better Purchasing: High Rewards at Low Risk," *Journal of Purchasing and Materials Management* Vol. 12 (Summer 1976): 3–9.

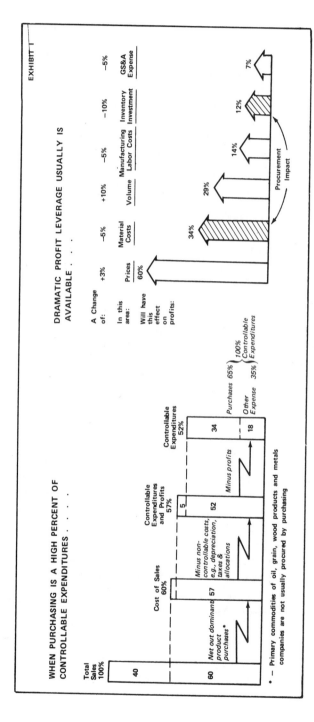

Figure 1-2. Sensitivity analysis demonstrates that the profit potential in improved purchasing may outstrip potential gains in other areas.

8

Such instances obviously show faulty or inadequate purchasing performance, which could be avoided by giving more and better attention to the buying function. But there are other cases in which purchasing may be done strictly in accordance with stated requirements, on time, and at a favorable price, yet the end cost may be unnecessarily high. This occurs, for example, when the specifications for a material or component are so rigid that the purchasing department cannot exercise its special talents in procuring the item. There may be a limited number of suppliers for the product—possibly only one. The specifications might automatically exclude commercially standard items or otherwise acceptable substitutes. Factors such as these are inherent in the economics of purchasing decisions. An organization can expect to get the most advantageous end costs only when purchasing factors are balanced against factors of utility and usage, when materials cost is considered in its relation to other costs.

Sound purchasing frequently discloses cases in which it eventually costs less to buy more expensive materials, as either product components or operating supplies, when the additional cost will be offset by manufacturing economies. The reverse may also be true in other cases. It may be economical to incur some additional manufacturing cost to take advantage of substantially cheaper materials that are adequate for the purpose. Or it may be found economical to abandon certain manufacturing operations that are presently performed in the plant, when parts so produced could be bought at lower cost from an outside supplier.

PURCHASING'S PART IN THE TOTAL SYSTEM

Purchasing is not an end in itself. Materials and supplies are bought because they are needed. Because the activities of purchasing have the primary purpose of implementing the work of other departments by procuring these goods, it is sometimes regarded as merely a service function. Purchasing can be carried on under this concept with partial effectiveness. The implication, however, is that purchasing considerations are subordinated to the aims, desires, and policies—or even to the preferences and whims—of the departments served. This is to sacrifice, by default, the larger benefits and full potentialities of scientific purchasing and decisions.

The modern view is that purchasing's role is coordinate with those of other major phases of company activity. It is neither subordinate or dominant, but works closely with other departments toward the common purpose of profitable operation. This viewpoint was well expressed in an interview over a decade ago by Mark Shepherd, Jr., president of Texas Instruments:

We look to our purchasing departments to support our engineering efforts with ideas and suggestions and liaison with vendors, to support our marketing effort by pointing out new business opportunities and suggesting marketing approaches (not reciprocity) which can be helpful. We expect our purchasing departments, because they are in the position to be so well informed, to be a source of innovations in their own operations and for the other operations within the company.

There is a tendency on the part of many to think that the purchasing mission is to buy things, whereas I think the purchasing mission is to be part of a larger system creating profits and growth. I'm not satisfied to have buyers sit at their desks waiting for paper requisitions to arrive and then converting these into other papers and sending them out to vendors. I want them to become more informed and influential and less simple data transmitters.[3]

Other chief executives have voiced similar sentiments over the years. Another typical top-level view of purchasing's "mission" was voiced by I. Andrew Rader, president of Allen-Bradley Company:

Purchasing provides feedback on changes that are going to affect key decisions on new product selection, product design, choice of materials and planning . . . . especially cash planning.[4]

Where the purchasing officer is thus "a member of the management team," the principles of economical, scientific purchasing can be applied without hindrance, on their own merits, and there is a constant incentive for improved purchasing methods and performance. Also, suggestions regarding materials and policies can be initiated in purchasing, with the assurance that they will receive consideration and be weighed against other facts in arriving at a final decision.

In this sense, purchasing is a function of management. In yet another sense, purchasing is in itself a true management function. It involves the management of materials in flow, from the establishment of sources and "pipelines," through inventory stores, to the ultimate delivery at production stations as needed. At every stage there are decisions to be made as to quality, quantity, timing, source, and cost. And these decisions must be keyed to constantly changing business and economic conditions that alter the immediate objectives and policies of purchasing from month to month, even from day to day.

[3] Mark Shepherd, Jr., "Buyers Must Be More Than Data Transmitters," *Purchasing Magazine,* January 11, 1968, p. 61.

[4] Denise Brootman, "Top Executives Can Add Punch to Purchasing," *Purchasing Magazine,* January 21, 1975, p. 34.

A review of the varied conditions that have prevailed at some time or other over a relatively short span of years shows how purchasing must be adjusted to current demands. Among these have been periods of extraordinary expansion and high activity; periods of recession and retrenchment; eras of "profitless prosperity"; prolonged "sellers' markets" and "buyers' markets"; material shortages during which manufacturing schedules were determined not by how much could be made and sold, but by how much raw material could be purchased; and great technological advances that introduced many new materials and processes, made others obsolete, and substantially changed the character of things to be purchased.

In the early 1970s, the industrialized nations of the world awoke to the realities of long-range shortages of materials, higher prices brought on by cartel-like agreements among producing nations (e.g., OPEC, the Organization of Petroleum Exporting Countries), and the sluggish growth of new capacity for the production of important raw materials.

Applied to changing conditions such as these, today's good purchasing policy could cause trouble tomorrow. In the materials crisis of 1973–1974, purchasing managers occasionally resorted to tactics that they would have resisted in normal times: barter transactions with suppliers; payment of black or gray market prices; and agreement to favorable payment terms to suppliers, such as prepayment, accelerated payment, or lower than normal discounts. On the positive side, however, as shown by a survey among the *Fortune* 500 companies following the crisis, purchasing absorbed new responsibilities. There was a trend toward giving individual buyers more latitude to negotiate terms with vendors, seek out new supply sources, commit company funds, and specialize on certain products. In addition, many companies gave their purchasing departments such additional duties as forecasting, and storeskeeping and inventory control. Purchasing also participated in certain general management activities in which assurance of future availability of materials is an important factor—for example, new product development and long-range corporate planning.[5]

The lesson of all this is that purchasing is a function in which maximum flexibility to adapt to changing circumstances is essential. Changes must not only be recognized, they should be anticipated, and purchasing methods should be adjusted, or developed, to cope with them.

[5] Stuart U. Rich, "Coping with Shortages: The Past as a Guide to the Future," in *Guide to Purchasing, Supplement 1.10* (New York: 1975) National Association of Purchasing Management, Inc., New York, N.Y.

RESPONSIBILITY FOR PURCHASING

Purchasing responsibility, as with other major management and operating functions, is generally delegated to a specific person or a special department in the company organization. In few concerns of any substantial size today do individual departments do their own buying, of either production materials or operating supplies. In some cases, the specialized purchasing department comes under the jurisdiction of the production manager. This is a carry-over from earlier days, when purchasing was regarded primarily as a service to the manufacturing department. Most companies set up purchasing, or materials, management as a completely separate department, with the chief purchasing officer reporting directly to the executive who has the overall responsibility for profitable operation, that is, the president, executive vice president, general manager, or plant or divisional manager.

The advantages of this system of allocating responsibility and concentrating authority for buying are inherent in the economic principle of the division of labor and in all functional organization:

1. Better control is assured by isolating the materials factor, with one person or department directly responsible to management for handling this function and one complete set of records pertaining to purchase transactions, commitments, and expenditures.
2. Concentration on purchasing develops specialized knowledge, skills, and procedures that result in more efficient and economical procurement.
3. Better performance may be expected in other departments when engineers, production executives, office managers, and other department heads are relieved of the detailed buying responsibility and of the interruptions and interviews incidental to buying. The same principle holds in a nonindustrial organization, such as a hospital, in which the professional staff is often the target of strong selling efforts.
4. Divorcing the purchasing function from the influence or domination of other departments, whose primary interests lie in other directions, affords a greater likelihood that the economic and profit potentials of purchasing will receive more consideration on their own merits and thus may make a greater contribution to overall profitable operation.

The purchasing responsibility is sometimes defined as buying materials of the right quality, in the right quantity, at the right time, at the right price, from the right source. This is a broad generalization, indicating the scope of the purchasing function, that involves policy decisions and analyses of various alternative possibilities prior to the act of purchase.

The significance of the definition depends, of course, on the interpretation of what is "right" and requires the consideration of many factors that are discussed in detail in later chapters. At this point, we are more concerned with the objectives to be attained.

The fundamental objectives of a purchasing department for a manufacturing industry may be summarized as follows:

1. To maintain continuity of supply to support the manufacturing schedule.
2. To do so with the minimum investment in materials inventory consistent with safety and economic advantage.
3. To avoid duplication, waste, and obsolescence with respect to materials.
4. To maintain standards of quality in materials, based on suitability for use.
5. To procure materials at the lowest cost consistent with the quality and service required.
6. To maintain the company's competitive position in its industry and to conserve its profits, insofar as materials costs are concerned.
7. To analyze and report on long-range availability and costs of major purchased items.
8. To continually search the market for new and alternative ideas, products, and materials, the adoption of which might improve company efficiency and profitability.

The same principles apply to purchasing in fields other than manufacturing. In a public utility company, for example, the first point would be to support the service, operating, and construction schedule rather than the manufacturing schedule; in purchasing for a municipal government, it would be to support the various services, such as police and fire protection, maintenance of streets, parks, and public buildings, garbage collection and disposal, and all other activities essential to a complete civic administration. In buying for a hospital, a university, or a governmental unit, in which the profit motive and competitive factors are absent, the sixth point could be rephrased to express a similar thought. It would relate to getting maximum value for the expenditure of a fixed budget appropriation for materials or, to take a word from the slogan of one eminently successful municipal purchasing department, to getting additional "mileage" out of the tax dollar. Purchasing is done to implement other phases of company operation. It starts, in every case, with a need that is established in the company's operating program.

Thus, a purchase requires authorization. This may be formal or informal. Sometimes it exists only in the form of a manufacturing quota for a given calendar period. The purchasing manager is apprised of this quota and all that it entails in the way of material and supply requirements. Sometimes it is embodied in the bill of materials, either for a standard line of products or for products built to special order. At other times it is expressed in the form of a purchase requisition for required material. For standard materials in common and repetitive use, the purchasing manager usually has considerable latitude to exercise judgment in purchasing for stock in advance of specific requirements. His or her decisions are based upon experience, rate of use, sales estimates, and other indicators and are usually in conformance with an established inventory policy.

In purchasing for a government unit or for institutions, purchases for a particular department or account are usually strictly limited by the annual budget or the unexpended portion thereof (which is another form of authorization). Specialized procedures and policies employed in buying for government and for nonprofit institutions are discussed in Chapter 19.

In governmental purchasing, and in about 20 percent of industrial operations, there is a monetary limit to the amount that may be spent for any single purchase without securing specific approval of the expenditure from general management. These monetary limitations vary from several hundred dollars to several thousand dollars. Frequently, in a single company, such limitations are scaled according to the type of purchase involved, being generally closer in respect to items of equipment and capital purchases and more liberal in respect to materials and supplies.

Purchases of capital equipment are usually controlled by special regulations, and purchasing department participation may be limited to procuring the basic data on what is available for the purpose, placing the order only after a decision has been reached by committee or executive action. In recent years, however, there has been a trend toward placing specialized equipment buyers in the purchasing department, giving these people relatively broad authority to recommend purchases of specific makes. Some raw materials may also be excluded specifically from purchasing department jurisdiction under certain conditions, although this is less prevalent than formerly. Again, the modern trend is to bring even the most specialized commodity buying within the general framework of the purchasing department, although with somewhat greater latitude and independence of action than for standard or routine requirements.

The general statement of purchasing objectives limits the purchasing department to procurement for actual or anticipated use. This rules out purchases made primarily for the purpose or in the hope of inventory value appreciation or speculative profits on materials. Such buying—though it may be effected through the purchasing department—is a matter for general management to decide. The outlawing of speculative purchases, however, does not preclude the exercise of purchasing judgment in adjusting the buying and inventory program to economic and market conditions. The purchasing manager may boost purchases in anticipation of rising prices and work closer to actual current requirements when a price decline is in prospect.

RESPONSIBILITY FOR SPECIFYING

Ultimate responsibility for the type and quality of materials to be bought must rest with those who use them and are responsible for results. In this sense, the using departments are in the relation of customers to the purchasing department, and they must be satisfied. But this does not place the responsibility or authority for selection in the using department. Rather, theirs is a responsibility of accurate definition or specification of the product, in terms of formula or analysis, accepted commercial standards, blue-prints or dimensional tolerances, or the intended purpose of the material. Most industrial materials, supplies, and equipment can be bought in competitive markets and from a variety of sources, and it is the function of purchasing to select the particular material and source most advantageous to the company, patronizing two or more alternative sources if it is desirable to stimulate competition or assure continuity of supply, always bearing in mind that the essential requirement, as defined, must be met.

In addition to quality, the request for materials involves a statement of the quantity desired and the date or time at which they will be needed. It is the responsibility of the purchasing manager to check these factors against the actual need, from his or her knowledge of the operating program or from his or her record of past purchases and use, and to question any apparent deviation from normal requirements, even though the authorization of the request may otherwise be in good order. This is a part of the purchasing manager's duty to avoid duplication, excessive stocks, and unnecessary rush orders that would disrupt the procurement program and incur extra transportation costs.

When the quantity and delivery requirements have been established, it is the responsibility of purchasing to decide whether the goods shall be bought in a single lot, or in a series of smaller transactions over a period of time from one or more suppliers or on a single long-term contract with delivery schedules to be specified according to the need. All these considerations, weighed in conjunction with quantity discounts, carrying charges, market conditions, and the like, have a bearing on the ultimate cost of the material, so that there is a considerable range of opportunity or advantage open to purchasing judgment, even within the strict specification of quantity and delivery requirements.

Commercial aspects of the transaction—negotiations as to price, delivery, guarantees, terms, and conditions of the contract and adjustments as to over- and undershipments or deficiencies in quality—are wholly purchasing responsibilities.

The extent to which the purchasing department is responsible beyond the point of issuing the order varies in different companies. Instances can be found in which this act marks the end of purchasing jurisdiction, but they are not typical; the test of purchasing performance lies in satisfactory deliveries against the order. In many companies, the purchasing function is interpreted to include the follow-up for delivery, reconciling receipts and vendors' invoices with the purchase order, and passing invoices for payment. In well over half the cases, it includes the responsibility of storekeeping and complete accountability for materials until they are issued to the using departments. Inspection and quality testing of deliveries for acceptance are sometimes included in the purchasing function.

TYPICAL PURCHASING ACTIVITIES

Operating a purchasing department to meet these responsibilities involves a variety of detailed assignments, of both an administrative and a routine nature. Typical activities of even the simplest purchasing program include

Basic Information
  Maintaining purchase records
  Maintaining price records
  Maintaining stock and consumption records
  Maintaining vendor records
  Maintaining specification files
  Maintaining catalog files
Research
  Conducting market studies
  Conducting material studies
  Conducting cost analysis

    Investigating supply sources
    Inspecting suppliers' plants
    Developing supply sources
    Developing alternate materials and sources
Procurement
    Checking requisitions
    Securing quotations
    Analyzing quotations
    Choosing between contract or open-market purchase
    Scheduling purchases and deliveries
    Interviewing salespersons
    Negotiating contracts
    Issuing purchase orders
    Checking legal conditions of contracts
    Following up for delivery
    Checking receipt of materials
    Verifying invoices
    Corresponding with vendors
    Making adjustments with vendors
Materials Management
    Maintaining minimum stocks
    Maintaining inventory balance
    Improving inventory turnover
    Transferring materials
    Consolidating requirements
    Avoiding excess stocks and obsolescence
    Standardizing packages and containers
    Accounting for returnable containers
    Making periodic reports of commitments
Miscellaneous
    Making cost estimates
    Disposing of scrap and obsolete and surplus materials

AUXILIARY FUNCTIONS

In addition to the activities that are distinctly within the province of purchasing, there are a number of responsibilities that are typically shared with other departments by means of recommendations or by decisions reached through conference or committee action in which the purchasing manager or representative has a voice. Among these responsibilities are:

Office practice	Materials budget
Determination of whether to manufacture or buy	Inventory control
	Selection of capital equipment
Standardization	Construction projects
Specifications	Production programs dependent
Substitution of materials	on availability of materials
Acceptance testing	

A typical position description detailing the functions and responsibilites of industrial purchasing executives is shown in Figure 1-3.

The list given here is not exhaustive as activities vary among different companies according to the character or the enterprise and its philosophy of management. Storeskeeping and traffic management, for example, are responsibilities of the purchasing department in some companies. Others make receiving and receiving inspection purchasing responsibilities. When the purchasing department's jurisdiction extends into these and other functions—such as materials control, warehousing, and materials handling (or when purchasing along with these functions is put under unified control)—what occurs in fact, if not in name, is the establishment of a type of *materials management* department. The concept of materials management and the different organizational forms that it takes are discussed in Chapter 6.

One point that is made clear in our review of the purchasing activity is that the buying operation has a significant relationship with almost every other department in the organization. The closest sort of cooperation must be maintained with production, finance, accounting, engineering, maintenance, sales, office management, and general management.

NEED FOR MANAGEMENT UNDERSTANDING

Top management has an obligation to see the total organization and profit picture and to see each part in proper perspective. It has an obligation to demand not only that each part function adequately within its own area of responsibility, but also that it make the greatest possible contribution toward the total operating and profit objectives. This entails defining the areas of functional responsibility and authority and correlating them in the larger scheme so that each will have scope to realize its full potential.

Purchasing is inescapably a part of that picture. Therefore, the

Title: Director of Purchases

BASIC FUNCTION:

Responsible to the Vice President-General Manager for directing the purchasing activities of the Company in accordance with established broad policies.

BASIC OBJECTIVE:

To secure for the Company its requirements of raw materials, purchase parts, equipment, and operating supplies at the lowest possible cost consistent with accepted standards for quality and service.

MAJOR DUTIES AND RESPONSIBILITIES:

1. Policies and Programs
   a. To recommend to the Vice President-General Manager broad purchasing policies and programs in accordance with his forecast of economic and price trends in the domestic and foreign markets.
   b. To establish procedures for the control of purchases.
   c. To coordinate Company specifications with those of the trade.
   d. To search for new materials of present or future interest to the Company.
   e. To promote standardization of all purchases.
2. Organization
   a. To develop and maintain a purchasing organization that adequately meets the needs of the Company.
   b. To carry out Company's personal relations policies.
   c. To approve position description of all immediate subordinates.
   d. To approve employment, promotion, change in compensation, or other employee movement personnel in the organization.
3. Negotiations and Procurement
   a. To engage in negotiations for materials requiring commitments over extended periods.
4. Sources of Supply
   a. To engage in the development of additional or alternate sources of supply for important materials.
   b. To direct Purchasing Agent and Assistant Purchasing Agent in similar activity.
   c. To promote, in collaboration with the Chemical Research and Mechanical Engineering Divisions, sources of supply for new or improved materials.
   d. To direct the maintenance of a list of acceptable vendors, a record of purchases, and a record of prices and terms of purchase.
5. Relations with Vendors
   a. To promote and maintain good Company relations with principal vendors.
   b. To direct Purchasing Agent and Assistant Purchasing Agent in similar activity.
6. Contracts
   To execute contractual agreements for the purchase of raw materials, purchased parts, equipment, and operating supplies, after view by the Company's Legal Counsel.
7. Purchase Forecasts and Budgets
   a. To prepare, in collaboration with the Controller's Division, purchase forecasts and expense budgets for approval and decision by the Vice President-General Manager.
   b. To submit such reports on the activities and future plans of the Purchasing Division as may be requested by Vice President-General Manager.
   c. To collaborate with Controller's Division in establishing purchase price standards.
   d. To review with Purchasing Agent and Assistant Purchasing Agent monthly material price variance statements submitted by the Controller's Division, and to recommend appropriate action.

LIMITS OF AUTHORITY:

1. To operate within established budget limits.
2. To implement major purchasing policy changes only after the approval of Vice President-General Manager.
3. To execute contractual agreements for the purchase of raw materials, equipment and operating supplies.
4. To execute Company purchase orders for items of capital equipment in excess of $500 and upon receipt of proper authorizations.
5. To approve recommendations of Purchasing Agent concerning employment, promotion, or change in compensation of personnel in the Division.
6. To approve expenses of Purchasing Agent and Assistant Purchasing Agent.
7. To present papers and make speeches to outside groups regarding Company activities and purchasing procedures only after obtaining approval of Vice President-General Manager.
8. To limit his line authority to his immediate subordinates.

RELATIONS WITH OTHERS:

1. Directly responsible to the Vice President-General Manager for the performance of the above duties.
2. Responsible for cooperating with all executives of the Company coordinating the activities of the Purchasing Division with other units of the Company.

MEASUREMENT OF PERFORMANCE:

The performance of the Director of Purchases will be measured by the effective degree with which he secures for the Company its requirements of raw materials, purchase parts, equipment, and operating supplies at the lowest possible cost consistent with accepted standards for quality and service, and the degree to which he satisfies the Vice President-General Manager with the performance of his duties.

Title: Assistant Purchasing Agent

BASIC FUNCTION:

Responsible to the Director of Purchases for purchasing new materials and purchased parts used in the manufacture of the Company's supply products.

BASIC OBJECTIVE:

To secure for the Company its requirements of raw materials and parts used in the manufacture of supply products at the lowest possible cost consistent with accepted standards for quality and service, and in accordance with established policies and procedures.

MAJOR DUTIES AND RESPONSIBILITIES:

1. Purchasing
   a. To purchase those items and materials for which he is responsible.
   b. To negotiate claims resulting from damaged or defective merchandise received from vendors.
   c. To negotiate the sale of scrap and surplus equipment only after approval of the Director of Purchases.
2. Sources of Supply
   a. To assist in the development of additional or alternate sources of supply.
   b. To promote, in collaboration with the Chemical and Research Engineering Division, sources of supply for new or improved materials.
   c. To maintain a list of acceptable vendors, a record of purchases, and a record of prices and terms of purchases.
3. Relations with Vendors
   To promote and maintain good Company relations with vendors.
4. Reports and Recommendations
   a. To submit such reports as may be required by the Director of Purchases on the activities for which he is responsible.
   b. To recommend to the Director of Purchases changes in policies, practices, and procedures.

LIMITS OF AUTHORITY:

To execute Company purchase orders in accordance with established schedules.

RELATIONS WITH OTHERS:

1. Directly responsible to the Director of Purchases for the performance of the above duties.
2. Responsible for collaborating with all departments of the Company in order to effectively meet their requirements and to achieve his basic objectives.

MEASUREMENT OF PERFORMANCE:

The performance of the Assistant Purchasing Agent will be measured by the effective degree with which he secures for the Company its requirements of materials and parts used in the manufacture of supply products at the lowest cost consistent with accepted standards for quality and service, and the degree to which he satisfies the Director of Purchases with the performance of his duties.

Figure 1-3. Typical position descriptions for purchasing executives reflect the broad scope of departmental responsibilities.

manager must be at least "literate" in respect to the objectives, opportunities, and methods of modern purchasing.

Without this understanding of purchasing principles, management lacks the means of even a rudimentary appraisal of purchasing performance. It is not enough to delegate the act of buying and to charge the buyer to procure needed materials at lowest cost. This quite literally authorizes the purchasing agent to become a "price buyer," the qualification for which is little more than the ability to recognize that a price of $99 for an item is lower than a price of $100. But the moment that we go beyond the concept of price buying, as we must, the matter becomes more complex. The questions for management become, "How much can we expect of the purchasing department? Where does it fit into our management and operating policies?"

There is no single, universal answer to these questions, as this study will show. But the answer in any given case may be surprising, for the developments in purchasing science and the experience of progressive purchasing departments reveal a potent profit tool that management can ill afford to ignore. The sharpness of that tool and the way in which it is used are matters that management, first, then the purchasing manager must determine. Viewed in this light, purchasing is more than just another job to be done; it is an integral part of successful management.

SOME PERFORMANCE OBJECTIVES

After studying this chapter you should be able to:

1. Explain the role of purchasing in modern industry and the importance of effective purchasing to the profitability and competitive position of a company.
2. List the major adverse consequences of ineffective purchasing.
3. Discuss the special demands that are put on the purchasing function in periods of severe economic change, with reference to current or recent abnormal conditions.
4. Enumerate the reasons why purchasing responsibility and authority should be delegated to specific persons in a separate department.
5. Name the fundamental objectives of an industrial purchasing department.
6. Give at least six activities normally and regularly carried on by a purchasing department.

In this chapter we have discussed the nature and importance of the purchasing function and the basic objectives and activities of a purchasing department. In the following chapter we will take up modern management policies on purchasing, the nature of the purchasing department's authority, what management expects of purchasing and its relations with other departments.

Purchasing And Management Objectives

2

Historically, purchasing in industry has been most closely allied to the production department. Purchasing also buys a host of items for other departments—such things, among others, as engineering materials; maintenance, repair, and operating (MRO) supplies; and office equipment. In the typical manufacturing operation, however, the bulk of purchased materials is used in the company's product, and its fabrication and procurement is the first step in the production process. This is the nucleus of the purchasing program.

SPECIALIZATION OF FUNCTION

The production department embraces a wide variety of activities that are subject to specialized and independent administration in large-scale industry. They include the design of the product to be manufactured (subsequently set apart as design and engineering departments); planning the schedule of operations (production control or planning department); procurement (purchasing) and stocking (stores) of materials and supplies required; and production itself. Other typical functions are plant engineering, power, maintenance, and the like.

The first step in specialization along functional lines is to assign the responsibility for each of these activities to a particular individual or group under the direction of the production manager. The second step is to set them up as separate departments, independent of the jurisdiction of the production manager.

A few decades ago, the purchasing department began to move beyond the intermediate stage of subordinate responsibility. It is now recognized as a specialized function equal to and independent of production and directly responsible to general management. Evidence of this change is offered in a booklet designed to attract job candidates to the purchasing field, in which it is reported that approximately 70 percent of the larger purchasing departments report to the president or vice president of the company.[1] A similar trend is indicated by the increasing number of purchasing executives being named corporate officers. At a 1978 meeting of thirty such executives, representing a broad spectrum of industry, exactly half the group were vice presidents of their companies.

The development of purchasing as a distinct functional responsibility, independent of production jurisdiction, paralleled the development of mass-production operations, large-scale corporate organization, and the increasing complexities of modern distribution. With a separate purchasing department, under the direction of a responsible purchasing executive, price consciousness and efficient procedures continue as matters of concern, but they no longer receive the primary emphasis as they did years ago. Price is balanced against the other factors of quality, quantity, and timing to the end that the greatest ultimate value may be obtained for purchasing expenditures. Procedure is considered as a means to an end, serving to implement an established purchasing policy. And techniques of research and analysis are added to help realize the full potential of purchasing toward making and conserving company profits.

WHAT MANAGEMENT EXPECTS OF THE PURCHASING DEPARTMENT

Having established purchasing as a separate department with specific authority, management expects, first, the competent performance of purchasing duties and the accomplishment of the basic purchasing objectives outlined in Chapter 1. It expects a department that understands and accepts the responsibilities of its function in the overall organization. It expects a department that is efficiently administered and that develops appropriate policies and procedures that will result in economical cost of procurement as well as economical cost of materials. It expects a well-informed department that can serve as an information center for the entire company on the commercial and market aspects of materials—

---

[1] National Association of Purchasing Management. *Purchasing As a Career,* 3rd ed. (New York: 1979.)

Xerox Procurement Philosophy

Objectives

The primary goal of the Xerox Corporate Procurement function is to insure the sound location, selection, development, administration and motivation of suppliers to Xerox for purchased components, materials, equipment, supplies and services, in order that a dynamic blend of the following technical, business and financial objectives may be achieved:

Balanced Value

Optimum Quality • Continuity of Supply
Minimum Final Cost • Supplier Know-How
Supplier Service • Good Xerox/Supplier Relations

Profit Contribution

Tight Economic Control • Constant Search for Value

Creative Business Leadership

Innovative Procurement Techniques • Highly Qualified and Creative People • Flexible Organization

Figure 2-1. Goals and responsibilities of a corporate procurement department as listed in a booklet distributed within a company and to suppliers. Courtesy, Xerox Corporation.

availability, costs, trends, and so forth—and so can aid in the formulation of broad business policies.

Management expects its purchasing people as well to put company interests and objectives ahead of departmental interests. It wants a department that can get along with other departments and work with them toward the attainment of company objectives without compromising sound purchasing principles.

Management expects the purchasing department, in its contacts and dealings with supplier companies and their representatives, to act with fairness, courtesy, and dignity and to maintain high standards of business relationships. This public relations aspect of purchasing is now recognized as one of the most important opportunities and responsibilities of the purchasing department.

With the development of purchasing science and the broadening concept of the scope of purchasing activity, the plaint of progressive purchasing managers is that management expects too little, rather than too much, of the purchasing department. It is well, therefore, at this point to note also what purchasing expects of management. It expects buying authority commensurate with its responsibilities. It expects a clear-cut definition of its activities and authority, particularly when they impinge upon the activities of other departments. It expects the backing of management in the enforcement of approved purchasing policies and procedures throughout the company. It expects management to provide the physical and technical facilities for efficient purchasing work.

Beyond this, purchasing expects management to understand the larger aims of progressive purchasing practice, so that the legitimate scope of activities may not be unduly circumscribed; to grant purchasing a voice in policy-making councils and decisions; to listen with an open mind to purchasing proposals affecting materials usage in other departments and company investment in materials; and to permit the department to extend its activities and influence when benefit to the company can be demonstrated.

The purchasing department should regularly make available to management and to all interested departments its special knowledge and appraisal of economic and market conditions. Purchasing is in a unique position to acquire valuable information. Through its study of markets and day-to-day contact with a variety of supplier industries, it can obtain insight into ideas and plans of suppliers (as well as those of suppliers' other customers). New products and processes, and new applications of old materials, typically come first to the attention of the purchasing department. Labor relations in supplier industries, and other factors affecting present and future supply, can be significant indicators in the formulation of sound business policies Purchasing department reports can be a valuable service to management, supplementing other research.

MANAGEMENT CONFERS AUTHORITY

We have referred in the preceding sections to the "authority" of the purchasing department and the purchasing officer, and more such references will be made in the balance of this chapter and in the discussion of organization for purchasing. It will be evident from the context that the authority mentioned is not standard or implicit in the function itself but is widely variable, in kind and degree, according to varying circumstances and individual cases. Before leaving the consideration of purchasing–management relationships, therefore, the concept of purchasing authority should be clarified.

Basically, authority is conferred by management along with the delegation of duties. The general management principle applied here is that authority should be commensurate with the responsibility and with the capacity to meet responsibility. Both these criteria are for management to appraise and decide upon. The first is the more important, for the presumption is that, if the person charged with responsibility does not have the required abilities, management will find or train one who has.

The scope of authority in any given case can therefore be interpreted, first, as corresponding to the functional responsibilities assigned by management in specific areas of decision and action. For example, when we say that it is outside the province of purchasing to decide *what* shall be bought for a particular purpose or need, but that purchasing does have the authority to select the *source* from which it is bought, the distinction is not one of privilege but of two different responsibilities—for suitability and for value.

The purchasing manager is given authority to buy, but the particular purchases must first be authorized by a specific evidence of need—a requisition originating in another department, a minimum stock quantity established by inventory policy, the bill of materials for a factory work order, or some other similar means of authorization.

Final decision as to the type and quality of materials to be purchased rests with the design or using departments, but the selection of source is a purchasing prerogative. Preference as to source or brand may be indicated and should be considered in purchasing so long as no sacrifice of other buying factors is involved. It should not be binding unless better reasons than personal preference or past usage can be presented. When required products are identified by a manufacturer's brand name or number, this description is usually qualified by the phrase "or equal," to give the buyer greater choice; the burden of proof is then on purchasing to show that alternative products are actually equal in suitability for the purpose. To increase the assurance of supply and to maintain competition, purchasing seeks to establish two or more sources for all items in regular use. Production and other using departments should therefore test alternative materials and supplies from various sources, at purchasing's request, and indicate those that are satisfactory for inclusion on an "approved list"; choice of product and supplier then is determined by purchasing, with the assurance that the selection will be acceptable to the user.

RESPONSIBILITY FOR ANALYZING REQUIREMENTS

In making requests to purchase, using departments are responsible for providing complete and accurate information on what is required. The purchasing department has the duty of buying to fulfill any legitimate, properly authorized requisition. It has the privilege of questioning any requisition as to the material or quantity specified for purchase, if in its judgment the request is out of line with current usage or best buying policy. This is in no sense a challenge to the authority of other departments. It is simply a prudent precaution, consistent with purchasing's position as a watchdog over purchase expenditures, against duplication, possible errors in description or estimating, or occasional misuses of requisitioning privileges. Usually, purchasing also has the privilege of revising quantities on a requisition for purposes of buying most advantageously, provided that the total requirement is procured in time to meet the need. Examples of this are the adjustment of quantities to conform with economical lot sizes, quantity discount brackets or standard packaging and shipping units, and the deferring or anticipating of purchases to take advantage of expected market fluctuations.

Where possible, product specifications should be so clear and specific that, when they are met, there is no question as to the acceptability of the purchased item. The purchasing department should have a voice in the preparation of such specifications to avoid special details that would restrict the sources from which materials might be procured or that would entail extra costs for unnecessary deviations from commercial standards and tolerances.

In ways such as these, flexibility and competition are made possible in purchasing for company benefit without prejudice to the interest of the plant personnel who have to use the material.

The scope of responsibility suggested in the preceding section is very broad. But even the simple delegated authority to buy may be limited *qualitatively* by stated exceptions to the general rule or *quantitatively* by placing a monetary limit on commitments made by the purchasing department. Limitations on authority may reflect basic management policy and philosophy. They may also be based on management doubts in the ability of the department to handle more than a certain degree of responsibility. In the latter case, the purchasing manager with initiative and ability, seeing ways to improve purchasing service and performance by broadening the scope of his or her activity, may persuade management to rewrite its definition of his or her authority. Or, in the absence of formal authorization, the purchasing manager may assume added responsibility, acting beyond the scope of his or her stated function, assuming that the manager does not infringe upon the authority of other departments.

PURCHASING VIS-A-VIS OTHER DEPARTMENTS

Although we have been stressing the independence of purchasing as a major function of business, clearly this independence should be merited only on the basis of the service and cooperation that it gives to other departments. It would be fatal to the department, and injurious to the company, if purchasing were to concentrate on its own "prerogatives" and procedures as ends in themselves, unrelated to the needs of the rest of the company. Excerpts from the purchasing manual of a well known office products manufacturer provide an example of how purchasing authority and responsibilities, as they relate to other departments, can be defined:

> The methods used by procurement personnel to fill the needs of other company personnel must clearly establish the procurement responsibility to purchase *total value* for the company. This is the basic criterion of all procurement activities. Relations with other company personnel must be established on that premise.
>
> Employees with procurement responsibility shall maintain maximum effort to assure that purchase transactions are processed promptly . . . . [They] are given the prerogative and held accountable to question all purchase requisitions, specifications and related matters to assure purchase of maximum value for the company.
>
> Procurement personnel shall cooperate fully in assisting other company personnel to obtain information, technical data, samples and visits from suppliers required to permit testing of alternative materials and services.
>
> Data shall be regularly supplied to interested personnel having a need to know regarding production plans, lead times, tooling requirements, shortages, material availabilities, price trends, new product technical data, supplier engineering and manufacturing capabilities, supplier publications and other information required to maximize effectiveness.
>
> Procurement personnel shall maintain and communicate to those having a need to know pertinent information regarding general economic data, marketplace conditions and other general management information deemed of value. Cultivating close professional association with those involved in the procurement cycle is invaluable. Cooperation is paramount to success and procurement personnel should make every effort to provide desired services required by other company personnel, subject to consideration of obtaining total value in the procurement transaction.[2]

Note that in the instruction communication of information is not considered a one-way street. Practical aspects of implementing the policy just outlined are discussed in the following pages.

[2] A.B. Dick Company, *Purchasing Manual,* 1975.

RELATIONSHIP WITH PRODUCTION

Insistence on the separation of purchasing from direct control by the production department does not imply any basic divergence of interest. It is still a primary function of purchasing to serve the production program, and the latter must be satisfied. The relationship between the two departments should be considered rather from the viewpoint of their common objective, which is to contribute most effectively to the company's overall advantage. From this viewpoint, there is excellent reason why neither should dominate the other. At the same time, there is compelling reason for the closest possible cooperation.

Support for this approach is found in official U.S. Air Force instructions for evaluating the procurement efficiency of defense contractors:

> The analysis of the contractor's organization should develop a clear understanding of the functional relationships of purchasing to manufacturing, quality control, engineering, etc. It shall be ascertained whether the organizational level of the purchasing department allows it to operate a maximum effectiveness. For example, unclear lines of responsibility or placing of the purchasing function subordinate to another management function may impair the capability to make objective purchasing decisions.[3]

Production or operating departments should advise purchasing promptly, and as far in advance as possible, concerning the program to be carried on, contemplated work schedules, special projects or contract jobs to be undertaken, new products to be produced, changes in design that will affect items to be purchased, and any significant changes in rate of production. In the absence of specific information, the routine guide of the buyer is the record of past consumption. This would be a misleading criterion in the event of a change of schedule, leading to possible shortages if requirements are increased without notice and to excessive inventories and losses through obsolescence if certain parts are discontinued or their use curtailed. The aim at all times should be to permit a planned program of procurement for systematic purchasing. "Lead time" in buying involves not only the supplier's manufacturing cycle and a normal period for delivery, but should also include a reasonable time for finding the best source and negotiating an advantageous purchase.

Data furnished to purchasing should also include a realistic statement as to when materials will actually have to be on hand for use. The safety factors of timing, anticipation of requirements, forward coverage,

[3] U.S. Air Force, *Air Force Systems Command Manual*, AFSCM 70–3, "Contractor Procurement Review Manual," p. S1–7.

and delivery schedules are matters of purchase policy and planning. A realistic statement of need fixes purchasing responsibility, whereas unwarranted requests for delivery in advance of the actual need tends to reduce the flexibility of the purchasing program, and generally to increase the risk of wasteful buying.

Purchasing, in turn, has the responsibility to keep using departments informed as to the status of their request for material. A copy of the purchase order is usually routed to the requisitioner to show that the need has been provided for. If the vendor's delivery promise does not meet the time specified on the requisition, or if later delays make it necessary to revise delivery schedules, using departments should be advised of this so that schedules can be adjusted.

PURCHASING AND ENGINEERING

Cooperation between purchasing and engineering departments is chiefly concerned with matters of product design and specification preliminary to the actual production requirements.

The purchasing manager and the engineer traditionally differ in their approach to the materials problem. The engineer tends to specify wide margins of quality, safety, and performance, whereas the purchasing manager tends to narrow such margins and work to minimum requirements. The engineer, by temperament and training, seeks the ideal material or design or equipment, frequently with insufficient regard for cost. The purchasing manager seeks adequate materials or equipment, with perhaps insufficient regard for desirable margins of quality. The two viewpoints have been brought much closer together in recent years as an increasing number of people with engineering training and experience have entered purchasing work. In a considerable number of companies, also, the appointment of a purchasing engineer, attached to the purchasing department staff for the express purpose of reconciling the two viewpoints with a full appreciation of both, has helped to arrive at an optimum solution of purchasing problems that involve technical considerations.

The purchase engineer is usually a staff adviser to the purchasing manager, directing research on qualities and costs, developing purchase specifications, and sometimes handling the purchase of such items as electric motors and controls to be incorporated in a manufactured product. Whether such a person is actually included in the purchasing department organization, it behooves the buyer to take advantage of the knowledge and advice of the engineering staff on any and all points where they can aid toward more effective selection of materials.

In some larger procurement organizations, arrangements for purchasing–engineering liaison are much more elaborate. Prior to the introduction of a new subcompact car in the late 1970s, Chrysler established a technical planning unit to work closely with the production planning, body engineering, general manufacturing, product cost planning, and design functions. A few years ago IBM San Jose formed a "procurement engineering" group within the procurement department to provide all the technical support required to assure that suppliers fabricate purchases to specification and schedule, at the proper price (see Figure 2-2). Both these developments are treated at greater length in Chapter 5.

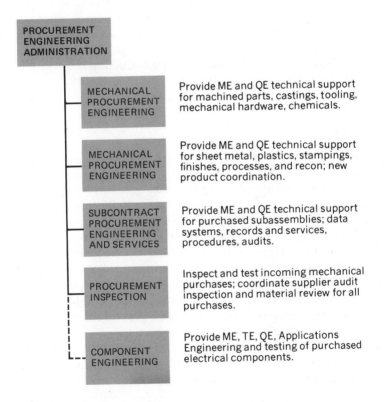

Figure 2-2. Procurement Engineering Group responsibilities in relation to other departments. ME, TE, and QE refer to mechanical, tooling, and quality engineering, respectively. Courtesy, *Journal of Purchasing and Materials Management.*

Engineering specifications may call for excessively close dimensional tolerances. These may add to product quality and uniformity, but they often place the requirement outside the scope of commercial standards, restrict the number of potential suppliers, raise costs, and increase the percentage of rejections, without any significant increase in utility. Cooperation with the purchasing department will frequently result in arriving at a more practicable and economical standard.

Standardization of materials and dimensions in product design is a field in which purchasing and engineering cooperation can yield very beneficial results. Such a program is logically initiated by the purchasing manager because of its possibilities in the direction of reducing the number of stock items, permitting the consolidation of requirements, increasing purchase quantities, and reducing inventory investment. The final decision is within the province of the engineer, whose judgment is invaluable in determining where, how, and to what extent the principle can be applied without jeopardizing product quality.

As in the case of the purchasing–production relationship, cooperation between purchasing and engineering is most effective if it starts at the planning stage, when designs and specifications are still formative and flexible.[4]

PURCHASING AND MARKETING

Sales departments should keep purchasing informed of sales quotas and expectations as a guide to probable quantity requirements of materials. Purchasing should also be advised when special contracts or new products are contemplated, so that the necessary preliminaries of the purchasing program may be undertaken well in advance of the actual need.

One of the functions of the purchasing department is to prepare estimates of the cost of materials for use in sales quotations and in the planning of product lines within a stated price range or cost limitation. The purchasing department can be of great assistance in determining how much quality or quantity can be built into a product or item within such limitations and in suggesting means of cost reduction or quality improvement to enhance the salability of the product, thus contributing to the competitive position of the company as compared with the rest of the industry.

Purchasing department files and daily mail provide a wealth of firsthand information on the sales policies, promotional methods, and similar activities of other manufacturers and examples of how other

[4] Arthur W. Brown, "Technical Support for Procurement," *Journal of Purchasing* (Spring 1976): 8–14.

companies handle special situations. This accumulation of material is particularly valuable because it has been objectively received and appraised by the purchasing staff and that it makes available a practical basis for determining what policies, what sales approach, and what type of sales material are most effective.

An interesting example of purchasing–marketing cooperation exists in a leading manufacturer of electronic business machines, the marketing department of which is responsible for selection and sale of peripheral equipment and supplies (bought from outside suppliers). It is marketing's function to seek out such new products using some conventional purchasing techniques, including vendor contacts. The purchasing department, however, is responsible for negotiating terms with suppliers, coordinating all contacts and transactions, and issuing the contract. Marketing is therefore expected to notify purchasing immediately of its requirements and to seek purchasing's assistance in its vendor contacts. Meanwhile, purchasing is expected to conduct simultaneous surveys of its own and keep marketing informed of all potential suppliers, substitutes, or equivalents.

PURCHASING AND STORES

The relationship between purchasing and stores departments is inherently so close and so basic that the two are combined in more than half of industrial organizations. The percentage is even higher in institutions such as hospitals and universities. Functionally, the effect is to extend the responsibility for materials from the point of acquisition to the point of issue and use. The activities between these two end points are chiefly of a custodial nature, including the receipt and care of purchased items and accountability for material stocks, both physically and in accurate record form. This is the continuation of a single process. Except for the verification of quantities actually received against purchase orders, there is no purpose of "checks and balances" to be served by separating the two functions. The administration of stores may be a job of considerable magnitude in itself, but widespread experience shows that it can be handled effectively within the general framework of the purchasing department.

There are cogent reasons for combining the purchasing and stores functions. Inventory stores are implemented wholly by purchasing action. A large part of the purchasing program is usually initiated by requisitions from stores departments, to replenish stocks. Duplication of records can be minimized. Stores records are essential to the buyer, not only as to receipts and quantities on hand, but also as to disbursements and rates of use. This information is vital to the formulation of a sound purchasing policy and program, for inventories and stock turnover are among the measures of purchasing performance and efficiency. The determination of maximum and minimum stock quantities is not primarily a control over purchasing, but a guide; it is purchasing's means of controlling inventory investment, of maintaining balance, and of assuring the adequacy of supplies in relation to the need. As a mere quantitative measurement, such figures have little meaning. As a matter of fact, they are effective only to the extent that they are adjustable—and adjusted—to the use requirements and purchasing policy which they implement.

To fulfill purchasing objectives, it is necessary also to know that materials are definitely correlated to the purchase order when received and that they are issued and applied to the purposes for which they are bought. Special attention should be given to inactive and slow-moving items, to avoid losses from depreciation and obsolescence and the accumulation of excessive carrying costs over a long period of time. All are properly chargeable to the materials account and add to the cost of materials up to the time of use or disposal, and thereby come within the scope of purchasing responsibility. The accountability for materials cannot be divided without sacrificing efficiency and control.

In any event, there must be a daily, detailed flow of information between the buying and the stores divisions. Purchasing must advise stores regarding orders placed and deliveries expected in sufficient detail so that they may be readily identified, promptly placed at the service of using departments, and accurately accounted for. Stores, in turn, must keep purchasing advised regarding the fulfillment of orders and the status of inventories, as noted above.

The most common point of issue in this general area is the responsibility for inventory control—the determination of quantities, coverage, and balance among items carried in stock. This is sometimes set apart from purchasing as a special, independent function. Inventory control is undeniably a major consideration in management policy, with significant effect upon the costs of operation. However, even more than the physical control of stores, it is inherently linked with purchasing. Determination of optimum ordering and inventory quantities is a part of modern purchasing science (see Chapters 9 and 10). In a purchasing department that understands the full import of its responsibilities, inventory control factors are weighed against commercial aspects of the transaction as a standard procedure in making buying decisions. To segregate this phase from the act of procurement is, then, a duplication of function. If it is imposed as the dominating policy, dictating or limiting decisions on quantity and timing, it can actually negate many of the opportunities and economic advantages of sound purchasing.

PURCHASING AND TRAFFIC

Purchased materials have to be brought from the supplier's plant or warehouse to the point of use, and transportation charges make up a distinct and sometimes substantial part of ultimate delivered cost. The purchasing department is therefore concerned with incoming traffic costs. Purchasing usually takes cognizance of this by giving preference to nearby sources or to those that are strategically located in relation to good transportation facilities, as one means of minimizing this cost factor. But the problem is not altogether so simple. The availability of a variety of alternative transport methods, proper freight classification, consolidated shipments, and the like offer additional means of savings. Further, the development of newer services, such as fast freight, truck–rail combinations, and air express, have materially extended the economical purchasing radius and are to be considered in buying policies and decisions. The purchasing department can therefore make good use of expert traffic knowledge.

Most purchase orders include shipping instructions for the vendor. A well-informed traffic department determines what is the "best way" for various types of shipments from various source locations, and this information is incorporated in the purchasing department's vendor file for quick reference and application when orders are issued. Other traffic services to purchasing include the tracing of shipments, expediting in transit, and the handling of claims on shipments damaged in transit.

Where no separate traffic department is maintained, purchasing usually has this responsibility in respect to incoming traffic. In smaller organizations, where a complete division of functional responsibilities is not practicable, the combination of purchasing and traffic is frequently found.

The purchasing of transportation is covered in more detail in Chapter 17.

PURCHASING AND QUALITY CONTROL

Purchasing's first responsbility in respect to quality control is to procure materials and products that conform to the specification. The quality control department usually handles acceptance testing of purchased materials. In that case, it should be made clear to purchasing, and through purchasing to the vendor, what test methods are to be applied and what are the criteria of acceptability. Such advance information minimizes the chances of misunderstanding and controversy and, in the long view, aids substantially in the procurement of consistently acceptable materials.

In the case of rejections, it is important to observe the principle previously stated—that complaints and adjustments be handled through the purchasing department and not directly between quality control and the vendor. Only in this way can satisfactory vendor relationships be maintained. It is also important from the standpoint of keeping purchase records accurate, for a rejected shipment means that the need has not been satisfied and the purchasing responsibility has not been ended.

Acceptance testing should be done promptly upon the receipt of a shipment, and the results reported to purchasing, rather than waiting until goods are issued from stores to production departments. Vendors' warranties are generally limited in time. Each day of delay makes adjustment more difficult, or even impossible if the warranty period has expired. Meanwhile, shortcomings in quality may multiply owing to the vendor's assumption, in the absence of prompt corrective action, that previous shipments have been satisfactory to the buyer.

Purchasing has a further insterest in the general field of quality control as practiced by vendor companies. It helps in the selection of vendors and can substantially reduce the necessity and expense of acceptance testing at the buyer's plant. To get maximum benefit from this buying technique, it should be correlated with the quality control practices and standards in the buyer's own company. (Quality assurance is discussed at greater length in Chapter 8.)

PURCHASING AND ACCOUNTING

Every purchase made represents an expenditure or commitment of company funds. It sets in motion a series of accounting operations, such as charging the expense to the proper contract or department account, the verification and approval of the invoice, payment of the charge, and final audit. In the case of extraordinarily large or unforeseen expenditures, it may require special financial arrangements or credit considerations. Under some forms of government contracts, there are further requirements that must be met to secure prompt reimbursement for the expenditure. The relationship between the purchasing and accounting departments is therefore a vital one, and it frequently starts before the purchase is actually made.

It is essential that purchasing forms and procedure be correlated with accounting requirements and methods, to avoid duplication of work on clerical entries and the necessary checking back to secure essential information. It is customary to have a carbon copy of each purchase order routed to the accounting department at the time that the order is issued for determination of cost data and distribution of charges to the department or job concerned. The carbon copy also provides original data for final checking and audit when the transaction is completed. Sometimes, as a matter of information, these order copies are supplemented by a daily or weekly summary report of commitments in dollar totals, to provide a quick view of the financial situation with respect to materials accounts. Purchasing reports to accounting are essentially automatic and comprehensively detailed in those companies at which procurement operations are computerized (see Chapter 4).

There are strong differences of opinion on which department— purchasing or accounting—should check invoices. In some companies, certain accounting operations are customarily handled by invoice clerks in the purchasing department, particularly the verification of prices and terms and in most cases the verification of extensions and totals as well. The receiving report is also routed through the purchasing department to denote completion of deliveries, and this is also checked against the vendor's invoice. When the proper entries have been made to purchase and stock records, the receiving report is attached to the invoice, and the latter is stamped or certified for payment and forwarded to the accounting department.

In other companies, invoices go directly to accounting to be matched with the accounting purchase order and receiving report copies. Any discrepancies noted are then referred to the appropriate buyer in the purchasing department for resolution.

In any event, prompt clearance is important so that payment can be made within the discount period. Invoices on which a cash discount privilege may be earned by prompt payment are sometimes flagged for immediate attention.

Another important phase of purchasing–accounting cooperation is the establishment of standard costs—that is, costs per unit of production developed in advance and used as a standard for a given accounting period. When standard costs are based on the cost of purchased materials, they are, in effect, a purchase materials budget. Standard costs and their relation to purchasing are discussed at greater length in Chapter 23.

PURCHASING PREROGATIVES

Four prerogatives of the purchasing department should be emphasized.

First, selection of the supply source is wholly a matter of purchasing authority. The need to buy originates in other departments, and required quality is defined. So long as these measures of *what* to buy are satisfied, the decision on *where* or *from whom* to buy is the responsibility of the purchasing manager.

Second, all contacts with vendors and their representatives should be made through the purchasing department, from the first sales interview, through the process of negotiation and ordering, follow-up for delivery, and correspondence relating to materials and purchases, to approval of the vendor's invoice or any adjustments that may be necessary. Legitimate contacts with technical and plant personnel should be arranged only with the knowledge of the purchasing department and are not to be conducted or construed as in any way prejudicing the purchasing department's freedom of negotiation or its latitude of choice in selecting the supplier. Some exceptions may arise in centralized purchasing for branch plant requirements (see Chapter 5).

Third, it is the duty of the purchasing managers and buyers to check purchase requests against the need. It is their privilege to suggest modifications of the requested quality for more economical or more expeditious procurement and to revise quantities on a particular order so long as the total quantity is procured in time to meet the need.

Fourth, the commercial aspects of the purchase are wholly within the jurisdiction of the purchasing department. These include the manner of purchase, the price, the terms and conditions of the order or contract, packing and shipping instructions and the like.

It will be recalled that the purchasing responsibility is defined as buying materials of the right quality, in the right quantity, at the right time, at the right price, from the right source. Quality is definable in the specifications; the other factors are matters of judgment and decision. In the buyer's constant search for the most advantageous purchase, these prerogatives must be reserved to him or her as the means of making his or her judgment and decisions effective.

SOME PERFORMANCE OBJECTIVES

After studying this chapter you should be able to

1. Contrast the concerns of purchasing departments of years ago—for example, in the period prior to World War II—with those of a modern department.

2. Compare management's expectations of purchasing and purchasing's expectations of management.

3. Justify the claim made by purchasing managers that their departments should have authority to question requisitions submitted by operating departments.

4. Explain the significance of the phrase "or equal" as it applies to purchasing requisitions.

5. Name the major departments with which purchasing should maintain close communication and coordination, and explain why.
6. Cite the basic prerogatives of purchasing discussed in the text.

Having focused more closely on the relationship of purchasing with management, and with other departments of the company, we move on in the next chapter to the "mechanics" of purchasing—the way in which the buying cycle operates and the specific procedures used by a purchasing department to carry out its responsibilities in that cycle.

Section II

PURCHASING DEPARTMENT ORGANIZATION AND OPERATION

Purchasing Systems

3

The procurement cycle, outlined in general terms in the two previous chapters, has several distinct phases: (1) requests for materials, supplies, and equipment from the using departments; (2) selection of suppliers and issuance of purchase orders; (3) follow-up of outstanding orders (expediting); (4) receipt and inspection of materials from suppliers; (5) and checking of suppliers' invoices. Thus a purchasing department dealing with hundreds of sources for thousands of items has a complex administrative job, in addition to its responsibility for skillful buying. In this chapter we will deal with the basic steps in the purchasing process and the forms and procedures (systems) necessary for proper control of each stage of the process.

BASIC FORMS AND PROCEDURES

A using department indicates its need for materials on a *requisition.* It uses a *stores requisition* to obtain materials that are in regular use in the plant and that are carried as normal stock. This goes directly to the stores department and the requirements are supplied from there. A *purchase requisition* (Figure 3-1) is used for materials that have to be ordered from suppliers. The person who needs the material fills in either type of form with the material name or code identification, the amount needed, and the desired delivery date. Before sending the requisition to either stores or purchasing, the person making the requisition must have it signed by a supervisor authorized to approve the expenditure.

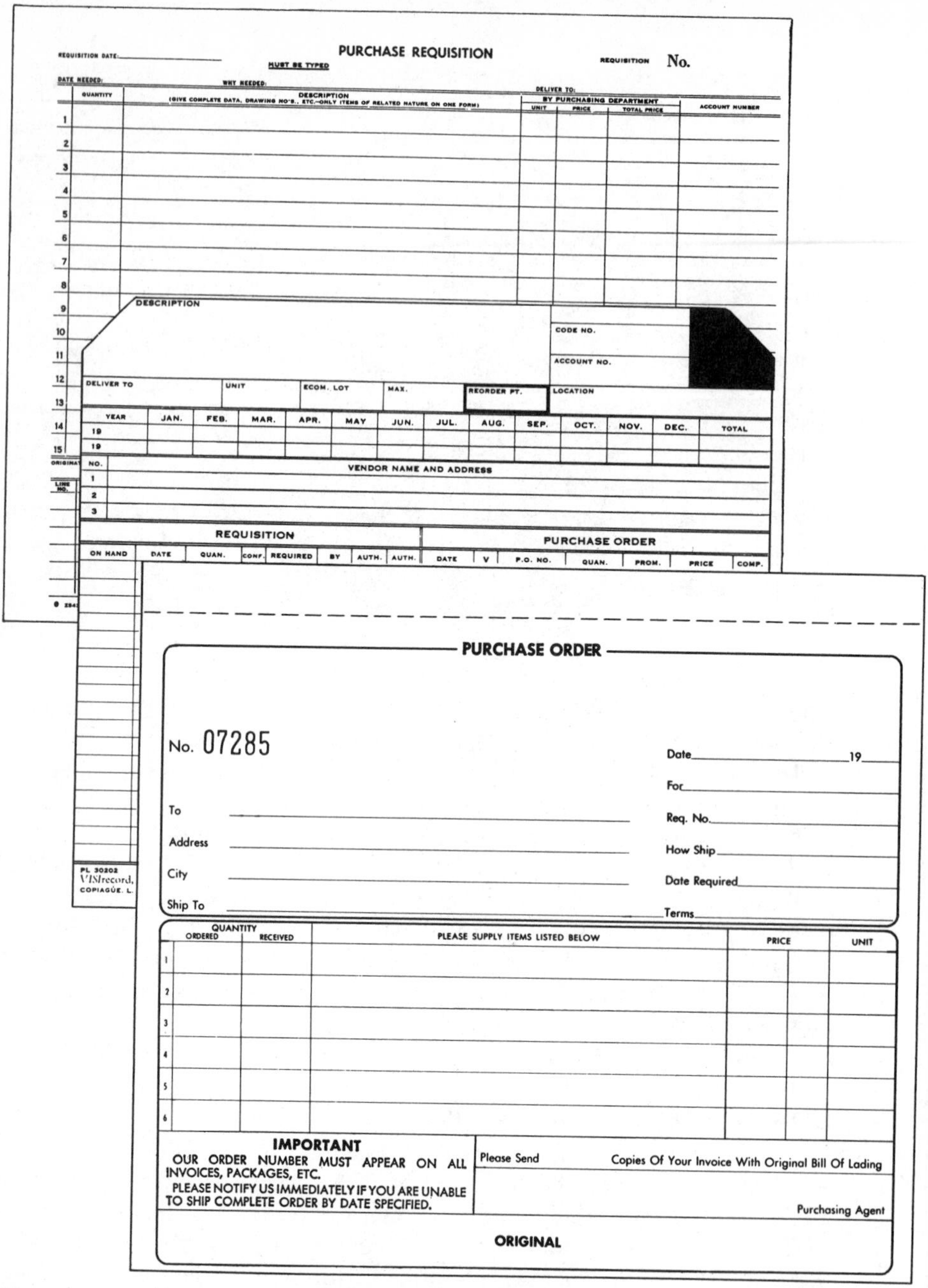

Figure 3-1. Samples of forms used in the requisitioning–purchasing cycle. Purchase requisition (top) is generally used to request purchase of items not in stock. Traveling requisition (center) is for stock items that are used repetitively; in contrast to the purchase requisition, it is printed on heavy stock and can be used up to thirty times for the same item. Form at bottom is a regular purchase order. Request for quotation (not shown) is similar in format to the purchase order but always clearly states that it is not an order. Company name is always imprinted on forms.

For items of a repetitive nature, and for those for which purchases are normally made to replenish stocks, a *traveling requisition* is used. The form is of heavy card stock so that it may be passed back and forth regularly between the requisitioning department, or stores department, and purchasing. A single card is made up for each item, and identification of the item is entered only once—in the heading of the card. But there is space provided for several (up to thirty) requests to purchase. The requisitioner or storeskeeper merely enters the date and the predetermined quantity desired and sends the card to purchasing. When the purchase has been made, it is recorded on the card, which is then returned to stores or the requisitioning department.

Sometimes purchasing is based directly on a *bill of materials,* which lists every item in a company's end product. When a manufacturing schedule is set by production planning, purchasing is notified and can set up its purchasing schedule or program to correspond with production plans. It receives a copy of the bill of materials, on which are indicated those items that are not on hand or ordered. This tabulation serves the same purpose as a whole series of requisitions.

ORDERING

The various processes of negotiation and decision that take place between the time at which a purchase is authorized and the time at which the order is issued are covered in Chapters 8 through 14. About the only routine procedure in the process as part of a purchasing system is the invitation to suppliers to bid and the evaluation of bids received. In industry, when such invitations are issued prior to ordering, the form used is generally called a *request for quotation,* and no obligation to buy from the supplier quoting the lowest price is implied. The procedure is employed in one or more of the following situations: (1) the intended purchase would involve relatively high expenditure, (2) not enough price information on the required item is available, (3) the product needed is complex and costly and the purchasing department has had little or no experience in procuring it, (4) there is intense competition among suppliers of the product or material, or (5) a major contract is up for renewal and purchasing wants to research the market for competitive prices and service.

In public agencies—governmental and institutional—*invitations to bid* are generally mandatory when a major purchase is planned. Except in unusual cases that require elaborate justification, the business must be awarded to the lowest bidder following public opening of the bids (see Chapter 19).

The *purchase order* is the instrument by which goods are procured to fill a requirement. It expresses in specific language the agreement between the buyer and the vendor. Once accepted, it has the legal force of a binding contract.

The essential information in every purchase order includes name and address of purchasing company, identifying order number, date, name and address of vendor, general instructions (marking of shipments, number of invoices required, and so forth), delivery date required, shipping instructions, description of materials ordered and the quantity, price and discounts, and signature. Terms and conditions are generally printed on the back of the form. The purchase order must bear some authorized signature—usually that of a purchasing manager or buyer.

Many companies try to get written acceptance of the order from the vendor. This is sometimes in the form of an extra copy of the order, known as the *acknowledgment copy;* sometimes it is in the form of a detachable stub on the original copy. It is actually more than an acknowledgment; it should constitute legal acceptance of the order. The law of acceptance is discussed in Chapter 21.

Simple purchase order systems usually require at least three copies of the order:

1. the original, sent to the vendor
2. the acknowledgment copy just mentioned
3. and a purchasing department file copy

The average number of copies in a typical department, however, may go as high as seven. These could include, in addition to the three listed above,

4. copy to the receiving department as notice that a shipment is expected and to facilitate identification
5. copy to the accounting department as notice of the commitment to be later reconciled with the invoice and receiving report as authorization for payment
6. copy to the requisitioning department to show that the request has been attended to
7. copy for the follow-up or expediting division of the purchasing department

As more purchasing department operations become computerized, a number of copies of the purchase order may be eliminated. Departments authorized to have access to information on an order can obtain it by means of readouts on the CRT (cathode ray tube) terminals that are part of a computerized system. The use of electronic data processing in purchasing is covered in Chapter 4. It is important to realize, however, that the computerized system incorporates the same basic steps involved in a manual system.

CLEARING THE ORDER

In some large companies, the normal responsibility of the purchasing department ends with the issuing of the purchase order. In such cases, the using department or a separate expediting unit follows up for delivery, the inspection department is responsible for acceptance, the stores department takes care of receiving the material, and the accounting department checks invoices and certifies them for payment from its own copy of the order. Usually, however, the purchasing department is involved in all of these duties, on the general principle that procurement responsibility ends only when a satisfactory delivery has been made and materials are actually on hand for use, and when the buyer's obligation to the vendor has likewise been satisfied, completing the contract.

If ordinary expediting methods fail to secure delivery as needed, the buyer who has had contact with the vendor and who made the original agreement is the most effective expediting agent. If materials are not in accordance with specification, the purchasing department must make the adjustment with the vendor. If there are discrepancies in quantity, price, or terms in the vendor's shipment and billing, it is the purchasing department that has the final responsibility for reconciling the matter.

The first step in follow-up is to secure an acceptance and delivery promise from the vendor. The vendor's promise is recorded, and provision is made for orderly follow-up without waiting for an emergency to develop if the vendor's promise is not kept.

ROUTINE FOLLOW-UP

Follow-up is selective. A study of prevailing policy shows that less than one third of all companies follow up every order issued for delivery. An additional one third follow up orders classified as "important" or production orders as distinguished from orders for stock. In the other companies, follow-up is restricted to those that are actually and seriously overdue and to special, rush, or emergency orders.

The mechanism for follow-up is a file of open orders arranged in numerical sequence so that those that are longest outstanding are in the front of the file, giving quick visual indication of the oldest ones. This, of course, is not an accurate indicator of the delivery dates requested or promised. Some further coding or signaling device is necessary.

A common method is to print a scale of numbers from 1 to 31 across the top of the sheet corresponding to the days of the month. A series of colored tabs, differentiated as to the various calendar months, can then be affixed at the proper point along this scale, on orders for which a positive follow-up schedule is desired. The combination of color and position shows the exact date at which follow-up action is to be taken. The receiving record must be posted against this file daily, and any completed orders must be removed from the file.

Routine follow-up according to such a schedule can ordinarily be effected by simple routine methods. A printed postcard requesting specific delivery information, with reference to date of order and vendor's promise, is the usual first step. A return postcard has been found useful in facilitating the vendor's reply. A somewhat more comprehensive form is sometimes used with provision for asking information on a variety of different points, according to the particular situation.

As the need for expediting becomes more acute, the tone and method of follow-up become stronger and more personalized, the usual sequence being personal letter, telegram, telephone call, and personal interview by expediter or buyer at the vendor's plant. The particular action and the amount of pressure brought to bear are adjusted to the circumstances.

FIELD EXPEDITING

In contrast to such routine expediting is the practice of maintaining a staff of expediters in the field, who keep contact with suppliers on important orders. Such expediters are usually made responsible for all orders placed with suppliers in a given territory; oftentimes they operate from the company's branch offices in these territories, but they report directly to the general purchasing office. Sometimes this function is combined with inspection of materials at the vendor's plant.

The field expediter makes regular progress reports to the follow-up department at purchasing headquarters during the life of the order or contract, and his or her reports, checked with the schedule of requirements, show at all times the prospect of satisfactory fulfillment of delivery dates or indicate in advance the likelihood and extent of any delay that may be encountered.

Buying for heavy construction or negotiating contracts involving long lead times and complex requirements has led to the development of what one writer calls "a new breed of professional expediter—the chief expediter or director of expediting."[1] Relying heavily on experience as the prime qualification, companies are "reactivating" purchasing retirees as expediting consultants or are moving staff engineers, plant foremen, or active purchasing personnel into expediting positions. The person must have initiative and native ability to relate to both line and staff personnel in the company and in its suppliers' organizations. The chief expediter must also be able to relate to top-level management in supplier companies.

CHANGE ORDERS

It sometimes becomes necessary to make changes in the original order—changes in quantity, scheduling, or specifications; changes authorizing some alternative product; or any other of the scores of possible corrections that may arise with changing design and changing conditions of business. Many companies accomplish changes by correspondence. Others make use of a form known as the *change order* or *change notice*. It is generally similar to the purchase order in form and is given the same number as the order it revises. In some cases it merely states, "Please change our original order of the above number to read as follows:" and lists the requirements as revised. In other cases, the body of the form is divided into two parts, the first restating the order as originally issued and the second giving the desired revision.

RECEIVING

The receiving department is usually an adjunct of the stores department, which may or may not be a part of the purchasing department. Its functions are to receive incoming goods, signing the delivery notice presented by the carrier or the supplier in connection with the shipment; to identify and record all incoming materials; to report their receipt to the purchasing department and to the stores, using, or inspection departments as required; and to make prompt disposition of the goods to the appropriate department.

To aid in identification of the materials received, the receiving

---

[1] Herbert J. Green, "The Future of the Professional Expediter," *Journal of Purchasing and Materials Management* Vol. 14 (Spring 1978): 30.

department is advised of all expected shipments by means of a copy of the purchase order.

All incoming materials are reconciled with the receiving department's copy of the purchase order. A record is kept of every delivery, and receiving reports containing this information go to the purchasing and stock records departments promptly.

INSPECTION FOR QUALITY

Not all materials require formal inspection for quality; in a large proportion of deliveries on a normal procurement program, simple visual inspection meets every practical need. But often, where a more detailed examination and certification of quality are required, materials are segregated by the receiving department pending inspection and are not permitted to be placed in stores, or to go into production, until the proper inspection is made. The receiving department notifies the department responsible for inspection that the shipment has arrived and takes whatever samples may be necessary or otherwise makes the material available for inspection. The *notification* may be accomplished by means of a copy of the receiving slip or by routing the receiving department's copy of the purchase order through the inspecting department on its way back to purchasing. In the latter case, the *inspection report* may be made on the same copy as the receiving report; otherwise, a separate inspection report is required, certifying that the materials are satisfactory or, if not, giving the reason for rejection.

When these two reports are received by purchasing, showing (1) a receipt of materials, including a check on the quantity received, and (2) a certification of quality, they are compared with the purchasing department copy of the order to see that they conform with what was ordered and are attached to it as evidence of a proper delivery.

CHECKING THE INVOICE

Meanwhile, an invoice for the shipment is, or should be, received from the vendor, and this, too, must be reconciled both with the original order and with the records of receipt. It is important that the invoice be received and processed promptly, in order that the order may be cleared and payment made within the discount period, or that necessary adjustments may be initiated without delay in case there is any discrepancy. It is customary to ask that invoices be sent in duplicate, one copy to be routed directly to the accounting department and one to the purchasing department, to allow simultaneous processing from both of these viewpoints in the buyer's company, to be correlated later in the accounting or accounts payable division.

A basic but very graphic illustration of a typical purchasing procedure is shown in the flow chart in Figure 3-2. The company in which it was developed had approximately fifteen requisitioning departments originally, each doing its own buying, inventory control, and stocking. Because their efforts were not coordinated, there were many problems: too many high-cost, low-value transactions, duplication of effort, unnecessary and time-consuming paperwork, lost shipments, and little opportunity to get the benefits of volume buying and professional purchasing. Following the establishment of the coordinated system with eight points of control, the problems were virtually eliminated.

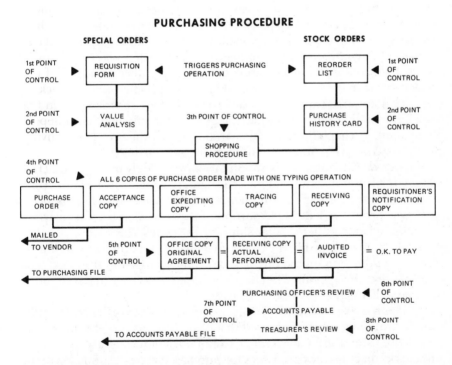

Figure 3-2 Flow chart of purchasing procedure at a large metropolitan newspaper shows basic movement of statement of requirements to the purchasing department and then to suppliers.

SIMPLIFIED METHODS

The procurement cycle obviously involves a great deal of paperwork and clerical detail. It just as obviously lends itself to simplification and "mechanization" in a number of areas. In those cases when the cost of requisitioning, ordering, receiving, and accounting for an item, for example, is greater than its value, use of complicated systems to procure it is foolish. Following elaborate procedures for every purchase of a part or material in regular use for which prices and vendors are established only once a year is costly and inefficient. As a result, many purchasing departments have set up simplified systems for handling this sort of buying without losing control of it.

One is a "small-order" system for the purchase of miscellaneous supplies of low dollar value—usually less than $100. A single simplified form is used. A typical small-order form will include requisition, purchase order, receiving report, and accounting copy. Most of the items are picked up by a purchasing department representative from local sources. In some systems, the pickup person pays cash; in others, selected vendors are permitted to bill monthly for all purchases picked up during the period. One company has simplified its small-order procedure to the point at which it includes a check drawn on a special revolving fund as a detachable stub on the order form. This eliminates invoices altogether.

This simplified approach to small orders is being carried to its logical conclusion and applied to a wider range of transactions by a number of companies. Perhaps the most outstanding development of this kind in recent years is the purchase order draft system instituted by Kaiser Aluminum & Chemical Corporation that is now widely used in industrial, commercial, and institutional purchasing departments (see Figure 3-3).

Under the system, the supplier receives a blank check as part of the purchase order—a detachable portion of the form that is an envelope in addition to being a check. After shipping the order, the vendor puts one copy of the invoice inside the check envelope, enters the net amount on the face, endorses it on the reverse side, and deposits it in the bank as an immediate cash payment. The check envelope comes back to Kaiser just as ordinary checks do.

The Kaiser plan was originally intended to cover orders up to $200 in value. But investigation showed that it could be extended to orders up to $1,000. Later, the limit was raised to $2,000; it now covers 92 percent of the checks that the company issues for purchased materials. Success of the system has eliminated an enormous amount of filing, retrieving, posting, check writing, stuffing, mailing, typing, and handwriting.

Another paper-saving order system in use by a number of com-

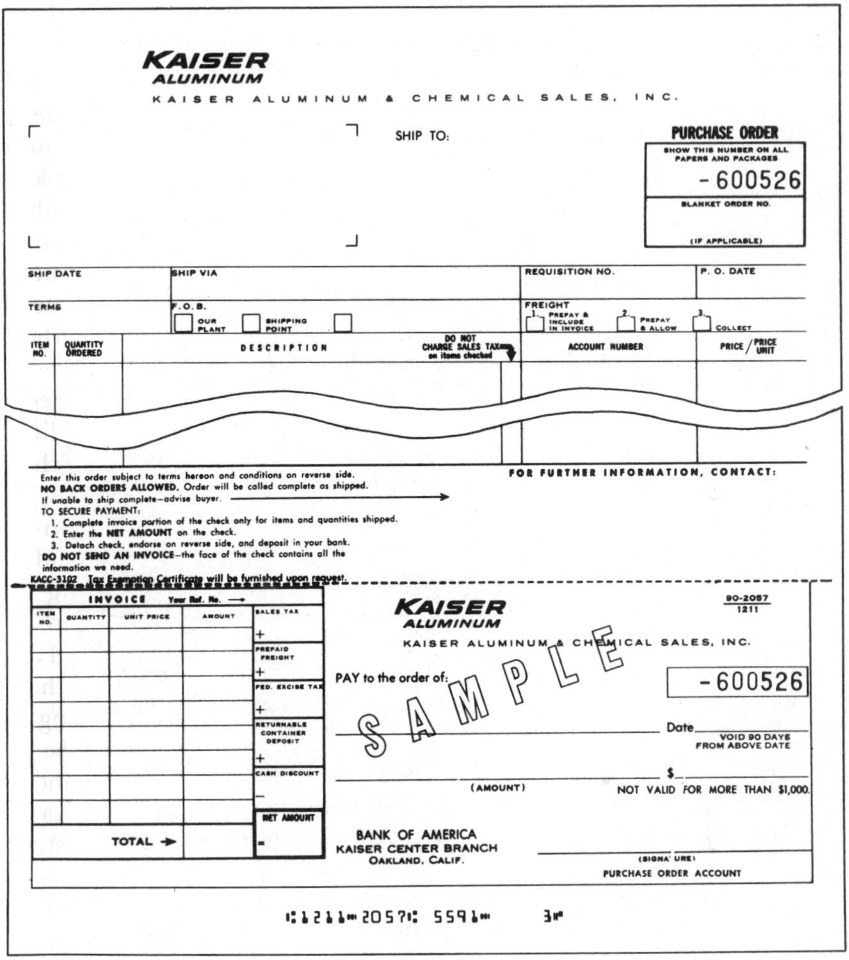

KAISER
ALUMINUM
KAISER ALUMINUM & CHEMICAL SALES, INC.

SHIP TO:

PURCHASE ORDER
SHOW THIS NUMBER ON ALL PAPERS AND PACKAGES
- 600526
BLANKET ORDER NO.
(IF APPLICABLE)

SHIP DATE | SHIP VIA | REQUISITION NO. | P. O. DATE
TERMS | F.O.B. OUR PLANT / SHIPPING POINT | FREIGHT 1. PREPAY & INCLUDE IN INVOICE 2. PREPAY & ALLOW 3. COLLECT

ITEM NO.	QUANTITY ORDERED	DESCRIPTION	DO NOT CHARGE SALES TAX on items checked	ACCOUNT NUMBER	PRICE / PRICE UNIT

Enter this order subject to terms hereon and conditions on reverse side.
NO BACK ORDERS ALLOWED. Order will be called complete as shipped.
If unable to ship complete—advise buyer.
TO SECURE PAYMENT:
1. Complete invoice portion of the check only for items and quantities shipped.
2. Enter the NET AMOUNT on the check.
3. Detach check, endorse on reverse side, and deposit in your bank.
DO NOT SEND AN INVOICE—the face of the check contains all the information we need.
KACC-3102 Tax Exemption Certificate will be furnished upon request.

FOR FURTHER INFORMATION, CONTACT:

INVOICE Your Ref. No.

ITEM NO.	QUANTITY	UNIT PRICE	AMOUNT
		TOTAL →	

SALES TAX +
PREPAID FREIGHT +
FED. EXCISE TAX +
RETURNABLE CONTAINER DEPOSIT +
CASH DISCOUNT −
NET AMOUNT =

KAISER
ALUMINUM
KAISER ALUMINUM & CHEMICAL SALES, INC.
90-2057
1211
PAY to the order of:
- 600526
SAMPLE
Date
VOID 90 DAYS FROM ABOVE DATE
(AMOUNT)
$
NOT VALID FOR MORE THAN $1,000
BANK OF AMERICA
KAISER CENTER BRANCH
OAKLAND, CALIF.
(SIGNATURE)
PURCHASE ORDER ACCOUNT

Figure 3-3. Purchase order draft with blank check attached, used by Kaiser Aluminum Corporation.

panies does away with the purchase order and vendor invoices. Requisitioners indicate the type of material and quantity needed by simply filling in a multiple-copy snapout form that serves all purposes in the order cycle. The requisitioner, in a typical case, removes one copy of the form for his or her records. The rest go to the purchasing department for checking. A buyer selects and calls a vendor, discusses prices and other terms, and places the order orally. No forms are sent to the supplier. The buyer keeps one part of the form as a worksheet and order record and sends three copies to the receiving department and one to finance. As soon as accounts payable receives a copy indicating that the material has been delivered, it issues a check to the supplier. The system is used on standard shelf items for which the total purchase cost is $2,000 or less. Price changes, partial or late deliveries, or substitutions of any kind are not permitted.

A significant aspect of the two systems described here is the assumption that both parties to the transaction are trustworthy and reliable and that both are interested in long-term association with each other. This is further evidence of the maturity of purchasing as an industrial function and refutation of the occasionally heard charge that the buyer–seller relationship is necessarily a dog-eat-dog affair. In the blank check system, the buyer puts full confidence in the supplier; in the no-purchase-order system, there is mutual trust, because the purchasing department knows the quality of material it is getting and the vendor knows that he or she will get paid.

Numerous other approaches have been used successfully in handling nonrecurring purchases efficiently, and with a minimum of paperwork. Because the cost of placing a formal purchase order runs anywhere from about $5.00 to over $25.00 (depending on the size and type of the company doing the buying and the nature of the material bought), the big advantage to these systems is the reduction of administrative cost rather than lower price.

Among the successful small-order techniques in use in industry are:

Petty Cash System: Designated individual visits local suppliers daily, picks up requirements submitted to purchasing the day before, and pays for them with either cash or check.

Cash on Delivery (C.O.D.) Orders: Buyers call in orders to local suppliers. Upon delivery, supplier is paid from petty cash fund by traffic manager or receiving clerk.

Telephone Orders: Orders are called in to suppliers. Vendor's packing slip that accompanies the order also serves as invoice.

Within these three systems there are many variations. For our purposes, it is sufficient to point out that all of them have the great advantage of eliminating many forms and a great deal of paperwork that in itself often cost more than the material being purchased.

BUYING AGREEMENTS

One of the most effective purchasing devices for cutting both material and administrative costs is the type of buying agreement variously known as the *blanket order, open-end order,* or *yearly order.* Essentially, it is an expression of the buyer's intention to purchase all or part of his or her requirements of repetitive items from one supplier during a given period of time. The requirements may be for a certain class of items (the term *blanket order* is generally used when maintenance, repair, and operating supplies are bought this way) or for a specific material or part. Terms are negotiated and an order is issued for a definite period—usually a year (see Figure 3-4).

As the operating departments need materials, they issue simple releases against the order, either through purchasing or directly to the vendor. In the latter case, purchasing is kept informed of what releases are issued. A refinement of blanket-order release system is the use of Bell System's Data-Phone, an electronic transmission device, for ordering material from suppliers. Transmission units are installed in both supplier's and customer's offices. Items under contract are listed on punched cards that are maintained in the purchasing office and are fed into the Data-Phone instrument as requirements arise. As price, quantity, and similar data are transmitted to the supplier, similar cards are produced on his or her unit, from which the supplier can fill the order.

A somewhat more sophisticated version of this type of purchasing is the computer-to-computer ordering used by a number of companies including General Electric, Gulf & Western, and Schlitz Brewing Company. In the G.E. system, more than two dozen plants throughout the country can order plant supplies directly from one distributor with whom a master agreement has been made. Buyers dial the supplier's computer direct, and all pertinent information is transmitted from the buyer's computer terminal to the supplier's.

This type of order generally carries no guarantee that the buyer will purchase a given amount of material during the term of the contract. It simply designates one company as the supplier for a class of purchased items, for example, plant supplies or office supplies. The order is usually revocable at the will of the buyer, although in practice this rarely occurs. Blanket orders are negotiated only after careful consideration and only when there is some assurance that they will be maintained until the end of the agreement.

Some orders, however, notably those of the open-end type used in the automobile industry, authorize the supplier to produce a certain number of items at various times during the life of the contract (for example, 10,000 crankshafts in the first two months, 15,000 the second month, and so forth). Such instructions then obligate the buyer to pay for the items produced in the specified time, whether or not the buyer is able to use them.

Vendor stocking agreements, in which the supplier agrees to maintain an inventory of an item, or a family of items and make regular shipments to the customer at specified times, are now widely used. Typical

Figure 3-4. Typical long-range purchase agreement, showing price advantage from volume buying and controls exercised by the buyer during life of the agreement.

conditions of such orders are described in Figure 3-5. In some cases, arrangements are made whereby the supplier stores and issues materials right in the customer's plant. The supplier owns the material until it is issued and bills the customer monthly.

MASTER PURCHASE AGREEMENT

This document is a Master Purchase Agreement covering the purchase by BUYER of the SELLER's products set forth in Exhibit A hereof. Except as modified herein SELLER's standard terms and conditions of purchase, as set forth in Exhibit B, shall apply to any orders released against this Agreement.

Ordering and Delivery: SELLER agrees to a daily delivery Monday through Friday to centralized receiving at time convenient to SELLER, with further agreement of delivery to various departments, should the BUYER's decision result in de-centralized delivery at a later date, the number and location of deliveries to be decided by mutual agreement.

Emergency Deliveries: As described in SELLER's operations manual, emergency delivery can be made. In the event of abuse and where the SELLER considers warranted, a charge of $_____ may be made for each delivery.

Stocking: SELLER will stock all items identified in Exhibit A with the guarantee to BUYER that there will be no stock-outs beyond the SELLER's control. Out-of-stock items will be provided with minimum delays; however, under these circumstances the BUYER is free to use other sources of supply to secure out-of-stock items. Delivery of items in Exhibit A are to be completed within 24 hours of order pickup.

Inventory Reduction: SELLER agrees to assist the BUYER in all areas of inventory reductions on all items supplied by SELLER. SELLER further agrees to make available to the BUYER, technical personnel as required to assist in any or all areas of technical service and technical information as required by BUYER's end users.

Price: Prices shown in Exhibit A will remain firm for ___ months. In the event of a general increase in the net cost of one or more items or product lines of the SELLER, the SELLER may increase prices by written notice and acceptance by the BUYER. The SELLER agrees that the BUYER may at any time audit records of the SELLER to determine if increases reflect a true cost to the SELLER. Price increases will become effective the first of the month following notice of increase by SELLER and acceptance by BUYER.

Term of Agreement: The term of this Agreement commences ___(Date)___ and shall end ___(Date)___.

Other Terms and Conditions:

- Order Form
- Packing Instructions
- Discrepancies
- Terms and Method of Payment
- Termination and Signatures

Figure 3-5. Standard terms of a master agreement by which vendor agrees to carry inventory for buyer and deliver specified amounts of the purchased product or material at certain regular intervals.

SYSTEMS CONTRACTING

A more advanced form of blanket or "stockless" purchasing devised by the Carborundum Corporation and known as "systems contracting." The company's headquarters buying staff draws up contracts or purchase agreements with suppliers covering large groups of materials or supplies generally bought from distributors. These would include office supplies, bearings, steel, mill supplies, and tools. Part of every contract is a detailed catalog of the items covered (see Figure 3-5). Suppliers are required to stock sufficient quantities of all items in the catalog.

Requisitioners in the company's plants are allowed to requisition items directly against the contracts. Material requisitions go directly to the supplier holding a contract rather than to the purchasing department. No invoices are required from the supplier, who simply mails a tally sheet (see Figure 3-6) to Carborundum's accounts payable department every ten days.

The blanket order and similar plans do a great deal more than eliminate much of the paperwork involved in requisitioning, buying, and invoicing. They enable the purchaser to get more favorable discount items on the basis of the increased volume that he or she is able to offer the supplier. And the buyer can get this discount without incurring the heavy carrying charges that he or she would be faced with if the whole order were brought into the plant at one time. By having material shipped in as needed, the buyer transfers some of the carrying cost to the vendor. This is not so burdensome or inequitable as it seems at first, however. The vendor, with some knowledge of what his or her customer will need over a given period, is in a better position to plan his or her own stocks or production and to eliminate the peaks and valleys in supply that often occur otherwise.

SOME PERFORMANCE OBJECTIVES

After studying this chapter you should be able to:

1. Trace the steps in a typical purchasing cycle.
2. Name the basic forms used throughout the basic manual purchasing system.
3. Distinguish between routine follow-up of orders and field expediting.
4. Explain the cash-with-order procedure used in many industrial and institutional purchasing departments.

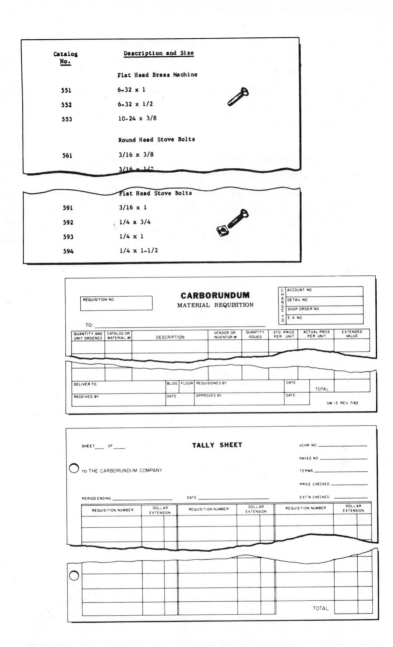

Figure 3-6. Systems contracting procedure includes a catalog (top) of all items bought under the contract, material requisitions that serve as releases and are sent directly by using departments to the supplier, and tally sheet sent to the buying company's accounts payable department in place of an invoice.

5. Discuss the small-order problem in terms of purchasing efficiency and identify three small-order techniques that have been used successfully in many types of purchasing departments.
6. Describe the major types of long-range buying agreements covered in the text.

The basic steps in the buying cycle discussed in this chapter are not likely to change substantially in the near future. The "mechanics" of the system, however, are changing rapidly under the impact of advances in electronic data processing. In the next chapter we show how that impact has been felt in purchasing and how the computer has speeded up the purchasing process and eliminated much of the detail necessary under manual systems.

Computerized Purchasing

4

The automated office has become as much a reality as the automated plant. Applied to purchasing operations, automatic equipment—specifically the computer—has helped to reduce paper-handling costs and free buyers from routine clerical work. The computer has also given the purchasing executive a continuing source of significant operating data not previously available to him or her without an enormous amount of hand calculation. The statistical information that the computer produces helps the purchasing manager in long-range planning, inventory control, evaluation of purchasing performance, evaluation of vendor performance, and reporting to management.

No machine can replace personal judgment and decision in purchasing. But the computer is a potent tool for eliminating drudgery and for improving performance in purchasing. The statistical data it provides give added authority to the purchasing manager's decision as to what and how much to buy, and it reduces the possibility of error in reference and calculation.

The computer is in effect a huge file, a calculating machine and a printer all rolled in one. It stores basic data in its memory—on reels of magnetic tape or on magnetic disks—and it translates the data for procurement action. A typical computer used in purchasing operations by an eastern office products manufacturer can compute economic purchase order quantities; vendor discount and lead-time information; produce requisitions; write hundreds of purchase orders an hour, if necessary; initiate follow-up orders; audit supplier invoices; prepare payment vouchers and checks. In addition, it turns out a wide variety of operating reports significant to purchasing and other departments as well as to corporate management, such as the status of open orders, commitments, and amount of expenditures. An idea of the amount and type of management information available from a computerized purchasing system can be obtained from Figure 4-1, adapted from an article on management information systems (MIS).[1] MIS is defined as comprehensive computerized data processing network that encompasses a wide range of individual computer applications that have been in existence for a number of years—for example, payroll, accounts receivable, general ledger, purchasing, inventory control, sales analysis, order processing, production scheduling, plant maintenance, and accounts payable.

There are three basic computer systems for gathering, interpreting, and transmitting information. In the *batch* system, information is collected in various departments during the day in the form of punched cards or tapes and keypunched in a batch into the computer at the end of the business day. An *on-line* system permits any department using a CRT (cathode ray tube) terminal with keyboard to get information on the data previously entered. The information might be as current as receiving reports a few hours old. In a *real-time* system, which also employs the CRT, the information is entered on line, but the data is updated simultaneously so that it is immediately available for display on the CRT of the interested department.

ON-LINE SYSTEM FOR PURCHASING

At the time of this writing, relatively few companies had complete installation of real-time systems in purchasing, but it was clear that the trend was definitely in that direction. A specialist in computer systems pointed out that the computer and the buyer were being brought into intimate contact with each other through the use of two already well established concepts: the CRT terminal, consisting of an integrated typewriter keyboard and video display unit linked to a computer and a computerized data base.[2]

Accepting the IBM definition of a data base as a "collection of data fundamental to an enterprise," this computer specialist pointed out that a purchasing department could be considered an enterprise in an on-line system. Its data base could include such information as buyer names and

[1] T. E. Shaughnessy, "Using MIS to Improve Supply Management," *Journal of Purchasing and Materials Management,* Vol. II (Winter 1975): 22.

[2] R. J. Cone, "Purchasing in the New Computer Environment," *Journal of Purchasing and Materials Management,* Vol. 14 (Summer 1978): 2.

MANAGEMENT PROBLEM	FORM OF MANAGEMENT ASSISTANCE	SYSTEMS APPROACH
Coordination of construction supply and equipment purchase with engineering department	Monitor supply aspects of construction project What is needed? When? Is it on order? When due?	Project management system with a supply interface
Recommend improvements in supply materials transport	Cost reductions or improved service via improved freight planning	Analysis of data on freight movements available from plant supply systems consolidated at headquarters
Techniques to measure supply function performance and effectiveness	Statistical data on volumes, trends and relationships to standards What is the volume of orders, dollars spent, dollars committed? Compare our price performance to published index for variance analysis	Data may be extracted from plant systems
Materials planning and control and pricing policy	Develop price indices for major product lines What is the price trend on important items or groups of items?	Using the central data base of supply data extract information and compute an index on key materials
Analyses of areas for concentrated effort, for value analysis consolidated purchases and negotiations	**Analyses of volume of** buying from key vendors and key materials bought Grouping of related materials as to where used and what volume	Extract information from a central data base of purchasing data
Buyer performance	Compare commodity purchase price to commodity index-track variance	Compare published index for commodity to the company experience
Obsolete inventory services	Disposition of obsolete material and equipment by publishing consolidated list of materials for disposition	Plant data describing obsolete items may be sent to a single location for processing a consolidated catalog
Vendor evaluations	Evaluate and rate vendors by field and total company performance using objective criteria	Field purchasing systems may capture vendor performance experiences via late delivery, rejected goods, and price changes
Contribution to profit via purchasing leverage	Derive statistical data to measure total volume of business by vendor and product to aid in evaluating leverage advantage	Central data base of purchasing data would produce necessary information
Inbound freight costs control	Any field location may be analyzed or groups of locations for consolidations or alternate route or carrier	Freight data on inbound shipments may be captured with purchasing data upon receipt of goods
Supply protection	Analysis of present sources related to high volume or sensitive items by using locations	Purchasing information may be extracted from a central data base
Price forecasts vs actual experience	Report comparing forecast vs actual prices with % deviations	Pricing information may be extracted from a central data base

Figure 4-1. Examples of information that a computerized supply system can provide, over and above basic purchasing data, to assist in the solution of management problems. Courtesy, *Journal of Purchasing and Materials Management.*

assignments, vendor names and addresses, descriptive data on repetitively ordered items, and a listing of open purchase orders with current shipping dates. The data base retains essential information in the computer and makes it available almost instantly, as already mentioned. The authorized person requiring the information simply enters a required sequence of digits and words on the keyboard, and the requested information is displayed on the screen in a matter of seconds in most cases.

This is in contrast to the situation in which information is stored on paper in conventional files or on tape or disks in off-line computer files. The batch system is characterized by extensive manual effort, heavy paper flow, and lengthy waits for information. A vendor's promised shipment date or a notice of received material might take a week to move through key punching and conversion to tape or disk storage to eventual appearance on a batch-produced report. However, batch processing is still suitable where the volume or frequency of information does not justify installation of costly, sophisticated systems.

RESULTS IN A REAL-TIME SYSTEM

In its planning to computerize the purchasing function, one midwestern company identified the problems that it had hoped to overcome with a new real-time system.

Current purchase order information was not easily accessible; the process of getting answers to inquiries was time consuming and inefficient; filing operations were often redundant and inconsistent; there was unnecessary duplication in transcription and posting, and errors were frequent; buying personnel were spending so much time on paperwork and clearing up delays in transmission of information that they neglected the most important aspects of their jobs, such as negotiation and planning; management information was difficult and costly to obtain.

The capabilities the company built into the system were as follows:

It generated purchase orders, releases against standing orders or contracts, and changes to purchase orders. Up-to-date order information could be both recorded and retrieved when needed. This included order acknowledgments from vendors, deliveries, changes, cancellations, and data on limited inspection and payment information. It permitted identification of received materials by part number, purchase order number, and supplier. Follow-up and exception reporting of selected purchase order processes was made automatic. Duplication of effort in the transcription, handling, and resolution of discrepancies caused by dissimilar data being used in two or more departments was reduced. Handling and filing of the receiving department copies of purchase orders was eliminated. Mistakes or discrepancies in quantities of purchased materials were reduced.

Following the installation of its procurement system, the company was able to report the following operational benefits:

Improved accuracy of information permitted faster decision making; duplication of purchase order files, which had been maintained in several places, was eliminated; problems in reconciling documents were reduced; accounts payable information was automatically transmitted; the clerical work load was reduced; paperwork delays were ended and the procurement cycle was shortened; delivered materials were positively identified at time of receipt; potential inventory level reductions were recognized; and commitment reporting was greatly simplified.

The company has repeatedly emphasized two significant points about the new computerized system: First, every action that takes place once the purchase order has been generated is available at all terminals (in this case, purchasing, receiving, receiving inspection, production control, and accounts payable) for reference. And, second, information generated and maintained by those departments is immediately available and accessible to them.

HOW THE SYSTEM FUNCTIONS

Following, in broad outline, is a description of how the company's computerized system functions.

The specific areas of the procurement cycle involved are the requisition process, the purchase order (or release) generation process, the receiving process, the accounts payable process, and portions of the operations report and analysis processes. The same information or data involved in the normal procurement cycle, which was discussed in the previous chapter, is the core of the automated system. It has, however, been organized into a formal structure of fields, data sets, programs, processes, and systems. All the information is kept in one place and is available to the various areas that may need it. All the interrelationships that exist in the purchasing cycle have been incorporated into the procurement system data sets; thus data entered by one department affects what happens in other departments. Consequently, no department can work totally independently of another without decreasing the efficiency of the whole system.

The purchasing cycle begins with requisitions for purchased materials and services based on requirements, planning and inventory replenishment, unplanned production manufacturing needs, demand for nonstocked items, capital items, expense items, specialized service requirements, and other types of needs that might arise.

A buyer in the purchasing department checks the requisition, selects a vendor, completes the requisition with the necessary information, and enters all the data including scheduled delivery time in the system. As the purchase order, or purchase order release or change, is generated, the data are being recorded on the procurement data sets, identified, and cross-referenced. Once all the appropriate information has been entered and verified, the purchase order (or variation) is automatically produced on a printer in the purchasing department.

As soon as the order has been produced, any authorized individual is able to inquire about the status of an order and have the information displayed on the appropriate CRT terminal in one of the departments just mentioned.

Three copies of purchase order documents are produced: one for the supplier, one for the originator, and one as a permanent record. Meanwhile, scheduled delivery information is recorded for later retrieval.

When a vendor's shipment arrives in the receiving department, it can be identified immediately, either by a purchase order number on the packing slip or by retrieving the part number or the vendor's name and address through the terminal (see Figure 4-2). When receiving records receipt of the material, the open purchase order data is automatically updated. The material is then moved to the inspection department for processing. Disposition of the material (accepted, rejected, partially accepted, etc.) is recorded, and again order records are immediately updated. From inspection the accepted material is moved to inventory.

All information entered is then available to all terminals, including that of the accounts payable department. Accounts payable receives invoices and, upon verification, enters a voucher number, the invoice number and date, and any other pertinent information. Payment of invoices is also recorded, thereby indicating completion of the procurement cycle for that order.

TIE-INS TO SUPPLIER COMPUTERS

Much of the computerized information in purchasing is intended for suppliers and can have a direct effect on their plans and operations. It is only logical that some highly computerized purchasing departments and some of their suppliers have developed systems by which their computers

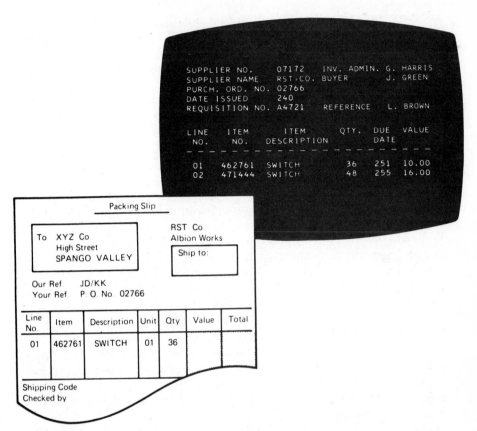

Figure 4-2. Purchase order details displayed on terminal in receiving department for verification against packing slip. Courtesy, International Business Machines Corp.

can "talk" repetitively to each other about purchases of materials that are bought. Automobile manufacturers, for example, were among the first to provide selected vendors with data output rather than with conventional purchase orders or releases against contracts. In the beginning of such exchanges, the data was supplied on magnetic tapes or punched cards generated by the buying companies' equipment, which in turn were fed into suppliers' EDP equipment to produce their internal documents.

The technique of providing data output has been widely adopted in other industries, but the exchange of information now involves direct telephone transmission from buyers to supplier computers. In a typical case, the buyer or assistant dials the supplier and then punches the necessary order data into his or her terminal keyboard. The supplier's computer responds through the buyer's CRT screen, acknowledging receipt of the information and requesting, when necessary, additional data. When that exchange is complete, the buyer signals the supplier to go ahead with the order.

The system also permits the buyer, on a given signal, to call out and review the details of any order that has been placed in a given period or determine the status of any open orders.

PURCHASING IN AN INTEGRATED SYSTEM

To emphasize the changes that computerization has brought to procurement operations, we have examined at some length an example that is limited to the basic buying and receiving functions. Purchasing, however, is only part of a complex of interrelated functions. Purchasing is, moreover, an execution system rather than a planning system, so that its operations must be directly coordinated with those of the planning departments.

Figure 4-3 provides a very general view of the position and relationships of purchasing in a completely integrated and computerized information processing system for production and other manufacturing operations. International Business Machines Corporation, which developed the Communications Oriented Production Information and Control System (COPICS), summarized the application areas outlined in the COPICS concepts as follows:

Engineering and Production Data Control creates and maintains basic engineering records.

Customer Order Servicing links the sales information system to manufacturing. Customer order entry and control of the order through to shipment are addressed.

Forecasting provides techniques to project finished product demand and establish management standards to control manufacturing activity.

Master Production Schedule Planning allows quick assessment of the impact of alternate production plans on plant capacity. The result is a realistic master production schedule, which is used for further detailed planning.

Inventory Management determines the quantities and the timing of each item to be ordered—both manufactured in-house and purchased— to meet the requirements of the master production schedule.

Manufacturing Activity Planning is used to plan detailed capacity requirements and to adjust the date of planned order release to be consistent with plant capacity. Its objective is to achieve a reasonably level load as well as to minimize work-in-process inventory and manufacturing lead time.

Order Release is the connection between manufacturing planning and execution. On the planned order release date, this function creates the documents authorizing production or purchase of the required material.

Plant Monitoring and Control traces the progress of each shop order as it moves through the shop. It coordinates many of the supporting activities, such as inspection, materials handling, and tools. Direct computer control of many phases of the manufacturing process is also within its scope.

Plant Maintenance addresses maintenance manpower planning, work order dispatching and costing, as well as preventive maintenance scheduling.

Purchasing and Receiving maintains current purchase quotations, creates purchase orders, and follows the progress of the order from the time of requisition through acknowledgment, follow-up, receipt, quality control, and deposit in stores.

Stores Control keeps track of material location and determines where to store the new material. Its objectives are to increase utilization of storage space and to reduce both picking time and picking errors.

Cost Planning and Control is addressed particularly to the financial executive and provides techniques whereby the information created and maintained for production purposes can be used for budgeting and accounting applications.[3]

FUTURE OF COMPUTERIZED PURCHASING

Computerized purchasing procedure follows, in general, the very same steps and procedures that make up the standard procedures described in the previous chapter in terms of a manual operation. It does not change the function of a procurement department, and it is necessarily based on exactly the same data for each purchase transaction and record. The special characteristics of the automated procedure are speed, the elimination of tedious and costly paperwork, the quick availability of information for almost any purpose desired.

This greater efficiency is in itself a tremendous asset. But even more important than the improvement in procedures is the improvement in management of the purchasing activity that this makes possible. The additional information gives the purchasing officer more tools to work with, a basis for better and faster policy decisions, and the means for extending the constructive aspects of materials and purchasing management. The abilities of the computer are by no means limited to the

[3] *Communications Oriented Production Information and Control System, Volume 1, page 2,* International Business Machines Corp. Figure 4-2, page 67, and Figure 4-3, page 70 are from Volume VII of the same series, and all are used with permission.

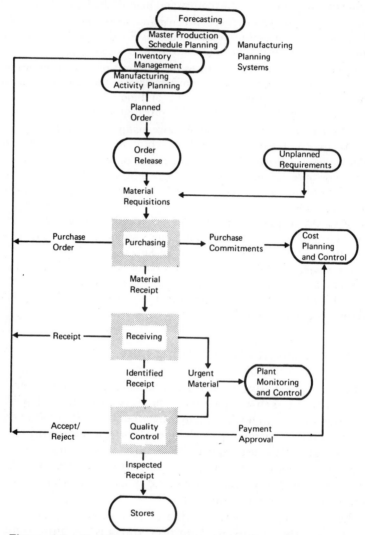

Figure 4-3. Relationship of purchasing and receiving to other application areas in a computerized materials system. Courtesy, International Business Machines Corp.

procedural operations. At least one automobile manufacturer uses the computer to take care of the almost infinite variations of color combinations and accessories that are encountered in purchasing and production for today's highly individualized "standard" models. The appraisal of vendor performance, studies of stock obsolescence, and the preparation of reports to management are other applications that come readily to mind. The possibilities of this sort are limited only by the ingenuity of purchasing and computer personnel in programming the operations to produce new types of information from existing data.

Further, automation of all routing and repetitive activities makes possible what is sometimes called "management by exception." It has been pointed out in the sections dealing with automated stock control, follow-up, and invoice checking, for example, that it is only the unusual situation, the emergency, the discrepancy of error, that comes to the attention of the buyer once the basic decision has been made. When the routine transactions proceed according to schedule—in perhaps as many as 95 percent of all cases, once the system has been properly installed and adjusted—the buyers' time, ability and judgment can be concentrated on the research, negotiation, policy, and special projects phases of procurement free from the burden and intrusion of routine details.

Not all companies need as elaborate a computerized materials system as that described here. As suppliers of EDP equipment constantly emphasize, each company has special requirements that may be met by installing a complex, tailored systems in some cases or simply by leasing time at a computer center serving a number of businesses in others. In any event, it is practically a certainty that the computer will be used universally in business operations of every kind.

Purchasing managers must recognize and understand the potential in computers, not only for improvement of their own functions, but for complete integration of all an organization's major functions. Thus, they should have some general knowledge of computer technology and vocabulary. More important, however, they must be able to see the computer as an overall tool for controlling the total resources of the organization. As Shaughnessy has pointed out, the use of computerized systems in material and supply management is an executive management issue, not a technical problem.[4] Purchasing and materials managers who want to stay in front of their competition must take the initiative in exploiting the capabilities of the computer.

The key problem in management use of computers has been described by one authority in the following terms:

> A common point of view of managers at all levels is that the computer group should come up with its proposals for computer utilization and present these proposals to the managers for their acceptance or rejection. Meanwhile, presumably, the managers go about their regular operational business. A different point of view—and one with far greater merit—is that

[4] Ibid.

it is the initial responsibility of managers to identify to computer personnel their objectives and the specific problems and factors with which they are contending as they seek to achieve these objectives. The identifications then become the basis of a continuing dialogue as computer personnel seek to apply computer capabilities to the attack on these managerial problems. Why is this not done to a greater extent? One reason is undoubtedly that managers do not have the proper initial attitude as discussed above (recognizing computers should be exploited). Another reason may be that they are too busy with day-to-day operational pressures—a problem which can be resolved through a reassessment of priorities. A third reason, however, may be that managers are not able to identify the problems adequately. If this latter reason is controlling, one may well ask whether the manager himself is properly qualified for his particular job.[5]

SOME PERFORMANCE OBJECTIVES

After studying this chapter you should be able to:

1. Explain why purchasing operations are particularly suited to computerization.
2. Name the principal elements in a purchasing department data base.
3. Describe briefly how a buyer–seller computer-to-computer system works.
4. List the typical operating benefits derived from the computerized system described in the text.
5. Name the units in the integrated COPICS system described in the text.
6. Discuss the possible reasons for the inability or unwillingness of some managers—including purchasing managers—to make more effective use of computers.

Having covered the basic responsibilities of a purchasing department and the operations of both manual and computerized purchasing systems, we next discuss the organizational structure through which the policies must be implemented and by which procedures must be directed and controlled.

---

[5] Victor Z. Brink, *Computers and Management: The Executive Viewpoint* (Englewood Cliffs, N.J.: Prentice Hall, 1971), p. 109.

Structure of The Purchasing Organization

5

Efficient conduct of purchasing presupposes a department specifically assigned to this duty that is (1) headed by a responsible purchasing officer who is accountable to management for performance of the function and (2) adequately staffed to carry on procurement activities. At one time, when purchasing was just emerging as a specialized function, it was described as "centralized" if the two conditions cited were present in a given organization. The term is still used in some organizations for example, in hospitals, to indicate, in this case, that a purchasing department—not the medical staff, or the laboratories, or the nurses, or others—has the authority to issue purchase orders. Generally, however, the terms centralization and decentralization refer to physical location of purchasing organizations within a multiplant company. (The two concepts are discussed later in this chapter.)

In a small company, with a limited volume and variety of purchases, the department may consist only of the purchasing agent or manager and a clerical assistant. In some cases, the head of the department is also office manager or manager of building and office services, but the assignment of dual or multiple responsibilities to the head of purchasing is becoming increasingly rare. Even in smaller units, such as educational and health care institutions, it is being recognized that procurement is too important to be handled on a part-time basis.

In very large companies, purchasing departments may have up to several hundred employees. There is no clear correlation between the dollar volume of purchases and the size of the purchasing staff. This varies widely according to the character of the enterprise and its purchasing problem, the scope of purchasing responsibility, and the extent to which related activities—such as expediting, storeskeeping, traffic management, and materials control—are included. Figure 5-1 shows the position of a purchasing department in a medium-sized company.

PURCHASING IN THE GENERAL ORGANIZATION PLAN

As noted in Chapter 2, the majority of organized purchasing departments report directly to the top executive officer who is responsible for profitable operation—president, executive vice president, or general manager. This includes plant and divisional purchasing departments in multiplant organizations in which the plant purchasing manager is apart from the general purchasing department at company headquarters, has considerable independence of authority, and reports to the branch or divisional manager responsible for that operating unit. This situation is discussed in greater detail later in this chapter.

Wherever the purchasing manager reports directly to top management, that individual is in the first tier of executives, on the same organization plane with the production manager, sales manager, comptroller, manager of industrial relations, and the heads of other functional divisions.

In a small number of manufacturing companies, the purchasing department is under the jurisdiction of the production or manufacturing division, and the purchasing manager reports to the production manager, who is in turn responsible to top management. Here the purchasing manager is in a secondary tier of executives, and the function is regarded as a subordinate one. It is considered primarily as a service function, not as a management activity with a responsibility to contribute to profit, however.

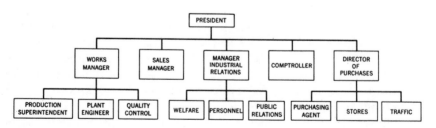

Figure 5-1. Place of a purchasing department in the organization of a medium-sized, single-plant company.

A third type of organization, used primarily in very large companies and diversified industries operating under a single management, separates the operational and managerial phases of purchasing. Separate buying departments are set up at the divisional level as parts of the division organization plan (see Figure 5-2). A general purchasing department at company headquarters serves the entire organization as a staff facility. It counsels top management on broad purchasing and material policies, conducts general and specific purchasing research programs that are made available to all buyers, sets policies for the guidance of divisional purchasing departments, coordinates purchasing policies and activities throughout the company, and gives assistance on specific purchasing problems where needed. It does little or no actual buying and has no responsibility for the details of procurement beyond evaluating purchasing performance at the various divisions and pointing out means for improvement. In most cases, it has no jurisdiction over the hiring or firing of divisional purchasing personnel, although it usually sets up the buyer-training programs and has decisive influence in the transfer of persons with superior buying talent to positions of greater responsibility and opportunity among the divisions.

Figures 5-3 and 5-4 show typical purchasing departmental structures in small and large companies, respectively.

PLANT OR DIVISION PURCHASING

In multiplant operations, which are frequently found in enterprises of moderate size and are almost universal among the larger companies, the question arises of whether to do all purchasing for the entire organization

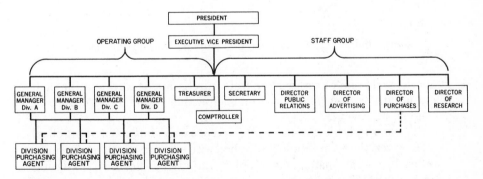

Figure 5-2. Place of the purchasing department under a divisional organization plan.

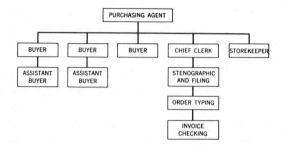

Figure 5-3. Organization plan of a medium-sized purchasing department.

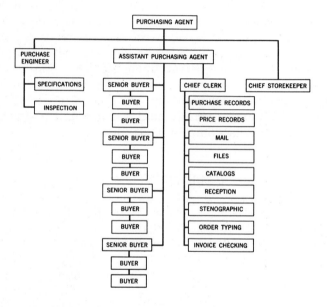

Figure 5-4. Organization plan of a large purchasing department.

at one central point or set up a separate purchasing department for each operating division or plant location, each with a considerable degree of autonomy in buying.

The latter plan is popularly referred to as *decentralization* of purchasing. However, the term should be applied with some reservations, because it refers to overall management policy rather than to the purchasing function itself. Centralization or decentralization of purchasing under these circumstances is usually a matter of degree. The branch plant or divisional purchasing department is organized on the same pattern as already outlined, and every principle of centralized purchasing is observed in its operation. Furthermore, the system is in no way inconsistent with effective central management control.

The reasons for establishing separate plant or divisional purchasing departments may be summarized as follows:

1. The plant or division manager is responsible for the efficient and profitable operation of that company unit. On the principle that responsibility and authority should go hand in hand, the plant or division manager should have jurisdiction over purchases as well as production, because a large percentage of his costs and a major factor in the efficiency and continuity of production are represented in the procurement function.

2. If the branch or division is large enough to be considered an economical operating unit, it is usually large enough to realize the advantages of volume purchasing on the basis ot its own requirements. It is, in most instances, as large as or larger than many completely independent companies in the same field, in which centralized purchasing is profitably used, and the corporate relationship to other divisions is merely incidental in this comparison. The law of diminishing returns applies to centralization in the organization and procedure for purchasing as well as in the mechanical phases of industrial operation. Good management seeks to find the method of maximum efficiency, rather than to apply even a proven principle, such as centralized purchasing, arbitrarily.

3. When the distance between plants is significant, purchasing from a central office entails a time lag that may result in serious delays. It involves duplication of paperwork and records. It sacrifices the direct, daily contact with departments when needs arise and materials are used. It is poorly adapted to cope with emergency requirements promptly. These shortcomings tend to offset the benefits that might be expected from complete centralization of purchasing operations.

4. Each plant or division may have some unique requirements and differences in operating conditions that affect material needs and procurement. Transportation, climatic conditions, storage facilities, plant equipment and usage, local trade customs and ordinances, and suppliers' distribution policies all have a bearing on purchasing. The plant purchasing department is in the better position to understand and adapt to these factors. Where two or more branch plants have some common requirements, suggesting an advantage in joint procurement, it is entirely feasible to regard this as the exception to the general rule and to handle it accordingly, rather than the other way around.

5. The public relations aspect of purchasing must be considered, as well as the more objective factor of overall purchase volume. It is now generally conceded that a company has an economic responsibility to the

communities in which its plants are located. Goodwill can be fostered by purchasing from nearby sources or through local distributors and sales representatives, so far as is practicable. Although such policies can be carried out even though purchasing is done from a distant, central point, they are likely to be more effective, consistent, and personalized when locally administered. Certainly they are more closely identified with the local community, in the public mind.

COMPLETE CENTRALIZATION

The arguments for complete centralization of purchasing for a multiplant manufacturing company stress the combined requirements of the entire company and the consequent opportunities to combine these requirements for greater quantity purchasing advantages and outright purchasing power; the desirability of having a single buying policy and procedure for the whole organization; the need for central controls as a means of evaluating purchasing activities and maintaining high standards of performance. It is pointed out that the staff responsibilities of the chief purchasing officer can be handled more effectively through his or her direct administration of all buying.

In this view, plant location in itself is a relatively unimportant detail. The purchasing department is not necessarily located at the plant in any case. It is regarded more as a part of the general executive organization than as a part of the manufacturing operation. Particularly in metropolitan areas, it is not unusual to find a company's executive and purchasing offices in the business center of the city, whereas the manufacturing plants are located in outlying factory sections, sometimes several miles distant. With modern techniques of rapid communication and travel, the greater distance to plants in other cities need be no great obstacle to efficient buying service.

There are advantages other than mere volume in a single purchasing program for the entire company. For example,

1. Quality of purchased materials and parts is more readily controlled when they are bought on one contract from one source than when the orders are placed with several unrelated sources by as many different buyers.

2. There is added flexibility because shipments on existing orders or contracts can be allocated and directed to various plants as needed instead of initiating a new purchase. The transfer of materials from one plant to another may be the quickest and most economical way of meeting an emergency.

3. One plant's surplus may be used to fill another's needs without making an additional expenditure or commitment, at the same time getting a better return on the value of such surplus.

4. Losses from obsolescence of parts due to changes in model or design can be minimized by concentrating the "balancing out" process of manufacture on the existing model in a single designated plant.

5. A higher degree of specialization and consequent purchasing skill can logically be expected in respect to special commodities. This contrasts with a situation in which the same responsibility is delegated to several buyers at the various plants.

CENTRALIZED CONTROL

Judging from actual business practice over the years, there is no one best answer to the question of centralization versus decentralization of purchasing. In the period following World War II, complete centralization was generally considered the best form of organization. In the late 1950s and early 1960s, American industry, led by such large organizations as the General Electric Company, took a decided turn toward decentralization of operations, including purchasing. A marked return toward some form of centralization began in the late 1960s and picked up momentum through the 1970s. The trend has continued into the 1980s.

Management's decision to centralize or decentralize can be influenced by a number of things: fundamental economic trends, fashions in management philosophy, changes in the structure of business, mergers, and technological developments such as the computer. The computer, for example, has done much to accelerate the trend to centralization in purchasing. It makes possible the compilation and analysis of large amounts of significant purchasing and related data—on activity, volume, prices, inventory status, and so on—so that judgments and decisions can be made speedily and communicated just as quickly to all concerned.

The most widely used arrangement is a compromise designed to obtain the advantages of both methods of organization. This usually takes the form of a decentralized system with centralized coordination and controls. Some of the specific means of developing and maintaining such a system include:

1. Uniform policies, forms, and procedures at all plants, established through a company-wide purchasing manual; uniform quality standards established by company-wide specifications.

2. Continuing review of all purchasing activities by having copies of

purchase orders routed to the central office. Systematic monthly reports from all branch purchasing departments, correlated at the central office and redistributed to the branches in a summary report form, with buying recommendations.

3. Dollar value limitation on branch plant purchases. Orders or contracts in excess of the stated limit are subject to approval by the central department. This corresponds to the regulation in many purchasing departments that orders amounting to more than a stated dollar value must be approved by the head of the department or by some higher executive.

4. Certain items, usually major materials in common use at two or more plants, are designated as contract items and are purchased by the central department for all plants. In some cases, the initial requirement of a new item is purchased by the plant purchasing department, with subsequent review to determine whether or not it shall be classified as a contract item. A variation of this is to delegate the purchase of specified items to a designated plant purchasing department in which the item is used in greatest volume.

5. Contracts for items in common use are made by the central department, with provision for shipment to all company locations. Branch plant buyers are expected to issue release orders against these existing contracts, but have the option of buying independently if they can improve on the terms of the contract for their individual plant requirements through special local circumstances or for any other reason. This assures buying on the most favorable terms in all cases and may lead to revision of the central contracts to extend the benefit to all branches.

One interesting application of the centralized–decentralized concept is that used by the Gillette Company, which has thirty-five divisions in the United States and abroad, each of which has its own purchasing organization. Each purchasing department reports to the division president or manufacturing vice president. At corporate headquarters a corporate group of less than a dozen persons has seventeen distinct responsibilities to the divisions, including the following:

1. Development of uniform purchasing policies and procedures and the issuance and updating of a manual explaining them.

2. Training of personnel, particularly in smaller locations, and preparation of training aids.

3. Monitoring of purchasing performance and auditing of purchasing departments upon request.

4. Exchange of information among divisions—on price movements, availability of critical materials, and special materials problems of individual divisions.

5. Consultation on job-rating classifications.
6. Consultation on organization of division departments (including maintenance of a corporate-wide list of key personnel).

Common materials purchasing was one of the first responsibilities assumed by the corporate department when it was formed. Some materials in common use in all or many of the divisions are bought at headquarters; others are bought for all divisions in one manufacturing group (toiletries, for example) by the division consuming the greatest amount of a given material. All contracts are reviewed at the corporate level.

Other corporate responsibilities include research and data gathering on material common to all or a number of plants, issuance of a newsletter on political and economic conditions that may affect company operations, cross-fertilization of ideas among divisions, and consultation on standardization.

In some companies, centralized control of commodities used in a number of plants has led to more highly centralized purchasing organizations at corporate headquarters. One large metals producer, for example, has moved approximately 40 percent of all its purchases into central purchasing at corporate headquarters. Commodity specialists at headquarters handle all corporate requirements for commonly used items such as pitch binder, petroleum, coke, and corrugated boxes. Any item not specifically assigned to the central office is the direct responsibility of plant purchasing officers. Headquarters continues, however, to provide local purchasing agents with policy guidance and administrative assistance.

Even the largest manufacturing companies move quickly to restructure their purchasing departments to meet changing economic, social, and political conditions. Major changes occurred in the procurement policies and organizations of major automobile producers in the mid-1970s. In an informative series on purchasing in the leading car makers, writer Brooke Elliott listed some of the developments that helped to alter the tactics and operations of purchasing organizations that spend many billions of dollars (General Motors' expenditures alone amounted to about $19 billion in 1976). The decline in popularity of larger cars—the result, in large part, of the Arab oil embargo of 1973 and the subsequent rise in gasoline prices, escalating materials and labor costs, long-range prospects of severe materials shortages, and costs of safety and pollution devices—all helped bring about profound and significant changes in automobile industry purchasing.

The response of the industry to these influences was typified by General Motors' reorganization of its materials functions: Central to the reorganization was the naming of a corporate vice president for procurement, production control, and logistics. GM had never had a corporate officer with that responsibility before. Reorganization of the purchasing function began with greater emphasis on centralized policy control. Previously, all purchasing had been done at the divisional level or below. Plant purchasing staffs bought items peculiar to their own location, and local buying was done at the smallest plants.[1]

New conditions, however, called for new programs, and GM developed five new approaches to procurement: lead division sourcing, forward planning, regional purchasing, national contracting for nonproduct materials (maintenance, repairs, and operating materials), and materials committees.

Lead division sourcing is the assignment of purchasing responsibility to that division in which a divisional engineering group already exists. If the division has responsibility for designing and developing all brake systems for the corporation, then the division's purchasing group does all the buying for those systems. All purchasing requirements are negotiated once, rather than at five separate times with the five divisions that use the systems.

The forward planning effort involves a small group at corporate headquarters that collects information relating to future material needs and availability: supply and demand, capacity, government regulation, cost trends, and so on. The data are distilled into reports on the availability of specific materials for the next four to five years, and the reports are then forwarded to each divisional purchasing manager and to appropriate members of the corporate staff.

Regional purchasing offices were established to determine specific nonproduct requirements for divisions in a given area and then to determine if requirements can be combined and bought on one contract to gain the advantages of volume buying. A necessary part of the information gathering is the development of a common identification for identical items that had been purchased under different names, by different numbers, and by different descriptions.

The idea of developing national contracts for nonproduct supplies, to be negotiated and administered from corporate headquarters, is a further refinement of the regional purchasing approach. The decision to enter into such contracts is the responsibility of the divisional purchasing directors, acting as a materials committee, who come together to analyze the benefits of coordinating their purchases.

The changing economic environment of the mid-1970s also prompted changes in the purchasing organization of Ford Motor Company. Ford moved from a supply organization approach to procurement

---

[1] Brooke Elliott, "How Detroit Buys," *Purchasing World* Vol. 20, nos. 8, 9, 10, 11 (August, September, October, and November, 1976).

(similar to the materials management function to be described in Chapter 6) to a centralized purchasing group with its own vice president that handles all buying and planning for North American operations.

The materials management organization was responsible for five activities, three staff and two central purchasing: production planning and control; purchasing policy and planning; transportation and traffic; facilities and tooling purchasing; and metals, petroleum, and raw materials purchasing.

In the new Ford organization, a centralized purchasing department, with its own vice president, now has direct responsibility for buying. Staff functions—traffic and transportation, production planning and control, and supply policy and planning—remain decentralized with limited or no operating responsibility. The supply policy and planning group, for example, is responsible for coordinating Ford's purchasing policies and procedures in all divisions in the United States and abroad. The one operating group that was retained in the supply staff is facilities and tool purchasing, which serves the worldwide Ford organization.

North American purchasing was organized into six groups: three directly concerned with buying and three performing planning and administrative functions (see Figure 5-5). The body and assembly unit, power train and chassis group, and metals, petroleum and materials unit handle most purchasing for Ford's assembly plants. There are a few exceptions. Some plants with special requirements are permitted to purchase them, and some purchasing of nonproduction materials—maintenance, repairs, and operating materials—is done locally.

A planning and analysis unit works closely with an engineering materials committee to develop long-range forecasts of requirements for materials and components. The purchasing controller develops cost forecasts, establishes price targets and evaluates price increases, and develops streamlined paperwork systems. The third administrative group performs personnel and organization planning.

Both the other major motor manufacturers—Chrysler and American Motors—had moved to decentralization several years earlier. Nevertheless, the purchasing organizations of both companies undergo constant change to meet new requirements and new economic conditions. Both have been particularly concerned with commodity and planning (see Figure 5-6). At Chrysler, for example, the administration and financial planning unit makes financial forecasts of materials costs on monthly, annual, and multiyear bases. The commodity planning group analyzes long-term commodity requirements and availability, in some cases up to ten years out.

The foregoing descriptions are obviously meant to serve as examples of purchasing organization theory and practice, not necessarily as

Figure 5-6

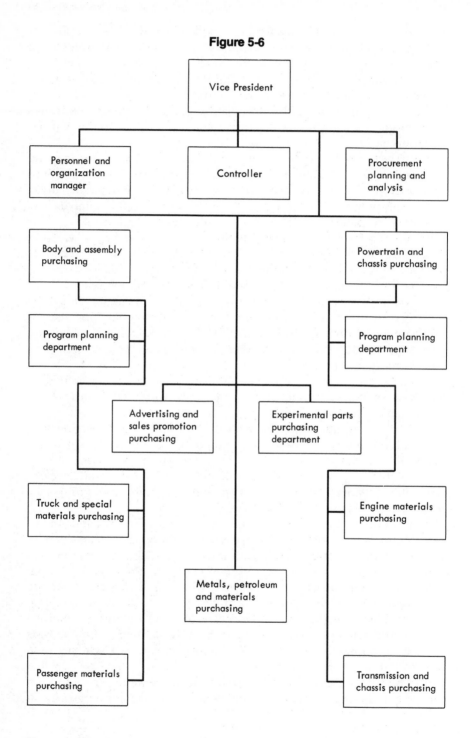

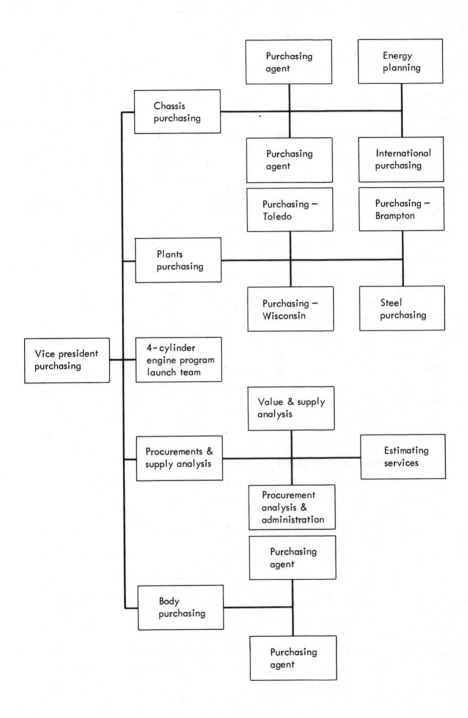

models for others. Most companies do not have the resources—personnel, management sophistication, economic power, and the like—that the motor companies can apply to their purchasing operations. Nevertheless, American industry at various levels has successfully adapted many of the car makers' business practices and philosophies, and their moves in purchasing bear careful watching.

It should be remembered that the automobile industry is both realistic and pragmatic—and in some cases almost modest—about its approaches to purchasing. In both public and private comments, top purchasing executives in the industry have tried to play down the widely held idea that Detroit has all the answers to purchasing problems. They have admitted that in some respects their previous approaches to purchasing methods and policies were far from ideal and they have not been averse to studying and adopting purchasing techniques developed in other industries.

The most significant lesson to be learned from the automobile industry's changes in purchasing organization and philosophy, however, is that there is no single, simple formula for organizing the procurement function. Economic necessity will eventually determine whether purchasing is to be completely or partially centralized or decentralized. The purchasing executives who presided at the reorganizations described in these pages are prompt to admit that their companies are not "locked in to" any particular form of organization and are flexible enough to switch back and forth to various purchasing structures to meet varying economic conditions.

SOME PERFORMANCE OBJECTIVES

After studying this chapter you should be able to:

1. Show what factors, in general, determine the size of a purchasing department.
2. Contrast the status of purchasing in companies in which the heads of purchasing report to the top level of management to the status in companies in which they report to middle-level management, in production and manufacturing, for example.
3. Review the arguments for and against completely centralized control of purchasing in the multiplant company.
4. Describe how a compromise system—partially centralized and partially decentralized—is organized. Refer to one of the companies mentioned in the text if you wish.
5. Discuss the reasons behind the changes in purchasing organization

that have taken place in the major automobile companies in recent years.

6. Identify the major lesson that can be drawn from the willingness of large companies to modify their purchasing organizations, even to the point of reversing themselves within relatively short periods of time.

Another form of organization integrates purchasing with several other functions related to the acquisition of materials and supplies and puts the combined departments under the direction of one executive. This type of organization, generally known as materials management, has been widely enough adopted (and debated) to warrant the full chapter treatment that follows.

Materials
Management

6

As we have seen in earlier chapters, purchasing has been given specialized departmental status along with clearly defined responsibilities and authority. But its role in an increasingly complex mass-production economy is not fixed, and we can expect to see continued evolution in the function. The main thrust of that evolution will be toward interdependence with other functions of business.

As purchasing continues to coordinate its efforts with those of other specialized departments—traffic, inspection, engineering, production and so on—all these activities will become more integrated than ever before. And the very process of integration may lead to a crossing of lines of authority in certain types of companies and under certain circumstances. This in turn would require new definitions of responsibility and new patterns of organization to administer them properly.

Does purchasing's responsibility in a highly integrated plant end, for example, with the issuance of the order? If purchasing's negotiations with the supplier involve transportation costs, packaging methods, and delivery dates, how far does its obligation extend in these matters? Should purchasing not have some interest in, or even control of, traffic and receiving to see that the supplier meets all requirements that were part of the negotiated price? Similar questions can be asked in regard to other phases of the materials cycle—whether, for example, purchasing's concern with ordering quantities and inventory levels should directly involve it in material control and production scheduling.

Such considerations have led many companies to adopt a broad concept of materials procurement that goes beyond basic buying. Known generally as *materials management,* the concept varies considerably from company to company, depending on the size of the organization, the nature of its products, and the customers that it serves. A review of some of the better known definitions and descriptions of the concept illustrates how flexibly the term has been used.

An early definition provided a general overview without getting into details of specific departmental responsibilities:

> Materials management is the planning, directing, controlling, and coordinating of all those activities concerned with material and inventory requirements, from the point of their inception to their introduction into the manufacturing processes. It begins with the determination of material quality and quantity and ends with its issuance to production in time to meet customer demands on schedule and at the lowest cost.[1]

Under that definition, materials management could include, in addition to purchasing, any or all of the following functions: (1) inbound and outbound traffic; (2) receiving and receiving inspection; (3) determination and control of inventories, including raw material, in-process, and finished goods inventories; (4) warehousing and shipping; (5) materials handling; and (6) production planning and scheduling.

In a comprehensive analysis done for the National Association of Purchasing Management, Dean Ammer said,

> In the broadest sense, materials management is concerned with activities involved with the flow of materials from supplier plants, through the manufacturing process, into finished goods warehouses, and on to the ultimate user of the product. In a more narrow sense, materials management is the process of getting purchased materials and services to the point where they are economically useful.[2]

He went on to list the functions typically included in a materials management system as "hard core"—inventory management, purchasing, traffic, and value analysis; "commonly accepted"—materials handling, physical distribution, production control, receiving, scheduling, shipping, stores, warehousing; and "fringe areas"—electronic data processing and market research and forecasting. Perhaps one of the most detailed explanations of what elements could be combined in a materials management system was offered by Paul E. Kindig, at the time manager,

---

[1] L. J. DeRose, "The Role of Purchasing in Materials Management," *Purchasing Magazine,* March 1956, p. 115.

[2] Dean S. Ammer, "Materials Management," in *Guide to Purchasing* (New York: National Association of Purchasing Management, 1971).

Material Resource and Traffic Operation, General Electric Company.[3] He pointed out that business objectives, information flow, and the manufacturing system and organization must each be carefully integrated. Using the flow chart in Figure 6-1, Kindig described the activities involved in two types of two customer orders as they move through the system:

A *finished goods order* is received and processed through order entry. It is then checked against the finished goods record. Assuming that the product is available, it is then withdrawn from finished goods, and the total order is accumulated and shipped, using information from traffic. The finished goods records are updated, and the customer receives what he or she ordered.

Following receipt of an *order for a special item* that requires engineering, the design and drafting are completed, a bill of materials is generated and planning and routing activities begin. Master scheduling controls the planning progress of the order and schedules the completion date. The master schedule is then converted into production and materials requirements. Materials requirements are checked against existing inventories, and materials requisitions are generated and sent to purchasing for negotiation and order placement. After receipt, purchased material is stored and made available for production. Production details can then be updated and the work released to the shop through dispatching. The job is then followed through the shop by job status reporting. When completed, the order is shipped, using information supplied by traffic.

Materials management, according to Kindig, combines a number of the above-mentioned activities into a major function. That function has the authority and responsibility for planning and controlling the material resources of the business. A logical nucleus for such a materials management system, he says, is a combination of the materials requirements, materials requisitioning, and purchasing functions. He then includes the requirements explosion, detailed production scheduling, and job status and resource loading as part of the system. Receiving, storage, and stockrooms also fall within the system because they relate to the availability of material. Traffic and shipping and billing, he says, are generally in marketing if finished stock is warehoused, but they are often considered part of materials management.

[3] Paul E. Kindig, "How to Build a Materials Management System," *New England Purchaser* Vol. 56 (May 1976): 11.

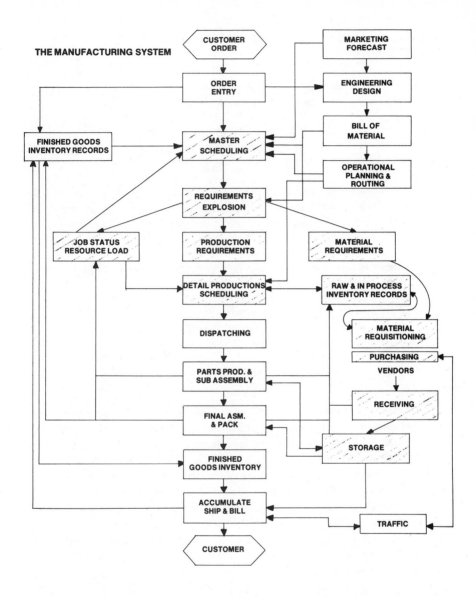

THE MANUFACTURING SYSTEM

Figure 6-1 Cross-hatched areas in this flow chart represent functions that are included in materials management system discussed on page 90. Chart shows how they interface with other functions and with each other. Courtesy, *New England Purchaser.*

PRACTICAL APPLICATIONS OF MATERIALS MANAGEMENT

In practice, the materials management concept has been interpreted in a number of ways. As Ammer said in the study cited,

> One major reason that the materials management revolution has been a quiet one is that there is no universal agreement on precisely what activities are embraced in the materials management organization.

In a research project conducted for a major U.S. corporation, two researchers surveyed one hundred top manufacturing companies (26 percent of which were using some form of materials management) and concluded:

> There is no typical materials management organization. [There is] a variety of structures used by different companies. Evidently, managers approach the materials concept pragmatically, choosing the organization that suits best their particular needs.
>
> This is what has undoubtedly led both proponents and opponents of materials management to find the concept an illusive one. They have failed to realize that the materials system is based on function rather than structure. It is a totally integrated approach to material control, not a rigorous form of managerial organization.[4]

The survey showed that all but one of the companies using materials management include purchasing in the system. Production control is part of 63 percent of the materials management organizations, and physical distribution of 81 percent. Significantly, most of the companies have incorporated a number of other functions: order entry, customer service, quality control, facilities planning, value engineering customer claims, and sale and disposal of surplus material. Three different types of materials management organization are illustrated in Figure 6-2.

Even purchasing executives, who are in the most logical position to assume the position of materials manager in the average industrial organization, are not completely in accord as to what materials management covers. Of fifty purchasing executives surveyed by the University of Wisconsin Management Institute, a high percentage (95 percent) said that materials management should include inbound traffic and receiving in addition to buying. But only 60 percent favored bringing outbound traffic, materials handling, and receiving inspection within the scope of

---

[4] Ron Baer and John Centamore, "Materials Management: Where It Stands . . . What It Means . . . ," *Purchasing Magazine,* January 8, 1970, p. 53.

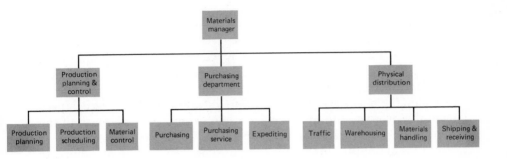

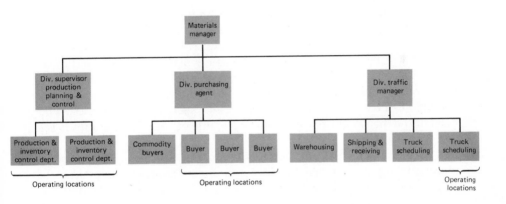

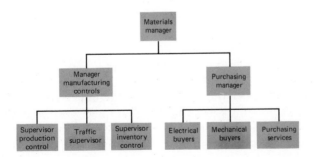

Figure 6-2. Three different organizational approaches to materials management. Courtesy, *Purchasing Magazine.*

the organization. And only 40 percent advocated making production planning and scheduling part of materials management.

Some of the more successful materials organizations in industry reflect these differences of opinion. The General Electric Company, for example, has pioneered in the use of materials management in the broadest sense of the term. Its Metallurgical Products Division has even extended the materials group's scope to include an order service department that handles and monitors customer orders. The inclusion of this function is not typical of the G.E. materials approach, however.

In addition to purchasing and customer service, the Metallurgical Division organization includes production and inventory control, receiving and warehousing.

A modification of the G.E. system is that used by Lenkurt Electric Company, San Carlos, California. It takes in buying, inbound traffic, inventory control, and receiving and stores. It has no control over shipment of finished goods or over production planning and scheduling. Purchasing personnel are divided into four groups, each headed by a senior buyer and each with its own responsibilities for planning, buying, routing, receiving, storing, and disbursing specific commodities. The head of the materials organization has the title of "Manager of Purchases and Materials."

Apparatus Division of Texas Instruments, Inc. also has a modified materials magagement organization, although it is not designated as such. It is headed by a purchasing agent and includes groups of buyers (assigned to specific division products, primarily defense items) and a material control group. The latter has responsibility for stores, collating and packaging spare parts and systems for the division's customers, and shipping and receiving.

ADVANTAGES OF MATERIALS MANAGEMENT

The great advantage of the materials management type of organization reported by those companies that have adopted it is the improved communication and coordination between departments that it permits. Materials management provides a central administration where conflicting function or departmental interests can be balanced out in the overall interest of the company. Centralized responsibility and control also make for smoother, faster flow of materials from the time they are requisitioned by using departments to the time they are shipped out to customers as finished products.

Among the more specific ways in which a centrally controlled materials organization has helped a number of companies to improve efficiency and to reduce costs are these:

1. Control of inventories is made easier and simpler. The traditional conflict caused by the efforts of manufacturing, on the one hand, to build up stocks of raw material and parts, and of purchasing, on the other, to keep them to a minimum, have been resolved. Production planning and control and purchasing have found it easier to come to agreement on minimum and maximum stocks when they are working more as a team than as separate groups with separate interests. Losses caused by obsolescence or deterioration of surplus materials are eliminated, as are the dangers of shutdowns necessitated by material shortages.

2. Clerical work is sharply reduced. As responsibility for materials moves from department to department, records are almost inevitably duplicated. Many production control departments, for example, retain file copies of the requisitions they issue to purchasing, and in turn demand copies of the purchase order. With production control and purchasing in one office under one individual, a single file copy of either form serves both. Similar reductions in the generation and filing of paperwork can be made in every department involved in the materials cycle, leading, in turn, to substantial cuts in the clerical force required. (Before the adoption of materials management in an eastern electronics firm, various functions involved in handling materials accounted for 10.5 percent of the total plant work force. A year after the new organization was formed, the percentage had dropped to 7.1. During this time the total work force had increased by 74 percent, but the number of materials personnel had gone up only 18 percent.)

3. Assorted problems of delivery scheduling, emergency orders, and storage are minimized. Purchasing can arrange delivery schedules on the basis of its knowledge of inventory levels and production requirements. Emergency or rush orders are less frequent because of understanding between production control and purchasing. Better regulation of the flow of materials into the plant permits better use of storage facilities and coordinated movement of materials into the production line.

Materials management is particularly suited to—and has been most widely adopted by—those companies that manufacture to customers' orders. Such operations often involve fluctuating inventory levels, engineering changes by the customer, and irregular production scheduling. Placing the responsibility for materials in one department enables management to keep informed on the status of every order by checking with one source. In a less coordinated system, basic information about a particular job—what materials had been requisitioned for it, the status of purchase orders placed against the requisitions, the condition of inventories, and manufacturing progress on the job—would have to be gathered from four different departments.

In those companies producing highly standardized items for stock, on the other hand, good communication and coordination between departments handling material generally have been developed by experience. Inventory levels and production schedules are usually established on the basis of sales forecasts and historical usage, and the manufacturing operation is generally more stable and predictable than is the case in the manufacture-to-order companies. In such cases, good control has already been built into the materials system, and the plant manager or vice president of operations or whatever top executive the departments concerned report to is, in fact, a materials manager already.

Another important consideration in the decision to adopt a materials management organization is the impact that the materials function has on profit and loss. Back when materials management was coming into its own and was being looked on as something of a panacea, a materials executive warned against indiscriminate adoption of the concept.[5] He pointed out that, in industries in which one or two commodities—textiles, tobacco, leather—represent the major investment, the skillful purchasing of these materials makes the difference between a profit and loss in a given year. The in-plant flow of tobacco, for example, however well managed it is, does not have anywhere nearly the impact of a buying coup, or a buying "flop."

It is important to recognize, Stiles said, that just as there are materials-oriented companies there are production-oriented companies, sales-oriented companies, and service-oriented ones. Rushing into materials management because it may be the fashion is always a serious step— and could be quite a serious error, he pointed out.

MEASURING MATERIALS MANAGEMENT PERFORMANCE

Because of the breadth and complexity of responsibilities in materials management, its specialized objectives, and the number of personnel involved, evaluation of performance in the function can be a lengthy process. The evaluation process has not received the same attention as that in purchasing (see Chapter 23) but there have been some attempts to establish measurement guidelines. One of the more comprehensive approaches was that suggested by Professor Gary Zenz, of Florida State University.[6]

[5] Edward M. Stiles, "Purchasing's Opportunity in Materials Management," *New England Purchaser* Vol. 57 (July 1967): 12.

[6] Gary J. Zenz, "Evaluating Materials Management," *Journal of Purchasing and Materials Management* Vol. II (Fall 1975): 15.

Dr. Zenz listed the major categories of materials management responsibility as planning and forecasting, integration of materials management into the total company operation, and performance of the individual functional areas of the materials management organization. He suggested that each of the areas of performance should be "budgeted" and that each actual results should be compared against the "budget."

Planning and forecasting responsibilities and areas of evaluation include:

1. Success in planning and meeting overall material dollar budgets
   a. Actual versus budgeted ratios for budgets involved
2. Accuracy of forecasts in the following:
   a. Commodity prices
   b. Interest rates
   c. General economic activity
   d. Specific corporate assignments
3. Organization and training
   a. Degree to which clear lines of responsibility and authority were established within the MM operation
   b. Degree of personnel turnover
   c. Success in implementing training and rotation plans for personnel
   d. Degree of self-development by subordinates such as attendance at lectures, conferences, seminars, and association memberships
   e. Rating of morale of subordinates

Integration with the total operation would include developing good relationships with and providing service to other departments and management personnel. Specific evaluation would consider success in providing:

1. Interfunctional management meetings
2. Understanding of MM principles throughout the company
3. Significant reports to management directed to proper audiences and providing useable information

Performance measurement of subfunctions would cover the following:

Inventory Control

1. Ratio of inventory investment to sales (by products)
2. Inventory turnover ratios for raw, in-process, and finished goods inventory

3. Relationships of direct materials cost to finished goods
4. Changes in "make or buy" dollars (dollars of this year's purchases that were "make" last year and vice versa)
5. Performance in establishing reorder points, that is predetermined inventory levels at which additional purchases or production should be instituted
6. The utilization of economic order quantities
7. A ratio of inventory control salaries and expenses to total manufacturing salaries and expenses

Production Planning and Control

1. Percentage of promises kept
   a. Of customer shipments
   b. Shipments to finished stock
   c. Shop operations
2. Establishment of a direct materials price index, using an appropriate base year, showing changes in internal and production costs
3. Changes in "make or buy" (dollars of this year's "make" that were "buy" last year)
4. Amount of dollars of indirect materials cost reductions
5. Ratio of production planning and control salaries and expenses
6. Changes in the average production cycle time for representative models or products including new models, standard models, and repairs)

Purchasing

1. A quantitative measure of idle machines and/or personnel resulting from a lack of purchased supplies
2. A measure of the extent of successful substitutes of materials and parts
3. Ratios of total purchasing salaries and expenses to total purchases and total manufacturing salaries and expenses
4. The value of purchase orders subjected to competitive bidding, as a percentage of total orders placed
5. Number of rush orders
6. Quantitative measures of expediting expenses
7. Ratio of rejected purchases to total purchases
8. Savings on discounts and quantity purchases
9. Measure of the extent of supplier technical assistance
10. Measure of vendors' keeping delivery promises

Traffic

1. Ratio of the cost of inbound freight to total purchases
2. Packaging costs, expressed as a percentage of hundredweight of shipments
3. Ratio of cost of outbound freights to total hundredweight of shipments
4. Trend of total transportation costs
5. Cost reduction
6. Measure of average intransit time of incoming and outgoing shipments
7. Ratio of total traffic expenses to value of shipments
8. Ratios of traffic salaries and expenses to total manufacturing salaries and expenses

Materials management, it has been said, is a matter of management philosophy more than of managerial organization. This view holds special significance for purchasing managers. As Dean Ammer said, referring to materials management generically, "While many companies may continue to enjoy the luxury of poorly coordinated materials management for years to come, the economic and social environment increasingly favors an integrated approach."

"The executive in charge need not have the title of materials manager," he concluded, "but he must function as one, if the company is to employ effectively the resources it devotes to materials management. For some purchasing managers, this means opportunity to test their managerial skills in a less specialized occupation that could serve as a springboard to general management responsibilities. For others, the coming decade may simply bring pressures with which they cannot cope."

SOME PERFORMANCE OBJECTIVES

After studying this chapter you should be able to:

1. Review some of the generally accepted definitions of materials management.
2. Describe the flow of a *finished goods order* and that of a *special order* through a materials management system.
3. Explain the difficulties in arriving at a universal, authoritative definition of materials management.

4. List some of the advantages claimed for materials management that could not be obtained with the conventional purchasing organization.
5. Discuss why materials management is less suitable in some types of companies than in others.
6. Offer a personal opinion on the future of the materials management concept in industry and its effect on the status of purchasing.

To function properly, purchasing must be organized in various ways to meet company requirements. But organizations do not exist by themselves; they must be staffed and operated by qualified people. The people in turn should be given assignments in which their particular skills or expertise will be most valuable. In the next chapter we discuss the staffing of a purchasing department and the kind of training that will enable staff members to improve or develop the skills required in their positions.

Staffing and Training For Purchasing

7

The overall corporate organization in which the average purchasing department operates necessarily varies from company to company, as we have seen in Chapter 5. The pattern of the internal organization of the department itself, however, is much more consistent.

As was previously noted, the one-person department presents no problems of organization, because all activities are embodied in the one person. In the two-person department, the situation is not much more complex. The assistant is exactly what that term implies, taking on such responsibilities as may be delegated to him or her by the purchasing manager. There is likely to be no more formal division of buying duties than the retention of major materials and contract items for the purchasing agent's attention while the assistant handles the procurement of supplies and routine requirements. Each would normally do his or her own follow-up on orders and clear the invoices for the goods that he or she purchases. In any such limited department, there is an advantage in having both buyers be familiar with the entire purchasing program, to gain greater flexibility of operation and to maintain continuity of work during the temporary absence of either person.

When the volume of purchasing has grown beyond the capacity of any such simple arrangement, organization becomes essential to efficient operation. The buying staff itself is necessarily larger, and the incidental services and paperwork of procurement increase proportionately. This requires coordination and direction. It is no longer efficient nor feasible to have each buyer personally responsible for the detailed procedures that make up the complete transaction. That individual is relieved of clerical and routine tasks so that he or she may become a specialist in buying—in the evaluation of quality, selection of sources, and negotiation—and usually a specialist in one or a few particular commodity groups. The other departmental activities are similarly divided and specialized and are generally assigned to clerical personnel, in support of the buying operation.

THE DEPARTMENT HEAD'S ROLE

In the fully organized purchasing department, the chief purchasing officer (usually having the title of director of purchasing or purchasing manager and, in an increasing number of cases, vice president of purchasing) is chiefly concerned with administrative and executive duties. This person establishes and directs overall purchasing policies, coordinates the purchasing program and procedures with the operating requirements of other departments, represents purchasing in plant management and policy meetings, assigns purchasing representation on interdepartmental committees and projects and is directly responsible to top management for departmental administration, morale, training, and performance.

The director of purchases may or may not take part in actual negotiation and buying. If he or she does so at all, his or her participation is usually limited to major contracts and items which involve substantial volume and dollar value and represent matters of policy as well as of procurement. The director of purchases may also take part in the initial consideration of new supply sources or of new materials that affect product design and manufacturing methods. For the most part, the director is concerned with summary reports of purchasing activities, order status, and cost trends rather than with the individual purchase transactions.

The director may have one or more staff assistants, for business and economic research, cost and value analysis, engineering counsel and coordination, or other specialized services.

The assistant director of purchases, or purchasing agent, is directly in charge of the buying staff and of general office operations. He or she assigns the buying responsibilities and directs the work of the buyers or buying groups. He or she is concerned with the actual day-by-day purchases, and in many companies all purchase orders pass over his or her desk for noting and review before they are released to the vendor. Through a chief clerk or clerical supervisor, the assistant director supervises the necessary office services of record keeping, filing, order typing, mail distribution, catalog library, and the like. The assistant director may also supervise separate sections for follow-up and expediting, traffic, and the disposal of surplus and waste materials.

If storeskeeping comes within the jurisdiction of the purchasing department, there will also be a chief storeskeeper, usually reporting to the director of purchases, on the same organizational level as the assistant director.

BUYING ASSIGNMENTS

Buying assignments are usually specific, item by item, with a definite responsibility for each item or commodity classification that is regularly purchased. So far as is practicable, items that are related by nature or by source (rather than by end product or using department) are grouped for buying purposes. In a department of moderate size, in which such assignments are made to individual buyers rather than to a buying group or section, this principle may have to be modified somewhat so as to distribute the work load evenly. But the major classifications at least will be identified with particular buyers—steel buyer, electrical goods buyer, and so forth—who have direct and sole responsibility for procurement of the stated products. For each such buying assignment, it is customary to name an alternate from among the other buyers, who can assist with or take over the buying in a classification other than his or her own as may be required from time to time.

In larger departments, assignments are made to commodity buying sections, each headed by a senior buyer or assistant purchasing agent, with one or more buyers and assistant buyers under his or her direction. When this type of organization is in effect, the commodity groupings and assignments can be completely consistent. Equal distribution of work load among the several buying sections is not essential, because the size of staff in each group can be adjusted to the load and understudies or alternates are available within the section.

The advantages of organization according to specific, related commodity assignments are:

1. Buyers become specialists in a particular field. Concerned with a limited range of items, they can acquire a better knowledge of the materials and products, their characteristics, and their applications, and greater familiarity with marketing practices, economic influences, and sources of supply in that field. All this makes for superior purchasing skill.
2. Duplication and overlapping are eliminated, and situations are avoided in which buyers in the same organization may in effect be competing with each other for supplies.

3. There is greater opportunity to review requirements of related items, sometimes resulting in beneficial standardization, and making it possible to combine requirements, gaining maximum quantity buying advantage, with fewer interviews and purchase orders.

4. Vendor contacts are concentrated, conserving time and effort for both the salesman and the buyer. The salesman of a given material or of a related product line usually needs to make only one contact in the purchasing department, and that contact is with a buyer having specific authority.

Some purchasing managers, however, prefer to rotate commodity buing assignments every year or two, switching a buyer from castings, for example, to plastic extrusions. They argue that rotation:

1. Gives the buyer a broader view of the overall purchasing operation and prepares him or her for greater managerial responsibility.

2. Assures smooth functioning of the department by providing capable replacements in the event that "specialist" buyers are absent due to illness or other reasons.

3. Reduces the likelihood of a specialist becoming so bored with his or her job or so "comfortable" with certain suppliers that he or she has little motivation to seek innovations or cost reduction ideas.

There can be no standard purchasing classification of commodities that will be applicable to all companies. Requirements vary widely among different industries. The item that is of primary importance and volume in one plant may be used in insignificant quantities, or not at all, in the plant next door. The division and assignment of buying responsibility must be tailored to the individual case.

In one of the large automobile companies, the buying sections in the purchasing department are organized by broad families of parts and equipment, such as

Production Parts. Chassis, Hard Trim, and Stampings—Bumpers, Diecastings, Exhaust Systems, Decorative Mouldings, Standard Parts, Plating, Radiators, Functional Stampings; Engine, Electrical, and Soft Trim—Electrical, Plastic, Rubber, Engine, Fuel Systems, Glass, Paint, Soft Trim.

Raw Materials, Nonproduction Supplies and Services. Steel, Nonferrous Metals, Foundry Supplies, Construction and Plant Engineering, Realty Construction Purchases, Office Supplies, Stationery, Machines, Miscellaneous Services, Disposal of Metal Scrap, Surplus and Obsolete Parts and Material.

Special Tools, Machinery and Equipment. Tools and Dies, Machinery and Cutting Tools, Manufacturing Supplies and Equipment.

A representative metal fabricating company classifies its purchases in the following groups:

Metals
Electrical Parts
Machine Tools and Mechanical Parts
Chemicals, Stores Supplies, Automotive Equipment
Office and Drafting Supplies
Printing, Office Machines, and Furniture

A public utility company uses the following basis of organizing its purchases:

Building Materials
Mechanical Equipment
Castings, Tools, and Hardware
Electrical Equipment
Fuel
Office Equipment and Supplies
Restaurant Supplies

These are specific cases, listing only the general group classifications according to which buying duties are assigned in the respective companies. Sometimes this is enough to set the pattern of responsibility. Usually, however, there would be a more detailed tabulation of the items coming under each group heading. And within each buying section, there would be definite buying assignments among the several buyers, for orderly administration if for no other reason.

A more comprehensive listing of representative commodity classifications and buyers' assignments is given below. Some of these may not be applicable at all in some companies. Some would be major classifications in one company and subordinate items in another.

Abrasives	Machined Parts
Accessories	Machinery and Plant Equipment
Automotive Equipment and Supplies	Maintenance, Repair, and Operating
Building Materials	Supplies
Castings	Nonferrous Metals
Chemicals	Office Machines and Furniture
Drafting Supplies	Office Supplies
Electrical Materials and Parts	Packaging Materials
Electronic Parts	Paint, Varnish, Lacquer, Finishing
Fabricated Parts and Assemblies	Materials

Fasteners
Forgings
Fuel
Glass and Glass Products
Hand Tools
Hardware
Instruments
Insulating Materials
Iron and Steel
Laboratory Equipment
Lubricants, Petroleum Products
  (except Fuel)
Lumber
Paper and Paper Products
Plastic Parts

Printing
Refractories
Rubber Products (except Tires)
Safety Equipment
Screw Machine Products
Services
Shipping Room Supplies
Stampings
Subcontracting
Textiles
Welding Equipment and Supplies
Wood Products

The diversity of products in this tabulation reemphasizes the importance of specialization in purchasing, through organization.

Special commodities.   In a number of industries in which the end product is made up largely of a single raw material, as in the case of cotton textiles, the procurement of that material constitutes a distinct activity quite apart from the general purchasing program and department. This is particularly true in the case of products of nature, where the evaluation of quality and the actual purchasing often must be done at markets or auctions at the point of production. For example, in cigarette manufacturing, the purchase and seasoning of leaf tobacco may be vested not merely in a separate department, but in a separate, affiliated corporation. Large users of wood customarily have a timber agent entirely independent of the purchasing department; the agent buys standing timber or leases timber rights and schedules cutting operations to provide the lumber for manufacturing needs. In the woolen textile industry, the wool buyer may spend the greater portion of his or her time in the distant wool markets of Australia, South America, and the Near East purchasing the particular types of staple desired.

Product purchasing.   In companies making a wide variety of products, usually in a number of different plants, the buyer in a plant manufacturing only one product or line of products may be responsible for all major purchased materials and components going into the product, rather than specializing in two or three. For example, a company that manufactures vacuum cleaners, waxing machines, and hand tools in several different locations and is constantly bringing out new models will use this system in the interest of time and efficiency. It is particularly useful in cases when there are a number of unrelated products in different stages of development at one time.

Usually, however, provision is made to take advantage of standardization and quantity buying. Items common to two or more products and items that can be bought in relatively large volume are generally assigned to a specialist buyer for purchase.

Project purchasing. Purchasing for special projects, such as new plant construction or highly complex made-to-order equipment, is frequently set up as a separate division within the purchasing department. This makes it easier to handle special requirements of the project, avoid delays, and obtain cost information in the early planning stages. Project purchasing calls for the use of buyers with a high degree of technical knowledge and training who can work closely with design and engineering departments.

Field operations, such as drilling and laying of pipelines in the petroleum industry, are customarily handled on a project basis. Purchasing for product development and research laboratories, in which requirements are highly specialized and there can be no consistent, continuing materials program, often come within this category also.

Project purchasing has received its biggest impetus in recent years, however, from military and related procurement. Defense contractors who must bid on such things as complex electronic systems have representatives of the purchasing department participate in the preparation of such bids. A well-known optical company that makes highly complex cameras and reconnaissance systems for the military uses the project buying approach. Procurement and purchasing engineers assist engineering, sales, and management personnel in the preparation of bids in several ways. They provide cost estimates on new materials and parts, analyze specifications that may cause suppliers trouble, and indicate probable lead times on delivery of materials. Without such specific procurement data, the planning group might make an unrealistic bid, and the company might end up losing money on the job or failing to deliver it on time.

Planning for actual purchasing goes on during the proposal stage in this system. Procurement engineers start searching for sources of new and unusual components and collect data for decisions on whether to make or buy certain items. If the company is successful in its bid, the purchasing program is then actually under way. The procurement engineers leave the actual negotiation and buying of parts to the purchasing engineers assigned to that project and move on to new projects.

Generally speaking, project buyers purchase only special items or materials used in the end product. Common items or standard components (fasteners, for example) used in both the company's regular and custom-made lines are purchased by the purchasing department's commodity buyers.

SELECTION OF PERSONNEL

The caliber and effectiveness of a purchasing department depend not only upon its organization and procedure, but even more upon the personnel through which its policies and systems are carried out. To maintain a high standard of personnel, there should be a consistent plan of selection and training for key positions and for progress upward through the department to the positions of responsibility. It is true that a departmental staff reflects the leadership of the department head, but the department that is bound up in the person of the one "indispensable" individual is a weak department. There must be delegation of responsibility and the capacity to accept responsibility. Consequently, one of the important characteristics of leadership is attention to sound training.

EDUCATIONAL REQUIREMENTS

Having set up one specification for purchasing personnel in the form of a list of responsibilities, the next step is to seek a source of supply. First on the list of prerequisites is a college education. A logical first source then, is among college graduates having the necessary academic background. Such persons are regularly cultivated in the standard personnel recruiting programs of many large companies. Where this method is a part of company policy, the recruiting for purchasing is usually handled as a part of the general program, with the specific assignment to purchasing following a screening and training program during which special aptitudes are disclosed.

The indicated preference for graduate engineers is consistent with a trend that has been in evidence for a number of years, but it is by no means an absolute requirement. This trend reflects the increasing complexity and importance of technical knowledge of materials and products purchased, but generalization is likely to be misleading. There are many positions in purchasing in which engineering training is but a marginal requirement and certainly not essential; there are other assignments in which very specialized technical qualifications are important—a textile engineer, electronics engineer, or metallurgical engineer, for example.

The case for the graduate engineer is well stated by the purchasing executive of a large company manufacturing technical products, who has made technical education a requisite in the personnel policy of his department. He stresses the point that it is more practicable to take a technical specialist and train him in the application of that knowledge to problems of procurement than to take a nontechnical person whose qualifications may otherwise be excellent and try to supply him with the required technical knowledge and training of the specialist. This argument has additional force in the particular case, because his large organization, like many other large organizations, has provision for an executive training program extending from twelve to eighteen months before the specific assignment to purchasing or other duties is made. Other companies, especially smaller ones, may require more immediate results. It should also be pointed out that highly specialized technical knowledge, although extremely valuable in a particular application, may also be a limiting factor. The broader the base of academic training, the greater is the opportunity for advancement to more general responsibilities.

The second academic qualification cited—training in economics and business administration—points to another preferred source for purchasing personnel, namely, the colleges of business administration. This is direct training for managerial positions. The majority of such schools now offer basic courses in the principles of procurement as a standard or elective part of the curriculum, and a few offer such courses as a major field of specialization.

Probably the most practical guides to what industrial companies look upon as the best educational preparation for those interested in a purchasing career are the recruiting brochures that many have prepared for distribution at colleges and business and engineering schools. Following are excerpts dealing with eligibility requirements from a number of such brochures prepared specifically to attract graduates to a purchasing career:

> Candidates for the Procurement Management Development Program must have an accredited bachelor's degree, preferably with a major in engineering or business administration. *Raytheon Company.*
>
> Do you have a superior academic record? Are you a candidate for a B.S., B.A., or Masters degree? Although a major in engineering or science is preferred, you will be considered regardless of your major, if your qualifications are exceptional. *Radio Corporation of America.*
>
> Graduates in the fields of economics, business, industrial management, engineering, or chemistry will be considered. Candidates must have performed in an above-average manner academically and have demonstrated a leadership record either in extra-curricular activities or in outside work. It is extremely desirable that candidates have an ability to get along with people, a pleasant personality, and an interest in purchasing. *Owens-Illinois.*
>
> New graduates will be hired this year . . . including . . . engineering majors with business interests; science majors with business interests; economics majors with science minors; business administration majors with industrial management minors. *Union Carbide Corporation.*

CERTIFICATION IN PURCHASING

In 1974, the National Association of Purchasing Management (N.A.P.M.) established a certification program through which individuals could earn the designation Certified Purchasing Manager (C.P.M.) Later on in the program, the kind of academic disciplines suggested for undergraduate students interested in a career in purchasing were described by the executive in charge of the program as follows:

"An 'ideal' undergraduate program in preparation for a career in purchasing should be a broad one with approximately 50 percent in business subjects; approximately 10 percent in the physical sciences, such as chemistry, physics, engineering, and electronics; and approximately 40 percent in liberal arts and humanities, such as literature, philosophy, psychology, history, and fine arts. It is recognized that some subjects, such as economics, English, and mathematics, can be oriented toward either a business or nonbusiness context. Such subjects should be classified according to their content to determine the proper balance between business and nonbusiness subjects.

"It is also recognized that in some industries an engineering or physical science education is desirable to equip purchasing people for the technological aspects of their task. Students should, wherever possible, weigh such special considerations in determining the 'ideal' subject mix for them. They may possibly need to supplement their undergraduate work with postgraduate studies to give them both the technological and business management backgrounds desired to enable them to develop competence and proficiency as purchasing and business managers."[1]

Dr. Bierman and the certification committee of N.A.P.M. recommended that the business core of the undergraduate program include: accounting, business law, data processing, economics, finance, industrial management, cost accounting, management and organization, marketing, purchasing, materials management, traffic and transportation, production planning and control, inventory control, and statistics.

The three examinations that candidates for the C.P.M. are required to take, however, deal primarily with functional operations in purchasing. To assist candidates to prepare for the examinations, N.A.P.M. has published a handbook, or study guide, the format of which is similar to that of the examinations. The table of contents of the handbook is shown in Figure 7-1. Each module of the handbook is followed by sample questions in the examination format. Each module also contains a bibliography, to aid in additional study.

[1] From an unpublished manuscript by Edward J. Bierman, Ph.D., director of certification, National Association of Purchasing Management, New York, 1978.

Figure 7-1. Contents page of N.A.P.M. certification study guide, showing subjects covered in examinations.

In addition to passing a series of examinations, candidates for certification must have had a certain amount of work experience in purchasing and have made contributions to the purchasing field, as outlined in the application form shown in Figure 7-2. Undergraduates are permitted to take the examinations, but they would not qualify for certification until the experience and contributions requirements had been met.

Full details on the purchasing certification program are available from the National Association of Purchasing Management, 11 Park Place, New York, NY 10007.

GENERAL TRAINING PROGRAM

The first objective of a general training program for any new employee is orientation—an understanding of the job in terms of its own activities, objectives, and responsibilities, and in relation to overall company objectives and operations.

If the new employee in purchasing comes to his or her work without previous experience in the company, or without previous business experience, so that all his or her practical training must be acquired on the job, one part of that training should be the opportunity to see the workings of other departments and their relationship to purchasing. Such assignments as internal tracing and expediting of materials, the investigation of complaints regarding materials and deliveries, and even messenger service that takes him or her out into the plant, the storeroom, the laboratory, and the drafting and accounting departments on missions concerning materials, purchasing service, and records—all contribute effectively to this end.

The objectives of this general training, which may be carried on coincidentally with specific job training, include:

Knowledge of the company's processes, equipment, and product.

Knowledge of production and maintenance materials and how they are used.

Knowledge of the flow of materials and of form and record controls.

Knowledge of other departments and their work, and of the purchasing department's relationship to them.

Knowledge of company policies.

Knowledge of purchasing policies.

NATIONAL ASSOCIATION OF PURCHASING MANAGEMENT
APPLICATION FOR CERTIFICATION AS CERTIFIED PURCHASING MANAGER
(Submit to: Program Administrator, N.A.P.M., 11 Park Place, New York, NY 10007)

Name: _____ Date of Application: _____
(as it should appear on certificate)

Home Address: _____ Tel. No.: _____
No. & Street   City   State   Zip

Employed By: _____ Position Title: _____

Business Address: _____ Tel. No.: _____

Member of N.A.P.M.? Regular _____ Associate _____ Non-Member _____

Name of Local Association _____

IMPORTANT
Do not submit this application without having passed all four field examinations

Years of Purchasing or Related Experience _____
(Minimum 5 years experience in purchasing or a degree from a recognized college and 3 years of related experience)

Application Fee Enclosed $ _____ or $ _____ Recertification fee enclosed $ _____
(NAPM Member $25)   (Associate or Non-Member $30)   ($10)

Request for Lifetime Certificate ($5 additional if 15 years experience and 55 years of age): Years of Experience _____ Date of Birth _____

POINTS EARNED TO APPLY TOWARD THIS CERTIFICATION
(Circle Points Earned)

I EDUCATIONAL CATEGORY (Attach official transcripts or other documentation.)

A. College Level (Circle points for highest level achieved—Maximum 30 points)—based on highest degree attained. Not on accumulative basis.

DEGREE PROGRAM	NAME AND LOCATION OF INSTITUTION	Course or Major	Year Graduated	Degree Received	Points Earned
Doctors Degree					30
Masters Degree					25
4 Year College					20
2 Year Community College					10

B. Specific College Courses Taken or Taught (2 points for each purchasing and materials management course, and 1 point for all other college courses. These must be profession related, may be in-residence or correspondence and must not be included in degree progam). Instructors get credit only once for a specific course taught more than once. Attach certificate of completion or other documentation.

COURSE	WHERE TAKEN	DATE COMPLETED	POINTS EARNED
			X2
			X1

C. Continuing Education Seminars and Courses

TYPE OF ACTIVITY	WHERE TAKEN	DATE TAKEN	POINTS EARNED
2-week Executive Seminar	Harvard University or other		4
1-week Management Seminar	Cornell, Michigan State, N. Carolina, Stanford, or other		3
N.A.P.M./Local Association Seminar or Courses (15 hrs. or longer)			X2
N.A.P.M./Local Association Short Seminars (8-14 hrs.)			X1
Seminars & Courses Equivalent to the above sponsored by other recognized organizations			

D. N.A.P.M. Examinations (all required—total 35 points)

SUBJECT	WHERE TAKEN	DATE PASSED	POINTS EARNED
Principles of Purchasing			
Materials Management			35
Principles of Business & Economics			
Quantitative Areas of Business			

Total points in Educational Category (A, B, and C) _____

Figure 7-2. Basic requirements for certification in the N.A.P.M. Professional Purchasing Certification program, as shown in application form. (Form continued on following page)

II EXPERIENCE CATEGORY (Circle Appropriate Points and Title and submit verification of employment.)

(Applicant must have at least 5 years experience in purchasing if he does not have a degree from a recognized college, or 3 years experience with such a degree)

	Annual Gross Purchases Responsible for * or Gross Sales Billed by Organizational Group Served by your Purchasing Function * (Mil. $)					Times Number of Years	Total Points Earned
		'Under 5	5-49	50-99	100 and over		
Class I (Vice President of Purchases/Materials Mgt. Director of Purchases/Materials Mgt.) Employment from: _____ to: _____ Employer:		4	5	6	7	x	=
Class II (General Purchasing Agent: Materials Manager) Employment from: _____ to: _____ Employer:		3	4	5	6	x	=
Class III (Manager of Purchasing: Purchasing Agent) Employment from: _____ to: _____ Employer:		2	3	4	5	x	=
Class IV (Supervisory Buyer: Senior Buyer: Administrative Buyer) Employment from: _____ to: _____ Employer:		1	2	3	4	x	=
Class V (Buyer: Junior Buyer: Assistant Buyer) Employment from: _____ to: _____ Employer:		1	1	2	3	x	=

*For position titles and functions not shown use equivalent position as best you can judge and explain in IV below.

Total Points in Experience Category _____

III CONTRIBUTIONS TO N.A.P.M. OR PURCHASING PROFESSION CATEGORY *(Submit verification of activities)*

Activity	Where Performed	When Performed	Total Points Earned
A. Affiliated Association (1 point per year) Officer, Director, Committee Chairman of professionally oriented standing committee			
B. N.A.P.M. (1 point per year) President, Vice President, National or District Committee Chairman of a professionally-oriented standing committee			
C. Published Articles (2 points each) List title, publication and date.			

Total Points in Contributions Category _____

SUMMARY

1. Total Points in Education Category (A, B, C) _____
2. Total Examination Points — 35
3. Total Points in Experience Category _____
4. Total Points in Contributions Category _____

GRAND TOTAL OF ALL POINTS (70 required) _____

IV COMMENTS OR EXPLANATION OF ANY ENTRY ABOVE DEEMED NECESSARY FOR CLARIFICATION:

_____
_____
_____
_____

V I hereby certify that the information submitted above is true and accurate to the best of my knowledge. I further agree to abide by the N.A.P.M. "Code of Ethics" and "Principles and Standards of Purchasing Practice", as listed on the Application for Examination form, whether or not I am a member of N.A.P.M.

Signature of Applicant _____

FOR USE OF NATIONAL OFFICE ONLY

APPLICATION NUMBER _____

APPROVALS _____

Program Administrator
Date Certificate Issued _____   Chairman, Certification Board

Expiration Date _____   5M 6-76

Figure 7-2, continued. Part of application form showing requirements for certification.

PURCHASING IN DIFFERENT INDUSTRIES

The general course of training outlined in the preceding paragraphs is predicated on the supposition that the new employee in the department is without specific experience in purchasing work. The case of the employee who comes with a background of purchasing experience in some other organization presents a special case. The functional job analysis quoted stresses the fact that basic qualifications and training are applicable to purchasing in any field. Many examples of successful transfer from purchasing in one industry to purchasing in another very different type of industry could be cited to support this statement; such cases present the most convincing evidence of the essentially professional nature of a purchasing career. The trained and experienced purchasing person is presumably capable of stepping into any purchasing assignment. But, although this may seem to obviate the necessity of further apprenticeship in preparation for the jobs, it does not eliminate the need for general orientation. Products, processes, and equipment vary rather widely even among individual companies within the same industry; material requirements or standards vary; systems and controls, although following a generally standard pattern, have individual peculiarities developed to adapt the plan to particular conditions and types of organization; and, finally, company policies are likely to be highly individualized. The new person, however competent and experienced in procurement, must adjust himself or herself to all of these factors to achieve maximum effectiveness in his or her new responsibility.

TRAINING ON THE JOB

Although the popular conception of a purchasing job is that of buying, this is a culmination rather than a starting point. It is generally accepted in the field that a minimum of two years' experience is required to fit a person for a position at a buyer's desk. This would include both the general phases of orientation and training plus work at other duties within the department. Extensive experience in other departments, of a nature pertinent to the knowledge and consideration of materials and their procurement, would naturally accelerate progress in the purchasing department itself, but it does not take the place of familiarity and experience with the actual mechanics of processing a requisition or carrying out a purchasing transaction. There is a practical advantage for every buyer in knowing not only how, but why, procedures are handled as they are. This knowledge gives significance to details that might otherwise be slighted, perspective to the process as a whole, and smoothness and coordination to the whole procurement operation.

In the earlier chapters on departmental organization, it was pointed out that, although the purchasing function is in the position of a staff assignment with respect to the company organization as a whole, within the department it is adapted to the "line" type of organization, with definite lines of authority and responsibility integrating the entire operation. In most purchasing departments, whether large or small, there is a well-defined sequence or relative rank of the various assignments, affording a logical course of progress without necessarily cleaving to a rigid pattern of seniority in promotion. Typical stages of such progress would include the following:

1. Routine clerical, file, and mail distribution duties: Reports to the chief clerk; provides general familiarity with departmental procedures and records, how and why used.

2. Invoice checking: Reports to chief clerk; provides familiarity with purchased materials list and with receiving procedure, contact with receiving and accounting departments; stresses importance of accuracy and demonstrates purchasing responsibility in committing the company to expenditures. Detecting and correcting a single, simple error at this stage is practical and valueable experience in showing what can happen to an order after it has been placed and the transaction is apparently closed.

3. Requisition checking, stock records, internal expediting: Reports to buyer; provides familiarity with purchasing program and flow of materials, contact with stores and using departments; demonstrates purchasing responsibility and policy in respect to stated requirements and how these needs are filled.

4. Follow-up and expediting: Reports to buyer or head of buying group; provides familiarity with specific materials from the procurement angle, first direct contact with vendors, evaluation of vendors' service and reliability, first independent responsibility.

5. Assistant buyer: Reports to buyer; first direct dealing with vendors' sales representatives, first decisions on supply sources, first responsibility for negotiation and terms committing the company to a purchase agreement. This work generally starts with standard catalog items, bought on established maximum–minimum stock basis, or issuance of release orders and shipping instructions against contracts in force, all under direct supervision of the buyer who is responsible for the items. Scope of items bought and independent authority are broadened as capacity is demonstrated, up to the point at which the employee is ready to serve as a buyer with certain commodities or items definitely assigned to him or her for procurement.

This regular progression of duties, with actual experience in the major phases of purchasing department operation, provides a comprehensive course of training on the job that should equip the buyer with the necessary knowledge of policy and procedure to think and act in accordance with that policy and to coordinate smoothly with the overall buying program. It should provide a foundation of general preparation in and for purchasing that can later be applied, at the "buyer" stage, to almost any group of items in the company's list of requirements as the need for such an assignment may arise. For, as was pointed out in the summary of qualifications, familiarity with particular commodities and products is something that can be acquired and superimposed on the basic purchasing knowledge. If there is a specific opening or buying assignment in view as the objective of the training, it would, of course, be logical to take it into consideration at the "assistant buyer" stage, so as to have a definite apprenticeship in the handling of these particular items. Typically, however, the objective of training up to this point is more general in nature, and versatility or flexibility is an important factor. Although specialization is a characteristic of purchasing department organization and operation, there is likewise a need for interchangeability of personnel in respect to commodity responsibilities, and there may also be an element of progression from one product group to another group of greater importance. Thus, the basic training is the essential feature of the training program.

Training away from the office desk is highly important. The trainee should be encouraged—and opportunities made, if necessary—to visit suppliers' plants, to develop a diversity of personal contacts in the trade, in supplier industries, and in purchasing associations, and to acquire a firsthand knowledge of how materials are made, marketed, and used. The value of these outside experiences can be greatly enhanced by following up each one with a personal conference or a written report to his or her immediate superior.

A CONTINUING PROGRAM

A proper conception of training recognizes the fact that it is never a completed job. The experience of many successful departments, even when the staff is stable and well established and its personnel reasonably experienced and competent in their respective positions, shows that there is much benefit to be derived from a continuing program of training, whether or not it is referred to as such. The emphasis placed upon education and discussion forums in the program of the National Association of Purchasing Management and the policy of that organization in making advanced study courses available to its membership are testimony to the fact that even those who have arrived at positions of leadership in their company organizations and in their profession can profit by such projects. N.A.P.M.'s Continuing Education Unit, working with universities and local associations, offers a varied educational program that attracts a broad spectrum of purchasing personnel from all parts of the country. The courses range from short sessions for newly appointed buyers to two-week executive seminars at leading business schools, including those of Harvard University and Michigan State University. One-week purchasing and materials management seminars are presented at such universities as Cornell, Stanford, North Carolina, Houston, and Texas. These feature instruction by university faculty and prominent purchasing and materials executives. N.A.P.M. also works closely with companies in planning and presenting in-plant seminars and training sessions.

There are several ways in which a continuing training program can be handled. Among those that have proved most effective are the following:

Refresher courses.   These may be conducted annually, or biennially, for a three-month period. Meetings are held weekly on company time, from four to five o'clock on Monday afternoons, for example. Attendance is usually compulsory for specified grades of personnel throughout the entire department. A formal course of study is followed, based on the department manual or selected from some standard text on purchasing. The class is generally led by some senior officer of the department, but not necessarily by the department head himself. Free discussion is encouraged but is held to prescribed subjects for each session so as to cover the topics in an orderly and comprehensive manner.

Periodical staff meetings.   These are less formal than the organized refresher course and do not have the "schoolroom" atmosphere that is sometimes resented by older and more experienced members of the department, but they can be made equally effective from the training standpoint with careful planning and good leadership. Meetings are held regularly, monthly or twice a month, on company time, for example, from eleven o'clock till noon on the specified dates. Attendance is limited, but it is compulsory for those eligible to take part, all other appointments being subordinated to this conference. Eligibility is defined in some cases as including all buyers and all those who have other workers coming directly under their supervision. Such a plan brings in the heads of the various sections such as filing, invoice checking, and expediting, whose attendance is usually of value in a discussion; at the same time, it keeps the group and its programs and deliberations distinctly above the elementary and theoretical plane.

A group of this kind provides an excellent opportunity for indoctrination in policy matters and for setting up uniformity of practices. It is a logical and effective place to have representatives of the company management and of other departments explain the work of the organization as a whole, what is expected of purchasing in relation to these other operations, and how it can be coordinated to best advantage.

Outside training. Earlier in this chapter it was pointed out that the chronology of training is variable—that academic or formal studies can be superimposed on departmental experience, if such happens to be the need in an individual case, with the same effectiveness as if the normal sequence were followed, taking basic academic qualifications and supplementing these with training on the job. This principle is well worth consideration in its application to the continuing training program. Facilities for the study of purchasing, and of related business and economic subjects, are available in many cities, scheduled for evening classes to meet exactly this need. One of the objectives of the educational program of the National Association of Purchasing Management has been to foster the establishment of such courses.

The facilities can be effectively used in the company training program, especially for the smaller departments where specific company training for a limited personnel would be impracticable. It is generally taken for granted that this type of education is a responsibility of the individual, and not of the employer, but there is much to be said in favor of encouraging such studies and of providing an incentive in the form of partial or complete payment of tuition charges. Unlike the company programs cited in the preceding paragraphs, these courses are not on company time. Therefore, although it is not proposed that trainees be compensated for time spent in such studies, it is logical to regard the actual costs—for designated trainees and for approved courses—as a legitimate training expense.

CAREERS IN PURCHASING

Up to this point we have considered the matter of purchasing personnel only from the viewpoint of management—the company with a purchasing job to be done and the executive responsible for administering the department. The discussion is not complete without a consideration of the subject of all this concern, the person entering upon purchasing work. What does purchasing promise him or her that will lead that individual to accept the job offer or the assignment to purchasing duties? For what sort of business life does this training equip the prospective purchasing manager? What opportunities and rewards are available if he or she chooses a career in purchasing?

Purchasing is an occupation of wide variety and interests. The buyer deals with a wide range of materials and products, and these are constantly changing, in themselves and in their economic relationships, through technological developments and progress. The products are procured from many different sources, affording the buyer direct and stimulating contacts and familiarity with a range of supplier industries far broader than the experience of workers concerned only with the internal company operation. In the regular course of his or her activities, purchasing personnel deal with many people—those for whom and from whom he or she buys—in a variety of business and personal relationships. And the economic conditions under which he or she does buying are constantly changing, so that one day's problems are never quite the same as those of the day before.

Purchasing is a challenging and competitive occupation, with large responsibilities in both the quality of supply service provided and the magnitude of expenditures. It calls not only for knowledge and routine efficiency, but also for resourcefulness, for skill in negotiation and good judgment in decisions, and for imagination and initiative in the continuing search for greater value.

Purchasing is a useful, essential part of the company activity. It offers the satisfactions of pride in the end product that embodies purchased materials and in the profit results made possible through wise and effective procurement.

Purchasing is a growing field, soundly established but still in the developmental stage, with many horizons yet to be explored and many opportunities yet to be fully realized and exploited as the function moves toward the broader concept of materials management. The person in purchasing has the opportunity for constructive service to industry and management by contributing to the knowledge and techniques of procurement science, to the broader scope of purchasing service, to higher professional standards and management status, and to a share in the rewards of such advances.

Purchasing is steadily winning increased recognition in every progressive company as an integral and important part of industrial management. It has prestige within the company organization. It participates in management councils and policy decisions and has the authority to administer and carry out the programs to fulfill its functional responsibilities.

ADVANCEMENT THROUGH PURCHASING

The work of procurement brings the buyer intimately into touch with the requirements and operations of virtually every other phase of the business. The qualities required and developed in purchasing work—analytical skill, foresight, organization and punctuality in meeting responsibility, ability to deal with people, imagination, resourcefulness, and respect for ultimate values—are precisely those that make for success in the broader fields of management. And with increasing reliance being placed upon purchasing as a vital part of profit potentialities, there is little chance that the really competent purchasing person will be unnoticed or overlooked in general management plans.

The recruiting brochures previously mentioned give strong support to this view of purchasing. RCA, for example, invites graduates to "join our Purchasing Career Development Program . . . be part of this broad management function in the leading growth industry . . . electronics." In the section entitled, "Purchasing . . . how it plays a major role in our corporate growth," the brochure goes on to say

> Purchasing makes you knowledgeable about many different types of businesses and products. You learn about business, not in a narrow sense of statistics, but in day-to-day contact that gives you the broad picture that leads to a comprehensive background for executive management positions . . . .
>
> You assume responsibilities and challenge rapidly . . . . There are few areas that can offer a more stimulating career. Look into this sometimes overlooked path to a high level management career.

SOME PERFORMANCE OBJECTIVES

After studying this chapter you should be able to:

1. Compare the relative merits of giving buyers specific commodity assignments in which they are expected to specialize and rotating commodity buying assignments.
2. Decide which type of assignment you would prefer, assuming that you are interested in a purchasing career, and explain why.
3. Distinguish between product purchasing and project purchasing as described in the text.

4. Estimate how well your own course of study might prepare you for a position in a purchasing department.

5. List the requirements that an applicant must meet to qualify for the designation Certified Purchasing Manager.

6. Discuss purchasing as a career in itself, as well as its relation to possible advancement in other corporate functions.

With its basic position established, its organization and systems in place, and its personnel requirements defined, we can turn now to the core responsibility of the purchasing department—making decisions on the procurement of materials and supplies. In the next several chapters, we will deal with the elements that affect those decisions, beginning with quality.

Section III

MANAGING BASIC PURCHASING DECISIONS

Quality
Assurance

8

What, when, how, how much, from whom, and at what price to buy are decisions that must be made in the purchasing department. The rightness of these decisions determines how well the responsibility is being carried out.

This and Chapters 9–14 deal with the principles underlying these decisions, which, together, made up the process of purchasing. Strictly speaking, they are not "steps" in purchasing, for the factors are so completely interdependent that in most cases they must be considered simultaneously. To take a very simple example, the buying decision may involve a choice between one quality of material at one quoted price and another quality at a different price, from another source. Obviously, in this case, it is impossible to consider quality, price, or source without considering the other factors at the same time. There is no fixed chronology or sequence. Nevertheless, each factor has its own characteristics and values that must be separately understood and weighed in arriving at a right decision before we can balance them in seeking the inclusive objective—value.

The three major factors entering into every purchasing decision are (1) quality (of the item purchased), (2) service (provided by the supplier), and (3) price (paid by the purchaser). Buyers generally state that they consider quality first, or of first importance, service second, and price last, in making a purchase. This is another way of saying that, unless the quality of the purchased item is adequate to satisfy the requirement, superlative service on the part of the supplier and all-but-irresistible price appeal are both in vain. Quality, then, is a logical starting point in consideration of the purchasing process.

QUALITY MUST BE DEFINED

In the vocabulary of purchasing, *quality* has a special meaning. It is not a generalization or an attribute to be characterized simply as "high" or "poor." It is specifically the sum or composite of the properties inherent in a material or product. These properties can be measured and defined. The significant ones must be defined so that the buyer may know what he should ask his or her supplier to furnish and may know what he or she is getting. This definition of quality, in greater or less detail, becomes the ordering description for every item—the essence of the purchase order.

Significant elements of quality for materials and components that go into a manufactured product include (1) analysis and dimension; (2) physical, chemical, and dielectric properties; (3) workability; (4) uniformity of analysis and dimension, to ensure uniform results in standard processing and to permit the use of mass-production methods with a minimum of spoilage or readjustments of machinery; and (5) special characteristics tending to increase the salability of the purchaser's product, such as appearance, finish, finishing properties, desirable bulk or weight, and the acquired quality of popular acceptance.

When dealing with maintenance and operating supplies, significant properties would include utility, ease of application or use, efficiency, economy of use, and durability.

When dealing with machinery and equipment, the properties to be considered include productivity, versatility, dependability, durability, economy of operation and maintenance, and time- and labor-saving features.

For purchasing purposes, quality can be defined in a number of different ways, appropriate in varying degrees to various types of purchases. Among these ways are (1) complete and detailed specification; (2) reference to established market grades or particular brand-name products that sum up certain combinations of qualities; and (3) actual sample, in which case the product itself is its own definition of the quality desired. Purchasing by each of these methods is discussed in following sections of this chapter. Of course, for many common items, such as hardware, for example, a simple statement of type and size is usually sufficient.

VARIOUS MEASUREMENTS OF QUALITY

Every definition of quality is predicated on some standard of measurement, understood by both the buyer and the supplier. Chemical analysis is one method of measurement. The composition of a compound determines its physical properties and its adaptability for a specific use. The formula of an ink is important in relation to the surface upon which it is to be used, the conditions to which it will be exposed, and the necessary permanence. The formula of a cleaning compound measures its usefulness and safety on various types of material and its efficiency in removing various types of dirt or foreign matter.

Physical tests provide a measurement of quality in respect to such properties as the tensile strength and shearing strength of metals and fibers; the bursting, folding, and tearing strength of paper; dielectric properties; elasticity; ductility; opacity; resistance to abrasion or shock; resistance to sunlight or moisture; and many others.

Dimensional measurements indicate such quality factors as precision finishing and conformance to stated tolerances. The thread count of a woven textile and the thickness of a leather belt are quantitative measures that are significant in respect to utility and quality.

The most obvious measurement of quality in the purchasing sense is the measure of performance. In each of the foregoing methods, it has been pointed out that the units of measurement of these various properties are primarily useful as a guide or indicator of suitability or performance. They provide a means of comparing various degrees of quality. Sometimes it is desirable to use all quality measurements available in evaluating a product. In some cases it may be possible and more practicable to measure performance directly rather than to go through the intermediate step of measuring specific properties or quality factors that may be expected to give the desired results.

Machinery is a common example of this situation. It is possible to describe and define a piece of complicated equipment in terms of dimension and design, given the component elements of each part. As a matter of fact, this is a necessary step for the designer and builder of the machine. But dimensions, design, and structural materials are means to an end, which is performance or productive ability; and it is this latter characteristic that interests the buyer and is the measure of quality for him or her, because the buyer is essentially purchasing what the machine will do. All the other factors are meaningless if the equipment turns out to be inefficient or unsuited to his or her purpose. Consequently, performance or guaranteed output is the basic measure of quality, and a proper "use specification" or description of quality would make this the responsibility of the machine builder, rather than mere conformance with the physical factors involved.

POPULARITY OF "USE SPECIFICATION"

There are sound and practical reasons why the "use specification" is becoming increasingly popular as a method of defining and measuring quality. As a general rule, it is good purchasing policy to inform the supplier or bidder as fully as possible regarding the specific use for which his or her product is intended, how it is to be applied, and the performance it is expected to give. There is no compulsion on the buyer to do this, and there are some cases in which it might not be desirable to do so, as in the case of special applications developed in the user's company or other confidential or competitive situations. However, these are the exceptional cases, not the general rule. Ordinarily, by enlisting the cooperation of the seller and inviting his or her suggestions and advice, a more satisfactory purchase can be made. Another point to be considered is that the law places the basic responsibility on the seller that goods must be reasonably adapted to the purpose for which they are sold; if the seller is not advised of this purpose, and if the goods conform to other stated quality requirements, the buyer has no recourse in the event that they do not live up to his expectations in use.

Inviting potential suppliers to prescribe a product or material for a particular purpose does not relieve the purchasing manager of specific responsibility of selection and purchase; the judgment and decision are still a part of his or her function and cannot be delegated to the seller. Nor does this policy condone the purchasing policy often urged by sellers, to select a responsible supplier and leave the problem in his or her hands. Up to a certain point, the principle expressed in this suggestion had merit, but its acceptance as a complete buying policy is a direct negation of purchasing responsibility.

One further point, of a negative nature, must also be stressed. Quality is *not* measured by price. The assumption that higher price in itself denotes higher quality has been disproved so often and so thoroughly that no thoughtful buyer can proceed on this basis. Examples are legion, in every selling field, that identical material is available at varying prices from different sources and that, if a thorough search is made, higher quality can be procured from sources at a lower price than is asked for the lower quality offered by others. The old saying that "you get just what you pay for" is a half-truth whose shortcomings have often been demonstrated and learned by the hard and costly method of experience. It can be expected only with the modifying influence of careful and objective judgment. Under competitive conditions, variations in quality tend to be reflected in varying prices, but this is the broadest sort of generalization.

SUITABILITY—THE BASIC CONSIDERATION

Purchases are made to meet specific requirements. Quality must therefore be related to the need. In the purchasing vocabulary, "right quality" means the best quality *for a purpose*. That involves both economic and physical considerations.

The measurements of quality previously cited presuppose that, for most materials, a considerable range of quality is available to the buyer, from superior quality at one end of the scale to inferior quality at the other end of the scale, with numerous gradations in between. Which grade is "right?" For intelligent and effective purchasing, it is assumed that the buyer knows, or will learn, the quality required and the qualities available. The buyer's task will then be to correlate his or her information, to compare and select.

It has already been stressed that suitability and adequacy of material for the intended purpose are the basic requisites of quality in a purchasing decision. This is absolute, and it substantially reduces the area of choice by eliminating everything that does not measure up to this standard. Thus, the buyer's definition of right quality starts with establishing the *minimum acceptable quality*. He or she may not actually purchase this minimum-quality material, though in many instances this would be the proper course. Before making that decision, the buyer makes a further study of values. Superior quality may be desirable, although not actually essential. Sometimes the buyer can find such superior quality at no additional cost, or at merely a nominal increase, that represents better value received for his or her expenditure. But real value, too, is value for a purpose. If the buyer pays premium prices for quality in excess of the need, the extra dollars spent are sheer waste. The purchasing responsibility is to procure adequate quality at the lowest cost. The purchasing manager who searches for the less expensive quality of material that will yet be suitable and acceptable for the purpose is still making quality the first consideration. There are some uses for which the lowest and least expensive grades of material will be entirely suitable. In that case, the lowest quality is the right quality, for the concept of value is rooted in utility rather than in intrinsic worth.

On the other hand, there are instances in which the best quality available is not too good. The purchasing manager may look for a highly refined material or the product manufactured to the most exacting precision standards, if that is what the company needs, and no price may be too high. Indeed, the buyer may be justified in making every effort to induce suppliers to extend the upper quality range and to encourage improvements that would enhance the highest qualities presently available.

IMPORTANCE OF RELIABILITY

As technology in industry becomes more sophisticated and complex, the quality of purchased materials and components becomes an integral part of the overall concept of product reliability.

Product reliability has been defined as the probability of a product's performing a specified function under given conditions, for a specified time. The reliability of any product, as *The Encyclopedia of Management* points out,

> will be dependent on the level of performance required as indicated, for example, by the position, speed, size, etc. of the target for a guided missile; on the levels of the numerous internal and external stresses which it must endure during operation; and on the length of time that the product must perform continuously without a failure.[1]

Reliability engineering first came into prominence in connection with the production of military equipment. In recent years, however, it has been increasingly applied to commercial manufacturing, particularly in the automotive and electric appliance industries. The quality of purchased items has a direct effect on the reliability of a company's end product. Consequently, it is important that the purchasing and quality control departments have a close working relationship.

Specifying the right quality in a purchased product is obviously pointless if that product is not available. As a practical purchasing matter, an item is available when it can be obtained readily at an economically acceptable price and can be delivered in a reasonable time. Ideally, it should also be obtainable from more than one source. If these conditions cannot be met, it is good purchasing practice to attempt to change the specification to bring it into line with what is available. Such an effort

---

[1] *The Encyclopedia of Management* (New York: Reinhold Publishing Co., 1963).

should, of course, be made with the cooperation of the specifying department and, as necessary, with the engineering and manufacturing departments.

Sometimes a change of this kind can be made simply by finding a suitable standard product in place of a specially designed one or one that can be bought from only one supplier. In purchasing, commercial standards are practically synonymous with product availability. Obviously, this easy answer does not apply to all items; but in any case, the specification should be reviewed to see if a product can be made of standard materials and can be produced or fabricated with ordinary facilities.

COST, THE ECONOMIC ASPECT

Beyond the considerations of suitability and availability, there is a third important factor in determining right quality—the factor of value. Cost of materials is a basic element of end product cost, and because of this it affects the competitive position and profitability of a company selling the product. To keep this materials cost at a minimum is the direct responsibility of purchasing.

The right quality to buy, then, is the quality that satisfies the requirements already described at the lowest cost consistent with the suitability and service desired. The buyer's first duty, then, is to explore the market to find the most favorable price at which the desired item is offered.

A thorough job of quality selection and purchasing, however, is not quite so simple as that. Cost is not measured by price alone, even after the cost of purchasing, transportation, and receiving have been added. Ultimate cost, the significant factor, includes the cost of operations involved in using or converting the purchased product. The cost of paint, for example, is not merely the price per gallon; ultimate cost depends also upon the labor required to apply it and the square feet of surface coverage that it provides. An expensive paint that is easily applied and gives good coverage is more economical than a cheaper paint that takes longer to apply and may require an extra coat to give the desired result. Similarly, a material having qualities of workability that save labor-hours and machine-hours in fabricating operations, or having superior surface qualities that eliminate a finishing operation, may cost more per pound but actually represents lower cost and greater value than a cheaper material that may otherwise be adequate but does not have these special properties. The balancing of all these costs is a necessary step in determining the right quality to buy.

RESPONSIBILITY FOR QUALITY

Quality must be defined for every commodity or product to be purchased, and it is expressed in such a way that:

1. The purchasing department knows just what is required.
2. The purchase order or contract is made out with a proper description of what is wanted.
3. The supplier is fully informed of the buyer's quality requirements.
4. Suitable means of inspecting and testing can be applied to see that delivered goods meet the stated standards of quality.
5. Goods delivered in conformance with the quality definition will be acceptable to the buyer's company.

Responsibility for the factor of suitability in the quality definition rests ultimately with the departments responsible for product quality and performance and for using the purchased items. This part of the definition should be restricted to minimum essential quality requirements, leaving the greatest possible latitude for considerations of availability and value in purchasing without sacrificing the necessary suitability. If, for any purchasing reasons, it seems desirable to modify the basic definition of quality, this is done only with the approval of design and using departments. In the preparation of formal specifications, even though they are primarily of a technical nature, the best practice is to approach the matter as a joint project of technical, manufacturing, and purchasing personnel, so that all phases of quality, use, and procurement may be considered from the start and full agreement reached.

PURCHASING BY BRAND NAME

The simplest method of defining quality, although not always the most satisfactory, is to identify a material or product by the manufacturer's own brand name. From the purchasing viewpoint, this method has the advantages of simplicity in ordering, normally well-organized distribution and, consequently, ready availability. Elaborate inspection and tests can often be eliminated, because the delivery of the specified brand fulfills the obligation of the contract and it may be assumed that the quality implications that are inherent in the brand name have been observed. It has the serious disadvantage of limiting procurement to a single supplier and thus eliminating the competitive element except insofar as competition may exist in the distribution of the product.

The greatest shortcoming of purchase by brand name is its restriction on the buyer's selection of supply sources and the elimination of competition. Most items and most types of materials and equipment are available in comparable quality from competitive sources or are in competition with adequate alternative items. This is one of the principal reasons for having a special purchasing department: to discover or develop such alternate sources of supply.

When it is desirable, for convenience or any other reason, to use a brand or trade name as the descriptive term or definition for a company requirement, prudent purchasing practice overcomes this restrictive factor by adding the phrase "or equal." On the initial requisition for a material or product that has not previously been used or purchased by the company, design or production personnel may be aware of a particular branded product known to be suitable for the purpose, and they naturally specify that brand as the product wanted. If the buyer lacks time for market search, analysis of products, and the development of a more definitive product description, it is good purchasing practice to order the stipulated brand. But there is no assurance that this is the only suitable material, or even the most suitable. It immediately becomes the purchasing manager's responsibility to seek possible alternatives. "Or equal" is his or her authorization to undertake this responsibility.

PURCHASING BY SAMPLE

The actual description or definition of quality is sometimes avoided by inviting prospective suppliers to match a sample submitted by the buyer. This may be the simplest method of indicating what is wanted, and sometimes, as a result, it is the lazy buyer's method. Unfortunately, the apparent saving of effort in the first instance may be more than offset by the necessity of detailed inspection and test to determine that the delivery actually does match the sample. Furthermore, no definite standards are set for the record or for future purchasers.

The practice is justified under certain conditions: in the case of special, nonrepetitive items; or when absolute quality requirements are not a significant factor; or when the size and importance of the purchase do not warrant the effort and expense of formulating a more definitive buying description. It is likewise justified when used in respect to particular aspects of quality, such as color, which is best defined by comparison with a standard sample.

FORMAL SPECIFICATIONS

There are some items, usually of a technical nature, whose quality cannot be sufficiently defined by any of the preceding methods, so that a more formal and detailed specification is necessary. Most technical standards (as, for example, the standards for composition and properties of the various alloy steels) are compiled in specification form and can be adopted and used in procurement. The same is true in respect to many manufactured items. Standard specifications of this sort are as easy to use as brand names and are more accurately descriptive and subject to analysis and test. Because they are widely accepted as industry standards, they have the same commercial advantages as market grades in that they are a part of the language of their respective industries or trades and represent materials or products that are directly comparable on the basis of equal quality.

However, because standardization has not yet reached universal or national status, and because there are different sets of standards applicable to various items, some cautions should be observed. One point that buyers must watch in purchasing on standard specifications is that some producers will quote on "our equivalent" for the industry standard. This is not necessarily to be interpreted as an indication of inferior quality; it does indicate that there is some deviation from the standard, although there is an implication that the quality is generally comparable and adapted to the same applications.

WRITING OF SPECIFICATIONS

As previously noted, the writing of a specification is best undertaken as a group project, with representatives of technical, manufacturing, and purchasing departments participating, so that the finished specification will be satisfactory to and in the best interests of all concerned, and in the best interests of the company as a whole. Although these viewpoints may sometimes be in conflict as to the details of a particular specification, they all have the common objectives of arriving at the best decision for the company. The work should be done in the spirit of cooperation toward that end, rather than in a spirit of conflicting aims and unwilling compromise. A standing committee on specifications is the approved agency for this purpose. This provides the orderly channel for initiating a specification whenever the need or desirability for such action arises, and also a means of review and revision as needs or circumstances arise. A provision for periodic review of all specifications is wise policy. For, although the specification itself is a very precise document, to be observed strictly in all its details, it should not be permitted to "freeze" quality standards to the detriment of product improvement or to rule out the consideration of new materials or methods. Working together on such a standing committee fosters an understanding and appreciation of all three viewpoints and makes for smoother, more consistent action.

From the purchasing standpoint, a satisfactory specification must:

1. State exactly what is wanted, clearly, definitely, and completely. This is necessary for the purchasing manager's own information and guidance in buying and also for passing along the information to the supplier.
2. Provide the means or basis for testing deliveries for conformance with the specification. Without this check on actual deliveries, the specification loses much of its force as a purchasing tool.
3. Avoid nonessential quality restrictions that add to cost and to the difficulty of procurement without adding to utility and value.
4. Avoid definitions that unnecessarily restrict competition.
5. Conform, so far as possible, to established commercial and industrial standards and to company standards for other materials in regular use.

ROLE OF SPECIFICATIONS IN PROCUREMENT

As in all purchasing, the consideration of the material or part to be specified should begin with an analysis of the function it is to perform, rather than writing the specification around a particular design or merely describing some predetermined quality. When the quality factors necessary to fulfill the functional need have been determined, they must be stated in such a way as to assure the procurement of the proper quality, yet with sufficient flexibility to permit the application of good purchasing practice in that procurement. Purchasing managers have a major responsibility at this stage in making the specification a practical and effective tool for achieving ultimate value as well as precise suitability.

For example, one of the important purposes for using specifications in buying, beyond defining the material, is to provide a uniform quality standard as a basis for comparing competitive bids. Many specifications, however, are so closely written around a particular product that all competition is effectively excluded. Such specifications, of course, should be avoided if that is in any way possible. Generally it is possible, because, for the great majority of industrial requirements, there are a variety of products or sources wholly adequate for the purpose, and the restrictive features are frequently nonessential to the intended application even though they may be entirely consonant with it. They have frequently been included, either by accident or by design, because the definition has been approached from the standpoint of describing a product known to be suitable for the purpose rather than describing the basic requirements of the purpose itself. Thus, an engine may be specified with a prescribed number of cubic inches' piston displacement, which might limit the buyer's choice to a single make, whereas a definition in terms of the power to be developed would be inclusive enough to admit this model, as well as several acceptable alternates, without sacrificing any significant measure of desired quality. The definition should, therefore, be rewritten from the viewpoint of the requirement, and all nonessential limiting references should be eliminated. This is also a strong argument for the adoption of existing standard specifications and established commercial grades if these are available and suitable, in preference to setting up a new and special definition, even at the expense of some slight compromise in design.

SPECIFICATION OUTLINE AND USE

The drafting of the specification should follow a definite pattern or outline. This has a dual advantage. It is a guide for the specification writer or committee, indicating the full range of details that should be included, thus preventing oversights, loopholes, or omissions. It facilitates references by users of the specification because certain types of information are consistently found in a particular section or sequence. Such a pattern in common use is the following.

In the body of the specification, there are separate sections devoted to special areas of information:

1. Reference to applicable standard specifications, if any, which are thus incorporated into the specification and made a part of it without transcribing the actual text. Printed copies of the standard specification may be attached for the sake of completeness and for convenience in reference. The use of standard specifications is recommended, where appropriate to the purpose. They take advantage of the wealth of technical skill embodied in existing standards, save research time and effort required in the formulation of an independent, individual specification, and help keep purchase requirements in line with standard industrial practice.

2. Statement of the various types, grades, classes, and sizes of material covered by the specification. Where a material is used in a variety of forms or dimensional ranges, the repetition of identical quality standards is mere duplication, serving no useful purpose. It is therefore customary to have one specification covering an entire group of items where the same quality standards apply.

3. Statement of the use for which the specified material or equipment is intended. This is not merely a verification of the suitability of the purchased item. It is a guide to usage and a precaution against misapplication of materials.

4. Statement of the kind of materials and workmanship required in a fabricated item covered by the specification and of any special methods of production or manufacture that are required. Control of quality in a purchased item may involve control of the fabrication or processing as well as of the component raw material.

5. General requirements common to all of the types, grades, and classes of the material covered.

6. Detailed requirements peculiar to each type, grade, and class included in the specification.

7. Inspection and test procedure to be used in determining conformance with the specification, including location at which inspection will be made.

8. Instructions as to packaging, labeling, marking of shipments, and so forth.

9. Notes and special instructions to bidders, rules regarding submission of samples with bids, where and how additional copies of the specification may be obtained, and similar information.

Complete files of existing specifications are maintained in the technical, purchasing, and inspection departments; in addition, there will probably be copies of some purchase specifications in the hands of suppliers. With this wide dispersion of basic quality information, it is essential that all copies be kept strictly up to date to prevent confusion and errors in ordering and deliveries. Whenever a specification is revised or discontinued or superseded by a new specification, this should be made clear to everyone concerned. The new specification is identified by number and effective date, with the notation that it supersedes a particular previous one. As an additional precaution, all outstanding copies of the outdated specification should be recalled and destroyed.

In addition to these uses, specifications may be distributed to design and requisitioning personnel within the company so as to avoid requests for special, nonspecification items when there are materials covered by specification that are suitable to the purpose.

ALTERNATIVES AND SUBSTITUTIONS

Whenever quality is defined, whether by formal specification or by any of the other methods mentioned, it follows that no deviation from the stated quality definition is permissible on the basis of purchasing judgment alone without approval of the other departments concerned. In certain circumstances, however, some deviation is necessary.

The obvious and extreme case of this is a condition of material shortages that make the specified material or quality unavailable for purchase, or an urgent delivery time requirement that is less than the necessary lead time or procurement cycle. In such a case, the purchasing agent must find the most feasible alternate or substitute that is available and secure approval as to its suitability for the purpose. Such approval may be limited to the immediate quantity required and does not necessarily establish a continuing approval for the substitution, although it may be so extended.

A second case is that in which a delivered material or product does not conform to specified quality but is close enough to be usable, perhaps with some reworking or other adjustment. If the deviation is not too serious, if rejection would entail any considerable delay in securing a replacement, and if it is in the interest of maintaining the goodwill of the supplier, the purchasing manager will take steps to determine whether the delivered item is usable and suitable and what additional costs or inconvenience will be involved in using it. If this is a practicable solution, the purchasing manager will negotiate a price adjustment with the supplier. This should not set a precedent for compromising or modifying the quality definition on future purchases.

A third case arises when specifications are sent to potential suppliers with an invitation to bid, and a bidder submits an alternative proposal, offering a product that differs from the one specified but is intended for the same purpose. It is entirely possible that products so offered are suitable and that they may have superior advantages of economy, convenience, or end-product improvement. If they are acceptable to the other departments concerned, the logical step is to establish the nonconforming product as an approved alternate or to revise the original specification. Some companies, indeed, include on their inquiries a statement that they are receptive to alternative suggestions, for this is one of the potent means of improving specifications and buying practice in the light of suppliers' specialized knowledge.

When alternative proposals of this nature are accepted, on items for which bids have been solicited, some questions of purchasing ethics may be involved. First, there is a responsibility to vendors who have conscientiously bid on the exact specification, only to find that the order or contract is to be placed on a different basis. Should the bid invitation be reopened so that all may have an opportunity to bid competitively? At the same time, the originator of the improved suggestion is entitled to practical recognition for his or her imagination and initiative in the buyer's interest as well as his or her own, even though the buyer is not bound to commit himself or herself permanently to a single source of supply for the item and good purchasing practice demands that competition be invited. The matter is usually resolved by giving the initial order to the supplier who has earned it by his or her superior initiative and by giving that supplier preferential consideration, at least, on succeeding orders. His or her margin of advantage may be narrowed as other suppliers bid on the revised specification, but such initiative should be encouraged. It represents an element of value that is extremely important and is not measurable by the ordinary standards of quality definition and competitive prices.

RELATIONSHIP OF QUALITY AND VALUE ANALYSIS

The search for such opportunities, the scientific determination of right quality in terms of cost reduction through reduction of producers' costs, has given rise to an important purchasing activity known as *value analysis*. Although it questions—and sometimes challenges—existing definitions of required quality, it is not an encroachment upon the authority of the specifying departments, because the recommendations prompted by such analysis are still subject to approval and acceptance by those who are ultimately responsible for setting the standards of quality and suitability. Value analysis simply adds another dimension to the definition of quality. A more detailed description of the principles and methods of value analysis appears in Chapter 12.

INSPECTION—WHERE AND WHEN

Inspection of deliveries, including the use of appropriate tests in some cases, is essential to ensure that the quality of the delivery is in conformance with the order and is as represented by the supplier. A basic reason for inspection is, of course, assurance that no improper materials go into the production process. It is likewise a check on purchasing, for the responsibility for procuring material of proper quality cannot be lightly delegated or taken for granted. The most accurate and painstaking attention to the specification of quality factors in purchasing is wasted unless there is a positive check on the quality that is actually received. Consequently, a provision for inspection and testing is included in standards and specifications, and provision for inspection and tests is also made in the routine of receiving deliveries. The very fact that inspection is indicated tends to make the vendor more careful to see that goods of proper quality are delivered. See Figure 8-1 for a typical policy statement on vendor responsibility for quality.

Section 4

RESPONSIBILITY

It is the responsibility of the supplier to provide and maintain an effective and economical Quality System that will assure an acceptable product quality level.

Section 5

REQUIREMENTS

5. 1 ORGANIZATION

The responsibility for Quality Assurance shall be clearly designated within the supplier's organization. The person designated to have responsibility for product quality levels shall have sufficient functional independence to allow objective and unbiased decisions.

5. 2 DOCUMENTATION

The Quality Assurance Program employed by the supplier shall be documented in the form of operating procedures and/or inspection instructions. This documentation shall include as a minimum, but not be limited to, the following.

5. 2. 1 Statement of Policy

The supplier shall provide a Statement of Policy concerning Management's concept of the responsibility and authority of the Quality Assurance organization. Such a statement should bear evidence of Management signatures.

Figure 8-1. Excerpts from a manual, "Supplier Inspection System Requirements," issued to vendors by an aerospace company.

5.2.2 Drawing and Change Control

The supplier's system shall provide that the latest applicable drawings, technical requirements and contract change information be available at the time and place of the supplier's inspection and/or fabrication. All changes shall be processed in a manner which assures accomplishment on the affected articles.

5.2.3 Subcontracted Suppliers

The supplier shall provide an effective system for the control of:

Selection of sources.

Obtaining certified test reports and/or certificates of compliance for procured material and services.

5.2.4 Inspection and Testing

The supplier shall provide an effective system for the inspection, test, and control of articles in:

Incoming inspection.

In-process inspection.

Final inspection.

5.2.5 Sampling Inspection

The supplier is encouraged to adopt the methods outlined in MIL-STD-105 and MIL-STD-414 Sampling Plans, which utilize statistics for quality evaluation, control, and acceptance. The utilization of any other system of statistical control will require approval.

5.2.6 Inspection Status

The supplier shall provide a system for indicating the inspection status of articles throughout all stages of manufacture. Identification may be accomplished by means of stamps, tags, routing cards, move tickets, tote box cards or other control devices which are attached to, or travel with, the product.

Inspection is an expense to the buying company, and it is obviously unsound to incur an expense of this sort out of proportion to the value and significance of the purchased material. But, when the quality and salability of the end product are involved, when manufacturing efficiency is likely to be affected, or when large amounts of labor are to be expended on the material in the process of fabrication, when other component materials are to be used in connection with it so that material expense is multiplied, when personal safety of workers is at stake, or when purchase value is dependent on certain analyses—it is equally obvious that careless or inadequate inspection is just as inexcusable. Some purchases will warrant complete tests of the entire delivery; in other cases, representative sampling will be sufficient. As a general rule, any purchase important enough to warrant the preparation of a formal specification will call for inspection and test, to an extent and in a manner defined in the specification itself.

Sometimes inspection is made at the manufacturer's plant before shipment. This has the advantage of eliminating freight charges for return and reshipment in the event of rejection and is consequently adapted to purchases in which transportation costs are a considerable factor, such as heavy products and those procured from distant plants. The procedure is likewise indicated when shipments are to be made directly to a distant location or exported, when the return of rejected merchandise for adjustment is impracticable, or when inspection at destination is too late to do any good as far as receipt of satisfactory and usable deliveries is concerned. To generalize, this policy is the logical one whenever the possibility of commercial adjustments is not adequate and when initial shipments of assured quality are essential. The military services consistently inspect products at manufacturers' plants prior to shipment. Increasingly, manufacturers are requiring that components that they buy be inspected against military standards, even if they are not going into end products intended for military use.

Inspection at the source involves the cost of training and maintaining a staff of capable field inspectors. It also entails the delegation of authority to such inspectors for decisions as to the acceptability of product, because the system becomes excessively slow and cumbersome if reference must be made to the home office whenever a question or doubt arises.

Inspection at the Buyer's Plant

Typically, quality inspections are made at the buyer's plant on receipt of materials, on the basis of representative samples from each shipment. Standard methods are prescribed for securing a representative sample of such nonhomogeneous materials as coal for fair analysis. On unit items, this of course presents no serious problem. Bulk materials, such as those received in tank car deliveries, are generally tested before unloading. Other materials are received, and, if sampling and tests are required before acceptance, they are segregated pending the completion of these tests to avoid the possibility of their going into general stock or even into use before the proper inspection has been made.

On some items the entire lot is tested, but these are in the nature of special cases. Large castings would generally be included in such a category as would parts for which extreme precision is essential. Safety rubber gloves for use in connection with high voltages would be subjected to individual dielectric tests before acceptance—and, in cases in which such equipment is in common use, the same procedure would probably be followed after each use, before the equipment is reissued.

Considerable use is made of independent commercial testing laboratories and services, usually by agreement between the buyer and the supplier. Such establishments have the advantage of excellent facilities for a wide variety of tests—physical, mechanical, chemical, X-ray, electrical, optical, photometric, and the like—adapted to all sorts of materials and products, and their impartial findings are accepted as final.

It should also be noted that there is increasing use of a manufacturer's certification of quality to obviate the duplication involved in acceptance testing after careful tests have been made in the production process itself. Where such certification can be relied on, this phase of procurement is greatly simplified. A specific guarantee of this sort technically places the responsibility on the seller. It has been developed to the point at which some steel producers, for example, furnish an individual analysis and heat-treating specification with each shipment made from a given heat of steel. At the Home Laundry Products Division of General Electric Company, Louisville, Kentucky, for further example, 95 percent of all purchased parts are certified by suppliers as meeting quality standards; 100 percent of all critical parts are certified by suppliers.

RESPONSIBILITY FOR QUALITY CONTROL

In larger organizations, in which the volume of such work is greater and in which a higher degree of functional organization usually obtains, the tendency is to regard inspection as a wholly separate function to be carried out by a quality control or quality assurance department. Such departments are responsible for measurement of quality and precision of products manufactured by the company as well as for those purchased from outside suppliers. Among their duties are the determination of sample lot sizes for accurate measurement of conformance to quality standards to specified degrees, thus reducing the amount of unit inspection required and in many cases eliminating the need for 100 percent inspection; measurement of the range and distribution frequency of deviation from standards, within and beyond acceptable tolerances; analysis of this information for correction and control of manufacturing processes; and development of graphic methods for presenting the information (see Figure 8-2).

For routine inspections of quality, in which a simple visual inspection or reliance on package labels is sufficient, the responsibility is generally in the receiving or stores department, which may or may not be under purchasing supervision. It is coupled with the routine receiving responsibility of inspection for quantity delivered.

Acceptance or Rejection

It is probably academic to argue the point of where the technical responsibility for acceptance or rejection of a delivery lies. But it is important to bear in mind these two distinct stages of responsibility—the obligation of the purchasing department to procure materials of the right quality and the obligation of the vendor to deliver in accordance with the order. It is a basic purpose of inspection and testing to confirm or certify the action of the purchasing department and to guide the buyer in his or her decision as to whether the contract requirements have been satisfactorily met in the delivery. The buyer will naturally rely on these findings as an integral part of the procurement process. Certainly any prudent purchasing officer will always consult with technical and using departments in the event of any substantial deviation from specified quality before making a decision as to the disposition of the goods.

Several alternative methods of procedure are open to the buyer in respect to substandard deliveries. These include:

1. *Outright rejection.* The goods are returned to the supplier, at the latter's expense, on a shipping order and invoice issued at the direction of the purchasing department. The supplier is notified of this action and of the reasons therefor. It should also be made clear at this point

**QUALITY CONTROL
ACCEPTANCE SAMPLING**

SYMBOL and DEFINITION	LOT SIZE	SAMPLE SIZE	COMMENTS
☐ *Discovery	1-999	11	Failure to pass this sample indicates need for re-inspection using 1.5 AQL unless otherwise specified in the square.
	1000+	22	This re-inspection is to be done on a multiple sampling basis.
⬡ Multiple	→	→	See MIL-STD-105 breakdown cards under: Multiple sampling normal inspection.
◇ Single	→	→	See MIL-STD-105 breakdown cards under: Single sampling normal inspection.

*DISCOVERY SAMPLING

I. Instruction:
   1. Obtain sample.
   2. Check each part carefully-
   3. Accept lot if no rejects are found.
   4. When one or more rejects are found, revert to MIL-STD-105 multiple sampling at the AQL level stated within the square.
      Any B is a 1.5 AQL. Check only for that characteristic which has been rejected initially.
   5. Write on inspection record "DISCOVERY SAMPLING".

II. Exceptions. . Do NOT use discovery sampling on:
   1. .015 AQL; .1 AQL
   2. "C", "D", and "F" sampling plans
   3. O checks (100% sort operation)
   4. Visual check - "50 series" of inspection sequence numbers where an AQL is specified. Visual in combination - eg.plating or surface finish.
   5. High Reliability

III. Modifications
   1. Plastic Parts - The sample must contain at least one part from each cavity of the mold. Increase sample size, if necessary, to obtain one part per cavity.
   2. Thread Checks - Use .65 AQL multiple sampling (unless otherwise specified by a tighter AQL) on:
      a) All receiving reports
      b) All work orders first time in
      c) After threads are chased
      d) After kerf is milled thru thread, or straddle milled, or cross drilled
      Use discovery sampling:
      a) In sub-assembly (unless threads are chased)
      b) After plating unless otherwise specified
      c) Die cast housings

IV. Multiple Sampling may be used unless otherwise specified

Figure 8-2. Sampling form used to correlate information developed in the sampling process.

whether the original purchase order is considered as still in force and unfulfilled or whether the transaction is terminated through default of the supplier.

2. *Return for replacement.* This procedure applies particularly to fabricated parts, but it can be used for materials as well. Accounting procedure is customarily handled through a memorandum invoice or credit memo pending receipt of the corrected or satisfactory delivery.

3. *Technical or engineering adjustment.* It is frequently practicable for a qualified vendor representative to come to the buyer's plant to make necessary adjustments on faulty equipment or to work out a satisfactory application of nonconforming materials.

4. *Price adjustment.* If goods are usable, although not strictly in accordance with the purchase specification, a price renegotiation in line with the value actually delivered may be the simplest and most satisfactory means of adjustment, although it does not actually correct the condition of a faulty delivery. It should be noted that repeated instances of this nature, regardless of the vendor's willingness to make the adjustment, are indicators of an unsatisfactory and incompetent source of supply.

Whatever method of adjustment is decided on, two principles should be consistently observed. The vendor must be promptly notified that a delivery is unsatisfactory, and for what reason, and the negotiation or adjustment should be carried on by or through the purchasing department. The procurement is not complete until a satisfactory delivery has been made and accepted. The contractual relationship has been effected through purchasing, and the personal contacts, both with the vendor and within the buyer's own organization, to aid in effecting a proper adjustment or settlement are generally centered on the buyer who placed the original order.

TEAMWORK FOR QUALITY ASSURANCE

The continuing demand for better quality in purchased materials, upon which product reliability ultimately rests, has led to close coordination of effort between the purchasing department and the quality control department in many companies. Typical examples of such teamwork include:

—In a company making rocket propellants, purchasing, quality, and engineering personnel define quality specifications for purchased parts. Joint review of subcontracts and purchase orders by quality control and purchasing to align suppliers' quality performance with customers' requirements led to the assignment of a quality assurance analyst to the purchasing department. As official liaison person between the two departments, that individual checks all requisitions to make sure that they meet quality requirements; keeps quality specifications up to date; monitors suppliers' compliance with quality requirements; and coordinates inspections of suppliers' facilities.

—A farm equipment manufacturer's purchasing department employs the services of a team of experts from the quality control department to analyze suppliers' quality capabilities. Upon purchasing's request, the team will investigate a supplier's buildings and work areas, inspection procedures, gage control, laboratory and test facilities, tooling, and competency of the quality and manufacturing personnel.

—A West Coast electronics firm's purchasing department has a quality assurance group that concentrates first on the completeness and accuracy of the company's specifications. If the specifications are in order and quality problems continue, purchasing calls on a team of in-plant inspectors and quality technicians for "missionary work" at supplier plants. When the inspecting team, which includes a purchasing representative, discovers such problems as incorrect tooling, insufficient controls, or improper instrumentation, they suggest alternative approaches and, in effect, begin a quality training program for the supplier.

—An automotive company has appointed a purchasing quality liaison agent, who works out of one of the two major plants of the company, but reports to the centralized purchasing department in Detroit. The agent represents purchasing in the frequently scheduled meetings of suppliers and personnel from the company's engineering, purchasing, assembly manufacturing, and quality control departments. The agent has the authority and responsibility to make on-the-spot decisions on quality matters that involve such things as tooling, premium costs, and overtime. When suppliers request permission to deviate from specifications, however, the agent must seek approval from the engineering department, which, in turn, consults with quality control before making a decision.

SOME PERFORMANCE OBJECTIVES

After studying this chapter you should be able to:

1. Compare the concepts of suitability and reliability as they apply to purchased products.

2. Explain the meaning of "use specification" and its significance in purchasing.
3. Contrast buying by brand name to buying by specification. Give examples from your own experience with the two types of buying and the reasons for your having employed them in specific instances.
4. List the approaches that should be used in writing satisfactory specifications.
5. Recognize those situations in which deviations from specifications may be necessary and tell how the deviations should be handled.
6. List the alternatives open to buyers when suppliers deliver substandard goods.

Proper quality in its purchases is of paramount concern to the purchasing department. But assurance of quality is pointless unless the products required are ordered in the right quantity, at the right time, and at the right price. The next two chapters—on inventory management—are concerned with the first two of those three considerations.

Inventory
Management—I

9

The second decision that a buyer must make, after determining the right quality to buy, is how much to buy. The need for materials has a quantitative, as well as a qualitative, factor. When a requisition or request to purchase comes to the purchasing department, it generally specifies not only the item that is needed, but the quantity needed as well. However, except in the case of custom types of manufacture, or materials to be purchased for a particular project, or special, nonrepetitive requirements, this statement of quantitative need is by no means a complete answer to the buyer's problem. Purchasing can be done on the basis of immediate need or on individual requisitions, but for the great bulk of industrial purchases this is a cumbersome and uneconomical policy.

Most material and supply requirements for a manufacturing operation are continuing requirements, and the cumulative or total need is a far better guide to effective purchasing than the day-to-day needs. Most requirements can be forecast well in advance with a high degree of accuracy on the basis of sales quotas, bills of material for the end product, projected plant operating schedules, and records of past experience in respect to rates of use. But, even if a whole year's needs could be anticipated by such means, it would obviously be impracticable, as well as unnecessary, to purchase the total quantity at one time (although it is sometimes advisable to cover the total need by contract). It is the purchasing agent's responsibility to have sufficient quantities on hand as needed. Purchase quantities therefore must maintain a balance with operating needs and with the advantages of volume buying, aided by the cushioning effect of an inventory reservoir of materials, to which current purchases are added and from which currently needed quantities are withdrawn.

Thus, in purchasing, just as the term "right quality" has the special meaning of suitability or quality *for a purpose,* so "right quantity" has the special meaning of quantity to be purchased *at a time.* And, just as there is a most suitable and economical quality of material, there is a most economical ordering quantity.

OPTIMUM ORDERING QUANTITY

Because quantity is a mathematical figure, there have been many attempts to develop a formula for determining the most economical ordering quantity. Besides the basic need, there are many factors to be taken into consideration—unit cost of the item in various lot sizes, the average inventory resulting from purchases in different quantities, the number of orders issued, cost of negotiating and issuing a purchasing order, and cost of carrying materials in inventory. Calculation of the last item alone involves a number of additional factors, such as interest on the inventory investment, overhead charges on storage space, stores department personnel, insurance, depreciation, and the like. Some of the earlier formulas contain no less than fifteen variables. Consequently, although they were mathematically correct, they were too complicated and cumbersome for practical use in connection with any extensive and diversified commodity list.

This difficulty has been largely overcome with the development of computers that are able to relate variables far beyond the capacity of individuals to do so and to give direct readings of the answers to complicated calculations in a matter of seconds, whereas manual calculation would involve excessive time and effort. Computers are now widely used in a variety of purchasing operations; in some cases, indeed, they implement an entire purchasing system so far as standard stock items are concerned. The key to their value and effectiveness is their ability to determine optimum ordering and stock quantities from the data furnished and to control reorder points and quantities once proper inventory standards and policies have been established. We are here concerned with the principles of quantity determination, which must be understood to feed the required information into the computer. This is important, too, because many purchasing departments do not have access to computers, and the results must be obtained by simpler means.

Meanwhile, a number of practical working formulas have been developed, based on the known factors. The problem can be worked out to determine economical ordering quantity in terms of the number of units per order, the dollar value that this represents, or the number of weeks of coverage at a given rate of use. All these methods are equally serviceable, because they are merely different ways of expressing the same quantity and the answers can readily be translated into either of the other two units of measurement, as desired. One such formula that has gained wide acceptance and has proved its effectiveness as a purchasing guide is:

$$EOQ = \sqrt{\frac{2 \times \text{Annual usage} \times \text{order cost}}{\text{Unit cost} \times \text{carrying cost}}}$$

or, in abbreviated form,

$$EOQ = \sqrt{\frac{24 \, dB}{cI}}$$

where
EOQ = economic order quantity
d = monthly usage in units
B = order cost in dollars
c = unit cost in dollars
I = carrying cost as a percentage of inventory value

Note that the constant 24 includes a factor of 12 to convert monthly usage to annual usage.

As an example, consider a situation in which the cost of placing an order is $10, the cost of carrying is 20 percent of the cost of the material, monthly usage is 1,000 pieces, and the unit cost is $.10 per item. The economic order quantity, based on the formula, would then be:

$$EOQ = \sqrt{\frac{24 \times 1,000 \times 10}{.10 \times .20}}$$

$$= \quad 3,464 \text{ pieces}$$

Remember that carrying cost is expressed as a percentage, not in terms of dollars.

Once the factors of order cost and inventory cost have been determined for any given company operation, the determination of optimum ordering quantity is directly related to a single variable, the total annual usage of the item under consideration.

To give meaning to the formula it is essential, of course, to have reasonably accurate values for the two cost factors. Relatively few companies have detailed information on purchase order cost. In lieu of an elaborate cost analysis, a satisfactory working value can be found by taking the total cost of operating the purchasing department, including all salaries, expenses, and overhead charges, on an annual basis, and dividing this by the number of purchase orders issued during the year. (Rather surprisingly, perhaps, this will show an average cost in the neighborhood of $10 to $15 per order.)

Information on average inventory carrying cost is more generally available in most accounting systems. Here, however, the average cost is likely to be misleading, because the order quantity formula is to be applied to individual commodities, and there will be a wide range of actual carrying costs due to differences in the physical bulk of various items, the type of storage facilities and protection needed, rates of depreciation, and so forth. It would be excessively difficult, and would serve no useful purpose, to calculate a specific carrying cost for each individual item. But, instead of taking one average cost figure of, say, 25 percent on total inventory, it is quite feasible to classify the commodities into three or four groups having similar storage characteristics and to assign an average carrying cost to each group. This might range from as little as 10 percent up to 50 percent or more. Applying the appropriate group figure in the formula obviously gives added accuracy and value to the calculation of ordering quantity. An example of this method, and of the difference it makes in the resulting order quantity determination, is shown in the parallel columns of Figure 9-1.

LIMITATIONS OF THE FORMULA

The limitations of a formula such as this are readily apparent. Most important of these is that it does not give effect to changes in the unit price of the material or product concerned. A change in unit price changes the value of (A) annual usage, in dollars, and consequently changes the economical ordering quantity. This can be adjusted by inserting the revised value in the formula and making a new calculation. But this adjustment does not take care of the more significant fact that the direction of current price trends and the anticipation of price changes may actually be determining influences in purchasing policy regarding the quantity to be bought at any given time. Certainly, they would tend to modify any decisions predicated on a stable price situation. Similarly, the formula does not (except through a recalculation, as in the case of a price

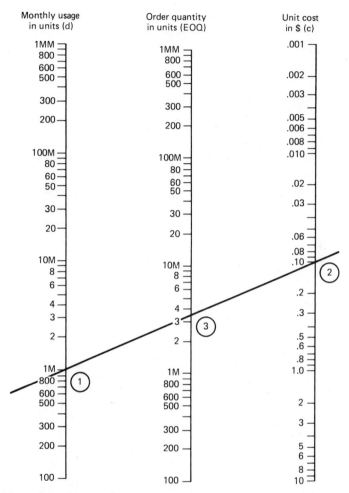

Figure 9-1. Nomograph for determining the most economical ordering quanity.

change) reflect the price advantages of volume buying and quantity discount schedules.

Even supposing that the price factor is stable and that the formula produces a precise theoretical determination of the most economical ordering quantity, it is quite likely that the resulting figure will have to be adjusted somewhat arbitrarily to bring it into conformity with commercial practice in respect to unit packages, established quantity discount brackets, economical manufacturing quantities, full carload or truckload quantities, and so on. This is somewhat analogous to the classic gibe at engineering practice that calculates a structural strain to three or four decimal places and then adds a 50 percent safety factor.

There are other limitations in which specific materials are concerned. Any formula must be interpreted and applied with common sense, and the ordering quantity formula is no exception. For example, no matter what the formula says, bulky materials, such as excelsior, cartons, and filler materials used in the paper and leather industries, must be ordered with available storage space in mind, because space may effectively limit the quantity that can be handled. Nor is it sensible to order materials that are subject to deterioration in such quantities that the supply will exceed the shelf life of the material. Portland cement, batteries, photographic paper and film, cellulose tape, and enameled wire are examples of items on which such caution must be exercised.

BENEFITS OF USING THE FORMULA

Despite these limitations, the mathematical approach to determination of best order sizes is steadily gaining in acceptance and usage, for sound reasons of policy and because of the very substantial demonstrable savings and benefits that have resulted where this method has been consistently used as a guide within the proper scope of its application.

It has already been noted that the decision on best quantity is quite a complicated one if all the pertinent factors are considered, and the list of purchased commodities typically runs up to thousands of items. Without some sort of approved mathematical procedure to simplify the calculations, an excessive amount of time and effort may be expended on this one aspect of the purchase for the larger and more significant items, whereas scant attention may be given to any accurate determination of best quantity for the great majority of items on the list. There will be a tendency to rely on other, less scientific standards of quantity, such as mere precedent. Experienced buyers may make a quick, intuitive appraisal of the factors and come fairly close to the right answer most of the time. The improved performance that results from using mathematical methods suggests that intuition is far from reliable when ordering quantities are concerned.

The ordering quantity formula substitutes fact for judgment. It establishes a definite relationship between the significant variables in the situation and eliminates the variable of personal judgment, so that quantity decisions are consistent and are in accord with policy. It can be used on computers or converted into tabular form for direct reference, so that the scientific method can be applied to every item on the list with a minimum of effort.

For the great majority of stores and supply items, the mathematical method can be relied on completely, relieving the buyer of all responsibility on this score, with the assurance of having correct decisions which are reflected in superior performance. For example, the purchasing department of the Bell Telephone Laboratories, as early as 1940, devised a series of conversion factors based on the formula that made it possible to reduce inventories automatically by 28.5–42.0 percent of dollar value while supporting the same volume of requisitions and maintaining a superior standard of service, as compared with the situation in which stock control, ordering point, and order quantity were based on the judgment and decisions of experienced stockkeepers and buyers. Thus, the often neglected area of operating supplies and standard parts, representing a great number of different items that must be purchased and stocked, sometimes in relatively small amounts but in substantial total volume, is readily brought under scientific purchasing control.

For production materials and other items in which the final determination of ordering quantity involves a consideration of price trends, seasonal factors, advance coverage, or other elements not provided for in the mathematical calculation, the formula nevertheless furnishes a useful starting point. Under stable conditions, it may be directly applied. In any case, the necessary modifications may be made more intelligently, and with a clearer understanding of costs entailed, than if there were no basic standard of optimum quantity.

In addition to these uses in quantity decisions, the formulas have established some important and hitherto unrecognized principles of costs and cost relationships in respect to inventory control, which is inseparable from the problem of how much to buy. Among these are:

1. Total cost is at a minimum at the point at which ordering cost is equal to carrying cost for a given quantity.
2. Within reasonable variation of order size (plus or minus 20 percent), the total cost varies very little; beyond these limits, total cost goes up rapidly either way.
3. Ordering too little usually costs much more than ordering too much.
4. A change in the cost of carrying stock has a much greater effect on the most economical order size than does a change in the cost of restocking. (Mathematically speaking, optimum size of order varies in inverse proportion to the carrying cost and in direct proportion to the square root of the reorder cost.)

USING THE FORMULA

It is only in unusual cases that the order quantity formula is calculated for each individual order. Once the optimum quantity is established for an item, it is valid until there is some change in one of the variable values—annual usage, carrying cost, or cost of ordering. The appropriate quantity is therefore noted on the purchase order record card for each item, along with maximum and minimum stock quantities and ordering point, so that the information is immediately available by direct reference when the item is to be reordered.

Also, there are some practical short cuts for making the actual calculation. One of these is the nomograph chart, a graphic device having parallel logarithmic scales so placed in relation to a reference line that the calculation can be made simply by laying a straightedge across the chart connecting the appropriate values in any given problem and finding the answer by direct reading at the point of intersection on the scale. This is essentially the same principle as in the operation of a slide rule, but it is even simpler for a specific type of problem. In some purchasing departments, such a nomograph is printed on the reverse side of the requisition form. Then, in the case of a new or nonstocked item, the buyer can use the requisition as a worksheet and determine the economical ordering quantity in a few seconds without going through the arithmetical process.

An example is given in Figure 9-1. In this case the cost of ordering is $10, monthly usage is 1,000 units, and the unit cost is $.10. To find the economic order quantity, the buyer draws a line from the usage quantity in the left-hand column to unit cost in the right-hand column. The point at which the line crosses the scale in the center column is the economic ordering quantity. Similar charts can be drawn up for different order costs.

The most widely used method is to make up a table based on constant values for ordering cost and carrying cost, calculating the economical order quantity for each of a wide range of annual usage values. This is permanent and universally applicable. All the buyer needs to know is the annual dollar usage of an item, and he or she can find the economical order quantity by direct reference in the table. In cases in which there are several different carrying costs for different types of material, a separate table is made up for each of the several values for this factor, and commodities are classified and coded to indicate which table applies.

ORDER QUANTITY TABLE

An order quantity table developed by the purchasing department of the Meter Division of Westinghouse Electric Corporation is shown in Figure 9-2. This was originally undertaken as a means of eliminating material

BEST ORDER QUANTITY MULTIPLIER

Annual Use $	Year's Supply to Order .11 / A	.25 / B	.50 / C	1.00 / D	Stock Carrying Rate	Annual Use $	.11 / A	.25 / B	.50 / C	1.00 / D
1	8	5.3	3.75	2.65	Code	260	.495	.328	.232	.164
2	5.6	3.70	2.62	1.85		280	.477	.316	.224	.158
3	4.6	3.08	2.19	1.54		300	.460	.308	.219	.154
4	4.0	2.65	1.87	1.32		325	.444	.294	.208	.147
5	3.6	2.38	1.69	1.20		350	.427	.284	.199	.142
6	3.26	2.16	1.56	1.08		375	.412	.273	.193	.137
7	3.03	2.00	1.42	1.00		400	.400	.265	.187	.132
8	2.84	1.88	1.33	.935		425	.388	.257	.182	.128
9	2.68	1.77	1.25	.885		450	.377	.250	.177	.125
10	2.52	1.67	1.18	.836		475	.368	.244	.173	.122
12	2.30	1.53	1.08	.765		500	.360	.238	.169	.120
14	2.14	1.42	1.00	.710		550	.341	.226	.160	.113
16	2.00	1.32	.936	.663		600	.326	.216	.156	.108
18	1.90	1.25	.885	.626		650	.314	.208	.147	.104
20	1.79	1.19	.840	.593		700	.303	.200	.142	.100
25	1.60	1.06	.750	.530		750	.292	.194	.137	.097
30	1.45	.968	.682	.482		800	.284	.188	.133	.0935
35	1.35	.900	.635	.448		850	.275	.182	.129	.0910
40	1.25	.838	.592	.419		900	.266	.177	.125	.0885
45	1.2	.790	.559	.395		950	.260	.172	.121	.086
50	1.13	.747	.530	.374		1000	.252	.167	.118	.0836
60	1.07	.682	.485	.342		1100	.242	.160	.114	.080
70	.960	.636	.450	.318		1200	.230	.153	.108	.0765
80	.896	.594	.420	.297		1400	.214	.142	.100	.0710
90	.840	.556	.394	.278		1600	.200	.132	.0936	.066
100	.800	.530	.375	.265		1800	.190	.125	.088	.063
110	.767	.508	.359	.254		2000	.179	.119	.084	.059
120	.730	.484	.342	.242		2500	.160	.106	.075	.053
130	.704	.468	.328	.232		3000	.145	.096	.068	
140	.675	.447	.317	.224		3500	.135	.090	.064	
150	.653	.433	.306	.216		4000	.125	.084	.059	
160	.632	.420	.296	.210		4500	.120	.079	.056	
170	.614	.407	.287	.203		5000	.113	.075		
180	.595	.395	.279	.198		6000	.107	.068		
190	.580	.384	.272	.192		7000	.096	.064		
200	.560	.370	.262	.185		8000	.089	.059		
220	.540	.357	.253	.178		9000	.084	.056		
240	.515	.342	.242	.171		10000	.080			

Application of the Table
(Using Stock Carrying Rate Code A)

If you use $10,000 per year, order 1 month's supply per order

1,000	3 months'
250	6 months'
65	1 year's
15	2 years'
5	4 years'
1	8 years'

Figure 9-2. Best order quantity table.

shortages that had occurred under the previous normal purchasing policy of buying repetitive stores items in lots representing a three months' supply. The accomplishment of this objective has been one of the great advantages resulting from its use, but it has also revealed previously unsuspected opportunities for economies in purchasing and inventory cost.

This table is calculated on the basis of four different rates of stock-carrying cost: 11 percent per year, 25 percent, 50 percent, and 100 percent. Annual usage, in dollars, is shown in a range from $1 to $10,000. The economical order quantity is expressed as a multiplier representing, decimally, the number of years' (fraction of a year's) supply to order. To use the table,

1. Find, by reference to the stock record card, in which of the four stock-carrying rate groups the item is classified (for example, code B, 25 percent per year).
2. Note annual usage of the item, in dollars (for example, $750 per year).
3. Find the figure in column B, opposite $750 in annual use column (.194).
4. Multiply $750 × .194 = $145.50.
5. Result: Best ordering quantity is the commercial quantity closest to $145.50 in cost, or about ten weeks' supply. To avoid repeated calculations, order quantity is entered on the purchase record card. It is subject to revision if the rate of use changes or if the item is reclassified.

Examination of this table clearly shows the error of applying one time-coverage standard (for example, three months' supply) to all items, regardless of the rate of use. It indicates that, for an item in the 11 percent carrying-cost classification, used at a rate of about $1,000 per year, the three months' supply is the economical quantity to buy. But, for items in greater use, or with higher carrying costs for the same dollar usage, smaller orders and shorter coverage are indicated. For less used items, it calls for orders greatly in excess of common practice.

The mathematical, or theoretical, calculation of most economical purchase quantity on these items of limited use, in which purchase of from one to several years' supply is indicated, runs counter to all the traditional concepts of prudent coverage and active stock turnover; yet the table has amply justified itself in actual use. It is easy to visualize mountains of inventory piling up under these schedules, but this did not occur. The reason for this is that the "long" orders are more than compensated for by closer scheduling on the major items that make up the great bulk of purchases. In this division, for example, there are about

8,000 different items purchased for stores, but 250 of these account for more than two thirds of the dollar volume; half of the total dollar volume is represented by only 40 items. The indicated purchase quantity for any item used at a rate of $10,000 per year is one month's supply per order, so that current investment is consistently low and turnover is high on this predominant portion of the inventory. Meanwhile, the elimination of frequent repeat orders on the minor items, purchased according to the table, reduced the number of purchase orders issued from 15,000 to 5,400 per year, with consequent substantial savings in the cost of purchasing, magnified by a corresponding reduction in the expenses of receiving and accounting.

Additional benefits resulting from this method of quantity determination are reported as follows:

1. During a period when the company was spending more dollars than ever before, fewer purchase orders were being placed.

2. Despite an all-time high of production volume, the buying staff was reduced by two thirds and total purchasing department personnel from 37 to 21.

3. Buyers were enabled to expend nearly their entire time on constructive negotiation, whereas formerly a significant portion of their time was devoted to expediting.

4. Follow-up action has been eliminated on 80 percent of the orders placed.

5. The record shows only one stockout[1] per account in seven and one-half years. On the average, there are only 15 to 20 items reported as delaying production out of more than 2,000 open purchase orders, as compared with a high of 325 items out of 3,000 open orders prior to the adoption of this system.

A variation of this method that puts the precalculated information into simple graphic form is shown in Figures 9-3 and 9-4. The first step is to plot the most economical order quantities as a curve on a chart having as its horizontal scale the value of one month's supply in dollars (corresponding to the annual use column of the table) and a vertical scale showing the number of months' supply to order (corresponding to the multiplier column of the table). The shape of the curve is such as to make a logarithmic scale most feasible on the horizontal axis. As a matter of policy, the scope of the chart is limited to purchase quantities of not less than one month's supply or more than a year's supply.

[1] A "stockout" is the inability to fill a requisition for a stores item from stock on hand, that is, the failure of the inventory policy or formula (or of purchasing performance) to anticipate fully the requirement for that item. In setting ordering points and quantities, this is a calculated risk.

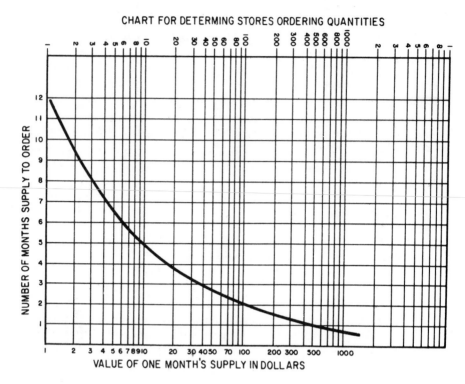

Figure 9-3 Curve showing economical stores ordering quantities.

The second step is to note the point at which the curve intersects the lines indicating best order quantity as equivalent to twelve months' supply, eleven months' supply, ten months' supply, and so forth and draw vertical lines from these points down to the baseline of the chart, showing the corresponding readings in terms of the dollar value of one month's supply. The result is shown in Figure 9-4, a simple and practical guide to determining economical order quantities according to the rate of use of the various items. As in the case of the quantity tables, this calculation is accurate for only the one value of inventory carrying cost used in the original formula; for different rates of carrying cost, additional charts must be drawn and commodities classified and coded to indicate which chart applies. In a moderately simple operation, two such values may be sufficient to cover all cases with reasonable accuracy. In large, complex operations, with a wide variety of items carried in inventory, the items can usually be grouped within not more than four classifications. Four charts, corresponding to the four columns of the multiplier table, will serve for the entire purchasing program.

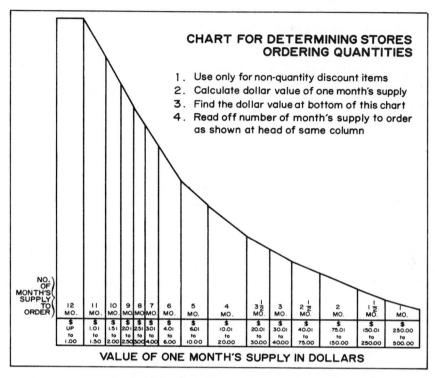

CHART FOR DETERMINING STORES ORDERING QUANTITIES

1. Use only for non-quantity discount items
2. Calculate dollar value of one month's supply
3. Find the dollar value at bottom of this chart
4. Read off number of month's supply to order as shown at head of same column

NO. OF MONTH'S SUPPLY TO ORDER	12 MO.	11 MO.	10 MO.	9 MO.	8 MO.	7 MO.	6 MO.	5 MO.	4 MO.	$3\frac{1}{2}$ MO.	3 MO.	$2\frac{1}{2}$ MO.	2 MO.	$1\frac{1}{2}$ MO.	1 MO.
	$ UP to 1.00	$ 1.01 to 1.50	$ 1.51 to 2.00	$ 2.01 to 2.50	$ 2.51 to 3.00	$ 3.01 to 4.00	$ 4.01 to 6.00	$ 6.01 to 10.00	$ 10.01 to 20.00	$ 20.01 to 30.00	$ 30.01 to 40.00	$ 40.01 to 75.00	$ 75.01 to 150.00	$ 150.01 to 250.00	$ 250.00 to 500.00

VALUE OF ONE MONTH'S SUPPLY IN DOLLARS

Figure 9-4 Ordering chart based on the economical quantity curve.

EFFECT OF QUANTITY DISCOUNTS

The best-order-quantity formula is predicated on a constant price factor. Fluctuations in price are taken care of by the fact that these are reflected in the figure of annual usage or value of a month's supply. But there is another important price variable that is closely related to order quantity—the quantity discount offered by many suppliers, by which the unit price of a product or material is reduced in successive stages as larger quantities are purchased. "Cheaper by the dozen" pricing is a common practice in industrial distribution as well as in retailing, and the price differentials may be very substantial and alluring. If the optimum quantity indicated by formula comes close to the point of such a price "break" or bracket, common sense would dictate adjusting the quantity purchased so as to take advantage of this extra saving. But, if the formula does not actually give the answer to this problem, it does suggest that the lower unit cost must be balanced against the extra investment and the extra cost of carrying inventory over a longer period, to determine whether the lower unit cost thus earned represents a real saving to the purchaser.

This factor does not lend itself to generalization or precalculation. Each case must be individually considered. However, there is a simple mathematical approach based on determining the return, or "profit," on the extra investment if the larger quantity is purchased. Figure 9-5 shows a worksheet for this purpose, by which a useful calculation can be made in a few minutes.

QUANTITY DISCOUNT ADVANTAGE WORKSHEET

TPFC-1135   DIVISION   DATE
MATERIAL

VENDOR   ADDRESS

1. COST TO BUY REQUISITIONED (SMALLER) QUANTITY NOW: 2. COST TO BUY RECOMMENDED (LARGER) QUANTITY NOW:

SMALLER QUANTITY .... LARGER QUANTITY ....
TIMES: UNIT PRICE ....PER............ TIMES: UNIT PRICE ....PER..............

EQUALS: COST OF GOODS .... EQUALS: COST OF GOODS ....
PLUS: FREIGHT .... PLUS: FREIGHT ....

EQUALS: TOTAL COST   EQUALS: TOTAL COST

3. ADDITIONAL INVESTMENT REQUIRED TO PURCHASE   4. ULTIMATE COST TO BUY LARGER QUANTITY, BY MEANS OF SMALLER
   LARGER QUANTITY NOW: QUANTITY RE-ORDERS:

TOTAL COST FROM 2 ABOVE .... QUANTITY (FROM 2 ABOVE) ....
MINUS: TOTAL COST FROM 1 ABOVE .... TIMES: UNIT PRICE (FROM 1 ABOVE) ....PER........
EQUALS: ADDITIONAL INVESTMENT .... EQUALS: ULTIMATE COST ....

                                               PLUS: FREIGHT (EST. FROM 1 ABOVE) ....

                                               EQUALS: TOTAL ULTIMATE COST

5. SAVINGS WHICH WOULD RESULT FROM BUYING   6. PERIOD OF ADDITIONAL INVESTMENT:
   LARGER QUANTITY NOW:

ULTIMATE COST TO BUY   LARGER (RECOMMENDED) QTY.= ....MOS. SUPPLY
LARGER QUANTITY (FROM 4 ABOVE) ....

MINUS: COST TO BUY SAME
QUANTITY NOW (FROM 2 ABOVE) ....   LESS: SMALLER (REQ'ND.) QTY.= ....MOS. SUPPLY

                                               EQUALS: MONTHS ADDITIONAL
                                               INVESTMENT MUST BE CARRIED   MONTHS

7. COST OF CARRYING INVENTORY IF LARGER QUANTITY   8. RATE OF RETURN ON INVESTMENT:
   IS PURCHASED NOW:

ADDITIONAL INVESTMENT (FROM 3 ABOVE)
X.01 (CARRYING COST PER MO' 1% OF INV.)........... DIVIDE   TOTAL SAVINGS (FROM 5 ABOVE) $
TIMES: MOS. ADDITIONAL INVESTMENT   BY   TOTAL COST OF ADDITIONAL
MUST BE CARRIED (FROM 6 ABOVE) ....   INVESTMENT (FROM 7, AT LEFT)

EQUALS: CARRYING COST OF INV. .... EQUALS: 0 _____ EQUALS _____ % RATE OF RETURN ON

                                               INVESTMENT
PLUS: ADD. INVESTMENT (FROM 3 ABOVE) ....

TOTAL COST OF
ADDITIONAL INVESTMENT

THE PERCENTAGE FIGURE DEVELOPED IN BLOCK 8 IS THE RATE OF RETURN ON THE EXTRA INVESTMENT REQUIRED TO PURCHASE THE
RECOMMENDED LARGER QUANTITY NOW. IT SHOULD BE COMPARED WITH THE PREVAILING RATE OF RETURN ON INVESTMENT IN THE
DIVISION CONCERNED, TO DETERMINE THE ADVISABILITY OF PURCHASING THE LARGER (RECOMMENDED) QUANTITY.

PREPARED BY

Figure 9-5   Work sheet for calculating quantity discount advantage.

For example, consider an item of stainless steel tubing priced at $42.20 per hundred feet in small lots and at $33.60 in lots of 1,000 feet or more. It is used at a rate of about 150 feet per month and is generally requisitioned in lots of 500 feet, or about three month's supply. Problem: To determine whether it would be more economical to buy nearly seven months' supply at the lower price. The applicable inventory carrying rate is 12 percent per year, or 1 percent per month. Freight charges amount to $4.00 on a shipment of 500 feet and $7.50 on a shipment of 1,000 feet.

Following the calculations on the worksheet, we find:

1. Total cost of an order for 500 feet is $215.00.
2. Total cost of an order for 1,000 feet is $343.50.
3. Additional investment entailed by ordering 1,000 feet at one time is $128.50.
4. Total cost of 1,000 feet, ordered in two lots of 500 feet, is $430.00.
5. Cost saving on 1,000 feet, ordered at one time, is $86.50.
6. Additional period for which the additional investment must be carried is (approximately) four months.
7. Additional inventory carrying cost is $5.30, making the total cost of additional investment $137.80.
8. Cost saving (5) divided by total cost of additional investment (7) represents a return of nearly 65 percent on the additional investment over a seven-month period.

Because this is many times greater than the normal return on investment, it would probably be advisable in this case to buy the larger quantity and take advantage of the price discount. This is not always the case, nor is the decision always in the hands of the purchasing department. In many companies the procedure is to submit such cost comparisons, with buying recommendations, to the inventory control department. There may be other considerations, such as maintaining inventory balance, or greater fluidity of assets, or conserving working capital for other essential purposes in the business. It is part of the purchasing responsibility, however, to determine the most economical buying policies and to follow them so far as is consistent with purchasing authority and within materials budgets.

QUANTITY DETERMINATION BY POLICY

Mathematical determination of most economical order quantities is a useful device, particularly in respect to inventory items in regular use, and is a guide in all quantity decisions, but it does not automatically provide the answer to the problem of deciding the right quantity to buy. It is not equally applicable to all classifications of purchased items or to all types of requirements. The decision on quantity may be a matter of policy, in which the economical lot size is only one of several factors to be considered. And there are a number of different buying methods, other than purchasing for the replenishment of inventory, especially adaptable to various types of requirements and having a definite bearing on the decision of how much to buy at a time. A complete purchasing program will probably make use of all these methods, according to circumstances and need. The more important of these are:

1. *Definite quantity contracts* with predetermined deliveries scheduled over a period of time. This method is particularly adapted to raw materials and components for scheduled operations and assembly, in which quantity requirements and rate of use are reasonably well known in advance. The contract quantity in this case is the total estimated need for the contract period, usually three months or a year, or a base supply to cover the bulk of estimated needs, to be supplemented by open-market purchases as required.

2. *Continuing contract,* similar to the above but without the specific limitations of quantity and duration, so that it has greater flexibility. In a typical arrangement of this sort, requirements are projected three months in advance; firm delivery instructions are issued for the first month, and the supplier is authorized to proceed with the manufacture of the second month's quantity at his or her convenience and to procure raw materials for the third month's estimated requirement. The quantity need is reviewed every 30 days and projected as before so that, in effect, there is a firm three months' contract in force at all times.

3. *Term or requirements contracts,* for a specified duration of time but not for a fixed quantity, this being subject to the buyer's needs as they develop. The quantity is usually estimated within stated maximum and minimum limits, with deliveries to be ordered and released as required. The method is used when requirements of a material or product are expected to be substantial, but total quantity and the scheduling of use cannot be accurately known in advance. It is particularly useful in connection with materials that are fabricated in two or more stages.

4. *Open-market purchases.* This method is indicated when quantity requirements of an item are either small or variable, when market and competitive conditions suggest the advisability of a flexible purchasing condition, when goods are readily available on short notice, when they conform to industry standards, or when special requirements are known sufficiently in advance to permit ordering and delivery time without endangering the continuity of operations.

5. *Group purchase of related items,* usually those that are used in small quantities as individual items but that make up a substantial order and commitment when combined in a single or "blanket" order to one supplier. It can be done either as an open-market purchase or on short- or long-term contracts. It calls for periodic review of stock by related classifications of items or the review of related items whenever a requisition is received for an individual item. A variation of this scheme is a monthly or quarterly contract on the "requirements" basis as outlined in the third case. This might cover a list of mill supplies or small tools, for example. Bids would be invited, either on an item-by-item basis or in the form of a generally applicable discount from list prices. After selecting the most favorable overall proposal, all requirements for these items are passed along to the successful bidder in the form of memorandum orders to be delivered as needed and billed on a single invoice at the end of the month or contract period. The advantages are that small and relatively unattractive "retail" quantities are consolidated into substantial business and that great savings in clerical and accounting procedure accrue to both buyer and seller because single small transactions are not made the subject of a formal purchase order and are not carried individually through accounting records.

6. *Special purchases,* applicable to nonrepetitive items—equipment purchases, special parts, items that are not regularly carried in stores, materials and supplies for a particular project. The quantity in such cases is, of course, determined by and equal to the specific need. The method of purchase depends on the nature and size of the project. No generalizations can be made for this broad and miscellaneous category; some of the more important aspects, such as the purchase of capital equipment, are discussed separately.

7. *Purchase strictly for requirements,* as indicated by requisitions received. Quantity is dictated by the individual request. This is the least flexible and least desirable of all purchase policies, affording a minimum opportunity for the application of sound purchasing principles and the development of a planned purchasing program. Except insofar as it includes the classification of special purchases outlined in the preceding paragraph, it is held to a minimum whenever centralized purchasing organization prevails.

BASIC QUANTITY REQUIREMENTS

The basic information regarding total quantity requirements and rates of use in a continuing operation comes from two sources: the record of past experience, which is available in purchasing department records and reflected in maximum and minimum stock quantities, and projected sales quotas and manufacturing schedules, which establish purchasing policies in the first place and are the basis of subsequent modifications. With modern scientific management, these projections of material requirements can be made with a high degree of accuracy. Sometimes manufacturing programs are set for an entire season or year in advance; more typically, they may be set for a quarterly period, with provision for review and revision monthly, so that there is at all times a reasonably accurate knowledge of what requirements will be for some time in advance. Manufacturing schedules can be broken down into detailed bills of materials, normal rates of waste and spoilage are known from past experience, and the normal ratio of nonproduct or operating supplies can be calculated to the operating rate. On the basis of this information, total requirements for the period can be forecast to take advantage of quantity buying, deliveries can be scheduled to meet the need, and purchasing policies can be established to permit the most economical and efficient procurement.

It is essential that the purchasing officer be completely and promptly informed of manufacturing or operating plans and schedules. The most desirable means of accomplishing this is to have the purchasing executive represented in, and participating in, the management councils where such decisions are made. His or her entire responsibility depends on such plans, and the successful execution of the plans depends on his or her knowledge and performance, to the same extent as on design, manufacturing, sales, and finance. In many cases the purchasing officer's special knowledge of materials and their availability, of new developments and trends in use, and of commercial standards can contribute much to the wisdom and practicability of the projected program.

MATERIAL REQUIREMENTS PLANNING

A relatively new management technique, material requirements planning (MRP), goes beyond the traditional bases for determining quantity requirements and purchasing schedules. In an MRP system, the (dependent) demand for components of a manufactured product depends on the forecasted (independent) demand for the finished product. Although statistical methods of inventory control—economic order quantities, safety stock, and reorder points—were part of early MRP methods, they are generally considered invalid by proponents of the more sophisticated MRP techniques that have been developed. The basic difference between the statistical methods and the MRP method of controlling inventory is that the former assumes relatively uniform usage of components and gradual inventory depletion, which users of MRP consider unrealistic. A more detailed discussion of material requirements planning and its relation to purchasing appears in Chapter 10.

EFFECT OF SPECIALS ON FORECASTING REQUIREMENTS

In operations in which products are made to special design and special order, forecasting of material requirements cannot be done with such detailed accuracy. In such cases the record of average requirements as reflected in purchasing experience, in which materials data are compiled and recorded, may be of even greater relative importance in planning. Under these circumstances it is even more essential that the purchasing department be apprised of needs and of projected activity than under a continuing schedule and at as early a stage as possible. To cite a typical example, orders may be received for three large installations to be built to special order, each one involving, as a matter of special purchase, a quantity of condenser tubing. Before a detailed bill of materials can be drawn off, these separate projects must go through the engineering or drawing board stage. One of these may take considerably longer to detail than the others, or the three may be engineered consecutively, coming to the purchasing department as three separate requirements, in limited quantity, within a relatively short space of time but each demanding separate and urgent procurement. If these three projects were known to the purchasing agent at the time at which the sale was made, with even approximate quantities, much time could have been saved; one order and one receiving operation, with all their attendant record and accounting detail, would have done the work of three; and a substantial saving in cost could have been effected by reason of the quantity involved.

FACTORS INFLUENCING QUANTITY

Having the basic information regarding scheduled quantity requirements, or any request to purchase, the buyer has several factors to consider in arriving at a decision as to the right quantity to purchase at a time—a quantity that will maintain continuity of operation according to schedule, that will represent the most economical unit cost, cost of procurement, and cost of handling, and that will take best advantage of commercial usage and market trends.

The first factor is the time required for delivery, from the time that the order is issued until the time that the goods are received. If the item is one that must be fabricated before shipment, this would include not only the time in transit, but the time required for manufacture and a prudent allowance for the supplier's own scheduling of production, because it is not safe to assume that production will start immediately upon receipt of the order. The sum of these three constitutes the procurement cycle, or lead time required in placing the order to ensure delivery when needed. The scheduling of purchase starts with the required delivery date and is calculated in reverse chronological order. In any time of scarcity and great demand, when production facilities are overcrowded and orders must wait their turn, the procurement cycle lengthens. Conversely, when markets are easier, the cycle shortens to actual production and transit time, and, on many standard items of the "shelf goods" variety that are normally carried in stock by suppliers, it may amount to the delivery time only.

For items that are in continuing use, and for which long lead times are involved, the quantity and timing of orders are calculated on the basis of the length of the procurement cycle and normal rate of use so that, ideally, stock will be replenished just as the last material from the previous order is being used. However, to minimize the risk of running out of stock, two prudent precautions should be taken. One is to supplement the lead-time calculation with a specific promise of delivery on the part of the supplier. The other is to maintain a reasonable reserve or "insurance" stock as a cushion for unexpected demands and delayed deliveries (see Chapter 10).

The second factor, or set of factors, affecting purchase quantity has to do with commercial usage in respect to manufacture, packaging, and shipment. There is a minimum economical manufacturing quantity, directly reflected in unit costs. The quantity will vary in respect to different types of products and the facilities of various suppliers, some being organized and equipped for long runs and mass production, whereas others can operate efficiently on a comparatively short-run or custom basis. There are basic costs of machine setting, tool and die changes, and the like incurred in every order and to be spread over the unit cost whether the quantity be large or small. It does not follow that costs and prices will be automatically or proportionally reduced as ordering quantities are increased beyond the minimum point. The cost of batch processing, for example, may be constant for any quantity that exceeds the minimum. The process may be such that it is feasible only in exact multiples of the minimum quantity, or new costs of reconditioning tools and dies may be incurred after a given volume of production has been accomplished. The supplier's schedule of quantity discounts is a fairly reliable indicator of the quantity economies that can be achieved.

Similarly, there are quantity economies in the cost of transportation, which is a definite part of the buyer's unit cost. Freight rates are quoted on the basis of carload and less than carload lots, and this differential must be taken into consideration in the quantity determination. As in the case of manufacturing costs, this factor tends only to set a minimum quantity advantage. If purchases are made in carload lots, there is rarely any saving in unit transportation cost to be gained by ordering two or more carloads. There are various ways of meeting the less than carload quantity problem. One possibility is an arrangement for mixed carloads or combination shipments of related products from the same supplier. Other methods of transportation should also be considered. Truckloads of various sizes, all less than the freight carload, are frequently feasible and economical.

Trade Customs and Quantity

The standard commercial unit of packaging also has a bearing on the purchase quantity. Although many items are procurable on a bulk basis or are specially cased or crated according to the quantity ordered, most products are packaged in standard unit quantities—wrapped reams of paper, bolts or rolls of specific or approximate yardage, barrels or drums of standard capacity, cartons of a hundred, or a gross, or a thousand, or multiples thereof. Insofar as purchase quantities can be made to conform with these standard units, it is advisable and economical to do so. Vendors customarily, and properly, make an additional charge for fractional or "broken" package units, and apparent savings from calculating requirements down to the last decimal place may be more than outweighed by increased unit costs.

There are other trade customs that must be considered in respect to quantity. In the production of special castings and some other fabricated parts, the manufacturing process is such that it is not always possible to come out even in the end, with precisely the number of units ordered. The producer's allowance for defective parts may not have been enough, or it may have been too liberal. Trade custom in these industries has established a reasonable leeway, plus or minus, for the producer in meeting this problem, that is, a stated percentage short of the quantity ordered is considered as satisfying the order, and a stated percentage of overage must be accepted by the purchaser. These conditions are generally written into the contracts in the industries to which they apply. This, of course, can result in either a shortage or a surplus for the buyer, and this possible variation in delivered quantity must be considered in addition to the buyer's own allowance for spoilage in his or her own company's operation, in determining the right quantity to buy. On parts that are regularly reordered, shortage or surplus on any particular lot can be compensated for by adjusting the quantity on succeeding orders. On parts that are procured for a specific purpose, a shortage can present a more serious problem. Experience may be the only guide as to which suppliers are most likely to come closest to the quantity actually needed and ordered.

The third factor affecting purchase quantity includes the storage facilities available and the cost of carrying inventory, both of which tend to set a maximum on the quantity to be purchased at one time. The importance and the effect of this factor have already been considered in discussion of the economical order quantity formula.

The fourth factor in determining how much to buy is the condition and trend of the market for the commodity. This is a major consideration in setting both purchasing and inventory policies. In periods of advancing prices, the indicated policy is to extend the period of coverage (that is, to increase purchase quantity), whereas in periods of declining prices the reverse is true. This is discussed in greater detail in the following chapter. The effect of price trends and changes is also reflected in the order quantity formula, because, for an identical physical quantity, the value of the annual use factor, expressed in dollars, goes up or down according to the unit costs prevailing.

SOME PERFORMANCE OBJECTIVES

After studying this chapter you should be able to:

1. Apply the economic order quantity formula discussed in this chapter (or one of its variations also in use in industry) to a real or hypothetical situation.
2. Discuss the limitations of the EOQ formula.
3. List the benefits derived from use of the formula.
4. Work out sample order quantities using the information given in Figures 9-2 and 9-5.
5. Explain the major methods of determining order quantity by policy rather than by mathematical formulas.

In the following chapter we will discuss company inventory policies and the control of inventories from the time they are purchased to the time they go into production.

Inventory
Management—II

No study of purchasing is complete without a consideration of the inventory phase through which most purchased materials pass between the time of acquisition and the time of use. In the present study, for example, this close relationship and correlation has already been noted in several instances. The purchasing responsibility to have materials on hand when needed implies the existence of an inventory reservoir as part of the procurement process. One of the principal reasons for standardization of quality is its effect in reducing the variety and volume of inventories. The whole science of economical order quantities and forward buying depends upon a knowledge of inventory costs, which constitute an important factor in the purchasing determinations. Finally, repeated surveys of actual practice show that in a preponderant number of companies, the responsibility for inventory control is vested in the purchasing department, entirely or in part, and in well over half the cases, administration and operation of the physical stores department are under purchasing jurisdiction.

OBJECTIVES OF INVENTORY CONTROL

Inventory stocks are the means of implementing many of the functions and goals of purchasing. They provide the assurance of having the items on hand when needed and afford the added protection of reserve stocks, theoretically untouchable but practically serving to fill needs when extraordinary demand develops or when current procurement fails, for example, when deliveries are delayed or rejected. They provide the flexibility that enables the purchasing department to apply economical buying policies that would not be possible in purchasing strictly according to current needs, for example, to take advantage of quantity discounts for lower unit prices, to make forward purchases in anticipation of price advances, and to adjust ordering quantities to conform to commercial packaging standards, economical manufacturing lots, and full carload or truckload shipments for minimum transportation costs. All these uses of inventory are taken for granted. They suggest the conclusion that proper inventory quantities are merely the result of scientifically determined purchase quantities.

In fact, however, inventory management has standards and objectives of its own, which importantly influence purchasing policy and quantity decisions. The relationship is a mutual one, working both ways.

The mathematical determination of economical ordering quantities (Chapter 9), by whatever formula or method, always involves an inclusive factor representing the cost of carrying inventory, and the variable rates for this factor found in some of the ordering tables show that this is not simply a matter of the interest on the inventory investment. There is, of course, the basic consideration of efficient stores administration and operation, and this depends in part on inventory policies. Handling and record-keeping costs vary, as do purchasing costs, with the size and frequency of orders and deliveries, and there are optimum quantities from the viewpoint of inventory management that do not necessarily coincide with the optimum quantities for purchasing. The limitations of actual storage facilities have already been noted as a modifying factor in purchasing policy. The whole area of the cost of providing and maintaining storage and handling facilities is a problem of inventory management. And, whereas the buyer may concern himself or herself with the summary figure of annual or monthly usage, the person responsible for inventory control analyzes the more detailed record of the number of demands per month or per day as a necessary item in setting order review points and minimum stock quantities. Thus stockouts are avoided when using departments call upon the stores departments to furnish their operating needs.

Company Policy and Inventory Control

Further, the investment in material is a factor of financial policy that may outweigh the considerations that pertain strictly to purchase quantities and costs. There may be excellent reasons of circumstance or policy that suggest a materials investment policy in which potential purchase savings are sacrificed for the sake of fluidity or conservation of capital resources or their application to other business purposes. Management decisions of this sort are often implemented through inventory policies and control.

Thus, it is true that purchasing and inventory policies usually go hand in hand, but they are not one and the same. They have the common objective of seeking the lowest practicable ultimate cost of purchased materials. But there are occasions when a company's inventory policy determines or modifies purchasing policy, rather than the other way around. This is one of the reasons for setting up inventory control as a joint responsibility, where such an organization plan is in effect. The purchasing department that has the responsibility for materials control in addition to procurement must have this broader viewpoint of the total function of material and be able to adjust both purchasing and inventory policies to attain the overall management objective.

Statistical Inventory Control

As with economical order quantities, appropriate and economical inventory quantities can be scientifically and mathematically determined. Also, as in the former case, the formulas must be applied with judgment and must be in a practical, workable form so that they can be readily used and so that the labor of calculation does not offset their value as a business tool.

At the outset, some facts should be noted about the nature of inventories. The typical industrial inventory comprises several thousand items. Every one of these is, in its own way, essential to the company operation, but dollarwise and in volume of usage, their significance varies widely. In a representative case, 25 percent of the items may account for 75 percent of total volume or the dollar value passing through inventory over any given period; the other 75 percent of items then represent a relatively small percentage (25 percent) of total dollar value. This is a conservative ratio. Instances are fairly common in which as few as 10 percent of the items account for as much as 80 percent of dollar value.

It follows that the same policies cannot be economically applied to both classes of items. If an inclusive policy of maintaining thirty days' supply of all items were adopted, it would entail the issuance of an unreasonable number of purchase orders every month. The vast majority of these would be for excessively small amounts in which the cost of purchasing is disproportionate to or actually greater than the value of the purchased merchandise. On the items of larger usage, the inventory investment would be burdensome or even prohibitive, and quantities on hand would tax normal storage facilities. A purchasing staff undertaking such a program, with the entire range of thousands of items coming up for procurement each month, could not possibly give adequate attention to all, or perhaps to any.

The economics of this situation, from the purchasing standpoint, is reflected in the ordering quantity tables (Chapter 9), which indicate that the items of smaller usage and annual dollar volume should be ordered less frequently, for longer forward coverage, up to a full year's supply, whereas the items of larger usage and value should be ordered more frequently, in quantities for much shorter-term coverage.

From the inventory standpoint, a similar conclusion is reached, expressed initially in a more general statement of principle in setting inventory policies. For the 25 percent or 10 percent of large-volume and -value items, the indicated policy of inventory control calls for careful analysis and planning, close individual attention item by item, and maximum flexibility to adjust stocks to current conditions. For the 75 percent or 90 percent of small-value items, in which individual analysis is neither practicable nor warranted, the indicated control policy is based on probability factors, which can be mathematically calculated and applied.

SIZE OF SAFETY STOCK

Probability, by definition, is not an exact science. A policy based on the laws of probability implies the calculated risk of deviations from the normal pattern — in this case, the risk of stockouts, which inventory control specifically seeks to avoid. This risk is minimized by providing safety or reserve stocks. The lack of even a small item such as a label or the tiny liner for a bottle closure can halt production just as effectively as can the lack of some major ingredient of the product to be packaged. Thus, it becomes even more important to make provision for a safety stock for the small items that are controlled by formula than for the larger items that are under continuous individual attention. It costs money to maintain safety stocks beyond the normal, expected usage. The effect, in total cost, is to trade this "insurance" expense for laborpower by releasing the time of buyers and inventory analysts for closer control of the larger items.

Determining the proper size of the reserve stock is a basic problem in inventory control. Too large safety stocks represent a wasteful expense and can be a very serious item. A fact about inventories that is not always recognized is that, although safety stocks may represent a relatively small percentage of the total value that passes through inventory over the course of a year, they can amount to 60 percent or more of inventory content at any given time, which is the basis of inventory carrying cost. On the other hand, too small safety stocks defeat the purpose. A study made in one large manufacturing company showed that its plants could operate successfully, without serious effect on production, if 1.5 percent of stores items were out of stock at any one time. If 3 percent of the items were out of stock, production losses were serious. At 5 percent, schedules were completely disrupted, and the purchasing department had a difficult time in providing the needed items.

The first step, then, is to determine the degree of protection desired, that is, not to exceed one stockout in two years, five years, and so forth. From this starting point, the calculation of necessary reserve stocks is a rather complicated statistical process. The number of demands per month, over a period of a year, is plotted on a Poisson distribution curve to establish a frequency-of-occurrence ratio, and from this an inverse accumulation ratio is calculated (see Figure 10-1). In this example, with an average or expectation of three demands per month, the inverse accumulation ratio table shows that .034 of the area of the curve (shaded area) lies to the right, or above six demands per month. This means that, 96.6 percent of the time, the number of demands will be six or less, and 3.4 percent of the time there will be six demands or more. Assuming a restocking period of one month, then, to limit the chances of a stockout's occurring more than 3.4 times in 100, the time to place a restocking order is when the stock balance reaches the equivalent of six demands, and the safety stock would also have to be six demands' worth, or three in addition to the expected three demands during the restocking period.

Going on from this relatively simple example, conversion factors can be calculated for various desired degrees of protection and varying numbers of demands per delivery period. These, in conjunction with the frequency of restocking orders, make it possible to determine accurately the required safety stocks and ordering points to provide the desired protection. A representative table of this sort is shown as Figure 10-2.

The determination of safety stocks by such a method is more than a means of scientifically implementing inventory policies. It is a guide to policy decisions, for it establishes a relationship between inventory investment and the quality of supply service at various inventory levels. For example, if management should wish to improve the service from 6 percent stockout to 4 percent stockout, it knows that this can be done only with an increase in inventory equivalent to a ten days' supply. Knowing the value of ten days' supply of inventory (for example $100,000) and the carrying cost (for example, 9 percent), it is clear that such a decision would cost $9,000, and this would be balanced against the cost savings resulting

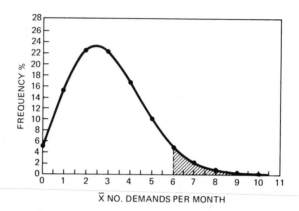

Frequency of Occurrences of Poisson Dist.
X = 3

No.	Frequency of Occurrence Ratio	Ratio (Inverse Accumulation)
0	.049	.951
1	.149	.801
2	.224	.577
3	.224	.353
4	.168	.185
5	.101	.084
6	.050	.034
7	.022	.012
8	.008	.004
9	.003	.002
10	.001	.001
∞	∞	∞

Figure 10-1. Poisson distribution curve for determining safety stock requirements.

from fewer interuptions to production or the additional profits or sales advantages resulting from better service to customers. The decisions would be based on actual cost data rather than on unsupported judgment, and it could be carried out easily by inventory clerks if they were issued instructions to use the appropriate inventory and ordering tables.

CONTROL OF WORKING INVENTORY

In the control of working inventory, exclusive of the safety stock, the basic formula is the one cited in Chapter 9 for the determination of most economical ordering quantities, which establishes certain relationships between annual usage, ordering quantity, cost of ordering, and cost of

ORDER REVIEW POINTS
TABLE OF PROTECTIVE STOCK FACTORS

Protection
1 Stock Out in 2 Years

RESTOCKING FACTOR		DEMAND FACTOR			
No. of Restk. Orders Per Year (N_r)	Factor (R)	No. of Demands During Delivery Time (N_d)	Factor (D)	No. of Demands During Delivery Time (N_d)	Factor (D)
1	.00	1	.85	13	3.00
1.2	.35	2	1.20	14	3.10
1.5	.75	3	1.45	15	3.20
1.7	.95	4	1.65	16	3.30
2.0	1.15				
2.5	1.45	5	1.85	17	3.40
3.0	1.65	6	2.00	18	3.50
3.5	1.85	7	2.20	19	3.60
4.0	1.95	8	2.35	20	3.70
4.5	2.10				
5.0	2.20	9	2.50	22	3.95
6.0	2.35	10	2.60	24	4.10
7.0	2.50	11	2.75	26	4.20
8.0	2.65	12	2.85	28	4.35
9.0	2.75				
10.0	2.85			30	4.50
11.0	2.90			40	5.20
12.0	2.95			50	5.85

Instructions:

A. RESTOCKING FACTOR
  1. Obtain (Nr) number of restocking orders per year from order quantity table and read Factor R.

B. DEMAND FACTOR
  1. Obtain number of demands during past three months from ledger and divide by 90 days to get demands per day.
  2. Obtain delivery time in days and multiply by number of demands per day to get number of demands per day to get number of demands during delivery time (Nd) and read Factor D.

C. PROTECTIVE STOCK
  1. Calculate protective stock; multiply the Restocking Factor R, times the Demand Factor D.

D. ORDER REVIEW POINT
  1. Add protective stock to the number of demands during delivery time (Nd) to get order review point in demands.
  2. Obtain past 90 days' issues or sales from ledger; divide by the number of demands in the past 90 days to get the average size of demand.
  3. Calculate order review point in units by multiplying the ORP in demands times the average size of demands.

Figure 10-2   Table for calculating order review point.

carrying inventory. The formula stands for a specific use, and it is not, therefore, an all-purpose answer to every inventory problem. But all the factors are present, or can be derived from the values expressed in that relationship. For example, number of orders is derived by dividing annual usage by order quantity; average inventory quantity is half the ordering quantity, assuming a constant rate of use and replenishment of stock at the time that previous inventory supply is exhausted; total inventory and total number of orders are the sums of these factors as applied to individual items. Any of these values can therefore be expressed mathematically in terms of the original factors, and the factors can be mathematically transposed in the equation without affecting its validity.

In establishing the economical ordering quantity, the problem was to arrive at lowest ultimate cost of maintaining the inventory supply, item by item. The formula showed that this could not be accomplished by applying the same ordering frequency to all items regardless of the total quantity (annual usage) involved. It was accomplished by increasing the frequency (decreasing the amount) of orders on items of large annual usage and by decreasing frequency (increasing the amount) of orders of small annual usage, to the point at which the cost of acquisition and the cost of possession were equal.

If lowest inventory cost were the only objective, if unit costs were stable regardless of quantity, and if usage were at a constant rate, this would be the whole story of statistical inventory control. But none of these conditions consistently prevails.

There are two variables in the formula — size (or number, or frequency) of orders and annual usage of items. The formula shows the relationship to be between the numerical value of the former and the square root of the latter. Mathematically, this is expressed by saying that order quantity is a function of the square root of annual usage. This can also be written as the formula:

$$Q = K \sqrt{A}$$

Standing by itself, this has little practical meaning. It is the problem of the inventory analyst and controller to find or assign appropriate values of the constant K to make that relationship meaningful in the attainment of specific inventory objectives and in the carrying out of current inventory policies. By standard statistical methods that are too involved for this discussion, and by taking cognizance of the additional factors pertinent to a particular problem, the skilled analyst can compute K values to adjust ordering frequency and quantity to desired inventory levels (at a sacrifice of purchase economy but to the advantage of total net cost of materials), or to reduce the number of orders issued, or to take best advantage of quantity discounts, or to cope with conditions of variable usage or variable lead times.[1]

Inventory control policies thus arrived at are translated into buying terms in the form of reorder points and quantities—maximum and minimum stock limits—for the various inventory items or classifications. It is a responsibility of the inventory control phase of management or procurement to keep these instructions up to date, consistent with current conditions and policies.

As in the case of optimum purchase order quantity, the calculations involved and the implementation of the entire program can be greatly expedited by use of the computer.

Inventory Classification

Successful inventory management is greatly aided by a logical system of classification covering all inventory items for purposes of control, cost accounting, storeskeeping, and issue. There is no necessary correlation between such a classification and the grouping of commodities for purposes of procurement; in fact the two types of classification frequently differ within the same company. For purchasing, the classification is logically based on the related nature and source of the various items. For inventory purposes, it is more logically based on the end use or function of the item, the purpose for which it is purchased. In both cases, the starting point is a system of standard nomenclature and identification, to avoid duplication in purchasing or stocking identical items under two or more different designations. The identification code or system, obviously, should be the same in both the purchasing and stores classifications.

There is no standard system of inventory classification appropriate for all companies, because of variations in material requirements. However, there are some general principles that apply.

For purchased inventory items, major divisions are usually set up for production materials (which are incorporated in the end product and are a direct material cost of that product) and nonproduction items (supplies, which are an operating expense). In some companies, depending on organization and policy, there is a third major division of capital expense items. Inventories of materials in process and of finished goods are outside the scope of this discussion, as purchasing responsibility usually terminates when goods go from stores into production.

The production material classification is generally subdivided into

---

[1] For a detailed exposition of these methods, see W.E. Welch, "Tested Scientific Inventory Control" (Greenwich, Conn.: Management Publishing Corp., 1956).

raw materials, semifinished materials, and fabricated parts and components; sometimes a fourth division is provided for items purchased for a special project or end use, as, for example, items bought to fulfill a government contract under which materials must be separately accounted for. If some parts are fabricated for stock in the company's own plant instead of being procured by purchase, they are classified in the same way as if they were bought from an outside source. The only difference in procedure is that, when the time comes for stock replenishment, a work order is issued instead of a purchase order.

Nonproduction materials are similarly subdivided. Major heading under this category would include fuels, operating supplies, maintenance and repair items, and stationery.

The process of subdivision is continued until there is appropriate classification for every item. If an item is used for both production and nonproduction purposes, like a common bolt that is a component of the end product and is also used in plant maintenance, it is listed only once, under the major use category. If an item is stocked in several different sizes, each size is treated as a separate item under the appropriate subhead.

One important purpose of inventory classification has been suggested — in accounting and distribution of costs for the various types of material. Another is in connection with the operation of physical stores, which are usually arranged in much the same way — raw materials, production parts, and supply stores, with related items in adjacent locations so far as is possible. Classification is especially helpful when mechanized accounting systems are in use and when identification is according to a numerical code, so that entries automatically fall into the proper group or account.

For control purposes, the summary figures, by groups, are useful in analyzing usage and in maintaining a properly balanced stock. Top management is more interested in such summary information than individual data, except for a few critical key commodities. It is obvious that inventory policies can be set collectively for many categories, from the standpoint of both investment and supply service. Thus, classification simplifies the mechanics of control.

The most comprehensive published inventory classification is that covering the wide range of materials used by the U.S. government in its various departments, bureaus, and establishments. This "Commodity Classification for Storage and Issue" was compiled under the direction of the Standards Division of the Federal Bureau of Supply and appears as Section II of the *Federal Standard Stock Catalog*. For comparison, see also Section III, "Commodity Classification for Purposes of Procurement," which is on a different basis altogether.

Inventory Records

The basic inventory record is the perpetual inventory. This is a continuing current record of receipts, disbursements or allocation of material, and balance on hand and on order, of every item in stock, showing the complete inventory position.

This information originates in the stores department, and the record is typically kept in that department, with some provision for making the data readily available to other departments as needed. In the small purchasing department, which also has the responsibility for stores and for stock control, it is a common practice to incorporate the inventory record directly on the purchase record card, showing also the maximum and minimum stock quantities, ordering quantity, and any other purchasing information required to implement the established, prevailing inventory policy for the item. Where this type of record is used, the record of disbursements is usually in the form of a summary figure obtained from the stores department, showing total monthly usage in a single entry instead of listing the individual issue transactions.

In the more specialized and completely organized systems of inventory control, whether under purchasing jurisdiction or in a separate department, mechanized or computerized records have almost totally replaced manual methods of record keeping. This has not only eliminated many hours of tedious clerical effort and minimized errors of transcription and calculation, but it provides a far more useful management tool by making it possible to present more complete information in analytical form, more quickly and at more frequent intervals. One particular system, for example, makes it possible to furnish the purchasing department with a weekly inventory recap that is automatically subtotaled by commodity groups (for example, plumbing supplies, machine parts, work clothing, and so forth), together with current cumulative, and past average usage data, information on open orders and split shipments, and indicated reorder and follow-up action. This is only a part of the information developed in this particular record. It establishes average prices that are used in pricing withdrawals, calculates inventory valuation, accumulates materials costs on specific job orders, and signals job closing for the invoice department. In providing more and better information of this sort, it has eliminated several individual records and forms previously required and has reduced travel and processing time on others.

All perpetual inventory records are periodically checked against actual stock for accuracy, and any discrepancies are adjusted in the record. In the system just described, the current inventory figure is verified by spot checks of selected items in each classification. In all cases, good management requires a complete physical inventory at least annually. The current record is accepted as adequate for control and operating purposes, but it does not constitute a real audit.

MRP AND INVENTORY MANAGEMENT

Material Requirements Planning (MRP) was mentioned in Chapter 9 as a management technique that goes beyond the traditional bases for determining quantity requirements for purchasing action. Originally an approach to inventory management, MRP has evolved into much more, so that it is now defined as

> . . . a set of priority planning techniques for planning component items below the product or end time level. It utilizes the manufacturing building schedule (master production schedule), which determines what components should be ordered and when they should be ordered. Taking this information, MRP will produce a schedule of specific component needs in a schedule sequence that plans for each component to be available when needed for the next level of assembly.[1]

Components in this definition would include raw materials, purchased components of assemblies, manufactured (in house) components of assemblies, subassemblies, and semi-finished items. The demand for such items (e.g., for small motors that power electric mixers) is described as "dependent" because it is derived from the demand for the end item (in this case, the mixer). The demand for an end item (the mixer, in our example) is considered "independent" when the demand is unrelated to the demand for other items, particularly higher level assemblies or products.

Dependent demand can be calculated and should not be forecasted. It can be better determined by exploding the bill of materials for products in the master production schedule and calculating demand for the components required in those bills.

Independent demand—for such items as finished products spare parts, production supplies and tools—must be forecast. Forecasting uses past experience as a guide to future requirements. Inventory control for independent demand items, therefore, involves time-phased "order points" for replenishment, since it is assumed that demand is uniform and that inventory will be depleted in small increments of the reorder quantity.

[1] W.J. Pierak, Jr.; Jon T. Rietzke; W.W. Wamsher; George Kolesar, *APICS Training Aid: Material Requirements Planning,* American Production and Inventory Control Society, Washington, 1979.

Proponents of MRP point out that no such assumption can be made about dependent demand components of assembled products. Inventory tends to be "lumpy," with periods of heavy demand alternating with periods of almost no demand, because end products are usually made in lot sizes to keep setup costs down, rather than in a perfectly continuous flow. If order points, (which are based on averages and assume a uniform demand for dependent components), are used to replenish inventory independently of the timing of end product fabrication, the results can be either severe shortages or overloaded inventories.

If, for example, a dependent demand item (say a small horsepower motor) that is bought according to traditional statistical inventory methods) is required in two or more end items (a variety of home appliances) simultaneously, a shortage could occur, and frantic expediting in purchasing would be necessary. What is perhaps a more prevalent problem in companies that use the traditional order point system is unnecessarily high inventories, with consequent higher costs.

BASIC STEPS IN MRP

Fundamentally, material requirements planning is a precise refinement and formalization of basic management techniques that have been used in manufacturing planning for many years. To quote the American Production and Inventory Control Society's MRP training aid:

> The techniques of MRP are not difficult or new. In fact, many of the techniques seem, on inspection, so simple that one might wonder why all manufacturing companies haven't always used them. The problem lies in the fact that the application of MRP rules to thousands of inventory items was not feasible until the computer was introduced into the manufacturing systems area . . . The main function of an effective manufacturing control system is to have the right materials, in the correct quantities, available at the right time to meet the demand for the company's finished products. The objective of MRP is to determine requirements accurately and quickly to enhance management's control over the complete manufacturing process. It does this by calculating the components needed to meet the master production schedule. On the basis of production and procurement lead-times, the MRP system calculates the time periods in which these components must be available. Traditional inventory management approaches could not go beyond the limits imposed by the information processing tool available at the time. With the introduction of the commercial computer with its ability to store data, manipulate it, and produce information at speeds previously unimaginable, industry now had a tool that could respond to our dynamic business environment.

The MRP process begins with the establishment of a master production schedule, (see figure 10-3) which is basically a statement of requirements for end items, by date (planning period) and quantity. End items are generally finished products, but they can also be major assemblies or parts used at the highest level in the product structure (e.g., replacement or service parts for the end product).

The next step is to explode manufacturing bills of materials, which list all components, including sub-assemblies, finished parts, raw materials and purchased parts that go into a given product or end item, and the amount of each required in each unit of that item. The gross quantity required in each time period, less the projected on-hand and on-order quantities, is the net quantity that is required and is to be ordered at that time. In calculating net requirements, the computer takes into consideration common usage of components in multiple products, changes to bills of materials, manufacturing and purchasing leadtimes, and order status. The requirements provide input not only to inventory planning and control, but to capacity requirements planning and shop floor control.

In brief, MRP produces "planned orders" that tell inventory planning and control what and how much to order, when to order, and when to schedule delivery, capacity requirements planning what capacities will be required by work center, by period, to meet the production plan; and shop floor control the priority ranking of the order against other orders in shop.

MRP and Purchasing

Oliver W. Wight, consultant on production and inventory control and a recognized authority on material requirements planning, explained the significance of MRP for purchasing in these terms:

> When the computer came along, people were delighted to be able to use it to do requirements planning, but for many years it remained just an ordering technique. Then two significant developments occurred...
>
> We began to recognize that MRP could be used not just as a way to order, but as a way to reschedule. The simple logic of MRP could be used to determine if the due dates on existing purchase orders were correct or needed to be pulled up or pushed out.
>
> Later on it was recognized that MRP is really a closed loop system where the master schedule must be constantly kept up to date to represent what really will be done, rather than what we planned to do sometime "or would like to do."[2]

[2]Oliver W. Wight, "MRP: An Aid to Professional Purchasing," *National Purchasing Review*, November-December, 1978, p. 16.

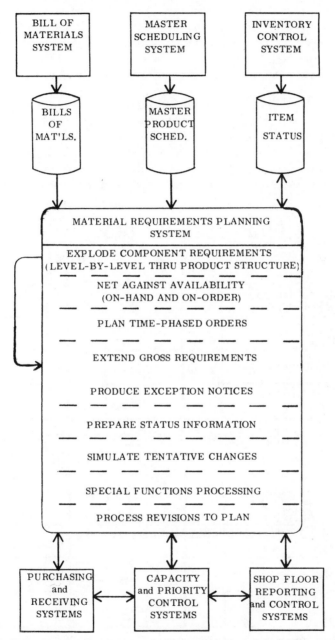

Figure 10-3. Flow chart showing basic processing of an MRP system, from *Production and Inventory Management, Journal of the American Production and Inventory Control Society,* Third Quarter, 1979.

Wight used a simple example to show how the system affects purchasing (see Figure 10-4). In the top chart, "MRP Used for Ordering," shows projected gross requirements, which are usually exploded from the bill of material. In this example, 90 bicycles are to be built in period one and the projected gross requirements for handle bars for the period is 90.

The second line shows scheduled receipts or open purchase orders. The next line shows the projected available balance, which in this case is the on hand figure. Line four shows the planned order releases, which generate lower level material requirements and the requirements for shop capacity planning. In each succeeding week, gross requirements are subtracted from the sum of the schedule receipts and the 250 cur-

MRP Used for Ordering

		WEEKS					
		1	2	3	4	5	6
PROJECTED GROSS REQUIREMENTS		90	80	100	110	90	110
SCHEDULED RECEIPTS	300						
PROJ. AVAIL. BAL.	250						-30
PLANNED ORDER RELEASE			300				

MRP Used for Reordering

		WEEKS					
		1	2	3	4	5	6
PROJECTED GROSS REQUIREMENTS		90	80	100	110	90	110
SCHEDULED RECEIPTS					300		
PROJ. AVAIL. BAL.	250	160	80	-20	170	80	-30
PLANNED ORDER RELEASE			300				

Figure 10-4. Basic method of computing requirements for ordering and reordering using the MRP system. From the *National Purchasing Review*, November-December, 1978.

rently on hand, and by week six, a negative, or net, requirement occurs. Used this way MRP indicates when to order.

The bottom chart shows how time phasing the scheduled receipt, i.e., showing the due date on the purchase order, permits the MRP computation to tell if that due date is correct when circumstances change—at the manufacturing level, for example. In the example, at least 20 of the 300 scheduled receipts should be moved from period four to period three, or the assembly scheduling call for 100 handle bars will not be met.

If the circumstances change on the purchasing side—for example, a vendor is unable to deliver the 300 required in week four—the system is programmed to change the due dates on all other matching components of the bicycle, such as wheels, gears, etc, once the information on the delayed delivery is fed back to the master schedule. As a result, purchasing will not be wasting time expediting things that are not needed when they could use the time to expedite things that are needed. When schedules are not properly updated, it is not always easy for purchasing to find out what is needed first.

MRP can not only predict shortages week by week, according to Wight, but when information on changing circumstances is fed back into the system it can repredict week by week. "As anyone who has worked in purchasing knows," he says, "if they could be working this month on next month's shortages, it would end a lot of the living from crisis to crisis that has become a way of life in so many companies."

Comparing the traditional "order-launching and expediting" system with material requirements planning, Wight says that with the old system the following conditions occur:

Thirty percent of open purchase orders are typically past due.

Purchase commitment reports are grossly overestimated in the early time periods.

Vendor performance reports mean very little—the shortage list is the real schedule.

The bulk of the purchasing effort is spent firefighting and expediting.

With MRP, he claims:

Less than three percent of the open purchase orders are typically past due.

Purchase commitment reports represent what actual commitments to spend with vendors are.

Vendor performance reports become a useful, realistic tool.

The bulk of the purchasing effort is spent in buying economically, doing value analysis, developing better sources, etc.

Material requirements planning, it has been pointed out by several critics, requires an enormous amount of planning, highly accurate bills of materials, complete and up-to-the minute inventory records, and a precisely realistic master schedule. It must be coordinated with the organization and operation of many other departments in the company. This brief outline provides only the fundamentals of MRP as they relate to inventory control and purchasing. A more comprehensive and detailed study would involve, at a minimum, a working knowledge of production control.

Disposition of Surplus

A final objective of stores control is the detection of inactive stock items that increase the inventory investment without contributing any corresponding service or utility. Such a condition may arise from any one of many reasons: overrequisitioning, overbuying, or overdeliveries; abandonment of projects or cancellation of sales orders; changes in design or specifications; undetected errors in materials accounting; materials stored in the wrong location and consequently "lost." These conditions rarely come to light of themselves. An alert storeskeeper familiar with his or her stock may notice particular items or lots that are not being called for and may question their place in the inventory. But, in dealing with a stock of several thousand separate items, complete reliance cannot be placed upon this chance. A comprehensive system of stores control therefore initiates action, which can be taken in three ways:

1. *Periodic review of stock records* on a systematic basis, taking a specified section each week or month so that the entire list is covered once or twice a year. Items that have not been called for during the past six months or for which the rate of use has fallen off so that stock quantities represent excessive coverage are noted and brought up for analysis and action.

2. *Analysis of physical inventory* at the time that the annual inventory is taken. Any material that has actually been in stock a year or more is noted and comes up for review.

3. *Periodic "clean-up" campaigns,* extending beyond the storeroom itself into all departments. This provides for review of materials that have been issued from stores but have not been used for the anticipated purpose, those held in subsidiary stockrooms and tool cribs and thus outside normal stores supervision, and capital items such as furniture and equipment that have fallen into disuse or have been replaced by more modern equipment.

Standards can be set to indicate the basis upon which an item should be declared surplus, for example, materials for which there have been no disbursements during the past quarter, quantities in excess of the past six months' requirements, equipment and tools that have not been used during the past year, and materials and supplies in manufacturing departments for which there is no open order.

If there is no reason for holding such items against some future contingency, a decision is made as to the manner of disposition. There are several alternative possibilities:

Utilization, as is, as a substitute for currently standard material or in some other product or model.

Utilization by transfer to another department.

Utilization by charge-out at a percentage discount from standard costs. (An oil company found this method effective in securing acceptance of outmoded models of pumps and other service station equipment by station managers whose compensation was calculated on the ratio of sales to investment and costs.)

Utilization by remanufacture.

Return to original manufacturer.

Sale as surplus material.

Sale as scrap.

The last three methods of disposal generally come under the jurisdiction of the purchasing department. Whatever disposition is made, it serves to convert a continuing liability into an asset, reduce the investment in stores, maintain a clean inventory, and increase turnover by eliminating inactive items.

SOME PERFORMANCE OBJECTIVES

After studying this chapter you should be able to:

1. Describe the relative roles of top management and the purchasing department in the formulation of inventory policy.
2. Explain how to classify inventory items.
3. Discuss the importance of safety stock and the relative effects of various frequency of stockouts.
4. Describe three methods used in a system of stores control designed to prevent accumulation of inactive stock items.

5. List the ways in which surplus material and equipment may be disposed of.

6. Describe the material requirements planning (MRP) concept and purchasing's role in an MRP system.

We have been discussing some of the basic elements to be considered in making a purchase decision: what to buy, how much to buy, and when to buy it. These are generally matters that are subject to internal company control. A fourth and equally important factor is price, which is more subject to market forces than the others. The next chapter covers pricing methods, and analytical techniques buyers can use to relate prices to value.

Price–Cost
Analysis

11

Price is without question of major importance in any purchase transaction, but, to the uninitiated in purchasing science, it is highly overrated. There is a curiously contradictory attitude toward this aspect of the buying responsibility. Management properly expects its purchasing manager to negotiate and buy at the most favorable price levels obtainable and is likely to judge the efficiency of its purchasing department on the basis of prices paid; yet the characterization of a purchasing manager as a "price buyer" is taken to be derogatory. Actually, price is only one of the terms and conditions of a purchase order, no more or less important than any of the other terms and conditions.

PRICE OBJECTIVES

Basically, price is rarely if ever considered alone, for its own sake; usually price is used in connection with other factors as a means of achieving certain objectives of economical and efficient company operation. A few simple concepts fundamental to all good purchasing should be noted at this point. Some of them have been suggested in previous chapters, but they should be specifically considered in relation to the price factor.

Low ultimate cost is the objective and responsibility of purchasing. Invoice price is one element of cost, but not necessarily the determining factor. This is readily apparent if a transaction is traced through its successive stages. The first checking point occurs at the time at which materials are received, when delivered cost can be ascertained. A low price paid to a distant supplier may be outweighed by packing and transportation charges, so that delivered cost of the low-price item is actually higher. The second checking point comes when materials are issued to the using department. The buyer may have paid a lower price by reason of taking larger quantities at a greater discount, but the expense of handling and storage may have outweighed this price differential by the time the materials are actually required, issued, and put to use. The third checking point occurs after the materials have been used or fabricated and incorporated in the end product. Manufacturing costs have now been added, and the extent to which such costs have been increased by reason of inferior workability or difficulties in application must be weighed against a price that would have procured superior materials. At all three stages there is a balance that must be observed, and, in considering the original or invoice price, the purchasing manager must aim at ultimate cost rather than immediate unit price.

PRICE AND QUALITY AS ELEMENTS OF VALUE

A common equation used in discussions of purchasing is that *value* equals *quality* divided by *price*. This is not a mathematical formula but rather, a means of expressing the general truth that value varies directly in proportion to the quality received and inversely in proportion to the price paid. It stresses the fact that the amount of investment in materials is less significant than what is obtained in return for the investment. If quality increases more rapidly than price in a series of offerings, the value is greater at the higher price—up to the point at which the buyer would be paying for quality in excess of the need. When quality has been defined in a specification, so that it can be considered as a constant in this equation, the comparison of values can be made in terms of price alone, and the lower price would represent the greater value. It should be noted, however, that this attention to price comes *after* quality has been fully considered and decided upon.

The purchasing responsibility is frequently defined as keeping the company in a favorable competitive position in its field, so far as costs of materials are concerned. Because this involves a consideration of what others are paying for similar materials, it carries the implication that there is a prevailing market price and that the purchasing manager must be familiar with market conditions to buy at or below their levels. The Robinson–Patman Act, for example, is aimed at eliminating price discrimination between buyers on the part of sellers, but the purchasing manager cannot rely on such regulations to assure him or her of equal price advantage. The purchasing officer will find differences of price between various potential suppliers in the same field and differences according to customer classification, quantity discounts, and the like. The purchasing manager must therefore exert himself or herself, to be sure that his or her company is in the most favorable customer classification earned by the nature and size of the business, and the manager must adjust his or her policies and buying methods to take advant ge of all available price economies. Otherwise, his or her company will have to overcome a competitive handicap as compared with another concern in the same field in which a more astute procurement program is followed.

The purchasing manager's concern for price properly extends to every item procured through his or her department, however trifling in unit value or however small the unit saving may be. This is a part of his or her function, to avoid any needlessly high cost and to keep expenditures at the lowest level consistent with attaining the desired results. The scorn that is sometimes expressed concerning penny consciousness in purchasing would be more appropriately directed at careless disregard of minor savings possibilities. For, in large-scale operations, the field of industrial purchasing, the cumulative effect of small savings amounts to substantial totals. This is particularly true in mass-production industries, in which even the smallest and least costly parts are magnified to significant proportions through repetitive use and large volume.

WHO MAKES THE PRICE?

In the philosophy of business, it is the seller's privilege to name the price at which he or she is willing to sell his or her product. In the economics of business, that decision depends on how many buyers can be found who are willing to pay the price; otherwise, there is no market. From this angle it could be argued that the buyer makes the price. As a practical matter, neither of these positions can be categorically supported. Although in theory the seller is under no compulsion to sell, nor the buyer to buy, at any given price level, actually that compulsion does exist if business is to be done. Business cannot be conducted on the basis of the irresistible force and the immovable object. It is a process of arriving at a mutual agreement resulting in sales and purchases. The seller must find an outlet for his or her product and the buyer must find the materials needed by his or her company. Markets and prices are not made by quotations or offers, but by actual transactions.

It is true, of course, that there are periods in which sellers can exert the dominant influence, and other periods in which buyers are in the more favorable position. But these "sellers' markets" and "buyers' markets" are basically economic in origin and nature, and the resulting price advantages are temporary in that they shift from one side of the transaction to the other as the imbalance is corrected. Realistically, pricing policies follow these changing economic fortunes, but businesses that are built on long-range, continuing supplier–customer relationships do not press the advantage beyond maintaining a normally competitive position. The supplier who consistently sets his or her price at "all the traffic bear" forfeits customer loyalty and can expect to fare worse than others when the economic tide turns. The buyer who is primarily an opportunist, looking for the hungriest supplier and capitalizing on that condition, can scarcely ask for consideration in price and service when problems of supply become more difficult.

For most standard materials and products, production costs and competition tend to establish a going market price that is approximately equal among all suppliers at any given time. This is presumably equitable and mutually satisfactory, representing a fair return to the seller and fair value to the purchaser under prevailing conditions. Buyers frequently test such markets, but rarely try to break them. The buyer is not a price censor. A generally established market price level is accepted as one of the economic facts of business life. The rightness of that price, from the buying standpoint, is largely a matter of being sure that regular supply sources are reasonably in line with the going market price and that the purchaser is getting the most favorable terms and discounts warranted by the size of his or her requirements and orders.

OBTAINING BIDS

For nonstandard materials, more complex fabricated products in which design and manufacturing methods vary and items are made to buyer specification, no such ready-made market level exists. Asking for competitive bids is the buyer's simplest way of exploring price under these circumstances and evaluating the rightness of the quoted prices. Figure 11-1 shows a typical form used to solicit price quotations from suppliers. To establish a right and realistic price, buyers properly insist upon firm bids, that is, the offer upon which a prospective seller will unequivocally stand in his or her bid for the order. If a bid is offered with the suggestion that the seller might revise it subsequently, offering a better price if necessary, the buyer can have no confidence that he or she will in fact receive the best, or right, price offer from that source.

If there is a wide range in quotations, the excessively high bid is clearly out of line, but the excessively low bid is just as much open to question on the grounds of its economic soundness and reliability. However, a reasonable variation is expected, for no two suppliers are exactly

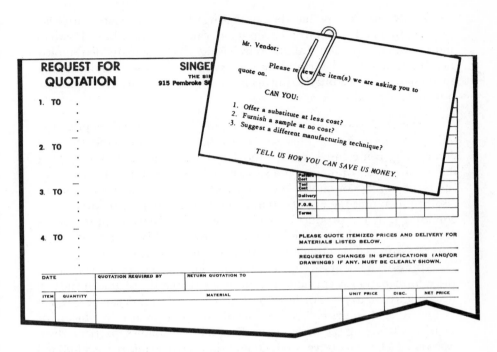

Figure 11-1. Request for quotation with special appeal to suppliers for help on cost reduction.

equal in manufacturing efficiency and competitive eagerness. If several or all quotations are identical, there is usually a suspicion of collusion to maintain an unjustifiably high price.

Having received competitive bids from a representative number of possible suppliers, the buyer can, of course, easily select the lowest price offer. Whether this is actually a "right" price he or she must judge by comparison with the other offers, with past experience, with the prices of similar products, and with his or her own knowledge of prices and markets.

A great deal of purchasing of both standard and special items is done on the basis of competitive bids. In governmental purchasing, which is very sensitive to charges of favoritism and patronage, which is specifically dedicated to the conservation of taxpayers' money, and in which the buyer as a public servant must operate "in a goldfish bowl" for all to see, the bid system is usually mandatory. When a purchase is contemplated, it is advertised so that anyone interested may have the opportunity to bid. Sealed bids are received and held, to be opened and made public at a stated time, in the presence of all bidders who may wish to come. The order must be awarded to the lowest responsible bidder. If no bids are deemed acceptable, the purchasing officer has no alternative but to reject them all and start all over again, calling for new bids. If two or more low bids are identical, the purchasing officer may divide the business or toss a coin to determine the successful vendor—scarcely a scientific method of making a purchasing decision. The entire transaction becomes a matter of public record.

The chief shortcoming of such a policy is that it makes price the only criterion of value. This can be justified on the principle that "all other things being equal" price is the determining factor, and by making the requirements of quality and service so definitive and clear that there can be no conflict or choice between suppliers on that score. Care must also be taken that the specification is not written so as to be preclusive, admitting only the product of one supplier. On important purchases, a performance bond furnished by the vendor with his or her bid is the buyer's assurance that quality and service will be as represented.

Industrial buyers are generally committed to the principle that bid price information is confidential, and they demand greater latitude in deciding where to place orders, so that due consideration can be given to factors other than price. They use the bid system primarily as a means of exploring or fixing the price factor. Frequently it follows, particularly in cases in which competitive products and alternative vendors are adjudged to be equally acceptable, or on standard commercial items on which "all other things" are equal, that business is awarded on the bid basis. But this is not necessarily so. Bids are a useful tool, but not the only tool at the buyer's disposal in determining the right price at which to buy.

Buyers and sellers alike are critical of strict adherence to the bidding system for another reason. It gives no weight to past performance and service. Continuity of supply and healthy buyer–seller relationships are important and valuable considerations to both sides. Yet both are disregarded when successive transactions are considered only on the basis of current bids.

NEGOTIATED PRICES

The alternative method of arriving at a price is through negotiation. Negotiation should not be interpreted as "trading" or compromise. It is the process of working out a procurement and sales problem together, to the point of reaching a mutually satisfactory agreement. Negotiation is not at all incompatible with competition. In almost all cases it starts with a competitive bid, a firm bid in respect to the conditions and requirements as known at the time. But it recognizes that this is by no means the last word and that many modifications may be made in all factors to arrive at the most favorable balance of quality, service, and cost. Negotiation can be carried on simultaneously with several suppliers on a given project, maintaining competition right up to the point of decision.

Most buyers agree that negotiated bids come closer to the right price than do merely competitive quotations, because all pertinent factors come under analysis and discussion in the course of the negotiation, and details of the requirement can frequently be adjusted to permit price advantages that would otherwise be missed. Most major purchases and contracts in industrial buying are negotiated. It is almost essential in the case of new products for which there is no prior manufacturing experience; otherwise, it is likely that a bidder will be impelled to include in his or her quotation a safety margin for contingencies and unknown manufacturing costs. These extra margins may or may not be warranted in the hindsight of actual experience, but the industrial buyer, unlike the federal government, has no legal recourse through renegotiation after a contract has been completed. Many of these problems can be resolved in the negotiating process.

In its military buying, the federal government has turned largely to negotiation rather than to bid-and-award methods. The practice has been sharply criticized as extravagant, wasteful, and discriminatory, but such charges are certainly open to debate. The fact remains that the massive, complicated, and urgent requirements in this field could never have been fulfilled by any other method.

Skill in negotiation is an important asset to the buyer. It includes a knowledge of costs and values, the ability to marshal facts logically and convincingly, to deal with people, to set realistic price goals, and to pursue these goals firmly and persuasively. It is the buyer's responsibility in negotiation to make sure that his or her company receives every price advantage to which it is legitimately entitled. At the same time, the buyer must understand and appreciate the seller's position. Although the buyer has no ethical responsibility to safeguard the seller's profits, the buyer is aware that the final price must be economically sound to make the price right for both parties. No purchasing program is stronger than its sources of supply and to drive too sharp a bargain is to weaken the supplier or to eliminate him or her as a potential, continuing source of supply for future requirements.

A more detailed discussion of the philosophy and techniques of negotiation appears in Chapter 15.

PRICE RELATED TO COST

There are three general criteria of what a fair price should be. They assume (1) that price should bear a reasonable relation to cost (material *plus* manufacturing cost *plus* overhead and profit), (2) that price is the result of economic conditions (supply and demand); and (3) that price is determined by competition. The purchasing manager must take all three of these influences into account in his or her analysis of price and in deciding what is the right price for a given product at a given time.

Cost sets a lower limit on the price at which a supplier can afford to make and sell his or her product. Prices based on cost plus a reasonable profit are fair to the supplier as well as to the buyer, but "cost plus" is a dangerous way to express price in a contract, because it tends to make the supplier careless of costs in the assurance that he or she will recover them, plus a profit, in any case. The cost basis of pricing should operate as an incentive for the supplier to reduce costs. Where price directly reflects cost, the buyer can select the supplier having the most efficient management and the most economical production and can share in those lower costs. The buyer can reduce costs by adapting the design and specifications of his or her own requirements to lower-cost materials and more economical production methods. It is not uncommon for large industrial companies to aid their suppliers in reducing costs by providing technical and management counsel, in the expectation of lower prices resulting from the cost savings.

The soundness of the principle of a price related to cost has long been recognized in certain types of contracts calling for price adjustments, up or down, in the event of changes in major raw material costs or prevailing wage rates. The standard coal contract endorsed by the National Association of Purchasing Agents and the National Coal Association contained such a provision, tied in with mine wage agreements, years before the idea was popularized under the descriptive term "escalator clause." Contracts of this sort have their place in industrial buying and selling. However, because one of the primary purposes of a contract is to fix risk and commitments, escalator clauses should be limited to long-term agreements or contracts involving a long production cycle, as in the case of power-generating equipment or special machinery, in which a period of years rather than weeks or months may be involved in filling the order. The cost basis of price escalation should be clearly defined in any case, and, because the risk is transferred to the buyer's account, provision should be made for downward adjustment on the same basis in the event that costs decline.

ANALYZING MANUFACTURING COSTS

Price analysis takes into account both materials and manufacturing costs. The first part is relatively simple, for even a complicated product such as an electric motor can be quite accurately broken down into quantitative terms of its major material components—copper, cast iron, and insulation. The spread betwen material cost and quoted price represents manufacturing cost and profit. To appraise this part of the price, the buyer should have a knowledge of manufacturing process and costs and the various operations and handling involved. The cost experience of his or her own company on comparable operations frequently provides a rough but useful comparison.

One of the things that consistent price analysis shows is that the manufacturing differential is by no means a constant factor; rather, it fluctuates in much the same manner as do materials costs. Sometimes that fluctuation may be justified by circumstances, and sometimes it is open to question. For example, if it is found that the differential is consistently on a percentage basis derived from materials cost, rather than representing a true unit manufacturing cost, the buyer may be justified in challenging the computation, for the percentage markup is not a sound method of estimating the cost of manufacturing operations.

Increasingly, industrial purchasing departments are either establishing their own price analysis sections or are using the services of specialists from the accounting or cost estimating departments to evaluate supplier prices. Automotive and aeronautical companies in particular have pioneered in the establishment of price analysis teams that have the capability to estimate what a supplier's material, labor, overhead, and general and administrative costs are. In many cases, particularly in purchases made under government contracts, such data are required of suppliers. In those cases in which suppliers refuse to provide such data voluntarily, the cost analysts use their own experience and judgment, as well as cost figures from their own companies' operations, to arrive at what they consider a fair price. This price is then used as a basis for negotiation.

These "in-house" cost estimates may be made before or after requests for price quotations are sent to suppliers. In some cases, requests for quotation are accompanied by a cost analysis form that the vendor is asked to complete (see Figure 11-2). Even when the quoting supplier elects not to complete the form, it has the psychological effect of letting him or her know that his or her quoted price will be subject to close analysis.

Basic Elements of Price Analysis

Five basic items are considered in analyzing supplier cost proposals:

Materials cost	General and administrative expense
Direct labor cost	Profit
Overhead cost	

```
International Business Machines Corporation
        Kingston Systems Manufacturing Div.
              COST AND PRICE BREAKDOWN


Part Number_____              Quantity_____
Inquiry Number_____           E.C. Number_____
Material                                    Unit Price
Base Material                       $
Packaging                             _____
   Sub Total                          _____
Shrinkage & Floor Loss_____%        _____
   Sub Total
Material Handling      _____%        _____
   Sub Total
General & Administrative___%         _____
   Sub Total
Profit                 _____%        _____
   Total Material                   $_____
Labor
Labor(Rate per Hr_____)
Overhead               _____%        _____
   Sub Total
General & Administrative___%         _____
   Sub Total
Profit                 _____%        _____
   Total Labor
   Unit Selling Price               $_____


Name of Company
_____

By                    Date
_____

Name Typed            Title
```

Figure 11-2. Some requests for quotation include a cost analysis form on which suppliers are asked to give cost and price breakdowns.

These general categories can, however, be subdivided extensively, depending on the complexity of the product, the relative influence of each item on the total cost, and the dollar volume of the order under consideration. Figure 11-2 provides an example of detailed analysis of a supplier's proposals, including comparisons with previous proposals made and prices paid.

Cost analysis requires a constant questioning—indeed, challenging—of all cost data, whether submitted by the supplier or estimated by the buyer's own plant personnel. Robert Logler, specialist in cost estimating for American Brands, has suggested, in a number of the seminars that he has presented, that the following information be sought on the various elements in a cost breakdown.

Direct labor hours. Is the item being manufactured subject to the learning curve (see Figure 11-3)? Has the same item—or similar items—been built before, and, if so, have the labor hours previously required been compared with those in the present quotation? Are there any contingencies in the labor hours? (Contingencies should not ordinarily be considered unless based on known conditions and reasonable estimates.)

Direct labor rates. What is the basis for rates quoted? Is it the same basis that the supplier has used in the past? If not, why not? What different kinds of labor are required and are the rates quoted reasonable for the effort involved?

Material costs. Are material costs for similar items available? Is a priced bill of materials available? In comparing quantities to blueprint requirements, do they reflect current requirements? Are major dollar items competitively priced? When competition is limited, what is done to assure a fair price? What are scrap allowances and spoilage factors?

Overhead rates. How are the rates computed? Do indirect loadings reflect current expectations over the period of performance? What are vendors of comparable size and manufacturing capability quoting? Are certain direct costs being included in indirect costs as well?

Profit. What is the basis for the supplier's profit margin—a percentage of sales, return on investment? How does it compare with that of other suppliers in the industry? Is competition strong enough in the industry to make it negotiable? Will an increase in order size reduce the supplier's unit cost and thereby open the profit margin to negotiation? Can agreement on how the profit margin will be compiled be reached before negotiations begin?

THE LEARNING CURVE

Probably the most difficult problems in cost analysis for the purpose of price appraisal and negotiation are those concerning new and nonstandard products for which there is no prior manufacturing experience. This is difficult for the supplier as well as for the buyer, but production management science has developed some useful techniques for coping with such problems, and the buyer should be familiar with these methods, too.

The first units of any new product are relatively costly to produce, but experience improves the efficiency of manufacturing methods and the productivity of workers, so that costs come down on succeeding products. The "learning curves" plotting this condition generally show rapid cost reduction on the first few units, then tend to flatten out as methods are standardized but continue downward at a lesser rate as workers steadily gain proficiency. When the curve is plotted on a log-log scale, it approximates a straight line (see Figure 11-3). This is projected to permit establishing a target level of production costs upon which a suitably profitable ultimate price can be predicated. The cumulative average line in this graph is higher than the unit cost line, because it includes the initial high costs, but eventually all these costs are recovered in mass production at the improved rates. The buyer who understands the statistical basis of this phenomenon is likewise able to project a target buying price. That buyer will reject the factual but unrealistically high costs of initial quantities and will base his or her negotiations on total quantities, in which long-run productivity has been established, or insist on a sliding scale in which the price of successive lots will fairly reflect the lower costs that result from "learning."

The 80 percent statistical curve shown in Figure 11-3 is fairly representative of average conditions in industrial production and is sufficiently accurate to be used as a starting point in most purchasing calculations. In general, the percentage to be used varies inversely as the amount of manual labor involved in the operation. The practical range for most production processes lies between 70 percent (assembly operations, showing steeper initial decline and 90 percent (machine work with long runs and few setups.) The 100 percent curve (no decline) implies complete automation.

SUPPLY AND DEMAND

The second, or economic, concept of right price is based largely on the law of supply and demand. As already noted, the operation of this economic law depends on freedom of market action, which has been so modified by modern political and business practices that the action of supply and demand is no longer the decisive factor affecting price, as assumed in classic economic and purchasing theory. Nevertheless, they are influences that cannot be ignored. Prices tend upward when demand exceeds supply and tend downward when supply exceeds demand.

In this equation, the purchasing manager represents demand. Individually his or her influence on the situation may be very small. Cumulatively, it may be considerable, but buying policies and action are not a concerted effort except insofar as they represent a common reaction to prevailing conditions. When demand is high, the purchaser must bid up in order to get the goods that he or she wants and needs. The indicated buying policies—to extend forward coverage in times of rising prices and

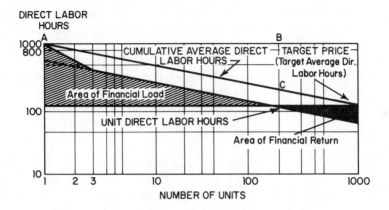

Figure 11-3. Effect of the learning curve on costs.

to buy only for immediate needs in times of declining prices—actually tend to exaggerate these price fluctuations rather than to modify or correct them.

In this concept, the rightness of prices at any given time is accepted as being determined by basic economic conditions outside any effective individual control. The buyer's role, then, is to collect and interpret as accurately as possible the facts of supply and demand, the outlook for economic and political conditions, and the psychological temper of the business community, to gauge the probability and reasonableness of prices, current and future.

COMPETITIVE PRICES

The third theory is that price is determined by competition. In a sense, this is predicated on the two price theories already discussed, for it assumes that supply and demand conditions are such as to create a market and to establish a general price level reasonably above the cost of production. Given these fundamental conditions, it is common knowledge that there will be some variations in price—sometimes substantial variations—as between various suppliers. The purchasing manager must discover and understand these variations so that he or she can place his of her company's business at the most favorable price that will not jeopardize the equally important considerations of quality and continuity of supply and that will not entail additional costs due to manufacturing or commercial difficulties, excessive spoilage, interrupted production, and so on.

Some of these variations are readily understandable. There may be lower manufacturing costs due to cheaper labor, cheaper power, strategic location in respect to raw materials or markets, better processes or better equipment, more complete mechanization, larger volume of operations, or highly specialized skills. All these are legitimate competitive advantages, in which the buyer can logically share.

Questionable Low Prices

Some low prices are of less desirable origin. The willingness to work on lower profit margins, for example, may be an indication of some essential weakness in the supplier's organization and entails the possible hazard of less adequate inspection or quality control, less attention to progressive research, and less reliable production and service. Low prices attributable to the exploitation of labor are now quite generally outlawed, but it must be kept in mind that any unsatisfactory labor conditions in a supplier's plant are likely to lead at any time to an interruption of supply through strikes and walkouts.

Low prices may be quoted on job lots and off-standard merchandise. This does not condemn the merchandise, which may be entirely usable. There is a legitimate outlet for such goods, but the offerings are generally avoided by purchasing managers who value product uniformity, the assurance of continuing supply from regular vendors, and loyalty in business relationships.

Competition may also be used as a selling weapon, as in the case of a special introductory price to capture a new market or a new customer. This obviously offers no permanent advantage to the buyer, and the temporary advantage may be more than offset by long-range considerations. There is also the vicious and destructive "price war" to discipline a competitor or to drive him or her from the field by forcing that person to sell below cost to meet price competition, a thoroughly uneconomic procedure and likewise, necessarily, a temporary measure. It can be argued that such situations do establish a market price, though it is temporary and usually limited to a local area, and that the buyer should accept it as such to maintain the company's competitive cost position. In any event, the choice of policy lies between opportunism and stable relationships, and buying decisions are made accordingly.

Purchasing policy, therefore, does not always seek the lowest price obtainable through competition. Yet it does seek competition as one means of evaluating the rightness of quoted prices and of keeping prices right. Competition is maintained by establishing acceptable alternate sources for purchased materials and products, by periodical checking of prices on even common, standard items, by the judicious division of business when quantities warrant, and by inviting competitive bids for comparison and analysis.

Discounts

There are three types of discounts that concern the buyer in his or her consideration of price.

Trade discounts. Many companies' pricing systems are set up with a series of discounts, on a graduated scale, that are applicable according to the company's classification of customers, without reference to the size of the particular order. Usually such a system is linked with the policy of distribution through franchised representatives, wholesalers, and local dealers; it makes possible an orderly chain of distribution by protecting the territorial rights, profit margins and incentives, and competitive equality of accredited middlemen. There are also other bases of customer classification for example, according to the purpose for which goods are purchased, whether for export, for domestic resale, for fabrication, or for end use. The price, then, depends to a considerable extent upon the classification in which a company is placed, and this involves an element of "rightness" from the purchasing standpoint.

This type of pricing sometimes comes in conflict with the logic of purchasing. This is the case when a buyer's purchases of an item are substantially greater than are all the distributor's other sales of that item, when orders are filled by mill shipments so that the distributor's role is only nominal, when the distributor does not actually perform the services associated with his or her function, such as maintaining stocks, extending credit, expediting deliveries, and the like, or when such extra services and conveniences are not needed or desired as a part of procurement. The force of these arguments (and of competition) is sometimes recognized by establishing special classifications for large users, by handling them as "house accounts" or "national accounts," or otherwise by modifying the discount system to bring prices in line with quantity and service factors.

Quantity discounts. The practice of offering lower unit prices on larger-quantity orders has already been discussed in connection with the determination of ordering quantities and forward-buying policies. It has its basis in the economies of volume production and the reduction of selling, shipping, and accounting detail, in the added business assured by the larger orders, and the large user's importance as a customer.

The buyer's responsibility in this case is primarily an internal one, to adjust his or her ordering practices to the most advantageous quantity price breaks. It is also a matter for negotiation in getting prices on products made to the buyer's specification, in the instance when quotations are asked on various lot sizes and when cumulative quantity discounts based on total annual purchases instead of individual purchases may be obtained.

Cash discounts.   The cash discount is quite a different matter. It is not a price concession or variation; it is an inducement for prompt payment of invoice charges, and it is earned only when payment is made in accordance with the stipulated terms. Nevertheless, because it affects the net disbursement, the discount is reflected in the total cost of materials, and purchasing must see to it that this potential saving is not jeopardized by carelessness in the terms of the contract or delay in the processing of invoices. The saving, though usually expressed in small percentages of invoice amount, is really a very substantial one. A commonly quoted discount, "2 percent, 10 days—30 days net," means that the seller is offering 2 percent for twenty days' use of the capital amount involved, which is at the rate of 36.5 percent a year.

Cash discount terms seem very simple, but they must be clearly defined by mutual agreement. For instance, in the absence of any other understanding, most vendors take the stand that the discount period starts with the date of the invoice. The purchasing manager can safeguard the position of his or her company by making it a condition of the order that the discount period shall be calculated from the date that an acceptable invoice is received by the buyer, thus anticipating and avoiding the loss of the discount when invoices are delayed or the lapse of the discount privilege pending necessary adjustments in the invoice charge.

SOME PERFORMANCE OBJECTIVES

After studying this chapter you should be able to:

1. Distinguish between price and cost as they relate to the purchasing department's responsibility.
2. Differentiate between a "sellers' market" and a "buyers' market," giving examples, current or otherwise.
3. Describe the bid system and some of the reservations that industrial buyers have about that method of procurement.
4. Explain the fundamentals of cost analysis. Show how you might apply the technique to estimate what might be a reasonable cost on some personal purchase or expenditure such as auto repairs, carpentry work, landscaping, and so on.

5. Give a brief explanation of the learning curve.
6. Describe the three types of discounts and explain the purchasing department's responsibility in respect to discounts.

From this discussion of price and cost we move in the next chapter to consider a technique for improving product value by relating its function to its cost to see how that function may be obtained at least cost. The technique, known as value analysis, is a logical extension of the purchasing operations described up to this point.

Value Analysis— Standardization

12

We have already suggested that the value concept breaks across the lines that divide functional responsibility and prompts a new purchasing activity—value analysis. To measure value, we balance what we get in our purchase against what we must pay. We get from the supplier what we ask the supplier to furnish; thus, we start with the quality definition and apply all our purchasing skills to procure that quality at a minimum cost. The essence of the quality definition is suitability. But, as soon as we enter the realm of price analysis and negotiation, we may find that a part of what we are paying goes for quality features that do not contribute substantially or proportionately to suitability of the material or product purchased. To that extent, the expenditure is wasteful. This brings us to a study of the purpose or function for which the item is purchased. That study includes a review of the specification for a possible revision of the quality requirement that may permit us to reduce costs without impairing suitability.

This process of study and review—value analysis—is not simply a routine part of the buying process. It takes time, special attention, and special talents. It is essentially a staff service to the buyer. In some situations, particularly in smaller companies, one person may have the dual role of value analyst and buyer. But any full-scale value analysis program is most effective when the purchasing department has its own staff analyst or analysis section or has a leading role in any company-wide value analysis program.

A SECOND LOOK AT THE SPECIFICATION

Value analysis is variously defined. One simple definition describes the process as "engineering unnecessary cost factors out of a purchased item." A more elaborate definition states,

> Value analysis is the study of the relationship of design, function, and cost of any product, material, or service with the object of reducing its cost through modification of design or material specifications, manufacture by more efficient processes, change in source of supply (internal or external), or possible elimination or incorporation into a related item.[1]

Carlos Fallon, a materials specialist on the RCA corporate staff, defined value analysis in an internal memorandum thusly:

> Value analysis is a performance-oriented scientific method for improving product value by relating the elements of product worth to their corresponding elements of cost, in order to accomplish the function of the product at least cost in resources.

DEVELOPMENT OF VALUE ENGINEERING

Originally, value analysis was intended to apply primarily to parts already in production. It soon became obvious, however, that the study of function could begin early in the design stages of a part or product. Gradually, the scope of value analysis was expended and refined to include pre-production functional analysis, which in turn became known as value engineering.

The Department of Defense, which enthusiastically adopted the value concept in the early 1960s, describes value engineering as:

> A systematic effort directed at analyzing the functional requirements of systems, equipment, facilities, procedures, and supplies for the purpose of achieving the essential functions at the lowest total cost, consistent with the needed performance, reliability, quality, and maintainability.

[1] Ammer, Dean S., *Materials Management and Purchasing.* 4th Ed. Homewood, Ill.: Richard D. Irwin, Inc. 1980.

The DOD goes on to state

> Although there are numerous other published definitions of VE, most are merely minor variations of this definition and none appears to contradict it. Others may refer to their value improvement efforts by such terms as value analysis, value control, or value management. There may be some subtle differences between these other programs and VE, but the basic objectives and philosophy appear to be the same for all.[2]

Thus, the various terms are generally considered interchangeably and are used so in this text.

Value analysis by purchasing does not encroach upon the functions or prerogatives of other departments. The cost-reduction possibilities that it discloses are initially presented as recommendations—perhaps only queries—to those who must ultimately define the need. Wherever changes in material, design, or process are involved, approval by engineering or manufacturing departments is essential before a specification can be changed. If a suggestion has merit, the actual changes are often worked out in those departments. If a suggestion is impracticable, or if there are other factors that outweigh the cost consideration, it can be rejected.

The application of value analysis to existing specifications is in no sense a derogation of the engineering skill and judgment represented in the original statement of need. Rather, it adds another criterion in defining right quality. It gives recognition to the fact that, in design and specification, as in every other field, there is an ever-present possibility of improvement and that the only way to achieve that improvement is through continuous, systematic effort directed toward that end. Characteristically, if any part or material is doing its job satisfactorily, and if the specification satisfies the requirement of suitability, there is no inclination on the part of the user to disturb the situation.

Value analysis also recognizes the fact that, in mass production, no unit saving is too small to merit respectful attention, because small unit savings multiplied thousands of times in the total production program quickly mount up to impressive dollar figures. The Ford Motor Company, a pioneer in promoting value analysis activities in purchasing, used a slogan pointing out that, with an annual output of millions of vehicles, "the difference of one cent per car represents a saving or loss of tens of thousands of dollars per year." Changing one small component from a forging to an equally serviceable screw-machine product saved four

---

[2] Department of Defense, "Value Engineering," Handbook 5010.8–H, September 12, 1968, Washington, D.C.

tenths of a cent per unit, an insignificant figure. But sixteen of these parts were used in every car. Annual saving: $64,000 per million cars produced.

Typical savings effected through value analysis actually run to many times greater than this very modest example. To anyone unfamiliar with the workings and results of value analysis techniques, the tangible savings reported may indeed seem fantastic, whether considered as a percentage of previous costs, dollarwise, or in relation to the cost of the activity itself.

A 1975 *Purchasing Magazine* survey showed that:[3]

1. The average goal for value analysis savings in the companies studied was 3.5 percent per year on dollars expended on purchases.
2. More than three fourths of the companies with programs met their value analysis goals.
3. The average payback ratio, that is, dollars saved compared with the cost of operating a VA program, is 26:1. One company, Black & Decker Manufacturing Company, reported a ratio of 100:1—savings of $1.2 million against an outlay of just $12,000.

Where accurate records of savings are maintained, it is almost universal experience that every dollar spent in value analysis work is returned many times over and that these savings are repeated and multiplied in succeeding years' purchases. For companies that have carried an intensive value analysis program for ten years or longer, there is no indication that the procedure is even approaching the point of diminishing return. Instead, the habits of mind engendered throughout an organization by this approach to value buying give added momentum to the program, with ever-increasing results. Value analysis is an integral, sound, continuing element of scientific purchasing. Such experience, more than any other factor, has brought about the realization that purchasing is, in fact, a profit-making function.

ELIMINATING UNNECESSARY COST FACTORS

Value analysis is a more fundamental and far-reaching concept than is the simple process of price analysis in that it goes to the causes of cost. Further, it has the practical objective of applying direct corrective action to minimize these causes and reduce costs, instead of leading only to comparisons and negotiation on the basis of existing costs.

The supplier's basic costs of manufacture are largely fixed by the

[3] "VA '75, A Plan for Survival," *Purchasing Magazine*, June 17, 1975, p. 58—125.

design, materials, and methods specified by the buyer for production of the purchased item. It may be that the item itself, which the buyer is asking his or her supplier to produce, represents an unnecessarily high cost for the intended purpose. If that is the case, and if it is recognized, the buyer and his or her associates can attack that hard core of basic production cost, seeking to eliminate or modify the unnecessary features of design and manufacturing operations. In this way they should arrive eventually at a part or specification that truly represents the most economical product to satisfy the end-use requirements. It is obvious that this concern for value adds a new and important dimension to the buyer's definition of "right quality."

From the standpoint of economical product cost, it would be difficult to overemphasize the significance and benefits of such an approach. Over a long period of years, the constant trend of economic factors has been to build additional costs into the basic cost structure of manufactured products in the form of higher labor rates, more expensive raw materials, and higher taxes and costs of doing business. Meanwhile, each increment in basic cost of manufacture reduces cost flexibility and tends to perpetuate the higher price plane. Under these circumstances, anything that can be engineered out of basic cost as a direct, item-by-item saving is doubly significant. Such savings permanently eliminate cost factors and conserve productive effort. They are repetitive, multiplied many times over in quantity requirements.

From the standpoint of purchasing practice and supplier relationships, the value analysis approach also has much to commend it in that it does not attempt in any way to "squeeze" the supplier, to reduce his or her normal margins of profit, or to exert extraordinary competitive pressure in dealings with that supplier. As a matter of fact, the supplier's own suggestions and cooperation may be enlisted in this effort, to mutual advantage. It is one of those happy situations in which everybody wins.

CHECKLIST FOR VALUE ANALYSIS

This approach to the problem of cost is well summarized in the checklist of ten "Tests for Value" originally compiled and used in the purchasing department of the General Electric Company and widely adapted throughout industry and the Department of Defense. This code, which has been widely circulated throughout every division of the company, among engineering and manufacturing as well as purchasing personnel, states that

Every material, every part, every operation must pass these tests:

1. Does its use contribute value?
2. Is its cost proportionate to its usefulness?
3. Does it need all of its features?
4. Is there anything better for the intended use?
5. Can a usable part be made by a lower-cost method?
6. Can a standard product be found which will be usable?
7. Is it made on proper tooling, considering quantities used?
8. Do material, reasonable labor, overhead, and profit total its cost?
9. Will another dependable supplier provide it for less?
10. Is anyone buying it for less?

Examples of this type of analysis, with a representative application of each listed test to a purchased component (most of which were bought in the hundreds of thousands) were cited early in the G.E. program as follows:

Test 1. (Condenser used across contacts of a relay to provide arc action as contact opens.) When cobalt became available after World War II, an alnico magnet was used to provide snap action. Analysis disclosed that the condenser was no longer necessary with this magnet—it did not add value to the product—and it was eliminated. The saving was 500,000 condensers per year, at 10 cents each.

Test 2. (Spacer hub for mounting light aluminum disks.) Considering the simple function of this part in the assembly, the cost of 90 cents per unit was out of proportion to its usefulness. The cost was high due to undercutting to reduce weight, which was an important factor. Analysis showed that, by making the part of aluminum, the undercutting could be eliminated, the weight still further reduced, and identical performance provided at a cost of 20 cents per unit. The saving was 77 percent.

Test 3. (Stainless steel disk used in dispensing machine.) These washers were formerly chamfered on one side. Analysis revealed that the chamfer made no contribution to value—the part did not need all of its features. Eliminating the chamfer reduced the cost from 18 cents to 5 cents per unit, a saving of 72 percent.

Test 4. (Mica stack used for insulation.) By changing from sheet mica to molded Micalex, the parts of the assembly were more rigidly mounted, resulting in a better assembly, and cost was reduced from $40 to $34 per M, a saving of 15 percent.

Test 5. (Hub assembly.) This part was formerly made as a two-part riveted assembly, at a cost of $30 per thousand. Study showed that it could be made as a one-piece casting, eliminating the assembly operation and simplifying production. At the same time, cost was reduced to $10 per thousand, a saving of 67 percent.

Test 6. (Stud contact.) This part had been made to special design, at a cost of $27 per thousand. Purchasing search discovered a standard-design stud, available at $14 per thousand, that provided identical performance. The saving was 48 percent.

Test 7. (Stainless weld nipple.) Because of relatively small quantities required, the former procedure had been to purchase a standard stainless fitting and machine away a part of it to provide the desired weld embossing. Cost by this method was 20 cents each. Value analysis disclosed the fact that production requirements had increased to the point where another process should be considered. It was subsequently produced in quantity on an automatic screw machine at a cost of 5 cents each. The saving was 75 percent.

Test 8. (Stainless dowel pin.) This part was purchased in large quantities, made to special design and specifications with close tolerances required. The cost of $3 per thousand seemed out of line with reasonable standards, but was justified by the vendor's costs. The manufacturer was invited to confer on details of the specification, manufacturing process, and inspection. As a result, some wastes of material and labor were eliminated from the manufacturer's operation. The identical part, produced to the same close tolerances, was subsequently produced at $2 per thousand, a saving of 33 percent.

Test 9. (Bushing.) Exploration of the market disclosed that this part, purchased from an established source of supply at $18 per thousand, could be procured from an equally reliable supplier at $13.50 per thousand, a saving of 25 percent.

Test 10. (Button.) This part, used by one division in large volume, was being purchased at $2.50 per thousand. Research within the purchasing department revealed that another division was using a similar button costing $1 per thousand. The latter was found to be applicable to the use under study, with equally good performance, at a saving of 60 percent.

The monetary values in the G.E. examples are, of course, not particularly meaningful in light of today's continuing price inflation. But the percentages of savings are still impressive, and the value techniques and principles on which they are based are more valid than ever.

THE ROLE OF PURCHASING

Value analysis for cost reduction is everybody's business and is more effective when its principles are applied throughout the organization, wherever requirements and specifications originate. But there are five important reasons why it is logical for the purchasing department to initiate and promote this activity (as in the case of standardization, which is one of the tools of value analysis, indicated in test 6 of the checklist).

1. Regardless of how much cost-reduction activity is carried on in other departments of the company, it is still a responsibility of the buyer to seek maximum value when a product requirement comes up to the point of purchase. It is his or her duty to challenge wasteful and avoidable costs inherent in the things that he or she is asked to buy. Thus, it is inescapable

that a large share of whatever value analysis work is done will be done by the buyer or in the purchasing department in any case.

2. Purchasing, more than any other department, must be cost conscious in respect to the materials and parts that go into the company's end product. This is a desirable attribute in every department, but it is an integral part of the buying responsibility. The purchasing manager is brought face to face with the cost factor in every transaction. Even when value analysis is not organized for special consideration, it is practiced to some degree, as a matter of course, in every purchasing comparison and decision.

3. Purchasing is costwise through experience in price analysis and comparisons, evaluation of alternative materials and methods, and the handling of many comparable items. The buyer learns why some products cost more than others and what features in a specification make suppliers' quotations higher. This knowledge is enhanced by the buyer's daily exposure to the product offerings and sales presentations of vendors, which can be directly related to his or her own requirements and often can reveal how cost reductions are being effected in other companies having similar needs.

4. Purchasing is objective in its attention to costs, to a degree that is difficult for the person or department whose first concern is the utility or performance of a product and whose judgment is understandably influenced by creative pride of design.

5. Purchasing is a natural focal point at which each individual requirement and specification, from whatever source in the company, must pass in review. It is therefore in a strategic position to apply the experience gained in connection with one item to other similar items, to recognize the areas in which intensive value analysis gives greatest promise of effective and profitable results, and to carry on such projects as part of a specific, comprehensive and continuing program.

Thus, beyond its own direct value analysis activities, the role of purchasing is to initiate and organize; to promote cost consciousness in all departments of the company, keeping this topic in the forefront of their thinking; to point out opportunities or to raise questions as to the possibility of cost reduction in purchased items; to develop practical techniques for product and value analysis; and to train personnel of other departments, upon request, in the application of these techniques, giving whatever assistance may be required.

TECHNIQUE OF PRODUCT ANALYSIS

The techniques of product analysis are as varied as the problems in this field, but particular attention should be directed to one method that has been exceptionally resultful. The examples previously cited have been concerned with individual components or small parts of a larger assembly. The more comprehensive approach starts with the complete assembly, considered as the sum of its parts.

A widely used technique is to take such an assembly, dismantle it, and mount it on a panel board of plywood or other suitable material in such a way that each of the component parts, down to the smallest screw or other fastening device, is shown in relation to all other parts. With this visualization, analysis is facilitated and the pertinent questions are more readily framed, leading to better and more economical practice.

A variation of this technique is to mount adjacently on a panel board, in corresponding position for direct comparison, the disassembled components of competitive or alternative products (for example, dashboard clocks) so that their relative designs and merits and costs may be analyzed, resulting in a revised specification that literally embodies the best and most economical features of each.

Still another technique that has produced excellent results is the "brainstorming" session. A problem or product is presented to a group of people for consideration. They need not be experts in the particular subject. If they represent a variety of special interests and experience, such as purchasing, engineering, and manufacturing, so much the better. The meeting is totally unrehearsed. The group leader presents the problem, stressing the function to be served by the product and showing current design or practice. The leader then invites suggestions for improvement. Each person makes whatever suggestions come first to mind, however unorthodox or impracticable the ideas may seem to be. These are listed and grouped, and, when the first flow of ideas has slowed down, they are explored in greater detail, again in open discussion and with the invitation for further ideas that may have been prompted by some aspect of those already presented.

In relatively large value programs, involving a number of specialists, a planned and systematic approach is generally more productive than an unorganized idea-swapping session. A popular procedure for analysis calls for a logical progression, moving from the collection of information, to speculation as to the function of the part or material, to consideration of substitutes or alternatives, then all the way through to recommendations and action. Called the VA/VE Job Plan, it is widely employed in industry and the Department of Defense. The basic principles on which the job plan is built can, of course, be adapted even when value analysis is carried out on a smaller scale, for example, by the individual buyer.

A diagrammatic explanation of the job plan is shown in Figure 12-1. A more generalized example of how an end product can be value analyzed component by component is presented in Figure 12-2.

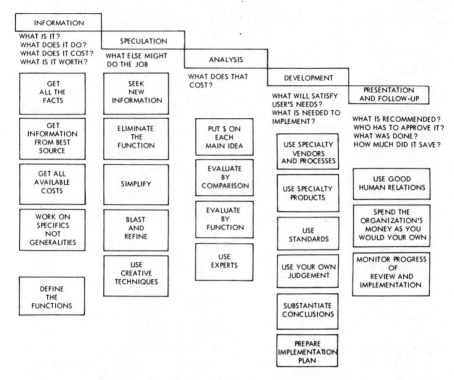

Figure 12-1.   Value analysis–value engineering job plan.

SCOPE OF VALUE ANALYSIS

The scope of value analysis is not limited to factors of design and man-ufacturing method. In chemical manufacturing industries, for example, the product is inherently and rigidly defined in its composition and grade, and variations or alternatives are obviously ruled out of consideration. Nevertheless, value analysis has been effectively applied in this field in respect to reagents, solvents, plasticizers, containers, bulk handling and distribution, and other elements in the process that substantially affect product costs.

The last three items in the General Electric Company's checklist for value relate exclusively to purchasing policies and methods and are applicable to any items of use in any company.

Because the concept of value is compounded of both quality and cost, the subject is not complete without reference to the criteria of buying

217

How to analyze a product

Even a good product
can be made better.
Value analysis provides
the approach.

PRE-CONCEIVED IDEAS are the biggest obstacle to value improvement. The design of the portable vacuum cleaner illustrated here is a good one—but even a well-made product can be improved.

The value analyst goes beyond normal buying steps and evaluates the total concept: from the standpoint of sales, engineering, production, cost. A fresh look can turn up additional savings.

No line of inquiry should be ruled out. Every question should be answered. Sometimes the "dumb" question is the one that triggers the best result.

Here's how a VA brainstorming session —designed to develop ways to improve the vacuum cleaner—might work:

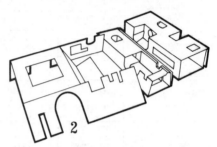

Parts must be fitted into three die-cut pieces of board. Would a molded plastic shell cut down packing labor? Can we redesign the spacers into a one-piece carrying caddy for the accessories?

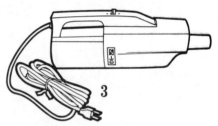

Vacuum unit has three-piece housing. Can this be made as two pieces? Why not mold the nameplate into the part instead of applying it in a separate operation? Could a standard metal tube replace the special molded housing?

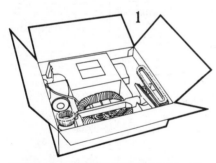

Interior packaging hides the product. Can it be redesigned for better visual display? Can the number of assembly operations be reduced in packing? Why not design the carton so that it can be used as a wall storage box?

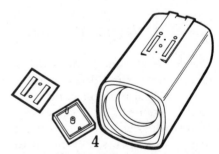

Seal for handle attachment must be assembled from inside housing. Can extra plastic piece be eliminated? Is there another way to achieve airtight closure?

Figure 12-2.　A basic approach in value analyzing an end product begins with identification of the function of parts and materials and consideration of alternatives. Courtesy, *Purchasing Magazine.*

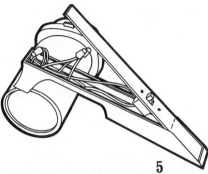

5

Plated metal handle requires extra operation. Can we use stainless or spun aluminum and cut out finishing operation? What about the switch? Can we buy it cheaper from a specialty supplier?

8

Rubber diaphragm on nozzle is fastened with metal plate and two screws. Can we mold protrusions on plastic and heat seal to eliminate screws? What purpose does the metal plate serve?

6

Blower assembly has too many parts. Why not combine into one? Do internal spacers have to be finished? Only purpose is to separate fins.

9

Brush housings and cleaning attachments are made from two types of plastic, rigid and soft. Can we standardize on one material? Washer in floor brush is brittle. Is there a better material? Nylon brushes set in metal rim; can they be all nylon and set in plastic? Do bristles have to be removable or can entire part be replaced? Two spring clips hold movable brush for upholstery cleaner. Is there a better way?

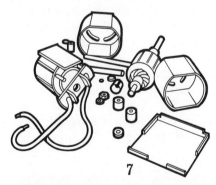

7

Is motor overdesigned for the job? Can we recheck the specifications? Is it possible to use a lighter housing to reduce weight? Can a standard base plate be used in place of special?

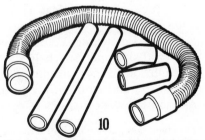

10

Two pieces of metal tubing must be chamfered on one end. Can they be made from rigid plastic, molded to shape? Flexible hose has wire core; what gage wire is needed?

at the right price (Chapter 11). Many of the methods used in that determination are properly included in the broad field of value analysis. The same is true of decisions on whether to make or purchase a part or item (Chapter 13) and, as will be shown, the whole field of standardization (see the separate discussion of standardization later in this chapter).

In the early days of value analysis, the function was generally performed by buyers themselves, particularly in small- and medium-sized companies. It soon became clear that this arrangement was unsatisfactory because of the additional load that it placed on personnel in terms of time, paperwork, and follow-up. As value analysis became more widely accepted, more formal types of VA organization developed. Among these are the following:

> Full-time analysts, generally assigned to the purchasing department, whose major responsibility is the study of purchased parts and materials offering the greatest potential for improvement or cost reduction.
>
> Value analysis committees made up of representatives of various functions, including purchasing, design engineering, manufacturing engineering, and accounting. The purchasing representative is generally the department's staff analyst, who acts as chairperson.
>
> A variation of the above, on which serve representatives of all functions in the plant. The purchasing agent or manager is generally the chairperson of the committee.
>
> Value analysis by project, in which VA teams are organized to work fulltime on specific VA objectives. When the project is complete, the committee is disbanded.

The use of value analysis techniques is not exclusively a matter for full time specialists, according to L.D. Miles, who set up the first value analysis program in the 1950's at the General Electric Company.

"Much good value can be achieved by everyday use of the techniques," he says "and large amounts of unnecessary costs will still be unidentified, however. Value activities must be enhanced by the use of specialized skill and knowledge.

"Obviously, the prevailing philosophy of a company's management, and the size and scope of the business, will determine the appropriate provision for value analysis effort."[4]

[4] Mr. Miles, now a columnist for *Purchasing World,* is widely known as the "father of value analysis" for his pioneering work and continuing contributions to the discipline. The quotation is from his book, *Techniques of Value Analysis and Engineering,* 2nd ed., published by McGraw-Hill.

REPORTING ON VALUE ANALYSIS

The results of the analyst's work are in the form of reports and recommendations. They are supported in every case by cost comparisons and the projection of anticipated savings, because this is the goal toward which value analysis is directed. The reports are made to the purchasing manager, and only through the purchasing department to other personnel or departments affected. This is the orderly channel of procedure and communication, because decisions based on the recommendations, involving changes in specifications, manufacturing methods, or shop practice, must be made at the executive level. To inject a third, independent factor and personality into interdepartmental problems of value and utility tends to confuse the issue, to give the impression of meddling, and in general to weaken the force of the recommendation and the consideration that is given to it. By contrast, a purchasing proposal based on the identical recommendation, and within the buyer's legitimate province of purchase cost reduction, must be weighed on merit even though the proposal may not be adopted for other reasons.

In addition to actual research and analysis projects, an important part of the program is to promote cost-consciousness throughout the entire organization, whether materials are specified and used. The publicizing of improved practice and lowered costs, through bulletins and employee publications, helps toward an understanding of what value analysis tries to accomplish and generates enthusiasm for the program. Cost reduction must be a team effort. When it is accepted that value analysis is not critical of previous decisions but is predicated on the principle that almost everything is capable of improvement, progress is made toward getting everybody on the team. A second step is to make available training in value analysis techniques. This is best done with small groups, in "workshop" sessions. Engineering, manufacturing, and other specifying departments, as well as buyers, should be invited to participate. The mixed group presents various viewpoints on the value and fosters understanding of the common objective.

Chief qualification for successful value analyst is an imaginative, questioning mind, backed with enthusiasm and perseverance. A knowledge of cost accounting and of manufacturing processes is desirable. The value analyst must have the ability to work with people and the willingness to share credit. Nothing can kill a value analysis program more quickly than a "credit-grabbing" attitude.

ENLISTING VENDORS' AID

One of the most fruitful sources of information and help in value buying is the cooperation of vendors. Here the buyer has at his or her disposal the advice of specialists who are expert and experienced in their respective fields to a degree that the buyer, concerned with many different products, can rarely hope to attain. The purchasing manager who can establish a relationship with vendors in which they make the buyer's problems their own, and will work with the buyer toward the objectives of cost reduction, enlists the technical resources and manufacturing experience of an entire industry. Such a relationship is, of course, predicated on the assumption that the cooperative vendor will be the preferred vendor and will profit through greater sales. This policy in itself represents a sound concept of value in purchasing. Figure 12-3 shows a checklist used by one company to solicit value analysis help from vendors.

In organized value analysis programs, this source of help is cultivated by means of "vendor clinics." A representative group of vendors is invited to come to the buyer's plant, usually for a two-day meeting, at which materials requirements, problems, and policies are explained to the group as a whole and sometimes in private conferences. The visitors are not salesmen in the ordinary sense, but are drawn from the higher-ranking management and operating officers of the vendor companies. A focal feature of the clinic is a comprehensive display of the company's important products and the purchased parts that go into them. Here vendors can see at firsthand how their own products are used in the buyer's assembly, which is not always clear from the specification or blueprint. It shows the reasons underlying certain terms of the specification, the need for close tolerances at one point or of extra strength at another, and the relationship of each part with other sections that may be procured from other sources. It stresses the idea that the parts manufacturer is in fact a participant in making the end product and that its quality, utility, and cost (and, hence, its marketability) are really the concern of all.

This is good education, but the clinics also have a more immediate and practical objective. When the vendors inspect the parts on display, they are invited to indicate those that they are equipped to furnish to best advantage and on which they would like to quote. At the same time it is made clear that the company is receptive to any suggestions as to parts design or manufacturing method that will improve quality or reduce cost, or both. Vendors are furnished with blueprints and specifications sheets on the selected items for further study and estimates.

ALLIS-CHALMERS PURCHASING DIVISION ———————— Works	VI₂P* SUPPLIER CHECK LIST FOR VALUE IMPROVEMENT

A-C PURCHASE ORDER OR INQUIRY NO. ——————————— BUYER ———————————

PART NAME ——————————————————————————————————

A-C PART NO. OR DRAWING NO. ——————————————————————

WE ARE CONTINUALLY ANALYSING OUR PRODUCTS FOR VALUE AND SOLICIT YOUR HELP THROUGH ANSWERS TO
THE FOLLOWING QUESTIONS THAT MAY BE APPLICABLE TO THE PART IDENTIFIED ABOVE. OUR AIM IS TO ELIM-
INATE UNNECESSARY COSTS WITHOUT ADVERSELY AFFECTING THE FUNCTIONAL INTEGRITY OF THE PART; WE
WANT YOUR SUGGESTIONS!

QUESTIONS	CHECK		SUGGESTIONS
	YES	NO	
1. DO YOU UNDERSTAND FUNCTION PRODUCT IS TO PERFORM?	☐	**	
2. COULD COSTS BE REDUCED BY RELAXING REQUIREMENTS AS TO:			
● TOLERANCES?	☐	☐	
● FINISHES?	☐	☐	
● TESTING?	☐	☐	
BY HOW MUCH? ———————————			
3. COULD COSTS BE REDUCED THRU CHANGES IN:			
● MATERIAL SPECIFIED?	☐	☐	
● ORDERING QUANTITIES?	☐	☐	
● MFG. PROCESS USED? I.E., CASTING, FORGING, STAMPING, ETC.	☐	☐	
BY HOW MUCH? ———————————			
4. CAN YOU SUGGEST ANY OTHER CHANGES THAT WOULD:			
● REDUCE WEIGHT?	☐	☐	
● SIMPLIFY THE PART?	☐	☐	
● REDUCE OVERALL COSTS?	☐	☐	
BY HOW MUCH? ———————————			
5. DOES IT APPEAR THAT ANY OF THE SPECIFI-CATIONS OR QUALITY CONTROL REQUIRE-MENTS ARE TOO STRINGENT?	☐	☐	
6. IN SUPPLYING THIS PRODUCT, WHAT IS THE GREATEST ELEMENT OF YOUR COST THAT WE MIGHT POSSIBLY HELP ALLEVIATE?			
7. DO YOU HAVE A STANDARD ITEM THAT COULD BE SUBSTITUTED FOR THIS PART SATISFACTORILY?	☐	☐	WHAT IS IT? ———————————— WHAT DOES IT COST? ————————————
8. OTHER SUGGESTIONS?			

SUPPLIER (COMPANY NAME)   ADDRESS

SIGNATURE   TITLE   DATE

* "VALUE IMPROVEMENT IN PURCHASING" AT ALLIS-CHALMERS
** IF ANSWER IS "NO," OBTAIN FUNCTIONAL INFORMATION FROM BUYER INVOLVED

Figure 12-3. Form used to solicit supplier help in a value analysis program.

STANDARDIZATION: TOOL FOR VALUE

Mass-production techniques are predicated on the principle of uniformity and interchangeability of materials and parts. To this extent, the vast

majority of manufacturing companies are committed to the policy of standardization in their product lines. This is reflected to some degree in the standardization of their purchase requirements. When this principle is carried one step further, to coordinate these "standard" requirements with the standard product lines and quality grades of supplier industries, additional advantages accrue in the form of quicker availability, alternative sources, and, again, in the economies of mass production.

These advantages are obviously of primary importance in purchasing and value analysis. Theoretically, it is possible to determine and define the ideal quality—in terms of composition, dimension, physical and electrical properties, and other attributes of a material or product—for each individual purpose. This ideal quality could be procured, at substantial cost of money and time. In some special instances, this may be necessary, but in most cases it is both impractical and unnecessary. Industry has found the answer in standardization of materials and products. Thus, the selection may be made not from an infinite number of possible qualities and sizes but, rather from a more practicable range, broad enough to meet the majority of requirements satisfactorily, yet sufficiently limited and well established as to acceptance and use to permit mass production and ready availability. Even so, there is a great deal of designing, manufacturing, and purchasing done on the basis of special specification, when reasonable standards could be adopted with no sacrifice of utility or satisfaction and with substantial advantages of economy and convenience.

Good purchasing practice extends the concept of standardization by promoting the consolidation of similar requirements into a single specification, wherever possible. For example, fewer types of cleaning compounds or fewer grades of lubricants than are ordinarily requested for specific applications might adequately serve the plant's maintenance needs. If so, there would be fewer items to buy and carry in stock, and those that are required could be purchased in larger quantities to better advantage. The same principle can be applied to production materials, as, for example, fewer sizes of fasteners, tubing, bar stock, and an endless list of other items.

Engineering Standards

The buyer's interest in standardization is of direct importance as it affects product fabrication. Standardization of screw threads makes possible the use of stock machine screws and bolts in standard tapped holes. Standardization of pipe fittings makes it possible to install plumbing and heating fixtures in existing piping systems and to alter or expand these as required. The list could be extended to great length, affecting many materials and products in common use in our daily living. It will be noted that in the latter examples cited, the principle of standardization has been extended to design as well as to simple dimension.

Standardization has also been applied to the composition of materials. A typical example of this is the SAE steels, a series of alloys of specified composition and known properties, defined, identified by numbers, and recognized by all buyers and producers of steel. The number of possible varieties of such steels, the nature and proportion of component elements, and the particular properties attained, are almost infinite.

Typically, such standards are developed through the cooperation of producers and users, taking advantage of the experience and technical skill of both groups and coordinating these efforts through various national technical societies or governmental agencies.

Among the agencies that have actively sponsored the development of industrial standards are the U.S.A. Standards Institute, American Society for Testing Materials, Society of Automotive Engineers, Amercan Society of Mechanical Engineers, National Electrical Manufacturers Association, and others. The Federal government has also taken an active and effective interest in such projects through the National Bureau of Standards and various procurement agencies.

The U.S.A. Standards Institute's catalog of standards lists almost 3,000 standards currently in force. A *Directory of Standardization* issued by the National Bureau of Standards (NBS Miscellaneous Publication 288) lists by product name more than 500 organizations concerned with standardization.

Government Standards

The federal government has contributed greatly to industrial standardization. As mentioned, it has placed the services and facilities of the National Bureau of Standards at the disposal of industry, on request, as a coordinating and sponsoring organization for the development of standards. This service is reinforced by the promulgation of such standards and by the sponsorship of a certification plan indicating adherence to standards by manufacturers, which substantially lessens the burden of individual tests. Figure 12-4 is a list of the benefits provided by the Federal government's specifications and standards.

Second, as a large consumer and buyer of a great variety of products, it has developed standards for its own purchases. These standards originate with the various procurement agencies, principally the armed forces and the Federal Bureau of Supply.

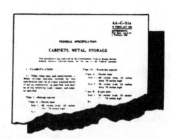

**BENEFITS
PROVIDED BY
GOVERNMENT
SPECIFICATIONS
AND STANDARDS**

1. Elimination of unnecessary types, varieties, and sizes of supply items, thereby reducing capital investment in inventories and storage space.

2. Utilization of nationally known and recognized technical industry standards.

3. Simplification of procurement procedures, better delivery service, and reduced procurement costs.

4. Utilization of regularly produced supply items to the maximum extent practicable.

5. Assurance to Federal agencies that the product being purchased has the characteristics and quality determined essential to the agency's requirements and will best satisfy the intended use--price and other factors considered.

6. Participation by large and small suppliers on an equal basis in supplying Government requirements, thereby broadening sources of supply and assuring greater supplier participation.

7. References to related specifications and standards, such as marking and packing requirements, by which the references become an integral part of the requirement.

8. Sampling, inspection, and test procedures for use in determining that requirements have been met, in addition to clear and accurate descriptions of the technical requirements for the material, product, or service, including design and construction, and component parts.

9. Purchase of supply items which will result in maximum value being received for the public funds expended.

Figure 12-4. Advantages of specifications and standards as outlined in a U.S. government booklet for businessmen.

An Industry Advisory Council has been established, collaborating with the Standards Division of the Federal Bureau of Supply to bring government standards and procurement practices more closely into line with industrial purchase requirements and prevailing manufacturing practices. The membership of the council includes representatives of the U.S.A. Standards Institute, the American Society for Testing Materials, the Society of Automotive Engineers, the Manufacturing Chemists Association, the American Society of Mechanical Engineers, and the National Electrical Manufacturers Association, technical experts from a number of leading industrial companies, and, significantly, the general purchasing manager of a large manufacturing corporation to represent the industrial purchasing viewpoint.

Another contribution of government to standardization has been the compilation of a directory of all standard specifications, including nongovernmental standards, those of the technical societies and of individual large manufacturers, for the benefit of producing industry and purchasing executives. The advantage of knowing what work has been done and what results are available is that duplication of effort is avoided and a multiplicity of similar but not identical standards eliminated. The cause of overall standardization is thus advanced.

STANDARDIZATION CUTS PRODUCT COSTS

Standardization, then, can be a potent tool of purchasing and value analysis. An adopted standard is essentially a definition of quality that becomes the purchasing manager's ordering description for the item. A standardization project or program must be effected through those in the company organization who design the product, thereby creating the need for specific materials and parts, and those who requisition and specify materials and supplies for plant use. The initiative and pressure for standardization, however, may logically come from the purchasing department, which has the responsibility for economical procurement and is in the strategic position of being a clearinghouse for the requirements of all departments, so that variations in usage and specification among various departments can be most readily detected here.

The most convincing argument for specifying and purchasing standard products, rather than those which are items of special manufacture, is the factor of cost. A survey of representative manufacturers of industrial products reveals the following significant cost comparisons: 23 percent of the manufacturers estimate that special items cost from 10 to 15 percent more to produce than comparable standard items; 47 percent estimate the additional cost at from 25 to 50 percent; 17 percent estimate that the extra cost runs even higher than 50 percent. Only 12 percent report that no substantial extra cost is involved. The type of product and the supplier's facilities and organization for handling special work naturally influence these calculations, but the general conclusion is clear that deviations from standards mean higher costs and less value received for the purchaser's dollar. This is confirmed by value analysis studies that show many instances where simply switching from a specially fabricated part to a standard part of equal utility results in cost savings of as much as 75 percent.

Along with this cost advantage is the factor of greater availability and more prompt delivery. Standard items are normally "shelf items" that can be promptly furnished from manufacturers' or distributors' stocks or those that have a regular place in the supplier's production schedule so that delays are minimized. Special items, on the other hand, must be fitted into the production schedule, often involving a delay of weeks or months. Thus, the normal procurement cycle or lead time is lengthened by the addition of scheduling procedure and the actual production cycle. Procurement of emergency fill-in quantities becomes excessively difficult, if not impossible.

STANDARDIZATION CUTS INVENTORY COSTS

One of the chief benefits of standardization is the possibility of reduced material and supply inventories. With fewer types and sizes and qualities of items to be carried in stock, a smaller total inventory can support the manufacturing program. The prudent quantitative safety margin on a single item protects requirements for all its various uses or applications. There is greater flexibility in meeting the demands of changing rates in the usage of any given item, and the danger of incurring losses through obsolescence is minimized. Reduced total inventories release working capital for other, more productive purposes. This is a constant objective of management.

At the same time, stock turnover is faster, so that there is less accrued carrying cost to add to the real cost of material up to the time of use.

STANDARDIZATION PROGRAMS

An effective company standardization program depends upon definite assignment of responsibility and continuing attention to the subject. In some companies it is set up as a function in itself, under the supervision of a standards engineer or of a director of standards. More common practice is to undertake standardization as a committee activity. This is perhaps the more logical procedure, because standardization is essentially a process of securing agreement among those responsible for specification and use of materials, those responsible for product design, and those charged with the procurement of the needed items. All these factors should be represented in any form of permanent committee organization, with provision for participation on particular projects by individuals or department heads directly affected. Where no standardization committee has previously existed, the purchasing department frequently is the one to initiate such an activity; often as not, the purchasing representative serves as its chairman.

One of the first objectives of the program is to establish standard nomenclature for all materials used. Analysis of stockroom inventories often reveals instances of duplication in which identical items may be carried under two or more identifying descriptions. This can easily happen when an item is requisitioned by and purchased for different departments, each of which uses its own term to describe the item; or, if a part is identified by the manufacturer's part or catalog number, or by the company's own part number for a particular end use in product assembly, it is often the case that two or more such parts are actually identical and interchangeable, although they may be independently requisitioned, purchased, and recorded. Effective standardization of materials cannot be achieved without standard means of identification.

Analysis of stockroom records reveals other pertinent information: excessively slow-moving items and materials carried in a multiplicity of sizes and grades. Data of this sort can be the starting point for study regarding the feasibility of standardization in particular areas. Another starting point may be found in purchase records. All materials do not pass through a central stockroom and do not appear on stores records. But, in the usual organization of a purchasing staff by commodity groupings, related items are generally handled by one buyer, and it is usually a simple matter to detect similar products used by several departments, excessive varieties of a single basic product purchased, and deviations from normal usage.

Aims of a standardization program are (1) adoption of company-wide standards for materials used for like or similar purposes, (2) correlation of these company standards with established industry standards to the greatest possible degree, and (3) reduction in the number of varieties and sizes to be purchased.

The Standard Stock Catalog

The work of a standardization committee generally results in decisions as to which materials and supplies are to be carried in stores as standard stock items. This information is frequently incorporated in a standard stock list or catalog, often a computer printout showing all stock items, identified by standard nomenclature with whatever cross-reference may be required, detailing all sizes of each item regularly carried in stores. Requisitions are expected to conform to this list, and users can expect immediate supply of listed items. The list is revised as new items are added by action of the committee or as standards are changed in view of changing requirements and usage. On common supply items, requests for nonlisted varieties are automatically questioned and are procurable only under exceptional circumstances, for good reason.

SOME PERFORMANCE OBJECTIVES

After studying this chapter you should be able to:

1. Give a brief definition of value analysis and explain the distinction, if any, between value analysis and value engineering.
2. Name the "ten tests for value" discussed in the text.
3. Use some or all of these tests in a simple value analysis of some product (and its components) that you use or are familiar with.
4. List the reasons for giving the purchasing department a leading role in a company's value analysis program.
5. Discuss the supplier's role in customers' value analysis program. Explain how a supplier might take the initiative in helping to organize a value program in a company that does not have one.
6. Explain why standardization is an important element in value analysis and standardization, employing, when possible, examples of standardization in some products that you use.

It has been obvious throughout this and previous chapters that the goal of purchasing is to obtain maximum value in acquiring company requirements from suppliers, using various forms of organization, methods, and techniques. But the process of locating, selecting, and evaluating suppliers is not automatic. The special expertise required in this extremely important phase of purchasing is the subject of the next chapter.

Selection and Evaluation of Suppliers

13

To make a satisfactory purchase, it is necessary to find a capable and willing vendor and to reach an agreement with that vendor on quality, service, and price. Scientific purchasing does not leave the matter to chance. The buyer seeks to find the best sources of supply for his or her needs. In some cases this will be a matter of making a choice from among many possible and approximately equally promising sources. In other cases it may be a problem involving extensive search to find one satisfactory supplier or even to develop a source where none had previously been available.

FOUR STAGES OF SELECTION

In the actual process of source selection, there are four stages: (1) the survey stage, in which all possible sources for a product are explored; (2) the inquiry stage, in which the relative qualifications and advantages of potential sources are analyzed; (3) the stage of negotiation and selection, leading to the issue of an initial order; and (4) the experience stage, in which a continuing vendor–supplier relationship is established or the earlier steps are reviewed in the search for a more satisfactory source.

As in all purchasing problems, the starting point is the need for a material or product. The exact specifications may or may not be fixed, but its general nature and purpose are known. What is available on the market? Who makes such a product, or who can make it? Who can supply it most satisfactorily and most economically?

The original survey of potential sources should overlook no possibilities, provided that they are reasonably accessible and that there is some assurance that they meet required standards of quality, service, and price. Trade directories provide comprehensive and well-organized listings of the whole range of manufactured products and manufacturers on a nationwide basis, usually with at least a general indication of size and commercial rating. Supplementing these are regional directories such as those issued by state Chambers of Commerce and, on a still more local scale, the classified section of telephone directories. Specialized trade directories are available listing concerns that do not have product lines of their own but provide industrial services, such as foundries, screw machine shops, heat treaters, custom fabricators of plastic parts, and the like. With the continued expansion of world markets, more and more directories of suppliers in foreign countries are becoming available (see Chapter 18).

The buyer's library of manufacturers' and distributors' catalogs is another reference source of prime importance, provided that the indexing system is adequate. Many purchasing agents also have a commodity information file in which they have collected vendors' mailing pieces and data sheets, advertisements, and new product announcements from business magazines. Some of this information is so new that it has not yet found its way into the standard catalogs, but the alert buyer has it on hand when needed.

Salespersons are an important source of information, both on their companies' products and capabilities and on their application to customers' processes. Experience has shown that the most successful salespersons are those who have not limited their service to buyers to merely selling the product at hand. Their psychology aims more toward meeting the buyer's need, not only with products but also with whatever information, service, and technical advice are available from their companies.

From the information gleaned from these various sources, the buyer can build a workable list of the most likely sources. The buyer will select those who seem to combine the attributes of reliability and stability, appropriate manufacturing ability and experience, and reasonably convenient location to avoid excessive transportation costs. Some of them the buyer may know by reputation or through their advertising. The buyer will exclude those having very low capitalization or credit ratings, those whose products are not in the general quality range that he or she requires, those outside his or her normal trading area, and any with whom he or she may have had previous unsatisfactory experience. If the product required is of a routine nature, the buyer may send out a request for bids from such a selected list. If the product is more significant, and one for which there is likely to be a continuing need, there will be an intermediate stage of inquiry and research.

STUDY OF SUPPLY SOURCES

The second stage of supplier selection narrows the field from possible sources to acceptable sources. Inquiry at this stage is directed toward developing more specific information on vendors' production facilities and capacity, financial stability, product quality, technical competence, manufacturing efficiency, general business policies, position in the industry, progressiveness, interest in the buyer's order, and cooperative attitude. The aim at this point is to find those suppliers who are capable of producing the item in the required quality and quantity, who can be relied on as a continuous source of supply under all conditions, who will keep their delivery promises and other service obligations, and who are competitive on price. Visits to supplier facilities are important in this stage.

Particular features to be noted at the plant of a supplier or prospective supplier are modernity and efficiency of equipment, facilities for technical controls and the importance attached to such controls, caliber of supervision and inspection, evidences of good management and good housekeeping in plant operations, practice as to the maintenance of raw material stocks, and the character of the operation, especially as it relates to purchasing requirements and practices. Personal contacts should also be established with key people in management and production as a very helpful asset in the event that emergency or special requirements need to be discussed later at long distance.

When the projected purchase involves substantial expenditure, or when the quality of the part to be bought is critical, inspection and evaluation of potential vendors is generally made a team effort. A typical team will include representatives from the purchasing, quality control, engineering, and production departments, although the makeup of the group may vary. A West Coast manufacturer of complex electronic controls, for example, requires that a team consisting only of purchasing and quality control personnel check out suppliers of critical parts before they are accepted.

Customarily, supplier survey teams follow a standard pattern of inspection and collection of information. The purchasing quality team just mentioned surveys ten areas:

1. written procedures
2. purchase order control
3. in-process control

4. final test and acceptance
5. shipping
6. contract drawing and specification change control
7. calibration control
8. control of nonconforming supplies
9. inspection control
10. records

Depending on the nature of the item being considered for purchase, the supplier's reputation, and other factors, other teams might give more attention to condition and capabilities of machines, shop methods, inventory, housekeeping, and so forth. The inspection can be speeded by having the supplier provide some basic information before the team's visit. One purchasing department, for example, asks suppliers to fill in the vendor capability survey form shown in Figure 13-1 before deciding on how extensive an analysis the evaluation team should make.

The result of the study at this point should be a list of several acceptable supply sources, not only capable of furnishing the requirements, but with any of whom the buyer would be willing to place his or her order. The list is not necessarily in order of preference. It may come very close to that point of decision, but, in the orderly process of vendor appraisal and narrowing of choice, there still remains the stage of negotiation in which details and terms are considered, to determine where the best ultimate value lies. Basically this will be in terms of quality, service, and price. Beyond that, it will be influenced by the intangibles of interest, cooperation, and goodwill that enhance the value of all these factors. Beyond that, the decision may hinge on special circumstances—the smaller company in which the order will have an importance that is lost in the larger operation, the company that has an engineer or superintendent particularly skilled in that type of production, or the company that has an open spot in its manufacturing schedule to accomodate the order.

As a matter of fact, there may be no *one* best source, for the buyer usually wishes to establish alternative sources for the products that he or she buys, both as an added assurance of supply and to maintain competition. Then the decision as to where the bulk of the business will be placed will be made on the basis of a fourth and convincing criterion—experience.

THE APPROVED LIST

Before taking up the evaluation and rating of vendor performance, the practice of buying from alternative sources should be examined further.

VENDOR CAPABILITY SURVEY

SURVEY DATE _____

COMPANY NAME _____ □ CORPORATION   □ PARTNERSHIP

ADDRESS _____ □ OTHER _____

PHONE NO. _____ DATE ESTABLISHED _____ STATE OF INCORPORATION _____

SUBSIDIARY OF _____ DIVISION OF _____

CREDIT RATING _____ SECURITY CLEARANCE _____

OFFICIALS (OWNERS)	TITLE	KEY PERSONNEL	TITLE

□ MASS PRODUCTION   □ JOB SHOP   □ MACHINING   □ FINISHING   □ ASSEMBLY

□ TESTING   □ ENGINEERING   □ RES. & DEV.   □ OTHER _____

NORMAL PRODUCTS OR SERVICES	DEFENSE	COMMERC.

CUSTOMER REFERENCES	ITEMS PRODUCED FOR THEM

FACILITIES	SQUARE FEET	OWNED	LEASED	LEASE EXPIRES	PERSONNEL DIRECT	INDIRECT	UNION	NON UNION
OFFICE AREA								
ENGINEERING AND LAB. AREA								
MANUFACTURING AREA								
TOTAL								

UNION AFFILIATION	LOCAL NO.	CONTRACT EXPIRATION DATE

EQUIPMENT:
ATTACH LIST OF MACHINE TOOLS, SPECIAL TEST AND OTHER EQUIPMENT. GIVE GENERAL CONDITION AND INDICATE WHETHER OWNED, LEASED, OR GOVERNMENT FURNISHED.   EQUIP LIST DATED

Figure 13-1. Front side of form used by some purchasing departments in evaluating potential suppliers is filled in by the company being evaluated. If preliminary data warrant further investigation, a survey team will be sent to the supplier's plant for more detailed analysis of operations and capabilities.

Purchasing policy in most companies traditionally requires at least two supply sources for each item, and management generally supports this policy as being in the best interest of the company. Whether there should be more than two, and how many, is a matter of purchasing judgment and the way in which the list is used. It depends partly on the importance of the item, on competitive conditions in the supplier industry, and on the quantities involved, which might make it practicable to divide the business among several suppliers.

In the preceding sections we have traced the finding and selection of suppliers, assuming the company has never purchased the item before. Acceptability of the source has been considered strictly from the purchasing viewpoint. It is assumed that the requirement has been defined or specified so that the delivered product, in accordance with the specification, will also be acceptable to all concerned. Deciding on the source, then, is entirely a responsibility of purchasing.

Now take another example. The company engineers have designed a product incorporating a common electrical part. For their development work they have selected such a part from a manufacturer's catalog or from an electrical supply house. Their main interest has been merely to find something that will serve the desired purpose. The selected part proves satisfactory and is incorporated in the product design. In drawing up a bill of materials for the first production order, the part is naturally specified by the manufacturer's name and catalog number.

When the purchasing manager receives the requisition to purchase, the manager is bound to conform to this request, and does so. However, he or she properly challenges the specification that ties the requirement to a single source and succeeds in having it modified by the addition of the words "or equal." Now the purchasing manager has leeway for choice on succeeding orders, but, because the original part was specified for its known successful performance, the buyer is not to be the sole judge of equality. The buyer is not authorized to make a substitution arbitrarily, without the consent of the specifying engineers. Neither is it practicable for the buyer to go to them for approval every time the item comes up for purchase and he or she wishes to consider an alternate.

So the buyer promptly starts a search for acceptable alternative products and sources. When he or she locates a promising new source, the buyer procures samples for inspection and test. Let us say that three such samples are approved as acceptable alternatives for the item first specified. Now, instead of a single source, the buyer has an "approved list" of four suppliers. The buyer enters their names, along with that of the original supplier, on the purchase record card for the item. It is now the buyer's privilege to patronize any one of the four at his or her own discretion. Or, the buyer has a mailing list ready-made for issuing invitations to bid, with the assurance that any one of the offerings will be acceptable as to quality and suitability.

It is quite likely that the buyer will continue to purchase the bulk of his or her requirement from the source originally named, provided that there is a real preference for the product and that the supplier's price and service are satisfactory. But the buyer will also make some purchases from the others or give them a chance to quote regularly to maintain their interest. An alternative source that is merely another name on a list represents no advantage either to the buyer or the seller. The approved list of supply sources must be used to be useful.

Sentiment in favor of approved vendor lists was strongly reinforced by purchasing executives' experiences during the extreme shortages of 1973–1974. A nationwide survey of purchasing managers in 1977 showed that 80 percent of the respondents were using approved vendor lists, and of those 37 percent had adopted the procedure in the previous five years.[1]

One purchasing manager explained his reasons for use of such lists:

> We feel that we must have the proper quality, pricing, and reliability that can be achieved only through the use of preapproved vendors. Reliability is the key—we cannot afford the disappointments of the 1973–1974 period a second time.

Another purchasing executive put his case for the approved list more bluntly:

> There were no good performers during the shortage crisis. But some suppliers were less bad than others. We want to make sure that, if we ever face a similar situation again, we'll at least have the less bad suppliers in our stable.

Two major criticisms are made of the approved list as a purchasing method. One of these is that it is discriminatory and serves to blacklist any potential supplier who is not included, whereas every seller should at least be accorded the privilege of quoting for business if he or she so desires. The other is that it imposes a limitation on the buyer himself or herself and that it restricts the scope of his or her choice.

Flexibility and periodical review will overcome both objections. As to the first criticism, it is assumed that all qualified sources of supply have been investigated and have been given an opportunity to present their story when the list was being built and that, if conditions have changed in any essential particular or if new sources enter the field, the opportunity

---

[1] "Vendors: Only 'Good Guys' Finish," *Purchasing World*, Vol. 21 (September 1977), p. 42.

will be given. If they can at any time establish any good reason why they should be added to the list, or replace one of the suppliers already included, that claim should be given full consideration, because the purchasing manager is naturally interested in maintaining his or her list at the highest possible standard.

As to the second criticism, the limitation on the buyer, if any, is a self-imposed one. In principle, that limitation is set by either of two conditions: the absence of additional competent sources, from technical or commercial angles, or the practical limits of a working list beyond the basic assurance of supply and reasonable competition.

EVALUATING SUPPLIERS

The real test of vendor selection is, of course, the test of experience, or satisfactory performance by the vendor once the order has been placed with him or her. It is listed here as the fourth step in selection because it does more than confirm or refute the buyer's judgment and decision. It is the deciding factor in whether the selected vendor will continue to receive the buyer's business or be replaced by another source.

Objective evaluation and rating of vendor performance has gained considerable acceptance in purchasing departments of all types in recent years. But, even when sophisticated, computerized systems are used to compile comparative statistics on vendor performance, interpretation of those statistics is left to the buyer's judgment.

Rating systems generally involve the three basic considerations in a good purchase—quality, service (delivery), and price—although any one of the factors named may be given more weight than the others. Quality is most important, for example, for a manufacturer of complex components for spacecraft. Price might be given equal weight in an evaluation system used by the manufacturer of highly competitive, "throw-away" items like party novelties. A typical vendor rating form is shown in Figure 13-2.

Formulas for rating suppliers vary in complexity, again depending on the nature of the item being bought, the quality required, and competition within the supplying industry.

One company that buys its requirements under blanket orders uses a relatively simple system to measure supplier performance on two counts: quality and delivery. (Price performance had already been determined when the contract was originally set up.) Each shipment against the order is rated as follows: by date requested, 100 percent; 1 day late, 98 percent; 2 days late, 95 percent, and so on down to 73 percent for 6 days late. If quality is to specifications, the supplier is rated 100 percent. If

VENDOR RATING REPORT

J. M. HUBER CORPORATION

COMPANY — DATE

Company:

	Excellent (4)	GOOD (3)	FAIR (2)	POOR (1)
Size and/or Capacity	4			
Financial Strength		3		
Operational Profit		3		
Manufacturing Range	4			
Research Facilities			2	
Technical Service		3		
Geographical Locations	4			
Management		3		
Labor Relations		3		
Trade Relations		3		
Total 32	12	18	2	

.63 x Total = 20.16

Service

	Excellent (4)	GOOD (3)	FAIR (2)	POOR (1)
Deliveries on Time	4			
Condition on Arrival		3		
Follow Instructions		3		
Number of Rejections	4			
Handling of Complaints		3		
Technical Assistance			2	
Emergency Aid		3		
Supply Up to Date Catalogues, Etc.				1
Supply Price Changes Promptly	4			
Total 27	12	12	2	1

.69 x Total = 18.63

TOTAL RATING

Products:

	Excellent (4)	GOOD (3)	FAIR (2)	POOR (1)
Quality	4			
Price		3		
Packaging		3		
Uniformity	4			
Warranty	4			
Total 18	12	6		

1.25 x Total = 22.50

Sales Personnel

	Excellent (4)	GOOD (3)	FAIR (2)	POOR (1)
1. Knowledge				
His Company		3		
His Products	4			
Our Industry		3		
Our Company		3		
2. Sales Calls				
Properly Spaced	4			
By Appointment		3		
Planned and Prepared		3		
Mutually Productive	4			
3. Sales-Service				
Obtain Information		3		
Furnish Quotations Promptly	4			
Follow Orders		3		
Expedite Delivery		3		
Handle Complaints		3		
Total 43	16	27		

.48 x Total = 20.64

Figure 13-2. Vendor rating form used by J. M. Huber Corporation. Evaluation categories are weighted according to importance (e.g., "Product" category is weighted 1.25, "Service" is next at .69). Individual factors (e.g., quality, delivery, etc.) have descending values, from four points for excellent to one point for poor. Total of points in each category is multiplied by the weight for that category.

using departments complain about quality of the shipment, the rating drops to 95 percent. For each complaint thereafter, the supplier loses 5 more percentage points.

Suppliers are notified periodically of their performance records. Suppliers falling below 80 percent on delivery and quality are warned that they are in danger of losing the business unless their performance improves.

A Comprehensive System

A more comprehensive mathematical vendor-rating formula has been developed in the purchasing department of a large manufacturing company. It is known as the "incoming material rating" rather than as a vendor rating because the calculation is based upon experience with a single item or product; this is its logical application as a buying tool when procurement of that product is under consideration. It is designed to provide a comparative evaluation of vendor performance in any case in which an item is procured from two or more sources.

This formula is based upon the principles that (1) the evaluation of a vendor's performance must embrace all three major purchasing factors—quality, price, and service—and (2) the relative importance of these factors varies in respect to various items. The first step, therefore, is to assign appropriate weights to each, adding up to a total weighting factor of 100 points. For example, in a given case, quality performance might be rated at 40 points, price at 35, and service at 25, and these percentages are subsequently used as multipliers for individual ratings on each of the three purchasing factors. The assignment of these weights is a matter of judgment. In the company in which this system originated, the importance of quality ranges from 35 to 45 percent, price from 30 to 40 percent, and service from 20 to 30 percent.

The quality rating is a direct percentage of the number of acceptable lots received in relation to total lots received.

In rating price, the lowest net price (gross price minus discounts plus unit transportation cost) obtained from any vendor is taken as 100 points, and net prices from other vendors are rated in inverse ratio to this figure.

The service rating is a direct percentage of the lots received as promised, in relation to total lots received.

These three ratings are multiplied by their respective weighting factors and the results are added to give a numerical "incoming material rating" for each vendor, for a given item. Perfect deliveries, on scheduled time, at the lowest net price earn a rating of 100 points. Any rejections, lapses in delivery, or prices higher than the lowest quotation reduce the rating. At the same time, there is an objective basis for determining the extent to which superior quality and service offset higher prices in overall value and satisfaction, or vice versa.

Example:

Vendor A has delivered 58 lots during the past year, of which two were rejected. The percentage of good lots is 96.5. Multiplied by the weight factor of 40, this gives vendor A a quality rating of 38.6.

The lowest net price from any vendor is $0.93 per unit. A's price is $1.07. By inverse ratio, A's price performance is 86.9 percent. Multiplied by the weight factor of 35, this gives vendor A a price rating of 30.4.

Of the 58 lots delivered, 55 were received as promised. This is 94.8 percent performance. Multiplied by the weight factor of 25, it gives vendor A a service rating of 23.7.

The sum of these figures gives vendor A a total performance rating of 92.7.

Vendor B, who furnished 34 lots during the same period, was the lowest-price supplier at $0.93 per unit, so has a price rating of the full 35 points. However, four of the lots were defective, giving B a quality rating of 35.3. Also vendor B was late with five deliveries, so B's service rating is 21.3, for a total performance rating of 91.6.

In this instance, therefore, vendor A is judged to be the more satisfactory source, and the buyer is warranted in placing the bulk of the business with A in spite of A's substantially higher price. If vendor B could be induced to cut delinquencies in either quality or service by one half, or if the price factor were deemed relatively more important in respect to this item, B would have the better rating.

ESTABLISHING THE SUPPLIER RELATIONSHIP

The aim of careful vendor selection is to find the one most satisfactory source, or a group of alternative sources with adequate and reasonably comparable qualifications. Thus succeeding orders for the same item can be placed with these same suppliers with confidence in the original selection. In other words, the decision as to a source of supply contemplates a continuing relationship.

It is to be expected that this relationship will improve with experience and growth in mutual understanding. The purchasing manager, on his or her part, should make every effort to foster that improvement. The elements that contribute to such improvement include:

Completeness and clarity of communication concerning the need, the application and usage of the purchased material or product. The scope and limitations of the product itself. The outlook for continued usage and probable quantities required, and any special requirements of either a technical or commercial nature.

Mutual understanding of the conditions and problems of both usage and production, resulting from that communication.

Mutual confidence in the statements and intent of both parties.

Mutual consideration—no unreasonable demands, as much notice as possible in the event of changes in schedules or instructions. A fair and open mind in the discussion of differences, and willingness to waive or modify nonessential details of the agreement if the modification does not impair quality of service and is substantially to the advantage of either party.

A genuine interest in the mutual problem of procurement and supply, rather than mere contract fulfillment. This includes suggestions for cost reduction in the product itself and in methods of packing, shipping, usage, and accounting.

Cooperation—an active effort to fulfill contract obligations, prompt shipment by the supplier to minimize the need for inquiries and expediting action, and prompt processing and payment of invoices by the buyer.

Continuous improvement of ordering methods and supplier service as the opportunities arise.

Cultivation of personal contacts in the buying and selling organizations, making for better liaison and goodwill.

Many companies have found it helpful to hold annual, or more frequent, suppliers' conferences, when vendors are invited to gather at the buyer's plant, to see at firsthand how their materials or parts are used, to share in the pride of product, and to be briefed on the reasons for certain buying policies and for the insistence on certain quality specifications. Conversely, buyers find it advantageous to make periodic visits to the plants of their suppliers to see at firsthand how the things that they buy are produced and to keep in touch with the problems and progress of supplier industries.

Loyalty to Vendors

A continuing buyer–seller relationship, based on mutual confidence and satisfaction, implies a policy (and, indeed, a responsibility) of loyalty to suppliers. This is the antithesis of opportunism and constant "shopping around" in purchasing. It is true that some cost savings can be made by such methods, but it is usually at the sacrifice of uniformity and continuity of supply and of most of the factors that have been cited as making up good supply service. Especially, it sacrifices the assurance of supply that is the first responsibility in purchasing. Without established and loyal sources of supply, every recurring requirement presents a procurement problem of the first order, and the work of the purchasing department is magnified beyond all reason and proportion.

Experienced purchasing managers are in practical agreement that the long-range considerations of reasonable cost and of satisfaction and value in respect to purchases are best attained through a consistent policy toward supply sources. And a sound purchasing program, like any sound business program, is based on long-range considerations. The buyer who relies on opportunism to gain an immediate advantage makes himself or herself and the company the vulnerable prey of opportunism in selling.

A high rate of turnover among suppliers suggests either that the purchaser's company is basically an undesirable customer or that wrong decisions as to supply sources have been made in the first place.

ASSISTING AND DEVELOPING SOURCES OF SUPPLY

So far in this chapter we have assumed that adequate sources exist to supply every need and that the purchasing agent's problem is merely one of selection from among the available suppliers. In the majority of cases, and under normal business conditions, this assumption holds true. However, the exceptions to the rule are equally important in the complete supply program and are likely to present difficulties that will put the procurement officer's resourcefulness to a severe test. The buyer's survey and search for the most satisfactory source may result in the discovery that no satisfactory or willing source can be found; yet the requirement exists, and it is the buyer's responsibility to meet it.

Products or parts that have not previously been made, intricacies of special design, unusual requirements in the specification or difficult conditions of application and use, and the utilization of new or unfamiliar materials for which there is little precedent in treatment and fabrication are some of the factors that may lead to a situation for which no established supply source stands ready at hand. Or, from the standpoint of practical procurement, the only available sources may be too distant, prices may be exorbitant or out of line with budgeted costs for the product, production capacity may already be fully occupied so that no new customers may be accommodated, or the potential suppliers may simply be unwilling or uninterested in additional business.

The process in its earlier stages is like that already described. However the emphasis of the search is placed on qualifications, equipment, and experience in a similar type of operation that might logically be applied to production of the material or part in question. Then, in place of a process of elimination or narrowing of the field, the buyer must concentrate on the most likely sources, persuading them to undertake the desired production and, if necessary, helping to implement their plant and personnel for such expansion or conversion of facilities as may be needed. In such cases, procurement is partly a matter of selling ability, seeking to establish the buyer's company as a desirable customer in the same way that the salesperson normally seeks to establish his or her company as a desirable supplier. Among the incentives offered are the steady flow of guaranteed orders over a period of time at a satisfactory price level, technical assistance in setting up the process on an efficient basis that will result in a satisfactory product, assistance in the procurement of raw materials even to the point of furnishing such materials for fabrication only by the supplier, so that risks of waste and spoilage in the initial stages are for the account of the buyer, and, sometimes, subsidizing the costs of new equipment and tooling until they may be absorbed by the volume of business that develops.

SOCIOECONOMIC FACTORS IN SOURCE SELECTION

The use of purchasing power as a tool in the achievement of certain social objectives came into prominence in the late 1960s and early 1970s. The social unrest of those decades, the growth of consumerism, the awareness of industry leaders that social health was linked to economic health, and the growing intervention of the government in the private sector—all contributed to complicating purchasing decisions that had been based primarily on economic considerations. Supplier selection, or the selection of the bidders' list, may well be influenced by community pressure for social reform or by regulations that restrict freedom of choice, it was noted in the *Purchasing Handbook*.[2]

As the *Purchasing Handbook* points out, most management policies and government regulations that deal with socioeconomic matters do not require the payment of premiums, but they do encourage competitive procedures. This is particularly so in the encouragement and assistance given to minority suppliers to help *make them competitive,* so that they may remain in the mainstream of the country's economic life. "Coddling" such suppliers with, for example, premium prices would only weaken them in the long run and defeat the whole purpose of the minority business program. (More details on management policy in respect to minority business are given in Chapter 20.)

The socioeconomic policies mentioned, the *Handbook* goes on to say, are aimed at legitimate objectives that society has come to accept as

---

[2] *Purchasing Handbook* (New York: Section 6, 3rd ed. McGraw-Hill, 1973).

desirable and necessary. However, the buyer should be aware, it is noted, that a supplier's freedom of choice may be restricted by the pursuit of social objectives and that the price paid, while competitive, may reflect the cost of the achievement of social goals.

Among the socioeconomic factors with which purchasing management has had to deal are (1) the use of small businesses as suppliers to government prime contractors, (2) placement of subcontracts in areas of labor surplus, (3) use of nonpolluting materials, and (4) placement of business with minority suppliers. The objectives and operations of one corporate minority purchasing program are shown in Figure 13-3.

SUBCONTRACTING

Defense purchasing brought into general business usage a term that had previously been largely confined to the construction industries but is now a permanent part of the vocabulary and policy of procurement. A distinction is made between "prime contractors," whose contract is directly with some governmental procurement agency as buyer, and "subcontractors," who contribute to the fulfillment of that contract but have no direct contractual relationship with the government. Their own specific contracts are with the prime contractors or with "subcontractors of the first tier," as the process of subcontracting is repeated in successive stages down the line. The emphasis in this terminology is on the end product called for in the prime contract.

Essentially, subcontracting is purchasing, and the subcontractor is a supplier. In the defense usage of the term, certain special characteristics of the relationship differentiate it from ordinary procurement and call for special handling. The purchased product is specifically identified with the project and end product of the purchaser; priority ratings on the material used follow through procurement and operations in both plants; and in wartime utilization of the purchased parts or products was definitely allocated. This presents a condition distinctly different from procurement of parts for stock or for application, at the buying company's option, to any need that might arise. Many of the terms of the prime contract are required to be passed along to the subcontract, by reference to the original document, even though there is no direct contractual responsibility between the subcontractor and the government, the ultimate recipient of the product. From the standpoint of the prime contractor's purchasing department unusually close contacts have to be maintained to see that schedules are properly and positively coordinated with the buyer's assembly program. Altogether, a much larger share of responsibility for the subcontractor's performance rests upon the pur-

What is Pfizer's Minority Purchasing Program

The Pfizer Minority Purchasing Program is a total Corporate effort to involve minority businesses in our overall purchasing of Goods and Services. Pfizer hopes to initiate and develop mutually beneficial and lasting relationships with minority owned businesses.

There is a strong commitment from Pfizer's management to see that minority economic development is encouraged on a continuing and long-term basis.

Pfizer is therefore seeking qualified vendors who can answer the call to provide a product or service of high quality at a reasonable price.

If you can meet these standards and are interested in selling to Pfizer, Pfizer is interested in hearing from you.

Who to see at Pfizer Corporate Purchasing Division

Corporate Purchasing
Pfizer World Headquarters
235 East 42nd Street
New York, N.Y. 10017

Steven Sheffield
Corporate Manager
Minority Supplier Program
212-573-2448

All inquiries about Pfizer's Minority Purc[...]
Program should be directed to Mr. Sheff[...]

Appointments can be arranged to revie[...]
discuss your potential as a supplier for [...]

Pfizer Inc.

Pharmaceuticals & Health Care
Chemicals
Consumer Products
Agricultural Products
Materials Science Products

Major Items Purchased

Raw Materials & Chemicals
Fuel Oil
Packaging Components
Promotional Items
Capital Equipment
Construction
Laboratory Chemicals
& Equipment

Janitorial Supplies/Services
Printing
Forms & Stationery
Electrical, Mechanical,
Plumbing Supplies (MRO)
Furniture, Office Supplies
Professional Services

Business Profile

Suggested Supplier information to provide at initial Sales Presentation.

General Information

A. Company Name, mailing address, phone number
B. Owner's Name, type of ownership

Current Services & Capabilities

A. Describe your product and/or service — supply a brochure if available.
B. Describe your facility, operation, equipment, etc. Provide samples of your work if applicable.
C. How long in business? Last year's sales? Number of customers?

Customer Reference

List Company name, address, phone number and key person to contact for representative major customers. Note: If you are a construction contractor include a brief description of recent projects and cost of projects.

Financial Reference

List the financial institution with which you are doing business. Give complete name, address, and person to contact.

Figure 13-3. Pages from a corporate brochure soliciting inquiries from minority businesses. Pfizer also offers technical assistance on a volunteer basis from members of management even though companies needing it are not participating in the minority purchasing program.

chasing manager than in normal procurement condition. Some variations from normal types of contracts have also been developed. For example, instead of contracting for delivery of a particular part or product, some companies contract for certain machine capacity and machine time in a subcontractor's plant, to be used as the buyer might direct. Under such an arrangement, the buyer furnishes raw materials, schedules production, and provides supervision.

As a result of these special conditions, the typical organization for subcontracting is a special division within the purchasing department for this purpose. In some companies, the procedure is considered as a separate managerial and administrative function, apart from the purchase of materials for use in plant production operations, and special subcontracting departments are set up outside the jurisdiction of the purchasing department. The reasoning behind such an arrangement is indicated by the fact that such departments are sometimes known as "outside production" departments.

In common industrial usage, the term "subcontracting" has reference to such parts or products as could be produced with the buyer's own facilities and would normally be manufactured within his or her own organization. Successful subcontracting, as suggested, regards the operations of the supplier as part of a continuous process, leading up to and including the operations in the buyer's own plant. In this concept, the supplier's material control, production efficiency, scheduling, and service are definitely the concern of the buyer and his company, to be handled with the maximum of cooperation and mutual assistance. So far as the subcontracts are concerned, the supplier's operations are a part of his or her customer's operation, even though they are carried on under a different roof and a different management.

"BUY" INSIDE THE COMPANY?

Normally, industrial requirements are satisfied by purchase of the needed product or material from some outside source. However, there is usually the alternative possibility of producing a needed part or product within the buyer's own organization, sometimes with potential advantages in cost, convenience, or control. This is not always feasible, but it should be considered. In a broad sense, the question "Make or buy?" must be answered in advance of every purchase, in the form of company policy if not by special analysis. This question may refer to a particular fabricated part for regular product use, or, on a broader scale, it may involve the decision of whether the company shall operate its own foundry department instead of purchasing castings or shall have its own printing department or undertake any one of a score of similar operations. It may likewise concern the making of special equipment, such as warehouse shelving, or major construction projects.

THE MAKE-OR-BUY DECISION

These decisions are presumably made before the requirement ever gets to the stage of a purchase requisition, and it is frequently outside the proper scope of purchasing department responsibility to find the answer. On the other hand, it is an ever-present consideration in determining the best method of procurement, even after a requisition has been received and regardless of previous practice. Therefore, purchasing is responsible for analyzing the relative merits and advantages of both procurement methods and of making policy recommendations if a change is indicated. Costs and conditions in the supplier industry may be such as to suggest very strongly the advisability of self-manufacture of products formerly purchased. It may also work in the other direction, when the possibility of advantageous purchase arrangements suggests the adoption of this method, even though such action may mean retirement of equipment and facilities formerly used in production. The whole program of subcontracting, discussed earlier in this chapter, is an example of procuring by purchase a wide variety of components, many of which would normally be produced in the purchaser's own plant.

The significance of the question "Make or buy?" and the amount of study justified in arriving at a decision depend largely on the dollar volume involved. If it concerns a product representing only a few thousand dollars of annual expenditure, it will not make much difference either way. If the amount reaches hundreds of thousands of dollars, it is frequently a matter of utilizing existing equipment balanced against the convenience and cost of procurement from outside sources. If the amount is more substantial, involving investment in new equipment, a full-scale analysis is indicated, going beyond direct cost considerations into matters of company policy, personnel, labor relations, plant layout, scheduling, and the numerous other details incident to any manufacturing program.

Cost Comparison

The decision of "make or buy" must be approached analytically and objectively. The company's own facilities must be considered as an alternative source of supply in competition with outside suppliers. A change in policy is not so simple as merely changing from one supply to another. When it is concerned only with manufacture of a particular part, utilizing surplus capacity or facilities already on hand, it may not be too serious a matter, and the policy could easily be revoked in case the results proved less advantageous than expected. But, in respect to larger and more significant items of supply, and particularly when new facilities are to be added or a new line of operation undertaken, it is likely to involve substantial tooling costs, investment in space and equipment, and enlargement of the organization, all of which represent a continuing problem of cost and efficient operation. A basic make-or-buy analysis worksheet is shown in Figure 13-4.

For this reason, a comparison of costs is one of the first considerations, though not necessarily the most important. Cost of purchased goods is accurately determinable. Complete cost up to the time of use is the significant figure: price, plus transportation charges, plus costs of handling and storage. This cost should be calculated on an annual basis and on the entire group of products that would be affected by a change in policy.

Against this figure must be balanced the total estimated cost of production. This should include not merely the cost of materials and direct labor, but investment and carrying charges, including depreciation on equipment, and overhead expenses, with due allowance for the possibility of idle time and production at less than capacity, normal waste and spoilage, and the other usual risks of management that are assumed by the supplier when goods are purchased. These costs should be calculated on the standard basis used throughout the company, because the new manufacturing operation will become a part of the company's general activities and must assume its share of the burden. Only when this has been done is a fair and accurate cost comparison possible. The factor of profit, which is necessarily a part of the supplier's price, is not a proper consideration for the buyer, because the buyer is concerned with costs, and the profit to his or her company accrues only in the sale of the finished product; however, efficient self-manufacture, elimination of sales expense, and consequent lower cost of components do enhance the profit potential in the eventual sales.[3]

---

[3] This is a controversial point in accounting. In vertically integrated industries, in which one division of a company manufactures components for another division and also sells to other consumers, it is customary to include a profit factor, with or without a differential in favor of the related plant when the product is transferred. In such cases the individual plants are responsible for their own overhead and must individually justify themselves by profitable operation as separate enterprises.

Dept. No. _____	MAKE OR BUY ANALYSIS WORKSHEET	DECISION
Project or Part #_____		MAKE ☐ BUY ☐
Quantity Needed_____		Date _____
Date Needed _____		Prepared By_____
		Approved By_____

	Purchased Cost	Manufactured Cost
A. Direct Variable Costs - Note A:		
1. Material - Include Variations for Major Products	$_____	$_____
2. Labor - Include Variations for Major Products		_____
Reroute		_____
Shift Premium		_____
Incentive Pay		_____
Etc.		_____
3. Subcontract	_____	_____
B. Overhead:		
1. Material Handling		_____
2. Indirect Labor	_____	_____
3. Hourly Supervision	_____	_____
4. Training - Include Special Skills	_____	_____
5. Set up	_____	_____
6. Overtime Premium	_____	_____
7. Vacation and Holiday Pay	_____	_____
8. Fringe Costs	_____	_____
9. Other Variable Costs:	_____	_____
	_____	_____
C. Semi-Variable and Fixed Costs - Note B:		
	_____	_____
D. Other Costs and Expenses - Note C:		
1. Purchasing, Shipping, Storage, Testing, Etc.	_____	_____
2. Division Administration	_____	_____
3. Division Engineering	_____	_____
TOTALS	$ (NOTE D)	$_____

NOTES:

A. Separate departmental labor hour and overhead rates may be preferable to the use of composite rates.
Total direct labor standard hours required _____

The divisional rate for overhead applied should be redetermined as substantial amounts of direct labor hours are absorbed in the make or buy products.

B. Semi-variable and fixed costs may be included for specific items.

C. These incremental and out-of-pocket costs are included only when quantities being considered are substantial in amount.

D. Includes vendor's invoice price and adjustments for out-of-pocket non-compensating costs included in the manufactured cost column.

Excess capacity costs should be included.   YES ☐ NO ☐

Tooling charges should be included.   YES ☐ NO ☐

COMMENTS:
_____ (Include vendor reference, delivery time, etc.)
_____
_____
_____

Figure 13-4. Worksheet for analyzing data on which the decision to make or buy is based.

Among the cost factors frequently mentioned as favoring the manufacture of parts rather than procurement by purchase is the possibility of spreading overhead charges over a greater volume of operations. This is more than merely an accounting device, but it is not always a complete answer. Where outside and inside costs are close, as they frequently are, other factors may be decisive. If a company is buying an item at, say, $40,000 but decides to make it at $50,000 to spread the overhead burden, a competitor who is still buying it at $40,000 acquires an immediate advantage that may alter the entire marketing situation.

The results of a complete cost comparison may seriously modify estimates of cost and other advantages based on casual judgment. Almost certainly, it will indicate the prudence of a highly selective approach to the question of "make or buy" based on detailed analysis of the individual case.

The Quantity Factor

Unit cost is not the only factor to be considered. The quantity of a requirement is important for several reasons. In the first place, it will help to determine whether or not the potential cost saving is sufficient to warrant the undertaking of a special manufacturing project or process. Second, it has an important bearing on actual costs through the economies of mass manufacture and the possibilities of absorbing initial costs. Third, as has already been suggested, it should be sufficiently large to ensure that any facilities that may be established or installed for the purpose will be kept reasonably fully occupied, so that overhead costs for idle time will not offset the unit-cost advantage.

A solution for the latter problem has been found in some cases by setting a basic production capacity that is large enough for economical production yet within the limit of minimum expected requirements. This is calculated to keep the facility running at capacity, any deficiencies being supplied by purchases from the outside. Many company printing departments are set up on this basis. The advantages, in addition to those of cost, include the convenience of having such facilities conveniently available, the possibility of producing rush jobs without waiting for an outside supplier to fit them into his or her schedule or paying premium prices for extra service, and the possibility of handling short runs and other special and commercially uneconomical requirements on a cost basis.

Any system of partial self-manufacture has the disadvantage of decreasing the desirability and the quantity purchasing appeal of that portion of the business that must still be procured from outside sources. In such a case, the outside vendor is likely to take the position that the buyer's company is a competitor and to give preference to other customers who purchase their total requirements.

Quality Control

The factors considered up to this point have been concerned largely with comparative costs and potential economies. This is not necessarily the determining factor in reaching a decision. It is quite possible that it will be found desirable to undertake, or to retain, the manufacture of a component part in the buyer's own plant when costs under this method are demonstrably and substantially higher than prices obtainable from outside sources.

Among the conditions that justify such high-cost procurement by manufacture, considerations of quality loom large. It is possible to have the assurance of strict quality control when the processing and fabrication of components are performed and supervised by the organization using them. In general, the greater the control required, either in analysis or in dimension, the more significant this consideration becomes. Close coordination and a single responsibility are frequently better than divided responsibility, and the maker's guaranty of the end product means more when control of the entire process and its component parts is in his or her own hands.

Furthermore, greater interest and effectiveness in quality development and improvement can be expected on the part of a producer who is following through from raw material to end product than from a supplier who is producing to strict specifications furnished by a customer.

Disadvantages of Manufacture

On the other side of the balance sheet, there are some disadvantages connected with the self-manufacture of component parts. Once the company is committed to such a policy, and particularly when special tooling or equipment has been installed for the purpose, an element of inflexibility is introduced into procurement. Freedom of selection is sacrificed, despite possible differences in cost or other factors. The assurance of supply that is gained by this additional control must be weighed against the loss of alternative sources.

The hazards of business and changing economic conditions, factors over which the buyer has no control but that affect markets and procurement, are now assumed by the buyer's company and may seriously alter the calculations upon which the decision was originally based. Such influences include cyclical and long-term trends in the supplier industry, changes in demand for the buyer's product affecting the nature and volume of requirements, technological advances, competitive conditions such as overcapacity in the industry, as well as a variety of unpredictable random factors such as war, government regulations, tax policies, and the like.

MAKE-OR-BUY CHECKLIST

One company that has made an exhaustive study of this problem as it applies to its own operations has compiled a checklist of six major sections to make sure that no significant factor is overlooked in the final decision. Every question in each category is weighed with the same question in mind, to arrive at these conclusions. The final step is to recapitulate six answers, to determine where the preponderance of reason lies, and to make the decision accordingly. The checklist asks the following questions:

1. Quality factors. Adherence to specifications? Quality control setup? Is proper equipment available? Experience in this type of work? Who pays for bad parts?

2. Capacity factors. Is space available? Is available space obtainable? Is machine time available? Must machinery be bought? Are outside finishing operations required? Is sales relationship a factor? Is stability of supplier relationships a factor? How much working capital is needed for inventory, and so forth? Is new capital investment needed? How much use have we for the new equipment? What return can we expect? Are our costs complete? Is absorption of internal overhead needed? Would total costs, including overhead absorption, be competitive?

3. Labor factors. Would layoffs be created? Would it help us hold the organization together? Must staff be increased? Is special training necessary? Are there union pressures? Is the labor rate comparative?

4. Scheduling factors. Can we get all necessary components on time? Have we the capacity to adjust to peaks or slowdowns? Would timing be surer with added sources? Are engineering changes frequent?

5. Skill factors. Is the best design experience available? Is the part natural to us? Is this the most profitable use of our executives' time? Is design–assistance relationship a factor? Do we have adequate measures of inside efficiency?

6. Cost comparison, on the basis of 100 pieces. Material cost, operations cost (direct labor, overhead, and profit), setup cost, tools repair allowance and spoilage, packing and shipping costs from outside supplier, tool charge (cost of tools per 100 pieces based on two years' run).

This is a very complete and scientific evaluation of the problem, dealing principally with the internal company factors involved. Before leaving this phase of the subject, however, it should be pointed out that make-or-buy decisions also have external effects and that there are some long-range considerations of this nature that should also have serious attention. The checklist section on capacity factors recognizes this by querying the effect on sales relationships and the stability of supply relationships.

It is not uncommon, in times of business decline, for manufacturers to switch from buying to making certain parts when excess capacity shows up in their own plants. Even if this is done as a temporary measure, rather than as a considered policy based on economy of manufacture, the immediate effect is to leave the suppliers of these parts stranded and to intensify for them the hardships of the business decline. The purchasing manager may well question the wisdom of such use of the make-or-buy alternative, especially if the decision is of a temporary nature. For, when business picks up and the buyer once again seeks parts and service from that vendor, the buyer will almost certainly find that the supplier relationship has deteriorated. In extreme cases, he or she may actually have lost that source of supply.

AUTHORIZING THE DECISION

It is apparent, from the many internal elements affected by the make-or-buy policy, that the decision is not one to be made by the purchasing executive alone, even though it is primarily a question of procurement method. It is within his or her province to make a recommendation for or against the method in respect to certain requirements of the materials program, and his or her recommendation should be supported with a detailed analysis of available outside sources, comparative costs, and other factors. His or her company, as is true for any other supplier, has the privilege of judging the profit potential and other advantages and disadvantages of the proposal that will determine whether it is advisable to undertake the production or to relinquish it in favor of outside purchase.

Production executives will naturally be in the best position to pass judgment on the equipment and facilities available or needed and on the practicability of the plan. Production and cost departments will check the purchasing manager's cost estimates. Financial officers will check the advisability of the capital investment involved. Technical and engineering advice will be sought on the advantages of quality control within the organization. Marketing executives are concerned with anything that will enhance the salability of the product and possibly with finding an outlet for surplus production from the new department. The final decision, after all these viewpoints have been presented, is a matter for top management.

SOME PERFORMANCE OBJECTIVES

After studying this chapter you should be able to:

1. List the important criteria used in determining (a) possible sources of supply and (b) acceptable sources of supply.
2. Identify the elements that make for stronger, longer-range buyer–seller relationships.
3. Explain the implications of a high turnover among suppliers.
4. Discuss some of the socioeconomic developments of recent years that have had an impact on purchasing.
5. Differentiate between purchasing and subcontracting.
6. List the major factors to be considered in arriving at a decision to make or buy a product.

With the selection of a supplier, the stage is set for one of the most critical activities in the purchasing cycle—negotiation. A certain amount of negotiation—working out a transaction that is mutually satisfactory to buyer and seller—is involved in every purchase, even the simplest one. Our concerns in the next chapter are the special negotiation skills and philosophies necessary in complex major purchases involving large dollar expenditures.

Art and Science of Negotiation

14

Negotiation, briefly discussed in an earlier chapter, was defined as "the process of working out a procurement and sales program together, to the point of reaching a mutually satisfactory agreement." Technically, this definition covers almost any transaction between a buyer and a supplier, from a telephone discussion about the price of a few gallons of lubricant to prolonged conferences on the terms of a major equipment purchase.

In practice, the term is generally applied in industrial purchasing to the more complex situations involving buyers and sellers, in which both make a number of proposals and counterproposals before an agreement is reached. The key word in the definition as far as this interpretation goes is *program,* which implies that something more is involved in the transaction than a simple comparison of bids or the acceptance of a catalog price.

NATURE OF NEGOTIATION

The nature of negotiation has been well defined in instructions issued to U.S. Air Force buying personnel:

> Procurement by negotiation is the art of arriving at a common understanding through bargaining on the essentials of a contract such as delivery, specifications, prices, and terms. Because of the interrelation of these factors with many others, it is a difficult art and requires the exercise of judgment, tact, and common sense. The effective negotiator must be a real shopper, alive to the possibilities of bargaining with the seller. Only through

an awareness of relative bargaining strength can a negotiator know where to be firm or where he may make permissive concessions in prices or terms.[1]

The process and techniques of negotiated purchasing deserve special attention for two basic reasons. First, the whole concept of negotiation is widely misunderstood, and in many cases suspect, even by persons engaged in purchasing. Second, technological change has made industrial procurement increasingly complex, particularly in defense-related industries. Simple, rule-of-thumb approaches to buying one-of-a-kind machines or systems, for example, are no longer adequate. Nor are they any longer satisfactory in the purchase of less complicated items like raw materials and maintenance supplies. The trend toward long-term purchase agreements (see the Buying Agreements discussion, page 54) on these commodities has placed special emphasis on many aspects of the transaction that are open to negotiation. Responsibility for holding inventory, timing of deliveries, methods of transportation, inspection, and prices are only a few of the factors that must be agreed upon before a purchase is complete.

BIDDING VERSUS NEGOTIATION

The confusion over the true meaning of "negotiation" is typified by the attitude of legislators and the general press toward the use of the process in government buying. A few years ago, when regular published Defense Department figures showed that over 90 percent of the dollar volume of purchases made by the military services was expended in negotiated purchasing, an outcry went up. Congressmen and editorial writers assailed negotiated purchasing as "secret buying" that all but eliminated competition for government business. The opponents of negotiation share an oversimplified view of purchasing: that the government would come out better in any purchase by letting its buyers select the lowest of a number of sealed bids rather than engage in negotiation. This approach is, of course, difficult and even impossible in the purchase of many types of military equipment—sophisticated electronic devices for which there is no existing model, for example, which account for a high percentage of the defense-procurement dollar. Buying by the bid system has its shortcomings even in relatively simple commodities such as uniforms and light vehicles. Among those pointed out in a study of defense procurement were

[1] Air Force Procurement Instructions, 3–101.50.

Unless the bid contains airtight specifications, the winning bidder will provide a product that meets specifications but does not always provide the performance the buyer expects.

The winning bidder often is the one who cuts quality to cut his price. The quality producer cannot afford to be competitive and is driven from the market. The buyer is than stuck with inferior merchandise that wears out or falls apart sooner than expected.

In industries like aircraft and shipbuilding, which depend heavily on government orders, the bidder good enough to get all or most of the government's business may drive competitors out of the field. He is then in a position to raise prices practically at will.

Many economists hold that, when an industry is dominated by two or three producers, the result can be an oligopolistic price structure, even without collusion. Producers behave in a rational manner on price and a follow-the-leader pattern develops. In this case, advertising bidding does not result in competition.[2]

Misunderstanding of negotiation is not limited to those who are unfamiliar with purchasing economics, however. Ironically, some purchasing agents put negotiation in the same category as haggling and consider it unethical or vulgar to bargain over prices. The president of the National Association of Purchasing Agents felt called upon to correct this idea—which is shared by some suppliers—in talks to his own organization. He said:

By negotiation the buyer takes the necessary initiative to optimize his position in any given purchase. Without negotiation, he is merely accepting the best offer given him.

Vigorous price competition is an essential ingredient of the free enterprise system. To refrain from seeking cost advantages through negotiation is to assume that the item price is priced right, that it is best for all concerned.

Much of the criticism of negotiation is directed at the methods used. But, within the limits of the law and the ethics of good business, the buyer is obligated by his position to aggressively go after the best price that will mean the least cost under the most favorable conditions available to his firm.

The unspoken criticism of negotiation is more likely to be leveled by suppliers who would like to find some haven for price protection where they would be immune to the results of sound, aggressive, and ethical negotiation. They want to protect their weakness of limited sales ability.[3]

[2] P. V. Farrell and D. S. Ammer, "The Truth About Military Buying," *Purchasing Magazine*, Vol. 43 October, 1957, p. 113.

[3] Russell T. Stark of Burroughs Corporation, in addresses to local chapters of the National Association of Purchasing Agents during 1962.

Negotiation as we have defined it—"the working out of a procurement and sales program together"—is generally used in the following situations, assuming that a relatively large amount of money is involved:

> When the purchase involves equipment of a unique or complicated nature that has not been purchased before and for which there is little cost information. A conveyor line for a new, automated food-processing plant would be a good example. Details of the construction, performance, and cost of such an installation would require involved technical discussions before a purchase were actually made.

> When prices on an item are fixed, by custom, "fair-trade" laws, or actual collusion among suppliers. If there are many suppliers in the field, good negotiating tactics are generally successful in winning concessions from one producer who is anxious to get the business.

> When there are few suppliers or only one in the field, but the product in question can be made in the buyer's own plant or bought from abroad or a substitute for it is readily available.

> When a number of suppliers have bid on an item, but none of the quotations is completely satisfactory. None may meet the buyer's requirements as to price, terms, delivery or specifications. In this situation, the buyer must be sure, before he or she attempts to negotiate, that all bids are unsatisfactory in terms of the requirements that he or she first placed before the suppliers. It is highly unethical to lead a supplier into committing himself or herself in a quotation merely to put him or her into a disadvantageous bargaining position. Responsible buyers will notify suppliers in advance that bids may be subject to negotiation.

> When an existing contract is being changed and the amount of money involved is substantial enough to warrant discussion. Major price changes on high-volume items, for example, are subject to negotiation.

NEGOTIATION STRATEGY

The strategy and tactics used in purchasing negotiations are similar in many ways to those used in labor negotiations. Both types of negotiations have been linked to military campaigns, in which the adversaries first try to outthink, then to outmaneuver, each other.

The basic step in preparing for negotiation is to establish one's own and the supplier's bargaining strength. The supplier's strength will be affected by how much he or she wants the business, how sure he or she is that the sale will be awarded to him or her, and how much time there is to reach an agreement. The buyer's strength will be affected by how much competition there is in the field, how good a price analysis he or she has made, how much business he or she has to offer the supplier, and how much time is available to reach an agreement.

A supplier anxious to establish himself or herself with a company or in an industry, for example, may be willing to make price concessions to achieve this end. A buyer under pressure from his or her shop to have an item on hand at an unreasonable date, on the other hand, is on the defensive and may be willing to pay a premium price for quick delivery.

A seller who is certain that he or she has no immediate competition (for example, a dealer with an exclusive franchise in a remote area) knows that he or she will have an advantage in a negotiation. A purchasing manager who has developed an alternate supplier, or who knows that a substitute material can be used, goes into the negotiation in a strong position.

Much of the art of negotiation consists of the ability to determine these strengths and weaknesses in advance and to exploit them to one's own advantage. At the same time, of course, one must try to conceal one's own weaknesses or at least avoid as long as possible having them put to the test.

In the first cases—buying a new or complex item, or refusing to take the lowest of a number of bids, or even negotiating a price change on a regularly bought item—supplier costs are a key area for discussion. A negotiator should come into such a discussion with a sound knowledge of costing methods and, if possible, comparative figures from his or her own cost estimates. Small- and medium-sized suppliers particularly—and some of the big ones—do not bother to develop accurate and factual records. Their cost figures are often pulled out of the air—on the safe side, of course. Their sales representatives are given a fairly wide range of prices to submit to prospective customers. Too many purchasing people go into negotiations with the rather vague attitude that the supplier deserves a price that includes cost plus a fair profit. But, if they don't go after those costs intelligently and aggressively, they may end up giving the supplier a fair profit and themselves an unfair price.

Just because a supplier has lower costs than the next highest bidder does not mean that his or her costs are low enough. That supplier may still be using his or her plant inefficiently. It is the purchasing agent's responsibility to help the supplier bring down his or her costs to an absolute minimum and still deliver the quality required.

Modern industrial pricing, however, is not based simply on costs. If the purchasing manager is unable to determine specific costs on an item under negotiation, he or she can always proceed on certain assumptions about the prices quoted to him or her. They may be based on any one or a combination of the following:

An attempt to get "all the traffic can bear," which is sound economic behavior on the part of a supplier.

Keeping prices just low enough to cut out competition.

Setting a specific rate of return—for example, as a percentage of sales or of capital invested—and pricing accordingly.

Any one of these areas is fertile ground for a skilled negotiator.

And even in the case of fixed-price or "fair-trade" items, there is room for maneuvering. A buyer can offer to buy other items, on which prices are not fixed, from the same supplier if the buyer can get a price concession.

The shrewd negotiator can also use the "unique specification" approach, which makes the component or material that he or she buys different from that bought by all other customers. The classic case is that of the automobile companies who buy tailpipes fabricated to their own specifications. The tube from which the tailpipes are made was selling at the same price to all buyers. But bent into special shapes, it is sold at a lower price than the basic product.

Among the fringe benefits that can be negotiated on industry-priced items are:

The privilege of bulking orders for quantity discounts.

Split shipments to one destination with the price based on total quantity.

Make-and-hold agreements which may lower the price and provide inventory protection without the cost of carrying it.

Concessions for methods of packaging and palletizing.

Lower shipping costs through a change in carrier.

Terms of payment.

Planning for Negotiation

Before the purchasing manager uses any of these general approaches in a specific negotiation, the manager should plan ahead to get a maximum advantage. Indeed, preplanning is as important as the tactics of negotiation, because the tactics are based on plans and objectives established before any meeting.

All good planning begins with the collection of essential data—and in the case of negotiation this includes not only economic but engineering, accounting, legal, and financial information pertinent to the particular matter to be discussed. These should be identified and ranked according to importance.

The collection of facts pertinent to the negotiation may involve several different departments, depending on the complexity of the matter at issue. Similarly, the negotiation itself may require the presence of a team of experts to participate in the discussions accurately and present the company's position and views. An experienced purchasing executive will always assume that the supplier is sending shrewd, well informed, and skillful representatives into any substantial negotiation, so he or she will try to match them when he or she selects his or her own team.

In an involved negotiation, a team might be made up of representatives from purchasing, engineering, accounting, marketing, industrial engineering, and legal departments. They should be thoroughly briefed on the nature of the negotiation and the technical and economic questions involved. They should understand or, even better, participate in the establishment of the company's objectives and alternative positions as described below.

It is absolutely necessary to designate a leader when negotiation involves more than one representative. The leader's authority to commit the company, and the limitations on the authority of other team members, should be clearly spelled out. Because the basic authority to commit company funds rests with the purchasing department representative, that person is generally considered the best choice to lead a negotiating team.

Guidelines for effective prenegotiation preparation, planning, and documentation that are issued to purchasing and materials management personnel of a large supplier to the automotive and aerospace industries are clear and comprehensive:

> The effectiveness of negotiation depends largely on the quality and thorough preparation of the prenegotiation effort, and the skill of the negotiation team. Although they are particularly applicable to critical procurements with complex technical and contractual situations requiring negotiation team effort, the basic elements and techniques detailed below apply equally to all procurements requiring negotiation.
>
> The buyer or subcontract specialist responsible for procurements requiring negotiation will, prior to such negotiation—
>
> a. initiate and develop a proposed plan for the conduct of a negotiation which will consist of but not be limited to the following:
>
> 1. definition of the negotiation objective
> 2. an agenda
> 3. clear identification of all issues involved
> 4. designation of the team captain
> 5. outline of the apparent prenegotiation positions of both parties
> 6. details on the key items and in-house analyses
> 7. requests for qualified specialists for evaluation of specific areas
>
> b. Document and submit the proposed negotiation plan, through super-

vision, to the individual authorized to approve the contractual agreement contemplated.

The size and composition of each negotiation team will vary according to the nature and complexity of each procurement situation. The negotiation team will include qualified specialists who are skilled and experienced in their specific areas to support negotiation.

The chief negotiator will:

a. select individual members for an effective, well-integrated team

b. outline individual team member responsibilities in the prenegotiation and negotiation efforts

c. brief team members on their respective roles in negotiation

The chief negotiator will:

a. determine and recommend, as a matter of strategy, optimum location and physical arrangements for the negotiation proceedings

b. incorporate these recommendations for location and physical arrangements into the negotiation plan

The chief negotiator, with the assistance of his team, will make a careful analysis of the relative prenegotiation bargaining positions of our company and the seller. Since negotiation can sometimes be simply a test of strength based on bargaining position every factor bearing on this position should be identified, understood, and properly evaluated.

After analysis and review of the procurement environment, the chief negotiator will outline the data developed, listing on one side the factors that tend to strengthen his position, and on the other side the factors that tend to strengthen the seller's position, and incorporate this information into the negotiation plan.

As a minimum, prenegotiation analysis should be performed to carefully evaluate the:

a. product work statement—to provide complete familiarity with the product and the various processes involved, and to ascertain their effect on cost and their relationship to the specific cost proposal submitted by the seller

b. seller's cost proposal—to ascertain the reasonableness of the seller's quoted price and cost breakdowns. The price/cost analysis function should be utilized to clarify all questions that affect costs

The selection and application of appropriate and effective cost/price analysis techniques will be dependent upon how well defined the specifications are, the extent of competition, the availability of cost and price history data and the reliability of in-house estimates.

As a final part of negotiation preparation, the chief negotiator and his team should meet to familiarize all members with the plans for negotiation, and the issues, objectives and data upon which such plans were based. He may conduct a dry run to develop the final negotiation strategy and techniques and to condition the team for the actual negotiation proceedings.

Defining Negotiation Objectives

The negotiator without clearly defined objectives is put on the defensive, as it must always be assumed that the other participant in the session has entered the negotiation with some definite goal for his company. Uncertainty or confusion over his or her objectives can lead a negotiator into making damaging concessions.

Such generalized objectives as "getting all we can out of the vendor" or attempting to get "the best possible price" are not much better than no objectives at all. A buyer must define his or her objectives more precisely in terms of what he or she and the company hope that they can get and reasonably expect to get if the negotiation is skillfully conducted. The objective may be a price or certain concessions on quality, delivery, or other factors.

The objective should be expressed in specific terms, such as a certain price, but it must always be subject to modification. Flexibility is at the heart of the negotiating art, and all objectives should be hedged by a minimum and maximum position to which a negotiator can move when he or she has the opportunity to, in the first case, and when he or she is forced to, in the second case. A buyer going into a negotiation with an objective, or "ideal" price, of $11,500 for a piece of equipment, for example, should have alternative prices above and below that figure that were deemed acceptable before the negotiation began. In the actual negotiation the buyer might use the minimum price the negotiating team agreed upon—$10,000, for example—as a first proposal without any real hope that the supplier would immediately accept it. Conversely, the buyer would be prepared to go to a maximum position—a $12,500 price, for example—but only as a last resort. The objective, maximum, and minimum prices would, of course, have been determined on the basis of cost analysis, need for the equipment, monopoly position of the supplier, or any of the other factors previously mentioned.

As a corollary to having an established objective and alternative maximum and minimum positions, a negotiator must try to estimate the supplier's objectives and maximum and minimum positions. One or more of these may already be apparent in a bid or proposal submitted, or they may have to be deduced from the buyer's own cost analysis or from previous experience with the supplier. In any event, a good negotiator will try to guess where a supplier will make concessions and where that supplier is likely to hold fast to his or her declared position. The negotiator will then prepare to act accordingly in the light of his or her own objectives.

Before entering a negotiation it is advisable for both parties—buyer and supplier—to come to some agreement as to what is being negotiated and put the agreement in writing. This tends to cut down on disagreements and arguments once the negotiation is under way, as reference can be made to a written statement or agenda. Similarly, both sides should clearly indicate who has authority to speak for them in the negotiation and the exact extent of that authority. There is no point in elaborate planning for a negotiation when one side's representative simply does not have the authority to agree on a critical point such as price.

Negotiating Tactics

Negotiation is often a highly technical matter, but it is always a very human matter as well. Because the essential element in a negotiation is bargaining between individuals, the process involves personalities, human motives, people's strength and weaknesses, and a great deal of psychology. In numerous addresses to purchasing groups, the authors have stressed these general rules for turning the human element in negotiations to one's own advantage:

Try to have the negotiation carried on your home ground, according to your own arrangements. There is a psychological advantage to having the other party come to the discussion. It implies that you are in control and have already won one concession. Provide a dignified, comfortable, well-lighted meeting place, free of distractions. Put the leader of your own negotiating team at the head of the table, and try to keep the members of the other team separated.

Let the supplier do most of the talking. At least, in the beginning. Let the supplier give the reasons for his or her demand first. If you use the proper restraint, he or she may talk himself or herself into making concessions that were never intended.

When your time comes to talk, don't fumble over facts and figures. Never send out for vital information in the middle of a discussion. Lack of information or lack of confidence puts you at a strong psychological disadvantage.

Try to avoid emotional reactions to the supplier's arguments or an emotional approach in presenting your own. Otherwise, you'll obscure the real purposes of the negotiation and possibly endanger your own position. A person who lets pride or anger govern his or her relations with others usually ends up by giving away more than he or she intended.

If the supplier has to retreat on a point, let it be done gracefully. If you spot something wrong in a cost estimate, for example, don't accuse the other side of trickery or ineptitude. Suggest that a revision is in order.

Avoid premature showdowns. You have to come to some sort of a showdown ultimately—that's the reason for the negotiation. But, if you force a supplier into a position in which he or she feels compelled to say, "Here are my terms, take them or leave them," that may end the discussion there. After that kind of an ultimatum it would be difficult for the supplier to give further concessions. So, before you make your final concession, be absolutely sure that is is absolutely final.

Satisfy the emotional needs of the people with whom you are negotiating. Most suppliers enjoy selling and persuading, but they are somewhat insecure. Give suppliers a chance to persuade rather than trying to head them off brusquely, and they will be better disposed to make concessions to get your business. And give them the impression that, despite your bargaining with them, you respect their position and regard them as members of your corporate team.

One of the country's leading authorities on purchasing negotiations has described the attributes of a good negotiator as follows:

1. *He must be a clear, rapid thinker.* The give and take of a complex negotiation requires a man with ability to think quickly.

2. *He must express himself well and easily.* In negotiation, what you know may not be as important as what you convey to others. The ability to communicate effectively is an absolute must. Ease of expression does not mean glibness. It comes from a knowledge of the problem at hand.

3. *He must possess the ability to analyze.* He must be able to analyze the statements of others and identify those who favor his position, those who oppose it, and those who favor another solution.

4. *He must be impersonal.* In the heat of a hard-fought negotiation, it is sometimes difficult to remain calm. But a negotiator must always approach the negotiation from the basis of the company objective, rather than his own personal inclinations.

5. *He must be patient.* Sometimes letting the other fellow talk himself out or explain his position fully helps resolve issues without argument.

6. *He must be able to consider the other person's ideas objectively.* He should be able to place himself in his opponents' frame of reference so that he can better evaluate their position.

7. *He must be tactful, have poise and self-restraint,* like people, and have a good knowledge of human nature.

8. *He must possess a sense of humor.* You can't win every point in a negotiation. An ability to make a concession and continue to display good humor will pay dividends in goodwill which will help in resolving the remaining issues.[4]

Negotiation is not, as is often charged, the purchasing department's technique for cutting down the supplier's profits. Nor is it an occult science whose practitioners are exclusively endowed with special gifts. It is the basic process by which competition is furthered in industrial buying and selling. It is the special responsibility of the purchasing agent to negotiate the best possible deal to achieve company objectives—just as it is the special responsibility of a sales representative ro negotiate for his company's objectives.

[4] Dean S. Ammer, in a letter to the author, 1978.

SOME PERFORMANCE OBJECTIVES

After studying this chapter you should be able to:

1. Explain the difference between buying by bid and buying by negotiation.
2. Describe the situations in which negotiation, as defined in the text, is considered the appropriate method of purchasing.
3. List half a dozen cost elements other than straight price that are subject to negotiation.
4. Cite some examples of negotiation from your own experience that involved the principles and techniques discussed in the text.
5. Demonstrate, with a theoretical example, the concept of minimum and maximum positions and its application by both sides in a negotiation.
6. Discuss some of the psychological aspects involved in negotiation.

The purchasing principles and methods we have described so far are essential in any purchasing organization, although the scope and degree of their application may vary with the size of the organization. There are others that theoretically should be applied in any size company, but are not because of time and personnel constraints. Two such activities—planning and forecasting—are described in the following chapter.

Section IV

SPECIALIZED PURCHASING OPERATIONS

Planning and Forecasting

15

Some successful businesses have been launched on a hunch, but few have survived solely on the instinctive genius of their founders or managers. If an enterprise is to continue to be profitable, it must be operated according to some plan. And the plan, in turn, must be based on some estimate of the future—of the demand for the company's products, of the size of its markets, of its requirements for materials, machines, and personnel. Whether this attempt to gauge future conditions is called "forecasting" or, more inelegantly, "educated guessing," it is essential in business. Good managers narrow the range of probabilities that they face and plan what action they will take to meet them.

Purchasing, as a management function, has a responsibility to participate in company planning and forecasting. The scope of its responsibility may vary, depending on the ratio of material cost to finished product cost and on the relative position of the purchasing executive in the managerial group. Regardless of the exact position of the purchasing department in the corporate hierarchy, however, the results of purchasing planning or lack of it have a very definite effect on overall company planning and the realization of company profit objectives. As noted in Chapter 1 purchasing's potential for affecting planning and profits received special attention from management in the wake of the 1973–1974 period of critical material shortages. Many companies—from the largest on down—gave their purchasing departments new or additional responsibilities for long-range planning and forecasting.

PLANNING AS A PART OF PURCHASING

The importance of purchasing to plan can be seen even in purchasing's most basic activity: forward buying to meet anticipated requirements for a given period. In any continuing manufacturing program, most material needs are reasonably foreseeable. A large part of purchasing can be done in advance of needs rather than according to individual current requisitions issued when the need arises. But consideration of forward buying immediately calls for some type of planning to allow for certain contingencies. The advantages of forward buying must be weighed against the disadvantages.

On the one hand, goods will be on hand when they are needed; requirements can be lumped together to obtain price concessions through volume buying; economic ordering quantities and other cost-reducing formulas can be applied; special market conditions can be exploited (see the section on speculative purchasing later in this chapter); and material costs will be stabilized over a stated period. On the other hand are possible disadvantages: The company must increase its financial commitments to cover the cost of the materials; corporate funds are tied up in inventory investment and carrying costs when they might be employed more profitably elsewhere; risks of losses through obsolescence are increased; unless provision is made for periodic review and revision of buying plans, the company may be left with a fixed commitment harmful to its interests if market conditions change drastically.

MANAGEMENT'S NEED FOR GUIDANCE

These points alone would justify the need for the purchasing department to make some organized effort at forecasting and planning. There are others, however. The most important is the value to top management of knowing the probable course of major material prices over a given period. Decisions on how to price manufactured products are much easier to make when material costs can be reasonably estimated. The significance of such information to certain manufacturers is obvious: Tire manufacturers must have some indication of the trend of rubber prices (and supply); similarly, soap makers should have a reasonably good forecast on market conditions in fats and oils. But even equipment makers— producers of electric motors and farm machinery, for example—find accurate forecasting of trends in such materials as copper and steel of great value in pricing their products.

Informed estimates of materials supply and availability of substitutes also aid management in its planning. Although studies of substitute materials and other technological developments that may lower costs or improve the quality of manufactured products are logically the concern of other departments, they often are the by-products of purchasing department forecasting.

Purchasing forecasting can be used in setting up departmental plans—setting materials budgets, setting up cost-reduction goals, particularly for the long range—and the establishment of reliable, competitive sources of supply needed for future company expansion and growth. Purchasing in many companies, both large and small, also participates in general forecasts of the general economic situation and their implications both for the purchasing department and for the enterprise as a whole.

Purchasing planning begins with what is essentially a short-term production forecast—the manufacturing schedule. The schedule indicates to the buyer the nature and volume of material requirements and the expected rates of use. In a large and highly organized company, it may come to the buyer in tabulated form from the production control or planning department. In the smaller company, the information may come to the buyer informally from the plant manager or superintendent. The schedule indicates the approximate volume and flow of materials that the purchasing department will be expected to provide. It should be communicated to the purchasing department systematically, for purchasing policies and plans must be keyed to it. Conversely, the purchasing agent should be informed of any changes in the anticipated operations, so that buying plans can be adjusted accordingly.

Regular access to at least a summary report of new orders received is important to good purchasing planning. Trends in this figure often provide a useful indicator of future operating rates in advance of actual changes in manufacturing schedules. For longer-range planning, the purchasing department should be kept informed of company sales quotas and forecasts.

In job shop manufacturing operations, the purchasing department is often called in before the bidding stage to supply cost estimates on parts and materials. This advance knowledge of probable requirements enables buyers to begin planning earlier than would be the case if they had to wait until the business was in the house and bills of material and requisitions all prepared. The collection of cost data in itself is an element in their planning. And without committing the company, they can begin to look for additional sources and alert regular suppliers to the possibility of new orders.

BASIC STEPS IN PURCHASING PLANNING

Collection and orderly presentation of pertinent information—including objectives—are fundamental to purchasing planning. Figure 15-1 shows some of the questions that might be asked in preparing a procurement plan for raw materials. The checklist, compiled by an industrial purchasing executive, was offered only as a sample of the kinds of information required for good purchasing planning; it can be adapted for specific planning programs involving a wide range of products or materials.[1]

Once significant data has been accumulated, it must be so organized that it can be put in written form in logical sequence for review and reference. A basic presentation for a purchasing plan on a relatively simple commodity, D'Arcy suggests, should be in outline form and contain—at a minimum—the following information: (1) suppliers' names and addresses, (2) past and present purchases from individual suppliers, (3) future purchases (based on estimated requirements) from individual suppliers in terms both of percent of usage and dollar volume, (4) reasons for the distribution of business among suppliers (supplier service, quality, price, lead times, etc.), (5) buying techniques being used or under consideration (blanket orders, contracts, spot buys, etc.), (6) purchasing department objectives embodied in the plan (improved products, higher quality, new suppliers, cost reductions, improvement of relations with vendors, etc.), and (7) economic advantages of the plan.

This relatively simple outline would, of course, be considerably more comprehensive when used in planning for more complex or more critical items. In any case, the plan is not complete until it has been presented, in written form, to key persons whose departments would be affected by it. Those, D'Arcy says, include the production manager, production planner, maintenance manager, or master mechanic, depending on what products or materials the plan covers. They may be able to provide additional data or opinions that would make the plan more accurate and more complete. More importantly, the review will help them to determine whether or not the plan reflects their needs. This in turn leads to a clarification of what their objectives are and how well they match up with the objectives of purchasing. Other departments that can help in rounding out a purchasing plan are receiving, accounting, and design engineering.

[1] Albert J. D'Arcy, "Planning for Buying," *Journal of Purchasing and Materials Management,* Vol. 7 (August 1971): 24.

QUESTIONS TO BE ASKED IN DEVELOPING A WRITTEN PROCUREMENT PLAN FOR RAW MATERIALS

1. What are the short and long-term objectives of the business involved?
2. Quantity required at each using location—by months for the next one to two years?
3. What specification applies at each location? What alternative might be considered?
4. Storage capacity available at each location? What ideas do we have on how much inventory to carry? Is inventory limited by storage facilities, working capital, deterioration with age?
5. Method of delivery preferred at each location? What alternative methods of delivery can be considered without new investment or with new investment? What is the maximum quantity per delivery?
6. Consumption and price by location, by month, for previous one or two years?
7. Current suppliers at each location, price being paid, and quantity supplied for previous one or two years? Production Department performance evaluation of current suppliers?
8. Prospective suppliers, their plant locations, capacities and processes? Desirable features of prospective suppliers relative to current suppliers? Is supply regularly available or subject to seasonal or other factors?
9. Total industry capacity/demand ratio for the product for past one or two years, with estimate of expected demand in next few years, by end use?
10. Supplier labor review—renewal date on labor contract?
11. Process economic data, such as estimated production cost, raw material cost, co-product values, batch sizes, yields, make-vs-buy? Rank suppliers from lowest to highest cost producers. Relative profitability of suppliers?
12. Objectives for value improvements sought in new buying period?
13. Preferred quantity statement in new agreement, i.e., fixed quantity or per cent of requirement, or fixed monthly minimum or fixed monthly maximum?
14. Specifications and methods of analysis to be described in contracts for use in receiving and accepting material?
15. Preferred length of contract period? What alternatives might be considered?
16. Is any option desired for contract extension?
17. Preferred terms of payment?
18. Method of invoicing?
19. What points of discussion must be explored between technical production men in buyer or seller organization?
20. What technical service might we require?
21. Who will provide transportation equipment? What alternatives should be considered?
22. Are suitable freight rates currently in effect? Do any new rates have to be established? Evaluate for each supplier.
23. Will all material move in bulk equipment or will some be required in containers? If so, how should it be packed?
24. Will purchases be negotiated or determined by bidding?
25. Distribution cost from the various suppliers' plants to each consuming location?
26. Do we want multiple suppliers for each consuming location?
27. How do we want to write our inquiry?

Figure 15-1. Typical questions to be asked in collecting data for incorporation into a purchasing plan. Courtesy, *Journal of Purchasing and Materials Management.*

BENEFITS IN "PLAN OF PURCHASE"

The experience of a well-known chemical company illustrates three important points about purchasing planning: the need for close cooperation between the using and purchasing departments, the variety of techniques available to purchasing in developing a plan, and the benefits that can accrue from good planning.

Forecasts for chemical raw material needs were not given to the purchasing department until after annual budgets were established in November and December. As a result, chemical buying for any year ran into the second quarter of that calendar year. Inevitably, there were delays in delivery, buyers spent much of their time trying to expedite shipments, and there was little time to investigate cost-reduction possibilities, better sources, or supplier and buyer performance.

With the cooperation of the production planning department, purchasing was able to get forecasts of consumption for twelve months at each midyear—from July 1 of the current year to June 30 of the following year. Production planning also agreed to revise the forecast annual rate on a quarterly basis. This gave the buyers at least three months more to complete their planning.

Buyers now use two approaches in planning their purchase. A "plan of purchase" is made up on all raw materials and chemicals with an annual purchase volume above $50,000. The buyer outlines the type of purchase that he or she plans—spot, contract, and so forth—and how the business will be split among various suppliers, both by quantity and by dollars. The buyer indicates the terms and past performance for each supplier and gives a brief description of supply conditions for the item, a price forecast, and data on previous price changes.

A more elaborate approach is used on all production materials costing more than $100,000 annually or on which there is only one supplier. A buyer complies with the following instructions in preparing his or her plan of purchase for the head of the department:

> *Raw Material Significance*—State percentage of raw material costs and manufacturing costs for the item and its function in the manufacturing process.
>
> *Market Condition*—Describe availability, price, economic factors of the market, and significant changes in supply-and-demand relationships which have taken place or are expected to take place in the foreseeable future.
>
> *Production*—Show total world production, domestic and foreign, broken down by supply company, if possible.
>
> *Buying Objectives*—What will be done to improve company profits on this item? Show what improvements, if any, can be made in relations with suppliers.

Significant Changes from Previous Plan—Indicate change from previous plan—in price, quantity, business split, suppliers, terms, and so forth, and their effects on supplier relations, profits, and method of purchase.

Reasons for Business Split—Explain the basis for split of business among suppliers and indicate what contributions suppliers have made to improve our profits.

General—Indicate unusual contractual liabilities or advantages and any other information pertinent to buying the particular commodity. When plan does not conform to plant recommendations, explain why.

The immediate results of the planning program were better performance in cost reduction and in service to the operating departments. With more time available, buyers were able to complete twice as many cost-improvement projects during the first year of the program as in the year before. The number of rush orders issued by the purchasing department was cut considerably, and relations with other departments improved accordingly. In addition, purchasing managers are now better able to appraise both buyer and supplier performance against the stated objectives of the purchase plan.

FORECASTING

Except in the larger companies, forecasting future price and availability trends is not generally a highly organized activity. Planning is often done on the basis of an informal forecast, often developed within the purchasing department itself. Increasingly, however, companies have turned to formalized forecasting, done either by their own economists or research departments or by outside consultants. Forecasting is identified as an educated assessment of the most probable course of events or a range of probabilities; planning is deciding what to do about them if they occur. (Someone once offered this simple analogy: a weather forecaster tells the radio audience to expect a cloudy morning followed by clearing skies and a sunny afternoon; some parents who are planning a picnic for the kids, pack raincoats and check the programs of local movie houses, just in case.)

Purchasing managers are, in fact, in a good position to act as company economists in situations that do not warrant a full-scale planning department. With a little extra effort they can collect and interpret basic information of the kind by which professional economists and forecasters try to anticipate future developments. However, we are concerned primarily with forecasts directly related to purchasing costs and availability of supply in listing the following elements that provide data for forecasting:

1. *General overall business conditions and the rate of growth in the economy.*
A rising population and a steady and substantial rise in the gross national
product obviously put pressures on supply and prices, for example.

2. *Growth and technological change in specific industries.* Activity in the
automobile industry has long been an important indicator of the direction
of supply trends in various materials. Booming auto sales push up demand for steel, rubber, copper and plastics. As auto makers try to cut
engine weight and meet emission control standards, their consumption of
aluminum and platinum, for example, will rise with subsequent effects on
the markets for those metals. A slump in auto sales and output such as
occurred in 1979-1980, will of course, have the opposite results.

3. *Labor conditions.* Strikes and costly labor pacts have a direct effect
on supply in the first case and prices in the second. Anticipated labor
turmoil in an industry—particularly the major ones such as steel,
aluminum, and other metals—pose problems for buyers, who must weigh
the risks of overbuying against the risks of production halts because of
materials shortages. Once- or twice-removed strikes against the suppliers
of a buyer's suppliers can be a matter of concern. These and other
possibilities call for close attention to the labor situation throughout
industry.

4. *Expansion or contraction of supply.* Major plant expansions in a
given industry generally indicate greater availability of supply. But, by the
same token, closing of plants or dropping of product lines by major
suppliers generally decreases availability. Changes in tastes or styles can
push up the demand for substitute materials—witness the tremendously
increased usage of plastic materials in household furniture.

5. *Cost trends in an industry* (and in that industry's suppliers). These
are of obvious significance. Improvements in productivity, usually
through the installation of new equipment, can often be a matter for
negotiation.

6. *The buyer's own "feel" of the market.* The buyer's abilities to judge
suppliers' expectations for the future are intangible but extremely important elements in a purchasing forecast.

Research in Planning and Forecasting

Forecasting plays an important part in the system described on page
276 but it is not explicitly given that label. In that program, the buyers
interpret market conditions and production outlook in their own studies
of conditions. In other companies, particularly the larger ones, a research
section might develop the necessary data and leave the interpretation of
the facts it collected to the buyers and their supervisors. The extent to

which research groups make specific forecasts followed by recommendations as to action varies widely. The smaller the company, the more likely it is that the buyer or purchasing manager is his or her own researcher and forecaster. In the larger organizations, it is generally a joint effort between purchasing research and the buyers. Figure 15-2 shows a format for informal monthly forecasts by a purchasing department.

In at least one large multiplant organization, the research organization is specifically charged with forecasting and making recommendations. The reports that it makes are, of course, the work of large numbers of highly trained specialists and, therefore, outside the scope of the small purchasing department. But the principles on which they are based can be used in modified form even in the smallest purchasing department. In

PURCHASING DEPT. MONTHLY REPORT _____

Purchase Orders (in 1000$)

SUMMARY	Drug Chem	Pkg Matl	Equip Supp	Total	FORECAST	Drug Chem	Pkg Matl	Equip Supp	Total
Open as of 10-1-	000	0000	000	0000	To be placed in Nov.	000	000	000	0000
Placed in Oct.	0000	0000	000	0000	Deliveries in Nov.	000	000	000	0000
Deliveries in Oct.	000	000	000	0000	" " Dec.	000	000	000	0000
Open as of 11-1-	000	0000	000	0000	" next 6 mos.	0000	0000	0000	00000
COMPARISON									
Total 10 Mos. 19	0000	0000	0000	0000					
Total 10 Mos. 19	0000	0000	0000	0000					

COMMENTS

VOLUME - Chemicals - The value of new orders and deliveries made
in October were within 5% of our buyers' prophecy. November
is expected to be about 15% less than October.

Packaging Materials - The value of new orders increased
sharply over the projection, chiefly due to hedging against
shortages that were developing in suppliers inventories as
a result of steel and glass strikes. Deliveries were nearly
20% greater than normal thus securing many important raw
materials against possible shortage.

INVENTORIES - Current inventories are obviously increased some and normal
operations can be expected for some time. However, we recommend
continued additions to our inventory of steel items (caps, drums,
band and wire) to protect against tight supplies expected for
several months after steel production is resumed.

PRICES - In spite of buyers' resistance to price increases, there is no
evidence that prices will hold at present levels indefinitely.
All indications are that labor costs will continue to contribute
to some inflation and reflect in possible increased prices in
many of our materials.

Figure 15-2. Format for a short-term, informal monthly forecast by a purchasing department.

the case of the small department, the reports would be prepared by rather than for the purchasing manager and directed to his or her management rather than to the buyer.

> *Materials Situation Bulletin*—An analysis of the current market situation in each of the major materials purchased by the company. This is accompanied by a short-term recommendation as to forward coverage.
> *Price Information Bulletin*—Market-price history of key purchased materials and short-term forecasts of price movements.
> *Advance Ordering and Inventory Bulletin*—A list of suggested ordering lead times and inventory levels in the light of current general economic and market conditions.

The group also issues long-term forecasts—sometimes as far ahead as ten years—on basic materials such as steel and aluminum. It also maintains price indices on all key materials.

SUPPLIERS AND FORECASTING

Suppliers are involved in any purchasing forecasting and planning operation in two important ways. First, they can provide significant forecasts of their own concerning market outlook, their plans for expansion (or retrenchment), and labor conditions in their industries. Second, they can in many instances help in or interfere with purchasing planning. During a period of steel shortage several years ago, one of the country's most prominent purchasing executives, a vice president of a large electrical manufacturing firm, spent a great deal of time "selling" his company to the steel companies as a good, long-term customer. The company, which was growing rapidly, was battling to get enough steel to meet its needs. But following custom, the steel companies were allocating their products on the basis of what share of production their customers received in normal years.

In a series of meetings with steel company sales managers, the purchasing executive outlined his case for more steel. He spelled out what his company was going to need in the way of steel for its planned expansion, and what it expected to get from the steel industry. His argument was based on an enormous amount of research on all steel purchases for several years previous. Every procurement factor had been thoroughly analyzed and correlated—types and amounts of steel purchased, mill locations, freight rates, and so forth. On the basis of his forecast, and his own aggressive "sales" approach, the purchasing executive got higher allocations of scarce steel from a large number of steel suppliers.

Suppliers can also be brought into purchasing forecasting and planning in a more positive way as well. The purchasing department is often counted on to develop sources of new components and materials that will be required years hence as a company grows and diversifies.

Purchasing forecasting and planning is initially concerned with supply, demand, and price conditions in specific commodities, but it also must consider general business conditions. Industry-wide use of basic materials—steel, for example—fluctuates with the business cycle. Thus, any forecast involving the steel market would inevitably have to include such factors as the outlook for the automobile industry and the construction industry. General business forecasting is a complex and highly specialized activity that most purchasing departments are not equipped to handle. Generally, the purchasing department will call on the company economist or the forecasting group for general economic data that relate to purchased materials for which forecasts are being prepared.

The flow of economic information is not always strictly one-way, however. In a number of companies, staff economists regularly obtain information from purchasing to incorporate in their regular economic reports. The chief economist of a large metals company recently added several sections to his quarterly reports on purchase costs, including an analysis of material costs in relation to the wholesale price index and the effects of material costs on breakeven points during sales rises. In at least one automotive company, a research and forecasting group in purchasing feeds information to a number of other departments. One is the corporate long-range planning office, which is responsible for planning of production facilities, costs of new models, and financial forecasts. The reports include such purchasing information as the outlook for commodity prices, long-range procurement problems, and the effects of wage rates on purchased materials. The purchasing department's forecast of materials and parts prices are also used as a part of the total financial forecast for the company. In a small company with no corporate economist, purchasing might well take over the role on an informal basis if it were already doing a good job in its own forecasting and planning.

THE USE OF PERT IN PURCHASING

Forecasting and planning usually proceed from the general to the very specific; from long-range considerations to very immediate needs. A company making products in which electronic parts are a major component, for example, relies on a long-range forecast of probable supply, delivery, and price of broad categories of parts when making its plans for the next three or five years. Competitive pressure is so great, however, that many companies are forced into introducing new products faster than they had anticipated. Time, then, becomes an extremely important element. Planning must be done in terms of weeks, not years; delivery forecasts must be more precise. Present market conditions—not trends—must be taken into consideration.

As long-range forecasting gives way to short-range planning (and market strategy), industry has turned increasingly to a relatively new planning technique known as Program Evaluation Review Technique (PERT). PERT is basically a method of scientifically scheduling a complex chain of events and activities which, together, will give a specific end result. A brief explanation of the technique, together with a typical time schedule for a new product based on the PERT technique, is shown in Figure 15-3.

Although the purchasing department is not responsible for the master scheduling involved in PERT, it is still in a unique position to feed information into every phase of the program. It can spell out the essential procurement steps and estimate the times needed to complete them (obtaining bids, negotiating, exchanging technical information with suppliers, inspecting sources, manufacturing and transportation lead times).

In a typical situation, a pharmaceutical company used PERT in the introduction of a new product to coordinate research, clinical testing, marketing, procurement, manufacturing, and government approval. Working with the PERT network, purchasing was able to advance a target date five months by getting permission to purchase raw materials four and a half months in advance of the company's normal schedule by committing for materials before testing was completed.

SPECULATIVE PURCHASING

Any discussion of forecasting and price fluctuations raises the issue of commodity speculation. This term has an unfortunate connotation. It is frequently argued that speculative buying is in the realm of business ethics rather than of purchasing science and that it has no place in any legitimate purchasing program. That generalization is not altogether sound. All forward purchasing is speculative to a degree, depending on judgment as to future probabilities. The analysis of these probabilities, and the adjustment of purchasing policies accordingly, are important elements of effective, scientific purchasing. The distinction between speculation and legitimate purchasing action hinges, rather, on the intent of the purchase and the extent of the risk involved.

What is PERT?
And what does it do?

PERT—Program Evaluation Review Technique—is basically a method of scientifically scheduling a complex chain of events and activities which, together, will give a specific end result. Originally used to coordinate the Navy's Polaris missile program, it is today more often encountered in such projects as construction of a building or plant.

PERT was first thought to be of value only for extremely complex projects, but it is increasingly being used for simpler tasks which can be broken down into logical steps.

Probably the most critical step in a PERT program is to make an initial checklist of every function that will be needed. Each task ("activity" in PERT nomenclature) is bounded by two "events." The first event must be completed before an activity can start. The second event occurs when the activity is finished. Activities and events are plotted on paper. Several will be interdependent; others parallel.

By estimating the time each task will take, one related series of activities will emerge as the longest. This is the "critical path", along which there is no leeway. Some purchasing activities will almost certainly lie on the critical path. The expediter must watch these orders closely.

Each path surrounding the critical path will be a slack path. Some loss of time here can be tolerated, depending, of course, on the slack. If such loss of time occurs, it's easy to decide whether to do nothing, whether to delay related activities, whether to "rush" that particular activity through overtime, etc., or whether to eliminate that activity and proceed with another one.

At Rockwell Mfg. Co., PERT is used to schedule each step in getting a new product on the market. With the system, the company has been able to introduce 36 new products in two years without a hitch.

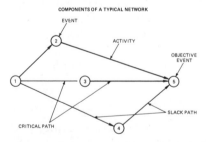

COMPONENTS OF A TYPICAL NETWORK

SIMPLE BUILDING blocks of PERT network are events (circles) and activities (arrows). Jobs which have to be completed consecutively form paths, the longest of which is called the critical path. Any delay along this path would hold up the entire project. All other paths are slack paths and have extra time built into them. At Rockwell a typical PERT network may involve between 50 and 100 activities.

Figure 15-3. Basic explanation of Program Evaluation Review Technique (PERT). Courtesy, *Purchasing Magazine.*

Keeping materials costs at a practicable minimum is one of the functional responsibilities of purchasing. Procurement of goods beyond the immediate need in anticipation of an expected price advance is a means of keeping down material costs. The purchasing manager buys for use, on the basis of reasonably foreseeable requirements. The manager is not a trader, seeking profits in the resale of what he or she buys or in the form of inventory appreciation. Most of the accepted methods of inventory valuation figure this asset on the basis of cost or market, whichever is lower. This effectively precludes any claim by purchasing to take credit for speculative profits from this source. The fact of materials cost, however, remains, and this is the purchasing manager's responsibility. In the event that the price rises as expected, it is of course outside the province of the purchasing department as to whether or not management and sales will take advantage of the cost saving to price their own end product for a more favorable competitive position in the current market or for a wider profit margin.

Some commodities are much more sensitive than others in respect to price and are subject to considerable fluctuations from day to day. These price movements are of concern to the buyer, for in the large quantities that are characteristic of large-scale industrial operations the difference of a fraction of a cent per pound amounts to substantial sums in the aggregate. Buying on the short price swings is actually more speculative in nature than when the long trend is considered. In the great bulk of purchases making up the industrial procurement program, and in the final evaluation of purchasing competence as a contributing factor to profitable operation, the long trend is the more important. Every transaction is, of course, reflected in the total purchasing record, but the measurement of price performance in a purchasing program is average cost as compared with average market at the time of use, not any single purchase or the difference between the extreme low and the extreme high price.

Responsibility for Speculative Buying Policies

Profit and risk are primarily the responsibilities of management. It has already been noted that inventory profits, though resulting from purchasing action, do not customarily accrue to the credit of purchasing in the company audit and accounts. Purchasing science seeks at all points to minimize risk—risk of shortage or surplus, of physical or financial depreciation, of overextended investment in materials. In many cases, the purchasing manager's authority to take risks is definitely circumscribed by the placing of a monetary limit on the value of orders that may be issued without specific authorization of a superior officer.

Management, however, can and does take risks for profit. In respect to materials procurement, in addition to the routine review and authorization of large purchases, such risks include decisions to risk shortages by deferring purchases in the expectation of lower prices or, at the other extreme, decisions to invest a large proportion of the company's financial resources in materials inventories, perhaps at the expense of other business purposes.

Usually, such decisions are implemented through the purchasing department, but the policy and responsibility lie with management. In some special cases, as when one or more key commodities are inherently volatile in price behavior, characterized by short-range fluctuations or wide market swings, when their role in the cost structure of the purchaser's product is significant and correspondingly volatile, speculative purchasing may be indicated as the rule rather than the deviation. It is in such commodities that the greatest problems, opportunities, and hazards of speculative purchasing occur. Because the objectives and techniques of this sort of buying have little in common with the general purchasing program, such procurement is sometimes set up as a separate assignment, handled by a commodity specialist close to management or by an executive in the management group, where the responsibility for speculative risk actually lies.

Most cases, and those most pertinent to a study of general purchasing principles, arise in connection with items that would normally be bought in the course of regular purchase procedure. Here a situation may develop that, in the judgment of the purchasing manager, calls for forward buying beyond the scope of his or her established policy and authority and justifies the additional risk. The commonsense way of handling such a situation is for the purchasing manager to make a recommendation to the general manager or other executive to whom he or she is responsible, with the reasons as to why he or she considers the extraordinary expenditure advisable. If management concurs in this judgment, the purchase is authorized and made through regular purchasing channels. The purchasing manager who is alert to recognize a special situation and does not hesitate to recommend special action to take advantage of it fulfills his or her function intelligently without arrogating to himself or herself authority beyond the usual scope of his or her office and without sacrificing sound basic policy. The ultimate decision reflects both purchasing and management judgment and objectives.

Some companies have established purchasing committees, consisting of the purchasing agent and top executives in general management, sales, and finance. The function of a purchasing committee is not to buy but, rather, to review and set purchasing policies on major requirements.

They usually concern themselves with only a dozen or so particular commodities that are the key materials required in the conduct of the business, and they determine the period of coverage that is desirable or make specific purchase authorizations.

Minimizing Speculative Risk

Commodity exchanges, providing facilities for trading in "futures" (contracts calling for the delivery of goods in some specified future month), exist for a number of leading commodities subject to daily price fluctuation. Among these are barley, cocoa, coffee, copper, corn, cotton, cottonseed oil, hides, lard, lead, oats, pepper, rubber, rye, silk, soybeans, sugar, tin, wheat, wool, and zinc. These exchanges serve a useful function, not only in facilitating actual purchases for future deliveries at a firm price, but in minimizing, through the practice of "hedging," the risk of necessary forward purchasing.

Speculative purchasing is sometimes inherent in the nature of a business, particularly when the process of manufacture is a lengthy one or when orders must be taken far in advance, so that there is a possibility or probability of market change between the time of procuring the raw materials and the sale of the product. For example, a cotton textile manufacturer must buy cotton now to start the production of goods to be sold three or four months hence, knowing that the price that can be obtained for his or her product will be in relation to the cost of raw cotton at the time that he or she makes the sale, and not to the cost of his or her actual purchase, which, for purposes of actual production, cannot be deferred to see what the applicable price will be. If the price of cotton should decline during this period, the manufacturer may incur a loss not recoverable in the price of his or her product.

"Hedging" in the Futures Market

To meet such a condition, the buyer may "hedge" his or her purchase in the futures market. In its simplest form, such a transaction would be as follows. The buyer purchases the required amount of cotton on the spot, or open, market and at the same time sells an equivalent amount in the futures market, contracting to deliver it at the future date when his or her own product comes upon the market, at the currently quoted price for that future period. When that time comes, the cotton itself will have been used up in manufacture, but the buyer will make a second purchase at the then current market to satisfy his delivery contract. Thus it makes no difference to the buyer whether the price has advanced or declined, because the two transactions offset each other and leave him or her in the position of having acquired the cotton at the price level prevailing at the time at which his or her goods are sold. If the price has advanced in the meantime, the buyer will have to accept a loss on the hedging operation, but will have a corresponding profit in the market value of his or her product. If the price has declined, the buyer will have a loss on his or her manufacturing operation, but an offsetting profit on the hedge. As used for commercial purposes, hedge transactions seek protection rather than profit. The expense of this protection is the relatively small brokerage fee and the use of capital for margin deposits pending the completion of the transaction.

In a large percentage of future sales, actual delivery is not called for, and the transaction is closed by issuing a transfer notice. For this reason, plus the fact that such sales and purchases do not refer to any specific lot of material, the transactions are sometimes referred to as "options." This is inaccurate, for they are bona fide contracts, and deliveries may be demanded and taken.

SOME PERFORMANCE OBJECTIVES

After studying this chapter you should be able to

1. Explain why the importance of purchasing planning extends beyond the purchasing department itself.
2. Construct a set of preparatory questions to be asked in preparing a hypothetical procurement plan for a product or material—one with which you are familiar or one that may be designated by the instructor.
3. Distinguish between planning and forecasting, giving examples of each as they are employed in a purchasing department.
4. List the major elements to be considered in forecasting for purchasing.
5. Name and describe three types of reports that a purchasing manager, even in a small company, can submit that would be of value to company management.
6. Compare speculative purchasing and hedging in the futures market.

Another specialized type of procurement activity in which purchasing participation is limited (but important) is the acquisition of major equipment. This is the subject of the next chapter.

Purchasing's Role in Capital Expenditures

16

The status of expenditures or investments in machinery as a part of the company's capital structure has an important bearing on the purchase of such equipment. It brings financial departments and policies more intimately into the picture than is the case with purchases of production materials and expendable supplies. And it has an important effect on real cost, owing to taxes and the possibility of "write-offs" in the capital account. Many purchases of new equipment, whether for expansion or for replacement and modernization, are approved or disapproved, accelerated or deferred, chiefly on the basis of this factor. Thus, the government's tax policy which is of minor influence in day-to-day purchasing, is a very substantial consideration in cases of capital purchases.

Even though the company may have a policy of replacing machines whenever production can be improved by more advanced models, the objective is to acquire equipment that will give maximum useful life. Thus, it is regarded as a one-time or nonrepetitive purchase, which goes beyond the ordinary delegation of responsibility to the purchasing department, though purchasing still has an important role to play in the procurement process.

PURCHASING DEPARTMENT PARTICIPATION

There is keen competition among manufacturers of machine tools, in the various classifications of lathes, shapers, grinders, milling machines, and the like, but this competition characteristically takes the form of individual features of design and application, so that competing makes are not directly comparable or interchangeable. Consequently, the purchasing devices of alternate sources of supply and approved lists of vendors from which a selection can be made are not applicable. In other respects, the purchasing problems and procedures are substantially parallel to those encountered for any other requirement. However, the selection and purchase of major equipment is by nature a special product rather than continuing program, and the decision involves the judgment of many persons.

Surveys of buying influences in respect to various types of purchases usually show more different executives participating in the selection of machinery than in the purchases of materials, components, or supplies. The reasons for this have already been indicated. The purchasing department rarely initiates such a purchase and is brought into the transaction at the stage at which technical, cost, and delivery data are collected. (See Figure 16-1.) Assembling these data is more than a routine factor of the purchase, because it provides the factual basis of evaluation. Furthermore, because the original request is likely to be in terms of a particular make and model, the collecting of data requires an intimate knowledge of the work to be performed and the various types of equipment available for this purpose. It is this point at which alternatives are explored for best value and greatest usefulness.

In large organizations, in which much equipment is purchased, there is usually a machinery buyer in the purchasing department specializing in these requirements, just as other buyers have specialized responsibilities for commodity groups. In large companies, which have multiple units of a given type of production equipment, there is likely to be more repetitive buying of machinery, and many such purchases are well defined by standardization in plant practice for simplification of maintenance, uniform training of machine operators, or coordination with other equipment in successive stages of manufacture. For example, once the basic decisions have been made, the replacement or expansion of a battery of identical screw machines or drill presses is distinctly a purchasing procedure.

There is an active trade in used and rebuilt machine equipment of all sorts, which become available as entire plants discontinue operations or as individual machines become surplus to a company. Such machines may be bought at auction or through established dealers. Aside from the element of cost saving, this is an important source because the machines so offered are available for spot purchase, whereas orders for new machinery, even of standard models, may take many months for construction

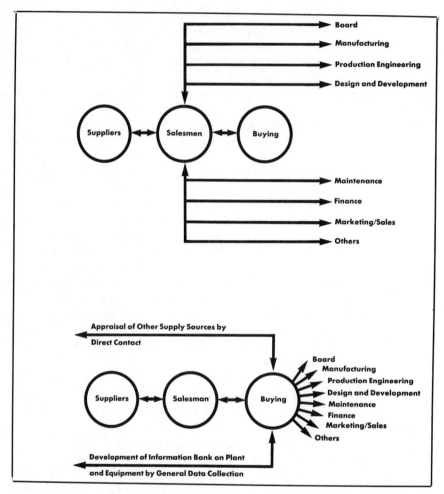

Figure 16-1. The "wrong" (top) and "right" procedures leading to selection of capital equipment suppliers as seen by John Stevens, British author and purchasing consultant. Courtesy, *Procurement,* official publication of the Institute of Purchasing and Supply, London.

and delivery. The purchasing department is familiar with these sources and should be alert to these opportunities as they are applicable to the company's needs.

When the possibility of purchasing used equipment is considered, and when there is no machinery specialist on the buying staff, the equipment is generally inspected prior to purchase by a two-person team, consisting of a buyer and a representative of the production department, to determine the condition of the machine, the tooling and other accessories included, and other details affecting its fitness for the intended purpose. Careful inspection is essential because used equipment is generally sold "as is," and the original manufacturer's warranty of quality and suitability no longer applies.

REQUISITION FOR EQUIPMENT

The requisition for production equipment originates in the operating division and, at the outset, requires the authorization of the plant manager, superintendent, or other responsible production executive. Similarly, requests for other types of equipment—medical, laboratory, cafeteria, or office machinery—must be presented or certified by the executive in charge of these respective activities.

The requisition alone does not always authorize the purchase. Usually, and almost invariably in the case of major equipment, a special appropriation is required. This serves the double purpose of safeguarding against promiscuous expenditures and major commitments without sanction of the financial department and of keeping management informed of developments that are essentially a part of the company's capital assets. Sometimes these appropriations are made at the time the need is expressed, in which case the requisition and procurement proceed along the normal course for any purchase; more frequently, a specific appropriation is made after the requisition has been translated into a detailed purchase proposal and approved by all those concerned. In companies for which a monetary limit is placed upon purchases that can be made without special approval, it is customary for this allowance to be less liberal in respect to capital equipment than for materials and supplies for current use. For example, in one company where a limitation of $5,000 applies to general purchases, capital purchases in excess of $15,000 require the general manager's approval. This makes it possible to procure a typewriter or a couple of bench grinders in the regular course of business, whereas a request for an elaborate bookkeeping or tabulating machine or a turret lathe would first be scanned by the manager. The logic of such an arrangement is obvious, not because of the money involved, but because any such major equipment would probably affect the capacity and the methods of the company for a long period to come.

For this reason, the requisition for equipment must either be a more detailed form than the ordinary purchase requisition described in the preceding chapter, or it must be supported by additional information to make possible more intelligent analysis of the need and the means by which it is proposed to satisfy that need.

Inside the tool specifier's mind

Does anybody out there have an organized approach to buying? You couldn't prove it by talking to William J. Doherty, manager of manufacturing engineering, Emerson Electric Co.'s Alco Controls Div., St. Louis.

Asked by the National Machine Tool Builders' Assn. to give a presentation on the buying of machine tools, he discovered that hardly anyone has formal procedures—and that he was no exception. This list is his preference, in order of diminishing significance:

1. Return on investment. But on special machines, he lists the reliability of the vendor as being more important. One reason is the pre-investment involved with special machines.
2. Reliability of the vendor and his equipment.
3. Equipment features. He says this is one of the most difficult things to tag with a dollar value. At Alco, features are selected by the engineer and the foreman involved.
4. The sales engineer. Mr. Doherty says he looks for product knowledge, helpfulness, patience, honesty—he demands more than a peddler.
5. Previous association with the product.
6. Service after sale. This is important because many tools can be in service ten years or more, says Mr. Doherty.
7. Turnkey responsibility. This can be especially significant in dealing with special machines. He knows of one bad example: lack of a turnkey responsibility is the major reason why a $20,000 machine system that was installed two years ago is *still* not operational. He is willing to pay a premium for assuming turnkey responsibility.
8. Engineering assistance. This includes such things as prototypes, requoting, and production estimates.
9. Versatility of equipment. "Our products can change rapidly," says Mr. Doherty.
10. Assistance with justification. "That takes more time than any other factor going into the purchase order. This is especially difficult on numerical control machines where it is difficult to put numbers on the indirect savings they make possible. The vendor must help."
11. Safety features. "On our purchase order, we state that the equipment must meet OSHA standards. One vendor refused to sell with that clause in the contract."
12. Manufacturing facilities of the vendor. "This is a matter of policy on all large purchases. It can raise some interesting questions. In one instance, we discovered a major builder didn't use his own equipment."
13. Location of manufacturer. "In specialized equipment we don't go foreign, and in the U. S. we have a bias in favor of the maker who is within a 300-mile radius of the plant."
14. Financial stability of the manufacturer.
15. Delivery.

Figure 16-2. Machine tool users and specifiers employ a variety of criteria in selecting equipment (and suppliers). This excerpt from *Industry Week* magazine, August 16, 1976, gives one department manager's views on the subject.

QUALITY FACTORS

As is the case with all industrial purchases, the requirement fundamentally consists of a purpose to be served or a job to be done, rather than the material or machine to do the job. Quality, in the sense of suitability for the purpose, therefore means the ability of equipment to do a particular job satisfactorily and efficiently over a period of time. The chief factors in selecting heavy machinery include (1) economy, (2) productivity, (3) dependability, (4) time or labor saving, and (5) durability.

These are all ways of expressing slightly different aspects of this same concept of quality; for, in the purchasing sense, quality of equipment is measured primarily in terms of performance and efficiency of operation, ultimately reflected in low cost of product, which is the result that must be balanced against cost of the equipment to arrive at the real value of the purchase.

There are, of course, certain basic descriptions or definitions to be considered first: the type of machine required to perform the desired operation—lathe, grinder, shaper, miller, drill, press, or other. Along with this comes the question of whether the equipment is to be used for a special purpose, continuously employed on a single operation, or for general purposes, adaptable to a greater variety of related operations. Special-purpose machinery may give better performance, and greater efficiency and output under conditions of large-quantity orders and mass production, where a machine is used continuously on one job with a minimum of setup changes. For small companies and for varied production, general-purpose equipment usually affords greater flexibility and a wider range of capacity and consequently offers greater possibilities of full-time utilization.

Within the general type are certain requirements as to precision, speed, power source, and the like. These are minimum requirements in the definition. Superior qualities may be desirable and useful; but, to the extent that extra costs are entailed by building these superior qualities into the equipment, they may represent the purchase of surplus refinements of performance that may rarely if ever be used.

There is also a quantitative requirement in the capacity of the machine. Certain output or productivity is needed to accomplish the purpose for which the equipment is desired. This is also a minimum requirement, a part of the definition.

Up to this point, the statement of the necessary characteristics of the machine is entirely a responsibility of engineering and operating officials. Now the element of competition enters. Whereas machine tools and similar equipment are highly individualized and have specialized features that make them particularly adapted to certain conditions of operation, the basic things that they will do and the purposes for which they are designed are entirely comparable. The issue of value has sometimes been confused and strong prejudices built up in favor of certain designs by stressing the points of difference rather than the fundamental similarity of purpose. It therefore becomes the responsibility of the purchasing department to see that the definition or specification is nonexclusive and to find all sources or makes that will satisfy the requirement. This is directly parallel to the purchasing process in respect to any other requisition. It is only when complete information is at hand regarding possible alternative equipment that will serve the purpose that competent consideration can be given to the points of comparison that lie beyond these minimum requirements and that are summed up in the buying motives listed here.

ULTIMATE COSTS

The five buying motives should be analyzed in some greater detail. Economy, productivity, dependability, saving of time or labor, and durability are all operating characteristics, and they are concerned with costs of use after the purchase, not with costs in the purchase price. But because the purpose of this procurement is the use of the machine rather than the machine itself, they constitute a cost increment that must be considered in the ultimate cost of performing the job. As an element of production cost, they frequently outweigh many times over the significance of the purchase price. Therefore, these characteristics of the equipment are constituents of quality and of value, in which the purchasing manager is vitally interested. The final decision is not entirely within his or her jurisdiction in this case, but it is highly important that these characteristics be interpreted in terms of the buying motives, without which no satisfactory selection can ever be made.

Economy of operation means that the added costs per unit of production will be held to a minimum. This is a generalization covering all sorts of factors that contribute to the end result; and other considerations are more specific.

Productivity or efficiency of equipment means that more units will be produced, or more successive operations performed, within a given period of operation, with the same result of lower cost per unit, plus the advantage of faster production.

Dependability means low maintenance cost and continuity of production, with a minimum of idle productive time due to breakdown. It is the assurance that the requirement will actually be satisfied and that continuity of use will avoid the increment of overhead charges without corresponding output against which they may be applied. It should be supported with adequate service from the supplier in respect to replacement parts and whatever special mechanical adjustment may be required.

Time- or labor-saving features of equipment point to the fact that important production costs are involved in addition to the cost of the equipment itself and its operation and that they may vary with different types of equipment. These costs may not be directly allocated to the equipment, but their effect on the overall cost should be given full consideration. Machines exist primarily to increase the productivity of human labor, and the ability of a machine to operate with a crew of three men instead of four or to increase the output of a single operator 5 percent or 10 percent as compared with his or her production at another machine is perhaps the most significant measure of the machine's efficiency and advantage as an investment.

Durability refers to the service life of equipment at high efficiency. This means a greater total output, a greater return on the investment, and more units of product over which the cost of the machine may be spread. As a matter of cost accounting policy, it is probable that this cost will have been fully depreciated before the useful life of the machine has been exhausted, but this does not alter the basic economy of durable equipment.

Life-Cycle Costing

A technique for evaluating the total cost of a piece of equipment, developed by the Department of Defense and gaining in usage in indus-try, is life-cycle costing. It is a method used to compare and evaluate the total cost received in bids, based on the expected life of the product. All costs are evaluated as a package: research, development, production, operation, and maintenance of the product or system.

The maintenance aspect of life-cycle costing has been used particu-larly successfully by the City of Chicago. For example, prior to buying refuse trucks with a life time guarantee of maintenance, the city spent an average of $293 per month to maintain each vehicle. When trucks were bought, by competitive bidding on a life guarantee basis, the monthly average was reduced to $183.69, a total fixed unit cost for the life of each unit of equipment.

The emphasis on operating costs does not imply that initial cost can be disregarded. As a matter of fact, it is highly important in that initial cost is the factor against which productivity, dependability, and durability must be weighed in seeking purchase value. Furthermore, as a capital investment, initial cost has a direct bearing on ultimate costs, because it involves carrying charges, determines the cost chargeable to depreciation, and provides the basis on which profitable operation must be calculated. Just as in figuring the true cost of materials, certain factors such as transportation and handling in and out of stores must be added to the invoice price, the total cost of equipment includes transportation, cost of installation, any extra foundations or other special expenses, and the costs of accessories and tooling.

THE BUYING TEAM

On the basis of the requisition and the comparative data and costs assem-bled by the purchasing department, the problem of selecting the right equipment is a matter for joint consideration by the plant engineer, the chief production executive, the head of the department in which the equipment is to be used, the purchasing manager, and a representative of general management. Expressed in functional terms, these are the individuals responsible for setting up the process, for overall efficiency of operation, for using the equipment, for economical procurement, and for the company's capital policy.

In the small company, the conference will probably be an informal one, leading directly to the purchase authorization. In the large company, it will lead first to a recommendation, requiring authorization by some designated officer of the company before the purchase can be made. For the purposes of this recommendation, a more formal analysis must be made and put into writing. It is presumed that, if the request is well founded and based on demonstrable need, the required authorization will be granted; nevertheless, there is a distinct value in going through this procedure. Putting the recommendation and supporting data into writing is evidence that an adequate analysis has been made and that the pertinent questions have been considered and answered. As a record of what the equipment is expected to accomplish, it provides a standard against which actual performance can later be measured. If this later comparison proves disappointing, and it is too late to do anything about the particular purchase, the analysis will still be a guide to judgment in later decisions, indicating whether too much or too little weight has been given to certain factors of selection, or whether excessive optimism or aggressiveness or superior selling ability on the part of any individual connected with the selection has prejudiced the decision to the disadvantage of the company as a whole. Such circumstances can be guarded against in later selections.

A typical form for analysis and recommendation consists of a letter-sized sheet mimeographed on both sides, with space for such pertinent data as the following:

Operation for which equipment is to be used

Part or product to be produced

Estimated annual requirements of this part

Estimated number of machine-hours that new equipment will be utilized in a year

Is equipment to provide additional capacity or for replacement of present equipment?

How is the part now being produced?

Present cost of producing part

Cost of procuring part from outside sources

Estimated cost of part produced on the new equipment

Total installed cost of new equipment

Itemized list and cost of accessories required

Age of present equipment

Salvage value of present equipment

Remarks: advantages expected from new equipment

Recommendations for purchase

Signatures of plant manager, chief engineer, purchasing manager, and department head

Machine size and power requirements, while not specifically part of the performance specifications, should be carefully defined in relation to a plant's layout and utility systems. These requirements are sometimes overlooked by suppliers. One company emphasizes their importance with a special amendment to its purchase orders for capital equipment (see Figure 16-3).

RECONCILING SPECIALIZED VIEWPOINTS

No recommendation requiring such a detailed analysis will be lightly made, and with these data in hand top management can make its decision intelligently and confidently.

In arriving at the recommendation, all parties to the conference are, of course, looking to the same result of satisfaction, efficiency, and ultimate economy. They approach the situation from somewhat different viewpoints and with certain special interests, and because of these special interests each is able to contribute something to the decision. The purpose of the joint analysis is to balance and reconcile these interests, to eliminate those that represent merely preference or prejudice, and to give proper weight to those that appear only when the problem is considered as a whole.

In the case of production equipment, the chief production executive will presumably exert the greatest influence, because he or she is the one ultimately responsible for efficient operation. The chief production executive is also the one best able to visualize the equipment and the producing capacity that it represents, in relation to the other facilities with which it must be used and in the light of the overall facilities, flexibility, and balance of the plant as a whole; but the engineers who have planned the process and are intimately familiar with its special requirements, and who may have further developments of a related nature in mind, can best

RHEEM MANUFACTURING COMPANY
EQUIPMENT SPECIFICATIONS

Date_____

TO:_____   (MAIL TO VENDOR
_____   IN DUPLICATE)

_____

SUBJECT: P.O.# _____

Gentlemen:

The equipment being purchased from your company on our order #_____
is to be furnished according to the following special information and specifications
which are made a part of the Purchase Order. Where compliance is impossible,
you are to notify the Rheem Manufacturing Company in writing of the variations.
They must be approved by our Plant Engineer before work can proceed.

    1.   Building Limitations
       A. Minimum Ceiling Height
       B. Maximum Door Width   _____
       C. Maximum Aisle Width   _____

       Equipment must be built to dimensions which will permit
       movement to installation through our Plant in accordance
       with these minimum and maximum dimensions, unless
       otherwise specified.

    2.   Utilities
         Power   _____   Volts
         Air   _____   Pounds Pressure
         Water   _____   Pounds Pressure
         Gas

               Natural   _____
               Mixed   _____   BTU _____
               Mfg.   _____   BTU _____

    3.   Paint
         Paint all body, frame and other fixed parts   _____
         Paint all guards   _____
         Paint all exposed moving parts   _____

ACKNOWLEDGED

_____   SIGNED:_____Plant Engineer

_____   _____Materials Manager

Figure 16-3.   Special instructions added to equipment specifications that accompany purchase orders for capital items. Courtesy, Rheem Manufacturing Company.

define the basic specification and can recognize and evaluate desirable special characteristics of the equipment under consideration. The head of the department in which the equipment is to be used, and which is to be charged with the expenditure and investment, has an important interest in the decision; the enthusiasm or reluctance of his or her acceptance may have a direct bearing on the efficiency of the equipment in actual use. The purchasing manager, in addition to surveying the market and seeing to it that both initial and ultimate economy are served, has the responsibility of negotiation and procurement once the decision has been made and the purchase authorized.

WHO SETS TERMS AND CONDITIONS?

The high value, technical complexity, and distinctive design features of many capital equipment items often complicate negotiation for purchase of such equipment. In requesting bids, purchasing departments forward their company's terms and conditions. Suppliers traditionally insist that their product has special features and that they are in a better position to evaluate its performance technically and in terms of experience and acknowledge the order using another set of terms and conditions. Consequently, a certain amount of haggling and byplay are often involved before the transaction is complete.

One large steel company has taken the initiative in setting terms and conditions from equipment suppliers and put it into the hands of its buyers. It has set up "Standard Conditions for Equipment Purchase Agreements" that are sent out with every request for quotation involving equipment or construction work costing more than $100,000. A broad range of subjects is covered. Particular emphasis is placed on terms of payment, indemnity for patent infringement, and warranties. In addition to the warranty against defects, for example, the company insists on a performance warranty with this clause:

> Seller acknowledges that Crucible has informed seller of the specific purpose for which Crucible will use the equipment. Seller expressly warrants and guarantees that the equipment is merchantable and is fit and suitable for the specific purpose for which Crucible intends to use the equipment.

Despite some initial resistance, suppliers have generally accepted the idea that their proposals will not be considered unless they agree to the standardized terms and conditions. The benefits for the company have been (1) more simplified analysis of bids, as identical terms make price and technical details a common denominator for competing vendors, (2) stronger negotiating position, (3) reduction in negotiating time.

EQUIPMENT RECORDS

Most purchasing departments make it a rule not to clutter up their files with reference records on nonrepetitive purchases, but equipment records are an exception to this rule. A detailed inventory should be kept in the purchasing department of all major equipment, whether actively in use or retired. This should include the manufacturer's name and address, the local distributor or other representative, model number, parts list and numbers, references to appropriate catalog data, date of purchase, and date of disposition if the equipment is replaced or retired from service.This is a record that increases in value with the passage of time by facilitating the identification and procurement of replacement parts. Changes of design in subsequent models frequently make such requirements difficult, as parts have become obsolete from the manufacturer's viewpoint just at the time when the need for new parts arises from the age and long-continued use of equipment. Cases can be cited in which the original manufacturer of the equipment has gone out of business, but, through accurate information, the purchasing manager has been able to trace the original patterns or drawings to the inactive files of some successor organization. One such record going back nearly sixty years is known. Reference to the older entries is not frequent, of course, but they have proved to be of invaluable aid on those occasions when they have been called into use.

The record has current usefulness, too, for replacement and repair purchases, for the procurement of accessory equipment, for interdepartmental transfers in place of purchasing additional capacity, for checking up on later and improved models, for reference in the consideration of subsequent equipment requirements, and, finally, for the eventual disposition of the equipment, which is a responsibility generally assigned to the purchasing department.

SOME PERFORMANCE OBJECTIVES

After studying this chapter you should be able to

1. Explain why the purchase of capital equipment is handled differently from that of materials and supplies.

2. Name and discuss the chief factors to be considered in selecting heavy machinery.
3. List the advantages and disadvantages of buying used equipment or leasing equipment.
4. Trace the steps involved in the purchase of capital equipment from the time that the need is known until the purchase order is ready to be placed.
5. List the items, other than price, that purchasing can negotiate with suppliers of capital equipment.
6. Explain the life-cycle costing concept.

Another form of buying in which purchasing should be deeply involved, but is different in several respects from conventional procurement of materials and supplies, is the purchase of transportation. Techniques for improving transportation services and lowering costs are discussed in the next chapter.

The Purchase of Transportation Services

In a recent internal report on the activities of its purchasing and transportation department, a large manufacturing company listed annual expenditures for materials at $686 million and those for transportation (primarily inbound and outbound freight charges) at $78 million. Cost-reduction efforts of the purchasing group resulted in savings for the year of $25.7 million, or approximately 4 percent; those of the transportation section amounted to $6.9 million, or almost 9 percent.

The figures are significant to anyone interested in purchasing because they dramatize a number of facts that are not always appreciated by individuals and organizations that otherwise show great interest in the cost of materials:

1. Transportation costs represent a substantial part of the price of a purchased product and therefore, a substantial part of the average company's expenditures on materials and services. (This holds true in governmental and institutional buying as well.) In the case cited, the amount is slightly more than 10 percent. This, in turn, is a little over 5 percent of the company's yearly income, as materials and services account for about half the company's sales dollar.

2. Use of transportation services is a form of purchasing, just as the acquisition of a material or product is. Recognition of that fact was the reason for combining the two functions in the company mentioned—purchasing and traffic and transportation—in a single department. The trend to this type of organization may be accelerated by recent new laws that deregulate transportation and stimulate competition among carriers.

3. The purchase of transportation, therefore, should involve the same techiques discussed in earlier chapters: careful evaluation and selection of suppliers, price analysis, value analysis, aggressive negotiation, and so on. A corrollary is that knowledgeable personnel, using those techniques, can effect substantial savings and, just as important, obtain greatly improved service from suppliers. As one expert has put it, because the basic purpose of the purchasing function is to secure goods and services in the most cost-effective manner, skilled purchasing professionals should apply their skills to the service that transports the goods.[1] It makes no sense, he points out, for a buyer to record a $100 savings obtained through negotiation, only to have part or all of it vanish because of improper carrier selection.

RELATIONSHIP OF PURCHASING AND TRAFFIC

Large organizations generally have separate traffic departments; others have some form of materials management system (see Chapter 6) in which traffic and purchasing are closely related parts. Even as late as 1976, however, a leading trade journal reported that most companies did not have professional traffic departments.[2] Often, it was said, the traffic "department" is staffed by a shipping clerk whose only knowledge of transportation is the telephone numbers of local carriers and the names of carrier sales representatives who call. A warehouse foreman who keeps goods moving on and off the shipping dock may also be considered part of the "department."

Purchasing personnel generally have little difficulty working with existing traffic departments. Nevertheless, it is important that they continually press their case for help on inbound shipments. Because the bulk of the transportation dollar is usually spent on outgoing shipments, particularly in industry, the tendency is to pay more attention to that area. Given the proper motivation, a traffic department can be of great assistance to purchasing on such matters as supply routes and rates for inbound shipments; routes, rates, and classifications for potential suppliers; rate adjustments; tracing, expediting, and reconsigning shipments; advice on most economical size of orders from the standpoint of freight charges; pooling of inbound shipments; auditing freight bills; changes in freight rates and classifications; and filing claims for loss and damage.

[1] Manfred A. Passman, "Are You Giving Freight Transportation Service the Proper Treatment?" *National Association of Educational Buyers Bulletin,* September 22, 1978.

[2] "Avoid Shipping Errors That Drain off Dollars," *Purchasing Magazine,* July 20, 1976. p. 97–101.

With the big increase in international trade, to be discussed in Chapter 18, the traffic department can be of even greater help, particularly in regard to shipping and clearance documents, tariff and custom regulations, and various forms of overseas transportation.

A purchasing manager intent on getting utmost value for the dollars that the purchasing department spends has a problem—and an opportunity—in those cases in which the traffic department, if it exists at all, is not much more than a couple of clerical personnel. The problem is that responsibility for traffic is generally dispersed among the accounting, sales, and purchasing departments, so that in the end no one is really responsible and significant cost savings are passed up. Purchasing and sales specify the carriers that they want for their shipments, accounting audits the freight bills, and no one bothers with the fine points of procurement, such as negotiation. Purchasing's opportunity in such cases is to assume full responsibility for setting up an organized traffic activity of some kind—be it under direct purchasing control or not—so that the company can get the full benefits of a "transportation purchasing" program.

CONTROL STARTS WITH FUNDAMENTALS

In some ways, the field of transportation is exceedingly complex: the number of carriers (and the specialized equipment and services available is huge; federal, state, and local regulations are voluminous; and the rate and classification data maintained by the Interstate Commerce Commission would fill a good-sized public library.

The buyer or purchasing manager, however, need not be an authority on every phase of the subject to exercise the same control over transportation costs that he or she does over material costs. The buyer can start with a working knowledge of fundamentals. Thereafter, he or she has access to a wide variety of information and help. The literature on traffic and transportation is extensive, and several authoritative trade journals in the field keep their readers current on all significant developments in the industry. We have already spoken of existing traffic departments as an excellent source of guidance and assistance; lacking that source, the purchasing manager can always call on the services of outside professional traffic consultants.

Leading transportation companies—railroads, airlines, and truckers, for example—have staffs equipped to provide all kinds of assistance, for general or for specific problems. Despite the element of self-interest that is involved, the knowledge and expertise that they make available is very valuable. In a more general way, associations—the Air Transport Association, the American Trucking Associations and the Association of American Railroads, to name a few—also offer help on a wide range of transportation problems.

A basic approach in coming to grips with transportation is to avoid leaving too much control over shipments in the supplier's hands. Vague purchase order specifications or instructions as to what mode and what carrier to use in shipping purchased goods are almost always open invitations to costly abuses, often unintentional, but still harmful to the buyer's interests. Buyers who take the easy way out and limit instructions to "Ship best way" and "Ship soon as possible" simply take too much for granted. To a supplier's shipping department, "best way" could mean whatever is the easiest, rather than the most efficient, way. It could also mean shipping by a friendly carrier who is generous at Christmas but costly and unreliable every other day of the year. The term could also be interpreted quite innocently as the fastest way at premium rates, even though the buyer may have had exactly the opposite in mind. An open-ended expression such as "Ship as soon as possible" is also open to obvious misinterpretation. Buyers should be specific about the mode of shipping—and carrier, if possible—and exact about delivery dates. The supplier is a specialist in making certain products; there is no assurance that he or she is a specialist in transportation.

F.O.B. TERMS

Buyers should have a basic knowledge of commonly used transportation terms, particularly F.O.B. (free on board). Many people assume that the term simply indicates that either the vendor or the buyer of the item is responsible for transportation charges to the buyer's plant. There is more to F.O.B. than just freight charges, however. Every purchase involves a transfer of title to merchandise from seller to buyer, assuming that the seller has title to begin with. When and where the transfer of title takes place are important because of possible legal complications over such things as damage and loss. There are several variations of F.O.B. terms, and the choice of a particular term will be influenced by trade custom, the nature of the item, the amount of money involved and the buyer's analysis of what costs are involved in each method—for example, would it eliminate paperwork, save time, and so on to simply have the supplier handle everything up to delivery at his or her plant? Following are the choices of terms of sale:

 1. *F.O.B. Origin, Freight Collect.* Title passes to buyer at the sell-

er's plant or warehouse. Buyer owns the goods in transit, pays freight charges, and files claims, if any.

2. *F.O.B. Origin, Freight Prepaid.* Title passes to buyer at the seller's facility, but freight charges are paid by the seller. Buyer owns the goods in transit and files claims, if any.

3. *F.O.B. Origin, Freight Prepaid and Charged Back.* Same as item 2 but seller collects freight charges from buyer by adding the amount to the invoice.

4. *F.O.B. Destination, Freight Collect.* Title passes to buyer upon delivery to the plant, and buyer pays the freight charges. Seller owns the goods in transit and files claims, if any.

5. *F.O.B. Destination, Freight Prepaid.* Seller pays the freight charges, owns the goods in transit, files claims, if any. Title passes to buyer upon delivery.

6. *F.O.B. Destination, Freight Collect and Allowed.* Seller owns goods in transit and files claims, if any. Title passes to buyer on delivery. Buyer pays the freight charges, but charges them back to the seller by deducting the amount from the invoice.

Larger companies generally pefer to buy F.O.B. the seller's plant, because their traffic departments (and often purchasing departments) are better equipped to do an effective job of carrier selection and routing. Smaller companies may not have the staff or the expertise to exercise that kind of control over transportation costs and service and, in a sense, may be forced to turn that responsibility over to the suppliers. Passive acceptance of such a policy weakens their whole purchasing stance, however. The fundamental criteria of right price and right quality at the right time apply to transportation just as much as they do materials, and any or all of them may be affected adversely by improper packing and shipping.

MODES OF TRANSPORTATION

The transportation industry offers a wide variety of modes to move goods of every size, shape and weight to practically any point in the country. ("Mode" is an industry term meaning a particular form of transport.)

Rail freight is the basic mode for large shipments, and it still accounts for almost half the freight shipped in the United States. Rates for full carload (CL), which run from approximately 30,000 pounds and up, are generally lower than those of other modes, with the exception of pipelines. Less than carload (LCL) rates are less competitive. Use of rail freight requires either a rail siding at the buyer's plant or an easily accessible freight yard or similar facility (in which case pickup by truck adds additional costs). Railroads, faced with tough competition from other modes, are continually upgrading their procedures, rolling stock, and special equipment for moving and handling, in an effort to retain the business of large shippers. The normal time for a rail shipment to move from New York to San Francisco is five days; times between other points vary proportionately.

Motor freight carriers handle either truckloads (TL) of approximately 20,000 pounds, or less than truckloads (LTL), which are considerably more expensive. The advantages of this mode include great flexibility in short hauls and door-to-door service (most plants are equipped with docks for loading and unloading trucks.) Generally speaking, truck freight moves faster than rail freight on short hauls, and it is competitive on a time basis on many long hauls.

Surface freight forwarders appeared on the scene as an economic response to the difficulty that shippers have had in getting railroads and trucks to move small (LCL and LTL) shipments at what they consider reasonable cost. Surface freight forwarders pick up relatively small shipments from a number of customers, consolidate them into carload or truckload lots, and arrange for their transport by rail or truck. The largest and best known surface freight forwarder is United Parcel Service.

Air freight, looked at in terms of total cost, can often be competitive with rail and truck freight, despite its higher rates. Deliveries by air reduce the need for large inventories of certain types of products; packaging requirements are simpler and less costly; delivery is fast (New York to San Francisco: five to six hours).

The airlines have steadily increased their share of the freight market with innovative ideas in packaging and handling, plus the addition of enormous carrying capacity in the new jumbo jets.

Airline parcel service, offered by the leading carriers, provides for fast movement of small packages 25 pounds or less and no larger than 90 inches in length, width, and girth combined). Packages must be delivered and picked up at the airport. The airlines guarantee that a shipment will go out on the next available flight.

Air freight forwarders provide the same types of services as their surface freight counterparts. They consolidate small shipments, move them by air at quantity rates, and through use of trucks at origin and destination can provide door-to-door service overnight to many points. Forwarders now offer service to about 8,000 communities. Rates are high but competitive in terms of total cost.

Parcel post is the most popular choice for inbound shipments of 70 pounds or under. Major problems associated with this mode are the general deterioration in postal service, shippers' or buyers' difficulty in determining delivery schedules, delays that occur during holiday periods, and the high rates of loss and damage in shipments.

Express mail, developed a few years ago by the U.S. Postal Service, offers guaranteed overnight delivery of letters and packages weighing up to 700 pounds. In 1979 service was available in approximately 1,000 U.S. communities. Items delivered to an express mail post office by 5 P.M. are available for pickup at the destination post office no later than 10 A.M. the following day. Delivery can also be made directly to the addressee for an extra charge.

Bus package express provides transport of relatively small packages between approximately 25,000 communities on the routes of major bus-lines. Total transit time on short runs—for example, New York to Boston—is comparable to that of air freight. Service is generally available twenty-four hours a day, seven days a week. Packages must be brought to and picked up from bus terminals.

Inland waterways transportation—by barges and scows drawn by towboats and tugs—has been enlarging its share of the freight market for a number of reasons: rates are considerably cheaper than those of any other mode, carriers have superior equipment for handling low-value bulk commodities and semifinished items, the number of industrial centers linked by navigable rivers has increased, and delivery is often as good as that of rail freight.

Piggyback and fishyback are neologisms for shipping methods developed by combining two of the modes just described. The first method involves pickup of a special trailer at the shipper's facility and then transport of the trailer to a rail facility, where it is loaded on a flat car. The longer part of the haul is then made by rail. The trailer can be delivered directly to a plant with a rail siding, or it can be moved again by tractor truck to its destination. Fishyback is a variation of piggyback, except that it combines movement by truck and water carriers. The combination of two modes permits reduction in handling costs as the handling of one unit— the container—is faster and more efficient than is handling a large number of individual items.

Pipeline transportation. Although technically they are common carriers and in terms of dollar value carry a significant percentage of the nation's freight, pipelines transport virtually only natural gas and petroleum products. Unlike other common carriers, pipelines usually handle the products of their owners, oil and gas producers. They are regulated by the Interstate Commerce Commission to protect the small producers or refiners who must use the pipelines of others to transport their products.

On a cost per barrel/mile basis, pipeline transportation is more cost efficient than any other form of transportation, with the exception of the largest supertankers.

Although primarily used to ship crude petroleum natural gas and refined petroleum products, pipelines have also been used to carry coal slurry—crushed coal suspended in water.

Private carriage describes company-operated as opposed to carrier-operated transportation. Technically, private carriage includes the operation of company-owned railroads, barges, ships and aircraft, but in general use, the term refers to trucks, both local and long distance. An estimated nine of every ten trucks in use are engaged in private carriage.

Companies operating their own trucks use them to supplement for-hire transportation. The reason most often given is that by running its own trucks, the company can obtain transportation equipment or service not available from, or superior to that offered by, for-hire carriers.

Yet companies who require neither special equipment nor special service also operate their own trucks. They find they can provide the same or better service at substantially less cost. Few companies who make the decision to operate trucks ever take them off.

Recent changes in Interstate Commerce Commission policy make private carriage more attractive and these changes are expected to spur the growth of private carriage. These changes are designed to save fuel and make maximum use of the nation's transportation fleet. They help private carriers by giving them more freedom to cope with a classic transportation problem—how to achieve a balanced operation, how to have a truck fully loaded in both directions for every trip.

Private carriers are not permitted to haul for the public, for hire, once they have applied for and obtained operating rights from the I.C.C. They can also haul, for hire, for subsidiaries of parent companies. These restrictions were initially placed on private carriage to protect the markets of the I.C.C.-regulated carriers.

No long-distance fleet can operate at a profit if it has freight moving only in one direction and must return to its base empty. Here is where purchasing, by pairing deliveries to customers with pickups from suppliers, can help make a private fleet operation profitable and reduce inbound transportation costs at the same time.

This need to provide a two-way loaded movement before a private carriage operation can be profitable is why companies use their private fleet for only part of their transportation needs. The unbalanced one-way moves, both outbound and inbound, are turned over to a common carrier on the assumption that the common carrier will have other customers offering freight to be shipped in the opposite direction.

FREIGHT RATES AND CLASSIFICATIONS

Contrary to a widely held belief, freight rates are not established and controlled by the Interstate Commerce Commission (ICC) or by any other governmental agency. The role of the ICC had been to determine that the rates proposed by carriers and shippers are just, reasonable, and nondiscriminatory. Rates are actually open to negotiation following deregulation of the transportation industry.

Classification of materials or products being moved is the basis for setting rates, that is, the higher the classification, the higher the rate. Plastic articles transported on LTL shipments, for example, have been classified as "Less than six pounds per cubic foot, Class 200; six pounds per cubic foot, but less than 12 pounds per cubic foot or over, Class 85." The rate for Class 100 is approximately one half that of Class 200; the rate for Class 85 is about 15 percent lower than that for Class 100.

Classes are printed in two publications that are essential parts of the business library of anyone involved in specifying or paying for various types of shipping: the *National Motor Freight Classification,* published by the American Trucking Associations, Washington, D.C., and the *Uniform Freight Classification,* published by Tariff Publishing Officer, Chicago, Ill.

To be sure they are charged the correct freight rates—and that they do not violate any Federal or state laws—shippers should thoroughly acquaint themselves with the descriptions of articles in the tariffs under which they ship. Commodity descriptions in shipping orders and bills of lading should conform to those in the applicable tariff, including packaging specifications, because there may be different rates for the same articles that are shipped in different types of packaging.

Precise descriptions of purchased items to be shipped to the buyer are essential then if the buyer is to get full value from his or her "transportation dollar." Because higher classes are shipped at higher rates, it is important that the buyer not assume that shippers or rate clerks will automatically protect the buyer's interests. Suppliers will often ship at the higher rate when there is some doubt about the exact classification to protect themselves, as there are legal penalties for falsifying billing. Similarly, rate clerks assess a shipment on the basis of what is on the shipping order and will often go to the higher rate to protect themselves.

Table 17-1 provides a few simple examples of how incomplete descriptions of purchased items can result in higher freight costs and ultimately higher total product cost.[3]

---

[3] Data courtesy *Purchasing Magazine.*

This need to provide a two-way loaded movement before a private carriage operation can be profitable is why companies use their private fleet for only part of their transportation needs. The unbalanced one-way moves, both outbound and inbound, are turned over to a common carrier on the assumption that the common carrier will have other customers offering freight to be shipped in the opposite direction.

General advice to companies considering the move to private carriage is to analyze the pros and cons of the move, by factoring in present transportation costs, the probability of balanced movements being available, the cost of equipment, availablity of labor, operating expenses, etc. Some transportation consultants specialize in fleet proposal analysis.

Table 17-1
Shipping Costs When Shipment Descriptions Are Incomplete

Specific product	If shipped with this incomplete description	Is rated	Should be rated
Cotton work shirts	Cotton shirts	Class 100	Class 77.5
Crude sulphate of soda	Chemical	Class 100	Class 50
Cotter pins, iron, or steel	Hardware	Class 70	Class 50

Examples of how analytical purchasing and traffic managers have reduced costs through changes in classification abound. Two from a large manufacturer of electrical equipment are typical. The company had been paying higher rates on electric meter sockets than on cable terminals and other items with similar transport characteristics. Application for a change in classification to the lower class and lower rate was successful, and costs were cut substantially. In another case, the company, as do many companies that discover that their product descriptions are incomplete or slightly inaccurate, asked for a change in classification of certain components of their generators from "electric generator parts." The traffic department had found that the components could more accurately be classified as structural steel parts. The change was agreed upon, and the rates went down.

Negotiation of freight rates is somewhat different from the type of negotiation described in Chapter 14. Efforts to obtain changes in rates begin with the shipper and the carrier. If agreement is reached on a new rate, the carrier proposes it to the appropriate freight rate bureaus that the transportation industry has established in various parts of the country—for example, the Southern Motor Carriers Conference or the Eastern Rail Freight Conference. If, after a public hearing, the appropriate bureau approves the change, the tariff is published and filed with the ICC, to become effective in not less than thirty days. The ICC reviews the tariff and, unless the commission believes it to be unreasonable or unjustified, or unless interested parties such as other shippers and carriers object, no further action is taken. If there are objections either by the ICC or interested parties, the commission undertakes lengthy procedural action in which the carrier and shipper making the application for a new tariff must prove that the rate is reasonable and justified.

An executive of a large eastern trucking company has offered the following basic suggestions to purchasing managers without immediate access to traffic information or training, who nevertheless want to purchase transportation as economically as they purchase materials and equipment.

1. Keep the freight classifications that apply to your purchases in your purchasing library. Local carriers will help in identifying which classification you need and where you can get it.

2. Determine if density is a factor in the rating of commodities that you buy. If so, instruct suppliers to specify density on all your shipments.

3. Whenever a "released value" provision applies to your purchased commodities (the information appears in the classification), make sure the supplier takes advantage of the provision.[4]

4. Make sure that your purchase order carries the complete classification description and insist that the supplier describe the shipment in the same way on any shipping documents.

5. Never permit incoming merchandise to be described by trade name. Very few classifications list trade names, so the shipper may be assessed higher charges.

6. Whenever more than one item is shipped on a bill of lading, see that a weight breakdown is furnished for each item. A basic rule of rating shipments is that whenever a weight breakdown is not furnished for each item, the entire shipment is rated at the highest rating that applies to any one article in the shipment.

---

[4] The ICC permits shipments of certain commodities at "released value," that is, at less than their actual value to limit the carrier's liability. The carrier in turn can offer a lower rate to the shipper. The "released" provision sets the maximum for which a loss or damage claim will be paid. However, many shippers who take advantage of the provision carry insurance policies to cover damage above "released value."

DEREGULATION OF TRANSPORTATION

Deregulation of transportation which, broadly speaking, is aimed at reducing the maze of rules governing carriers and introducing greater competition into the industry, began in earnest in the 1970's. Some of the major provisions of the laws passed follow.

—The Airline Deregulation Bill of 1978 made it easier for new carriers to enter the field and allowed carriers to raise or lower rates within certain limits without permission from the Civil Aeronautics Board.

—The Motor Carrier Act of 1980 made entry of newcomers into the business easier, permitted existing carriers to expand operations and raise and lower rates within certain limits without permission from the Interstate Commerce Commission, and permitted companies with private trucking operations to haul freight for subsidiaries and charge for the service.

—Proposed legislation for deregulating railroads was being debated in Congress as this book went to press. It would remove the railroad's protection against antitrust prosecution agreeing among themselves to set rates at certain levels, sharply reduce ICC control over certain types of rates, and allow railroad intermodal ownership.

The full effect of deregulation may not be felt for several years, but a prominent authority on transportation predicted these long-term benefits to users of transportation services:

Increased use of intermodal transportation, i.e., combinations of rail, truck and air transport.

Classification of trucking by service, rather than by the artificial legal definitions of common, contract, private and exempt.

Movement of freight under contractual agreements based on return on investment, rather than on myriad tariff classifications.

Increased emphasis on service, rather than on price discounts, lessening the impact of an influx of "Mom and Pop" transportation companies.

Disappearance of complex tariffs and classifications, interpreted by rate bureaus.

Setting commodity shipment rates according to the competitive marketplace.

Growing domination of long distance distribution by the railroads as the pricing of transportation services approached a true cost basis.[5]

[5] John J. Barry, "Clearing the Air on Transportation Deregulation," *Purchasing World*, January, 1980.

THE IMPORTANCE OF PROPER PACKAGING

Packaging is an important consideration in the transport of products and materials because it can affect the price, the quality, and to a degree the delivery of the purchased product. The buyer should be aware of these facts: (1) items should have adequate protection against jolting, rough handling, accidents, and all the other dangers inherent in the movement of goods—particularly when more than one carrier is involved; (2) excessive packaging can add unnecessary freight charges because it adds weight to a shipment; (3) properly designed packaging and containers not only minimize the problems mentioned here but can reduce handling costs at points of origin and receipt as well as in the customer's storage and production areas.

Whenever possible, agreement on the types of packaging and containers to be used for shipping the purchased products should be made at the time that the purchase itself is negotiated. The better carriers respond positively to appeals for assistance in holding down total purchase cost, just as reliable suppliers of materials and equipment do. Most of the innovations and improvements in packaging and handling that have been developed over the years were inspired by competition, which in turn is spurred by buyers of transportation, either in traffic departments or in purchasing departments.

The experience of a midwestern company that had to truck heat exchangers about 150 miles to another division for plating provides a good example of close carrier–customer coordination in overcoming problems and cutting costs. Protective packaging was needed on the units when they were shipped to the plating facility and when they were returned to the plant. But the packaging was costly and time consuming. Working together, carrier personnel and company personnel from both the traffic and production departments devised special equipment that would permit safe shipment of the heat exchangers without any packaging at all. But the group did not rest with that improvement; using skids and racks, they refined the system so that the heat exchangers could be moved from the plant to the trucks, from the trucks right into the plating process and then back out on the trucks for movement back to the plant, without being removed from the equipment.

DAMAGE CLAIMS

Despite advances in transport packaging and handling, however, damage during shipment continues to plague the transportation industry and its customers. Buyers should be particularly concerned about early detection of damage to inbound freight, not only because of the possible monetary

314

loss but because damage to production materials for example, could disrupt tightly scheduled manufacturing operations. Goods should be inspected as quickly as possible, both to ascertain the need for immediate replacement and to determine carrier responsibility, if any. If there is an indication that the carrier is at fault, claims should be made promptly, because even the most efficient and cooperative carriers can take up to several months to settle claims. Supporting evidence should always accompany claims.

SOME PERFORMANCE OBJECTIVES

After studying this chapter you should be able to

1. Discuss the similarities and differences between conventional purchasing of materials and supplies and procurement of transportation services.
2. List some of the problems that can be caused by indifference as to how products are to be shipped and by vague or incorrect instructions regarding shipment.
3. Differentiate between transportation "modes" and "carriers" and give several examples of each.
4. Explain the meaning of F.O.B. and its significance to the purchasing department.
5. Discuss the means available to purchasing managers without a background in traffic management for controlling the cost of transportation.
6. Explain the importance of proper packaging in respect to both inbound and outbound shipments of freight.

Another activity that was unfamiliar to purchasing managers in general until recently is purchasing in the international market. The problems and opportunities involved in this type of buying are covered in the next chapter.

Purchasing in International Markets

18

It is hard to believe now, but only a few decades ago the West Coast of the United States was considered a relatively undeveloped area, industrially speaking. Despite the growth of the aircraft industry in states such as California and Washington during World War II, major manufacturers seeking to establish plants in the area in the late 1940s had difficulty in locating adequate local or regional sources of supply for materials and components. In some cases, they resorted to various forms of subsidy or assistance to develop satellite industries and avoid the high cost of transporting materials and supplies from the Middle West[1]

Today, of course, the West Coast, and the even more "underdeveloped" South and Southwest, are all integral and significant parts of the one great continental U.S. industrial market. It is the rare industrial purchasing department that does not have regular suppliers in all major sections of the country.

This dramatic change in the American market is mentioned to point up the significance of an even greater and more rapid expansion of the industrial market—one that has taken purchasing managers and buyers far beyond national borders.

By the mid-1970s almost half of American industrial purchasing departments covered in a nationwide survey were buying some part of their requirements in foreign countries—an increase of 21 percent in less than two years.[2]

---

[1] "Ford's West Coast Purchasing Program," *Purchasing Magazine*, July 1948, p. 249.

[2] Somerby Dowst, "Nearly Half of Buyers Now Dealing Overseas," *Purchasing Magazine*, May 6, 1975, p. 49–51.

U.S. Customs Department figures for 1976 showed that in one year imports of typical industrial products rose as follows: motors, 34 percent; switches, 40 percent; gears, 27 percent; hand tools, 21 percent; electrical machinery, 17 percent; fasteners, 21 percent.

American buyers, particularly those of the large companies, had been dealing with suppliers in leading industrial nations of the world— England, France, West Germany, and Japan—for a number of years. Raw material imports—metals, petroleum, agricultural products, for example—had also been a big factor in U.S. industrial imports. But the huge expansion of the 1970s took in literally the whole world. This included such nations as the Soviet Union and the People's Republic of China, heretofore virtually off limits to U.S. buyers because of political considerations. When major corporations began buying in those two nations, it was big news; a few years later the establishment of purchasing offices in such places as Moscow and Peking by American companies was almost commonplace. The trend toward economic integration and the end of economic isolation seemed irreversible, despite political differences.

A powerful factor in the change has been the development of almost instantaneous communication and rapid transportation between any points in the world. A telephone call from New Orleans to Hong Kong takes little more time than a call between neighboring U.S. counties; air shipments from Europe are made overnight; a New York purchasing manager wishing to visit the Paris plant of a supplier can fly there by Concorde in less time than it would take him or her to drive to Boston.

Basically, U.S. buyers have turned abroad for a significant portion of their purchases because foreign sources offer them certain advantages that they find difficult to obtain from domestic suppliers in many cases:

Continuity of supply.   Increased worldwide demand for goods made it imperative that new sources of supply be developed. Industry has become sharply aware—particularly since the shortages of 1973–1975—that the long-range outlook is for continued scarcity of supply in a variety of materials. As the vice president of General Motors in charge of procurement, production control, and logistics put it,

> [There is] mounting evidence of worldwide shortages. For example, petroleum products, powdered metal, aluminum and some precious metals are approaching short supply, if they are not in short supply already... If we are to run our business properly we must be able to coordinate our worldwide needs with our worldwide availablity.[3]

[3] From an address by Thomas E. Darnton at the convention of the Purchasing Management Association of Canada, Quebec City, June 1978.

Suppliers may be customers. Virtually the whole world is a potential market for goods produced in the United States, so it makes good economic and political sense to buy in that market when it offers some of the competitive advantages listed in the following paragraphs. In addition, it is the policy of most multinational corporations to accept some responsibility for the economic development of the nations in which they operate. In the same speech, Mr. Darnton said:

> Producing for and selling to the world market is replacing the national market concept. General Motors will be responding [Authors' note: as part of the reorganization described in Chapter 5] to the new global concept of doing business through its new international purchasing program.

Greater competition. The growth of commerce and industry in relatively underdeveloped, or politically isolated, nations—added to that of the already industrialized countries—has opened up new sources and new productive capacity. Increased competition and availability have a powerful attraction for professional buyers, particularly when they appear to be waning in their normal markets.

Cost benefits. Generally, foreign sources have been able to offer American buyers lower prices, particularly on manufactured goods, because of lower labor, material, and overhead costs. Total landed costs, incuding the cost of transportation for thousands of miles in some cases, are often lower than are those of U.S. suppliers of a wide range of industrial supplies and equipment. Rising standards of living and pressure from labor may eventually nullify that advantage, but initially it has given tremendous impetus to the growth of the international market.

High-quality technological know-how. For years, many people had the notion that foreign producers were generally followers of U.S. industry in quality standards and product innovation. American purchasing managers consistently report the opposite in many cases. Foreign vendors have displayed great flexibility in adapting their manufacturing methods to special requirements; their products—particularly machinery—are often far advanced over American counterparts; and the quality of many products (e.g., stainless steel, high-tolerance forgings, precision ball bearings) is often superior to that of higher-priced domestic items.

Issuing a purchase order to a foreign supplier does not, however, automatically guarantee irresistible prices, better service, high quality, bright ideas, and so on. Suppliers must be as carefully researched—and often more so—as domestic vendors are. Dealing with heretofore unknown companies in foreign markets presents many difficulties and obstacles. Few are insuperable, however, and indeed present purchasing people with many opportunities for improving their skills in negotiation, research, and finance. A number of large companies with overseas purchasing operations have, as a matter of policy, used such operations as training grounds for younger personnel marked for advancement to high managerial positions, both in purchasing and in other executive areas.

These are some of the problems in overseas buying that require close attention and control:

Low costs may prove ephemeral.   Unless *total* costs are carefully considered and monitored, the economic advantage that seemed to exist in a low initial price may quickly evaporate. Rising freight costs, a high rate of reject in items purchased, labor troubles at supplier plants, delayed deliveries, the need for carrying heavier inventories to protect against such delays, and the possibility of having capital tied up in letters of credit are just some of the elements that may affect the final cost of a product purchased abroad.

Currency fluctuations cause trouble.   Extreme gyrations in the exchange rates between countries may cancel out the economic advantages expected. Half the cost increases in foreign purchases experienced in 1978 were attributed to the severe decline in the U.S. dollar in that period.

Cultural and language differences must be overcome.   Methods of doing business, social customs that are part of doing business, and, of course, languages can cause complications serious enough to upset the delicate negotiations that are often required in international trade.

Quality problems do exist.   As mentioned, quality standards vary from country to country and industry to industry. Rigid specifications are not always adhered to (or even understood) by some foreign suppliers. Rejects of foreign goods are more troublesome than are those of domestic items, because duty has usually already been paid on them and the process of returning them and getting customs refunds is costly and time consuming.

Paperwork is extensive and complex.   Import duties, insurance, and other administrative procedures require a great deal of time and effort, at least initially, and can be discouraging to those who buy abroad only sporadically and in small quantities.

SELECTION OF SUPPLIERS

Locating a supplier—once the determination to buy overseas has been made—can involve something as simple as a telephone call or as extensive as a small research project. Just as on home ground, buyers can get information on foreign products and producers from a number of sources. Thorough evaluation of the supplier, however, is somewhat more difficult and lengthy as it may require consultation with other customers of a distant supplier, obtaining and testing samples, or even visiting overseas plants if the producer's reputation is unknown.

Information sources include a variety of publications, from trade journals and newspapers to directories of manufacturers and distributors, to trade lists, directory reports, and surveys from the Department of Commerce. An exceptionally clear and comprehensive guide to international purchasing procedures lists twenty major directories on internationl trade.[4] They include such volumes as *The American Register of Exporters and Importers,* published in New York; *Jane's Major Companies of Europe,* published in London; *Dun & Bradstreet's World Marketing Directory,* published in New York; *Directory of Swiss Manufacturers and Products,* published in Zurich; and the *Bottin International Business Register,* published in France, which contains information on companies throughout the world. These and other directories are available in World Trade Center libraries that have been established in twenty-three leading American cities.

The Department of Commerce maintains up-to-date lists of names and addresses of foreign companies dealing in specific products in more than a hundred countries. The lists also identify importers and dealers, along with other pertinent information. The department also maintains trade centers in leading foreign cities such as Warsaw, Seoul, Milan, Paris, and Sydney. (U.S. district offices in forty-two leading cities are also excellent sources of information.)

There are also American Chambers of Commerce in fifty leading cities throughout the world, all prepared to help U.S. buyers and sellers. Embassies and consulates, both of foreign countries and the United States, are similarly equipped to aid businessmen seeking to trade in their respective countries.

Banks, airlines, and shipping companies have significant collections of data on businesses in the countries that they serve, as well as information on local customs and procedures.

When there is no competitive advantage involved, purchasing managers of other companies experienced in overseas buying are usually willing to help newcomers to the field.

A significant step in the promotion of world trade was taken by the

---

[4] C. L. Scott and Eddie S. W. Hong, "An Operational Approach to International Purchasing, in *Guide to Purchasing* (New York: National Association of Purchasing Management, 1975), pp. 1–31.

purchasing profession itself when the International Federation of Purchasing and Materials Management (IFPMM) drew up a list of member correspondents in twenty foreign nations. The correspondents have agreed to provide overseas buyers with data on suppliers in their respective companies. This list is available in the United States through the National Association of Purchasing Management in New York, a member of IFPMM. N.A.P.M., in turn, has compiled a guide, "How to Buy in the United States," for use by IFPMM member associations throughout the world.

DIRECT AND INDIRECT BUYING

Whether to buy directly from overseas suppliers or indirectly through intermediaries depends in large part on the volume and frequency of purchases, the anticipated length of a relationship with a supplier, and the availability of qualified buying personnel.

Small-volume or occasional purchasers most often use a variety of middlemen—wholesalers, brokers, selling agents—for overseas transactions. For a fee (which in the case of selling agents or representatives is paid by the supplier), they will handle the basic details of a purchase, including choice of a supplier when necessary. The breadth of services varies widely among these intermediaries, so it is important to know in advance whether or not their fees (which can run up to 25 percent of the value of the purchase) cover such important elements as research on vendors, shipping costs, insurance, customs, administrative expenses, and degree of financial responsibility, among others. Prudent buyers will also make an effort to determine, preferably from their other customers, the broker's or agent's performance record.

Trading companies are larger organizations that offer even more comprehensive services than do those of the specialists mentioned earlier. They usually handle a broad spectrum of products from one or more countries, ranging from small consumer goods on up to the most complex types of machinery. Some, such as Mitsubishi of Japan, have offices all over the world and maintain their own transportation and financial services. In advising buyers to consider trading companies as an alternative, the authors of "An Operational Approach to International Purchasing" cite these advantages: greater efficiency and convenience, lower costs, shorter lead times, and assurance of quality, as inspection is made before shipment and the trading company remains responsible in this country for unacceptable shipments.[5]

---

[5] *Ibid* p. 22.

Another authority, however, has at least one reservation about trading companies and, presumably, other types of intermediaries. The prices that they obtain, he says, are seldom established on the basis of costs but on market levels at the time of purchase, so that the buyer is denied the possible benefits of direct negotiation.[6]

The different points of view underscore the need for extra care and judgment in dealing in new and distant markets.

As transportation and communication improvements make the world market even more compact and accessible, middlemen will undoubtedly be relegated to a minor or highly specialized role in international trade. By the mid-1970s, indeed, most major American companies had well-established networks for buying directly in Europe, Asia, Latin America, and parts of Africa, after years of having sent purchasing personnel abroad on individual buying trips. Some assigned responsibility for purchasing requirements to existing buying departments in foreign subsidiaries; others established separate buying offices that report directly to corporate headquarters. Scott and Hong suggest these advantages to setting up a separate foreign purchasing office:

1. Lower operating costs. Foreign purchasing overhead is generally lower than the brokers fees. Communication is more effective and less costly.

2. Better control. On-site administration provides better control over price, quality, and delivery schedules. The foreign office is also better equipped to handle the intricacies of foreign exchange.

3. More current information is available. The ruless and regulations that govern foreign transactions in overseas countries often change, and an on-site office has access to the most current legal and economic information.

4. Better understanding. Foreign nationals in such offices can often negotiate better agreements than can many U.S. businessmen because of their familiarity with the territory, local business conditions, local customs, and, of course, language.

On the final point, there has been some disagreement, as many purchasing managers prefer to place American supervisors in any type of purchasing organization—subsidiary or separate office—buying products for use by U.S. plants. In most cases, however, on-site nationals have played an important part in the buying process because of their knowledge, as has been described. In recent years, however, nationality as such has become almost irrelevant. Experience has shown that purchasing executives with good professional skills and the ability to adapt to chang-

[6] Paul Combs, *Handbook of International Purchasing* 2nd ed. (Boston: Cahners Books, 1977), p. 161.

ing conditions can operate almost anywhere. It is not unusual, for example, to find a Brazilian heading the Rotterdam purchasing office of a large American firm. Similar situations can be found in many other functions of business. Managerial competence is the major requirement.

CULTURAL AND LINGUISTIC DIFFERENCES

Regardless of the type of purchasing organization or methods that a company establishes overseas, one cardinal rule must be observed: know and respect the culture and customs of the nationals with whom you wish to deal. A corollary is: Know how to communicate with foreign counterparts, preferably in their own language, but at least through skilled interpreters. Ignorance or disregard of these matters can lead to embarrassment at best and harm to your own interests at worst.

Examples of misunderstanding abound:

1. In preparing Hertz Rent-a-Car advertisements for the German market, an agency used the then widely known (in the U.S.) slogan, "Hertz Puts *You* in the Driver's Seat." When rendered into German by an unskilled translator, the idiomatic expression, intended to appeal to status-conscious American businessmen, came out as "Hertz Makes *You* the Chauffeur," which hardly made it appealing to the even more status-conscious German businessmen.

2. Even after a few years of doing business with a Japanese company, an American buyer sent the supplier's sales department a letter of cancellation, only to receive a reply stating that they did not know the meaning of the word "cancellation."

3. The purchasing director of a major U.S. company began preliminary negotiations with a Japanese company for the purchase of well over a million dollars worth of copper-fin tubing. At a critical point, the senior supplier representative at the session said flatly, "Mr. R_____ , tell us the lowest price you are paying any of your current suppliers and I guarantee we will cut that price by 20 percent." Trying to make the point that "auction" buying—that is, revealing other supplier's prices to obtain leverage in a negotiation—was not the way that he did business, the purchasing director replied, with typical American exaggeration. "Why, I could tell you that I am paying only 10 cents a pound" (the average price at the time was about 50 cents).

The Japanese took the reply literally, and obviously stunned, then highly agitated, they asked for a recess in negotiations. By the time the session was resumed the following day, they had flown in two top officials from Tokyo to add to their delegation. The misunderstanding was quickly cleared when the purchasing director explained that he was simply dramatizing a point. A mutually advantageous contract was worked out, although the purchasing executive came close to missing a substantial reduction in price, and the suppliers a lucrative sale because of a misunderstanding.

In an informative filmstrip/cassette produced by the International Group of the National Association of Purchasing Management, purchasing managers planning to buy overseas are urged to stay well informed on foreign business customs. The following set of "rules" for negotiating in the Japanese market is offered as a guide.[7] The "rules" are, of course, adaptable to purchasing in other foreign nations.

1. Have high level introductions
2. Maintain surface harmony
3. Avoid embarrassments
4. Understand the importance of appearance
6. Be patient—progress will be slow
7. Speak their language—if only a little
8. Have plenty of business cards
9. Give little mementos
10. Be generous with visitors

"Number 6—patience—is particularly important," the narrator of the program says. "Japanese business practice is not to meet and run, but to get to know each other first and to reach some form of consensus among themselves before finalizing a business venture."

Any analysis prior to the establishment of a long-range overseas procurement program should also include some consideration of politicoeconomic conditions in the country or area involved. There is obvious risk in doing business in national economies that are strike-prone, plagued by civil disorder, ruled by unstable governments, and subject to manipulation for domestic and international political purposes. Any one of these conditions, if extended for any length of time, can result in delayed or canceled shipments, revocation of price agreements, and destruction of property. Even the least of those problems—delayed shipments—could require heavy investment in inventory building to guard against plant shutdowns, thereby adding to the total cost of a purchase. In self-defense against such eventualities, some overseas buyers have resorted to double sourcing, that is, they place part of their

---

[7] "An Approach to International Purchasing" PAL 49, (New York: National Association of Purchasing Management, 1976).

business with one or more domestic suppliers to assure themselves some supply in the event of trouble overseas. This, however, dilutes the benefits that they would otherwise get from a foreign supplier's lower price.

NEGOTIATING WITH FOREIGN SUPPLIERS

It should be clear from points made earlier in this chapter that negotiations with foreign suppliers call for a good deal of understanding and insight in addition to the normal planning required for such sessions. Formal plans are needed, but they are not enough; negotiators must have more than ordinary skills to deal productively with people of different commercial and cultural backgrounds than theirs.

This is not to say that the principles of sound negotiation described in Chapter 14—thorough preparation, development of the negotiating team, precise definition of team members' responsibilities, establishment of objectives, analysis of relative bargaining positions, and so on—do not apply in overseas buying. They definitely do. But some must be modified and others intensified, and in every case they must be adapted to customs, practices, and perceptions that may differ from those found in American business.

Obviously, preparation for negotiation in a foreign country (or anywhere for that matter) begins with the designation of skilled negotiators who have sound judgment and can adapt readily to new or difficult situations. As a backup to basic negotiating techniques, experienced international traders suggest these approaches:

1. Observe local custom in business relationships. In Japan, for example, customers and suppliers customarily get to know each other on a personal basis before getting down to business, so a certain amount of socializing may be expected.

2. Because negotiations in direct overseas purchasing are generally conducted on the supplier's home ground, at least one member of the negotiating team should be fluent in the language and thoroughly conversant with normal business practices of the country.

3. Serious negotiations should be conducted whenever possible only with persons who have the authority to commit their companies. Anyone without that authority may simply drag out the negotiation, wasting valuable time and ultimately leading the buyer to reveal his or her bargaining strengths (and weaknesses) prematurely.

4. Some foreign negotiators, as Combs points out,[8] measure their success in negotiation by the number rather than the substance of the

---

[8] *Ibid.*, p. 175.

concessions they win. If they win on more than half the issues, they may consider the negotiation a success. In such a situation, good strategy on the part of the buyer would be to develop as many negotiation points as possible in the advance planning. This would give the negotiator flexibility in making minor concessions without endangering major objectives.

5. Businessmen in many foreign countries are extremely status conscious and consider it undignified to deal with lower-level personnel. Negotiating teams, therefore, should whenever possible be composed of—or at least led by—persons whose titles correspond with those of the supplier representatives.

6. Negotiators should avoid peremptory or abrupt actions and decisions that could alienate suppliers (who may also be customers of one or more divisions of the buying company). The kind of blunt talk that is taken quite objectively in American business discussions might be taken as a personal affront overseas. As previously mentioned, maintenance of at least surface harmony is essential.

7. No negotiation should be concluded without mutual understanding and firm agreement on product specifications, delivery schedules, prices, packaging and shipping methods, insurance, and terms of payment. This seems an elementary precaution, but, because of language and other differences, carelessness in ironing out details could lead to costly mistakes for both sides. Just the casual use of the term "ton" for example, can cause trouble unless it is made clear what kind of ton is meant: a short ton (2,000 lb) a long ton (2,240 lb) or a metric ton (2,204.62 lb). Similar confusion in describing complex items with close tolerances would present even more serious problems.

TERMS, SHIPPING, INSURANCE, CUSTOMS

Payment for goods purchased overseas can be made in a number of ways: payment in advance; payment after the seller has delivered the purchased materials to the buyer's plant, as in regular domestic buyer–seller transactions; and payment by letter of credit.

The latter method has for many years been the most common form of settlement in the international market. Letters of credit are issued by the purchaser's bank, and the supplier can draw against the credit upon presentation of the required documents.

Letters of credit spell out the total amount of the purchase, the currency in which payments are to be made, and what documents must accompany each draft. Because the foreign supplier is generally responsible for clearance of the shipment, the supplier must submit bills of lading or airway bills, commerical invoice, customs invoice, insurance certificate, and, in some instances required by U.S. Customs, inspection or analysis certificates.

The letter of credit mechanism, flow of goods and documents, and the relationship between parties to the letter of credit are shown in Figure 18-1.

Currency fluctuations can cause problems for overseas buyers. (As was estimated earlier, for example, at least half the increase in costs of buying abroad in 1978 was caused by the decline of the dollar in international markets.) Among the steps that buyers have taken to soften the impact of downturns in the exchange rate are (1) agreements with suppliers to split what exchange loss does occur, (2) the purchase of blocks of foreign currency to cover purchase requirements for a given period, (3) the purchase of currency futures, and (4) the negotiation of contracts that call for firm prices regardless of fluctuations in the exchange rate.

Buyers cannot be expected, however, to be financial specialists any more than they can be expected to be engineers and lawyers. When complications in payment terms and currency fluctuations are anticipated, overseas buyers should call on the company finance department for guidance and assistance. In a number of larger companies with extensive experience in overseas procurement, purchasing personnel meet at least quarterly with their financial people to assess the position of the dollar in relation to major currencies of the world, particularly those of the countries in which they are currently buying. They also have immediate access to financial assistance in special situations.

A number of terms are used in international trade to describe seller and buyers' rights, duties, and risks in respect to shipping. A complete list of terms and their definitions appears in the authoritative reference work, *Revised American Trade Definitions*, published by the National Foreign Trade Council, Inc. The overseas buyer should, however, be familiar with the following basic expressions as defined by Combs:[9]

> *F.O.B. (free on board) your plant:* supplier makes delivery to buyer's plant on a carrier and bears all risks and costs. F.O.B. the foreign port: transfer of title occurs when the goods are loaded on the carrier and buyer assumes costs and risks from that point.
> *Ex works* (factory, warehouse, etc.): seller makes delivery at port of origin, and thereafter all risks and costs are the buyer's.
> *F.A.S.* (free along side): seller bears all risks until the merchandise is placed within reach of the ship's tackle. Thereafter, all transportation risks and expenses are the buyer's

[9] *Ibid.,* pp. 84–89.

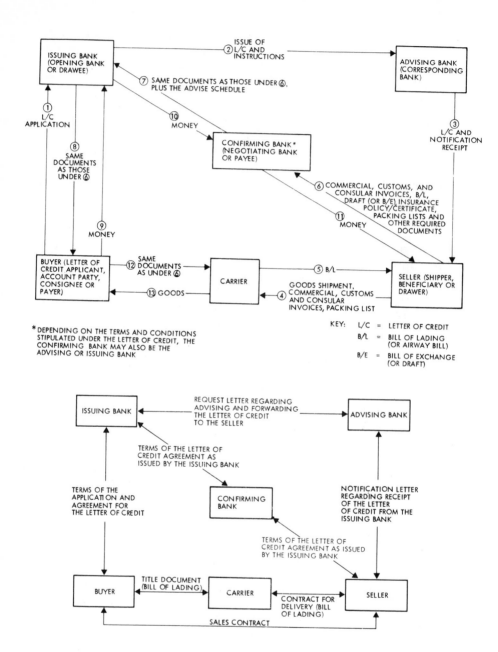

Figure 18-1. Letter of credit mechanism: flow of goods and documents (top) and governing relationship between the parties to the letter of credit (bottom). Courtesy, TRW, Inc.

Ex dock: seller bears cost and responsibility for placing goods on the dock at port of destination. There, buyer takes ownership and possession and assumes all further risks and costs.

C.I.F. (cost, insurance, freight): seller is responsible for all costs and risks until the ocean vessel ties up to the dock of destination. Unloading is the buyer's risk, as are the costs and risks of all subsequent handling, storage, importation, and transportion.

C & F (cost and freight): seller does not provide insurance or bear the risk for loss of merchandise while at sea. Otherwise the term is the same as C.I.F.

Proper packaging is an essential element in the safe arrival of overseas shipments. Specification of export packing ordinarily ensures that the goods will be protected despite multiple handling, lengthy in-transit time, and the possibility of pilferage. This should be written into the contract at the time of negotiations.

Several years ago, the newly organized International Group of the National Association of Purchasing Management suggested that one of the conditions of the purchase order be the following statement, or one similar to it:

All goods must be packed in an adequate manner to withstand the handling involved in export shipment by (specify type or carrier). There should also be agreement on the part of the supplier to number each package consecutively, and to indicate on each package the company's name, order number, port of arrival, and country of origin.

FREE TRADE ZONES

No discussion of overseas buying by American companies would be complete without some mention of special customs privileges extended to buyers in U.S. foreign trade zones, commonly know as free trade zones. These locations, considered outside customs territory, are available for activities that might otherwise be carried on overseas for customs reasons. The Bureau of Customs, U.S. Department of Treasury, describes the function of the free trade zones thus in its publication, "Exporting to the United States":[10]

On the import and re-export side, no duties are charged on foreign goods moved into zones unless and until the goods or their products are moved into customs territory. This means that the use of zones can be considered

[10] *Exporting to the United States,* U.S. Department of the Treasury, Customs Bureau.

for operations involving foreign dutiable materials and components being assembled or produced here for re-export. Also, in such cases no quota restrictions would ordinarily apply. There are now 12 approved foreign-trade zones in the United States. The facilities are available for operations involving storage, repacking, inspection, exhibition, assembly, manufacturing, and other processing.

Information on the zones is available from the Foreign-Trade Zones Board, Department of Commerce, Washington, D.C. 20230, or from the nearest Department of Commerce district office.

INFORMATION ON OVERSEAS PROCUREMENT

Purchasing in foreign markets is a complex, sometimes very delicate, and often frustrating, process. Only in its broadest outlines can it be discussed in the limited space of this chapter. There is, however, an enormous amount of information on various aspects of foreign purchasing available to both experienced and neophyte buyers. Immediately at hand are the finance and traffic departments of the buyer's company, with which the purchasing department should closely coordinate its overseas purchasing efforts. The foreign trade departments of major banks are an excellent resource. In addition to the publications, directories, and agencies already mentioned, buyers should have, or have access to, such reference books as the following:

Foreign Commerce Handbook, U.S. Chamber of Commerce; *An Introduction to Doing Import and Export Business,* U.S. Chamber of Commerce; *Export and Import Procedures,* Morgan Guaranty Trust Co. of New York; *Exporting to the United States,* U.S. Treasury Department Bureau of Customs; *Export and Import Financing Procedures,* First National Bank of Chicago; *Customs Information for Exporters to the U.S.,* U.S. Treasury Department, Bureau of Customs.

SOME PERFORMANCE OBJECTIVES

After studying this chapter you should be able to

1. List the advantages often claimed for purchasing some requirements overseas. Evaluate them in light of today's conditions.
2. Review the problems that may face buyers entering the international market for the first time.

3. Discuss your personal attitude toward and experience with foreign made products or components, particularly in those cases in which you chose them in preference to domestically produced products.
4. Explain the rules for negotiating in the Japanese market discussed in the text.
5. Give some recent examples of how socioeconomic and political developments can affect American companies' international purchasing programs.
6. Define the following terms as they are used in international trade: F.O.B., ex works, F.A.S., ex dock, C.I.F. and C & F.

Throughout this text heavy emphasis has been put on the policies and systems in industrial purchasing and how they can be employed to increase profits. Billions of dollars are being spent by purchasing departments in nonprofit organizations, however, and how efficiently this money is being spent has a decided effect on the national economy. The following chapter deals with the differences and similarities between purchasing in industry and in such service organizations as governments, and educational and health institutions.

Purchasing in Nonprofit Organizations

19

Buying for business and industry for many years received the lion's share of attention in purchasing literature, in business school classrooms, and in various educational and training programs, such as those of the National Association of Purchasing Management and the American Management Association. Relatively little attention was paid to purchasing for governments and government agencies, health institutions, schools and colleges, and other nonprofit or philanthropic organizations. The efforts of such organizations as the National Institute of Governmental Purchasing and the National Association of Educational Buyers and the excellent performance records by individual governmental and institutional purchasing executives received little notice in comparison with that given developments in industrial purchasing. (Procurement in the federal government is something of an exception, in a negative way. As pointed out in one of several studies,[1] from the time that the Second Continental Congress established a Commissary General in 1775, government procurement has commanded the attention of public officials and private citizens. All too often, it was emphasized, the attention has focused on individual abuses rather than on the overall system.)

The benign neglect seemed understandable at the time. The conventional wisdom was that because industry as a whole bought so much more and spent so much more than any other group of purchasers, it would by a process of natural selection have developed the most sophisti-

[1] Report of The Commission on Government Procurement, Vol. 1, Superintendent of Documents, 1972.

cated buying policies and procedures. These would then, "trickle down" into the nonindustrial sectors. After all, it was thought, the buying cycle—requisitioning, seeking suppliers, negotiating, ordering and so on was basically the same whether one bought for General Electric or for a local school district. The outstanding performance of a number of city, state, and university purchasing managers was cited as evidence that nonprofit organizations could use not only basic purchasing methods but such sophisticated techniques as value analysis as well. (Actually, the traffic in ideas was not all one way. Several advanced techniques—life-cycle costing, for example—originated or were refined in nonindustrial organizations before being adopted by industrial buyers. Such contributions were not recognized for some time, however.)

The apparent indifference could not last, however. As government activities and agencies proliferated, health care facilities multiplied, and educational and other types of institutions expanded, their costs came under increasing scrutiny from legislators and the general public. In the early 1970s, for example, Americans were spending $35 billion a year on health care, and that figure was increasing by $3 to $5 billion annually. Approximately 25 percent of these expenditures were going for purchased materials, supplies, and services.

The Comptroller General reported to the Congress in 1977 that large government agencies—such as Defense, Energy, Transportation, Space, and General Services—were spending about $80 billion a year for procurement. (No less than 60,000 federal workers were involved in these procurement activities.) The figure was also growing annually—at a rate of 5 percent or more. Total purchase expenditures of the thousands of local, county, and state government purchasing offices were estimated at over $100 billion a year—and growing at a rate of 3–5 percent. Even in an age of hyperbolic finance, this volume of spending attracted the attention of the public, which was paying the bills, and their elected officials, who wanted assurance that value was obtained for the public's tax dollars or philanthropic dollars. Because a large percentage of the money being spent was coming from federal grants to state and local governments, taxpayers had an additional interest in seeing that procurement was being conducted in an efficient, businesslike manner. As a result, governments at every level, hospitals, universities, and similar institutions have steadily upgraded the personnel assigned to the purchasing and materials management functions, have improved procurement policies and methods, and in general have begun to operate their purchasing departments on the same management principles that have been so successful in industry. This is not to say that individual purchasing executives and organizations in such areas as education, health care, and government at all levels were not the equals of their successful counterparts in industry. The problem was that in general the full potential in purchasing was not recognized. As a result, salaries were relatively low, buyers were subject to many kinds of restraints on imaginative and innovative purchasing of the type described in other parts of this textbook, and many people had a distorted view of the professional standing of nonindustrial purchasing personnel. These impediments to good purchasing were pointed out in a study of defense purchasing as long ago as 1957.[2] The authors decried, for example, the fact that "most Americans have an inborn distrust of the military and a mild contempt for the civil servant; not a few regard government service as a refuge for lazy unemployables." They declared that objective analysis shows that military procurement personnel are probably about as competent, level for level, as their counterparts in industry. "But this isn't enough," they concluded. "They should be more competent. The military establishment buys nearly ten times as much as the biggest private manufacturer. The money they use doesn't come from the voluntary demands of consumers as it does in industry; it comes instead from taxes. Consequently, the need for outstanding purchasing is that much greater."

Whether purchasing personnel in tax-supported bodies or other nonprofit units such as the health care "industry" and the education "industry" are now more competent than their business counterparts would be hard to prove or disprove, given the magnitude and complexity of the universe that would have to be analyzed. What is clear to most leading purchasing executives, educators, and observers, however, is that as a group their own efficiency and proficiency and that of their departments has shown steady and substantial improvement.

One of the most significant developments of recent years in governmental purchasing was the publication of a *Model Procurement Code for State, County and Local Governments* by the American Bar Association in 1979. The code was the result of several years of cooperative effort by government officials, procurement specialists, attorneys, and government purchasing officers. Despite some criticisms of individual sections, the code has been enthusiastically recognized as a major advance in helping states, counties, and municipalities to establish effective procurement policies and methods.

This chapter provides a broad overview of the general nature, problems, and significant developments in representative nonprofit organizations. Unless specific differences are noted, it can be assumed that well-organized and properly staffed purchasing departments in any milieu will have adapted the *basic* purchasing procedures, policies, and

[2] Paul V. Farrell and Dean S. Ammer, "The Truth about Military Buying," *Purchasing Magazine*, Vol. 44, October 1957 pp. 50–65.

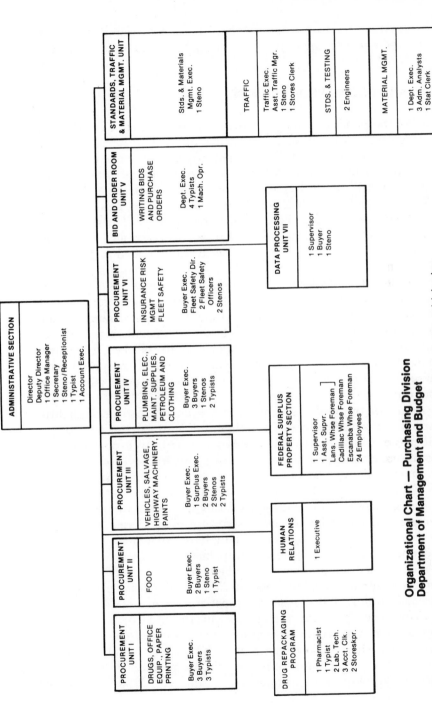

**Organizational Chart — Purchasing Division
Department of Management and Budget**

Figure 19-1—Organization chart of a typical state purchasing agency, which also indicates scope of its responsibility.

techniques discussed throughout this book to their special situations. To describe their purchasing cycles, for example, would be redundant.

STATE AND LOCAL PROCUREMENT

There are thousands of local government bodies, in addition to those of the states, and many differences in their requirements and the regulations and laws that govern their purchasing operations. (The legal references in the State of New York's *Purchase Handbook for Municipalities,* published in 1975, for example, include Town Laws 5, 20, 41, 64, 112, and 117; Village Laws 4-412, 5-520, and 2-526; County Laws 363, 371, 408 and 625; General City Law 20; General Muncible Laws, 103, 104, 105, 106, and 119; Second Class Cities Law 76.) Nevertheless, most of the purchasing agencies follow the basic procedures described in the following paragraphs.

Once requirements have been established, most state and local purchasing offices use competitive sealed bidding, also referred to as procurement by formal advertising, to obtain supplies, services, and construction from suppliers. Public notices of invitations to bid are posted and published a reasonable time prior to the date set for bid opening. Submitted bids are opened publicly and in the presence of witnesses at the designated time, and the bids are made part of the public record.

Award of the business is made to the lowest responsible bidder whose bid conforms in all respects to the criteria listed in the invitation to bid. Ideally, the invitation to bid should contain a complete description of the item or items to be purchased; testing, quality, and workmanship requirements; delivery terms; discounts; transportation costs, and any other element that will affect the *total* cost of the product. Theoretically, then, there is to be no negotiation with bidders after the receipt and opening of the bids. (The terms "responsible bidder" and "responsive bidder" are often interchangeable, although the ABA *Model Procurement Code* defines the former as having "the capability in all respects to perform fully the contract requirements and the integrity and reliability that will assure good faith performance" and the latter as "one who has submitted a bid which conforms in all material respects to the invitation for bids.")

In practice, some governments permit the head of a purchasing agency to negotiate an adjustment of a bid price and changes in bid requirements, when the lowest responsible bid exceeds available alloted funds and time or economic conditions do not permit resolicitation of bids. Such exceptions are recommended in the ABA *Model Procurement*

Code. In every case, preaward approval by higher authority and postaward justification are required.

Generally speaking, state and local regulations permit purchasing units to forego the bidding process for small purchases, emergency purchases, and purchases of certain types of proprietary products for which there is only one source. There has been, moreover, a strong effort to find—and to justify to regulatory bodies—alternatives to competitive bidding when it is clear that such bidding will not be competitive or economically rewarding. Among the conditions suggested by one state purchasing officer as legitimate bases for acting without a formal quotation process are the following:[3]

Requirements can be obtained economically on blanket orders covering specific time periods; purchases of standardized items such as furniture, equipment, and supplies can be negotiated; purchases might require duplication of investment when switched to another vendor (e.g., when duplicate printing negatives and plates or corrugated box dies would have to be supplied); a vendor has an established record of good performance on stock items and is considered better qualified to provide a given service or commodity. The writer urged fellow purchasing officials to "sell" such exceptions to appropriate management bodies or purchasing councils, so that they could be incorporated into a written purchasing policy.

Not all public purchasing officials would agree with Hartman's specific suggestions. Few, however, would disagree with his basic contention, that is, that the taxpayers' interests are not automatically and invariably served by statutory limitations on purchasing methods.

Reflecting the sentiment that public buyer should be given more flexibility in applying purchasing principles used successfully in industry are two provisions in the ABA *Model Procurement Code* that offer alternatives to competitive sealed bidding.

The first—providing for multistep sealed bidding—would permit purchasing agencies to solicit unpriced offers when they determined that it is impractical to prepare a purchase description to support an award based on the lowest-priced bid. Such offers might be solicited for a specially designed or nonstandard item or for a special service on which there was no purchase history or record of supplier performance on quality or service. Offers would be evaluated primarily in respect to the bidders' qualifications to meet the specified requirements. Competitive

[3] Boyd Hartman, "Alternatives to Competitive Bidding" *The Spanner,* publication of the Michigan Public Purchasing Officers Association, October 1978, p. 1.

sealed bids would then be invited from qualified suppliers and evaluated in the conventional manner.

The other alternative suggested by the ABA is the competitive sealed proposal system. Suppliers are invited to offer what are called proposals, but are actually the same as bids under the sealed bid systems, that is, they are offers to provide certain specified products or services at certain prices. Buyers are permitted, however, under this system to evaluate offers by responsible and responsive bidders and compare the quality of competing products. They are also permitted to hold discussions with suppliers as to how proposals might be changed to the advantage of the city, county, or state for which the product is being bought. These techniques are, of course, in common use in industry and are variations of the methods of negotiation permitted in federal procurement (see the next section). But they are strictly prohibited under the sealed bid system. In both industrial and governmental buying, it must be noted, ethical buying practice requires that (1) suppliers be notified that their proposals will be subject to such evaluation and (2) under no circumstances should information obtained from any supplier's proposal be disclosed, for any purpose, to a competitor.

COOPERATIVE PURCHASING

Governmental (local), educational, and institutional buying agencies may individually buy many hundreds of items, but very few buy in the tremendous volume that their industrial counterparts do. Hence they generally do not have the leverage to negotiate with suppliers as agressively and effectively as do those purchasing officers in nearby factories. One widely employed solution is group, or cooperative, purchasing in which individual requirements for products or families of products are combined and obtained through single purchases or contracts with competitive suppliers who offer substantial price reductions on the larger quantities involved.

Cooperative buying arrangements vary only slightly. Bergen County, New Jersey, for example, operates a cooperative buying program in which a majority of the municipalities and most of the local and regional school districts in the county participate. Among the commodities covered in the plan are fuels, tires, automotive products, certain types of paint, rock salt, and asphalt. County purchasing officers select likely commodities for inclusion in the program and then canvass each municipality and school district to determine their interest in pooling their annual requirements. The county purchasing department prepares and advertises the bid proposals and selects the lowest responsible bidder.

Each agency then decides for itself if it wishes to accept the quoted price and all other contractual terms. If the terms are acceptable, it then deals directly with the supplier.

Various states, for example, Michigan and New York, permit local agencies to participate in contracts negotiated at the state level for state requirements, without any canvassing beforehand. Typical commodities covered are fuels, office supplies and furniture. Voluntary (nonpublic) hospitals in many parts of the country have worked out group buying arrangements with other institutions in their areas, in which case committees made up of representatives from the hospitals decide on what items might be purchased in volume at more advantageous terms. The larger groups usually have paid staffs that negotiate volume contracts. Individual hospitals then buy against those contracts. The Hospital Bureau, Inc., founded in 1910, is a national cooperative buying agency for voluntary, nonprofit, healthcare institutions that negotiates national contracts on a wide variety of products. The Educational and Institutional Cooperative performs the same function for higher educational institutions. E&I member purchases were close to $30 million in 1974 and were growing at a rate of 8 percent per year. In both cases, members of the cooperative have achieved substantial savings over what individual purchases would have cost them. E&I is associated with the National Association of Educational Buyers.

FEDERAL GOVERNMENT PURCHASING

As mentioned, the Federal government was spending about $80 billion a year on procurement as the 1970s came to an end, and the figure was rising every year. Such an outlay has a tremendous effect on the economic and social structure of the country. Major contract awards can stimulate growth in various areas, and cancellations of contracts can have the opposite effect. The billions of dollars spent in such fields as atomic energy development, scientific research, space technology, housing, transportation, health care, and the like have resulted in development of products with commercial application, from automobile safety equipment and fire-resistant materials to solid-state computer components. Technological breakthroughs brought about by research and procurement by the Department of Defense and other agencies in such fields as electronics, metallurgy, and fuels have stimulated the development of entire industry segments. Meanwhile, the continually rising costs of government purchases, particularly those by the Department of Defense (which account for about 70 percent of all federal government procurement expenditures), must be met by continually rising taxes.

Governmental spending activity of such magnitude invariably arouses not only the interest but the concern of the taxpaying public and the legislators. For two centuries, the purchasing practices and policies of the Federal government have been the target of criticism, investigations, studies, and legislation, all with the declared purpose of making the procurement system less costly, more efficient, and less prone to abuse. At the risk of oversimplifying an enormous body of valuable work, it can be said that each successive effort to improve the system has had some, but not total, success. But the enormous growth of the government and its requirements and the rapid pace of military and space technology create new procurement problems faster than old ones can be solved.

Constant surveillance of the government's procurement system has resulted in an elaborate set of statutes and regulations that literally take volumes to list, describe, and interpret. Indeed, the volume and complexity of the statutory and regulatory restraints on procurement officials is one of the important contributing causes for whatever shortcomings exist in the system.

The procurement systems of the defense agencies, the Coast Guard, and the National Aeronautics and Space Administration are governed generally by the Armed Services Procurement Act of 1947 (ASPA). Those of many civilian agencies are governed generally by Title III of the Federal Property and Administrative Services Act of 1949 (FPASA). After statutes and executive orders, agency regulations are the most important written means for directing government procurement. The two primary procurement regulations are the Armed Services Procurement Regulations (ASPR) and the Federal Procurement Regulations. There are also semiautonomous procurement regulations for the Atomic Energy Commission, Central Intelligence Agency, National Aeronautics and Space Administration, and the Tennessee Valley Authority, each of which has some degree of independence from FPR.

The Commission on Government Procurement called the present statutory foundation a welter of disparate and confusing restrictions and of grants of limited authority to avoid the restrictions. (This problem has arisen in part because Congress has never been called on to focus its attention on the overall procurement process, the commission said. It added that the inaction of top managers of the executive agencies has aggravated the problems.)

Inconsistencies between the two statutes, the commission reported, involved such things as the following:

1. Competitive discussions. ASPA requires, but FPASA does not, that proposals for negotiated contracts (as distinct from competitive bids) be solicited from a maximum number of qualified sources and that discussions be conducted with all sources in a competitive range.

EXAMPLES OF BOOKS OF REGULATIONS
USED AT A LOCAL BUYING ORGANIZATION

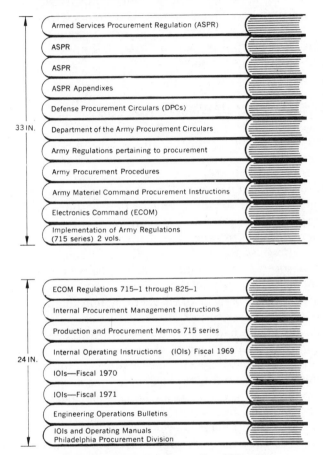

Source: Study Group 3, *Final Report*, Nov. 1971, p. 73.

Figure 19-2—Sketch showing the amount of regulatory material that governs Department of Defense procurement.

2. Truth in negotiations. ASPA requires, but FPASA does not, that contractors and subcontractors submit cost or pricing data.

3. Specifications accompanying invitations for bid. ASPA states that an inadequate specification makes the procurement invalid. Comparable language is not found in FPASA.

The commission has pointed out comparable gaps and inconsistencies not only between ASPR and FPR but in the multiplicity of regulations that have followed in their wake as subordinate agencies. (The volume of such regulations alone would intimidate the most seasoned executive, much less a newly appointed buyer; a contracting officer at the U.S. Army Electronics Command, Philadelphia Procurement Division, for example, has a five-foot shelf of procurement and procurement-related regulations for which he is responsible for knowing and applying insofar as they govern his area of responsibility.

THE FEDERAL PROCUREMENT PROCESS

Although there is some similarity in basic techniques, buying for the federal government differs markedly from buying for state and local governments. The volume of business placed is greater, to put it mildly; federal buyers generally specialize in one commodity or a family of commodities, and in so doing many often become more expert and knowledgeable about them than do supplier representatives, whereas governmental buyers at other levels are often responsible for a varied collection of products, from office supplies to fuel oil and have neither the time nor the incentive to become specialists in all or any of them. Federal procurement, particularly in the Defense Department, often must be planned for a yet-to-be-developed major system that involves research, development, testing, production, construction, installation, training, operation, and maintenance. Even the Federal Supply System (part of the General Services Administration), which buys supplies and services for all federal departments and agencies, gets involved in spurring new technology among its suppliers. A typical example is its development of performance specifications in contracts for home water heaters, ranges, room air conditioners, and frost-free refrigerators, as part of a campaign to design products that use less energy.

The needs that trigger the procurement system may originate from normal depletion of stock of a commercial item, on up to creation of a new and sophisticated weapons system, the complete specifications for which it would be impossible to put in writing at the time. The first requirement is generally handled using the same methods described elsewhere in this book. The second type requires complex planning and may have to be handled by a team that could include project managers, scientists, engineers, lawyers, accountants, price analysts, and other specialists, in addition to the procurement personnel.

The basic forms of procurement are similar to those used in the governmental units discussed earlier: formal advertising and the solicitation of competitive sealed bids; competitive negotiation, and negotiations with a sole source.

Contract types vary according to the degree of risk assumed by the contractor and the amount of profit incentive involved. At one end of the spectrum is the firm fixed-price (FFP) contract in which the contractor agrees to deliver the supplies or services for a specified price that includes profit. At the other end is the cost-plus-fixed-fee (CPFF) contract, in which profit is fixed in the form of a specified fee and the contractor is reimbursed for his or her allowable costs. Use of the CPFF type of contract is severely limited. Selection of contract type is influenced by such factors as the government's financial liability, the adequacy of cost information supplied by the contractor, the nature of the work, and the current market and competitive conditions.

The buying cycle begins with the issuance of an invitation for bid (IFB) or a request for proposal (RFP). The IFP is used in conjunction with formal advertising to solicit competitive sealed bids. The RFP is used to solicit competitive and sole-source proposals as a basis for negotiation.

The Armed Services Procurement Act requires that all procurement be done through formal advertising, with certain exceptions, e.g., purchases of $10,000 or less; purchase of personal or professional services; purchase of items impracticable to secure through formal advertising. There are 17 such exceptions. Most of the dollars spent by the Department of Defense, however, are expended on procurement by negotiation under exceptions to the basic law. Basically, this is because of the complexity and high cost of the equipment and weaponry bought by the department. In such cases, price can only be established after evaluating the estimated costs of performance, followed by bargaining to reach agreement on the amount of money to be paid for the work.

Generally, invitations for bid are sent to a number of suppliers and any company that requests an IFB may obtain one. When other competitive procedures are used, the purchasing agencies generally select the companies to which a request for proposal will be sent; however, additional firms may request an RFP and submit a proposal.

Invitations to bid are opened and recorded in public. The agency involved must determine how responsive bidders are to the requirements spelled out in the invitation to bid and identify the lowest responsive bidder. Once the agency determines that the lowest responsive bidder is capable of performing on the contract, the contract can be awarded.

Items purchased through formal advertising are generally clearly defined. In some cases, however, specifications for an item or service for which invitations to bid are issued may not be firm enough for conventional advertising. The procedure often used in these situations is two-

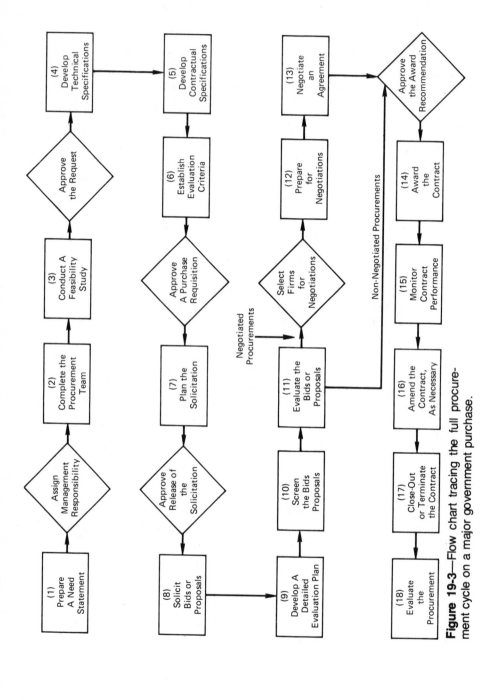

Figure 19-3—Flow chart tracing the full procurement cycle on a major government purchase.

step formal advertising. The first step is to issue requests for proposals and determine which are acceptable. In the second step, those companies which submitted acceptable proposals go through the sealed bid procedure followed in formal advertising. The responsible bidder whose bid is most advantageous to the government then gets the contract.

Sole-source or single-source negotiation is negotiation with only one supplier. It is estimated that approximately 40 percent of all defense contract dollars are placed by using sole-source negotiation.[4] There are two basic reasons: (1) price competition is impossible when the ultimate design of the product being purchased is not known; (2) the special equipment required to build a weapons system, for example, is so complex and costly that duplication of the equipment to obtain two suppliers is not economically justified.

PURCHASING IN INSTITUTIONS

As mentioned earlier in this chapter, basic procedures in the purchasing cycle in non-industrial or nonprofit institutions do not differ markedly from those in manufacturing or commercial companies. The similarity in purchasing for a hospital, for example, has been noted in a special study:

> Unlike many other features that the hospital does *not* share with business and industrial firms, the procurement function is one that is largely the same in most of its functional aspects.[5]

There are, however, significant differences in the two purchasing environments. Taking hospital and college and university buying as generally representative of institutional procurement, we can identify these differences as follows:

Purchasing Objectives.   Basically, businesses are organized to produce a profit; hospitals and schools of various kinds to provide service to society. Purchasing in each type of organization, then, has traditionally been measured on how well it helps meet the objectives of the organization. Thus purchasing, until recently, was often considered a mere clerical function that existed solely to assist medical personnel in their efforts

[4] Lamar Lee, Jr. and Donald W. Dobler, *Purchasing and Materials Management,* Third Edition, McGraw-Hill Book Co., New York, 1977, p. 560.

[5] *The Procurement Cycle: A Special Study in Hospital Systems and Procedures,* United Hospital Fund of New York, New York, 1968.

to protect the health and lives of patients. In the pursuit of those lauda-ble goals, and attitude of "money is no object" developed. Many profes-sionals felt it was irrelevant—even inhumane—to talk about cost-cutting, competition or businesslike methods when people's lives were at stake. Educational buyers fared somewhat better, but even in many universities and colleges efforts at economy or cost-effectiveness through better pur-chasing were considered inimical to instructional or research objectives.

Those attitudes have changed drastically in recent years. Soaring costs of education and health care have aroused concern among the public, legislators, and institutional administrators and trustees. There is growing recognition that good business methods and effective health care and education are complementary, not incompatible. Policies and techniques that have been successful in industrial purchasing are being adopted by institutions. The status of purchasing has been elevated and career opportunities and pay levels for purchasing people are being improved. Although improvement in these areas in hospitals has lagged somewhat behind that in universities, there has been a definite trend toward recruiting skilled purchasing personnel, particularly from indus-try and the armed services into hospital work.

The Scope of Purchasing.   In industry, 50-60 percent of the sales dol-lar goes for purchases; in institutions, purchasing accounts for about 25 to 30 percent of total expenditures. The dollar volume and quantity of purchases in the average institution are considerably smaller than those of even a small manufacturing company. Many institutions, particularly individual nonprofit hospitals, buy the great majority of their require-ments from distributors, rather than directly from manufacturers. In-stitutions buy a wide variety of products, many in very small quantities for very specialized purposes. A buyer for a university, for example, may be called on to buy exotic materials and even animals and insects, for research purposes, in addition to his or her regular pur-chases of furniture, athletic equipment, fuel, maintenance supplies, ve-hicles, band instruments, etc.

One-time or unique purchases, as well as low quantity conventional purchases, inevitably limit institutions' negotiating power. This limita-tion is at least partially overcome by the availability of cooperative pur-chasing organizations, such as the Hospital Bureau and the E&I cooperative mentioned on page 339. Another significant development in this regard is the increasing number of group purchasing units in the hospital field. Typically, a number of hospitals in a state or region will establish a centralized purchasing office to negotiate contracts for a vari-ety of products used by all the hospitals. The group purchasing office of the New Jersey Hospital Association, for example, buys, among other things, millions of gallons of fuel oil annually for about 50 member voluntary hospitals. Officials of the association have pointed out that savings made through group purchasing for the state's nonprofit voluntary hospitals have kept New Jersey patient costs consistently below the national averages.

A number of companies operating private hospitals for profit have, in effect, adopted group purchasing by centralizing procurement at company headquarters. Humana, Inc., for example, buys the bulk of the requirements for its 92 hospitals throughout United States from its main office in Louisville, Ky.

One of the oldest group purchasing organizations, the Joint Purchasing Corporation is a not-for-profit corporation founded 60 years ago to serve the purchasing needs of agencies and institutions supported by the Federation of Jewish Philanthropies of New York. It has since expanded its operations outside the Federation group, and now has 400 members, including hospitals, extended care facilities, child care agencies, camps and cultural, educational and religious institutions. Each year, JPC publishes an index of purchase agreements it has negotiated, listing about 450 contracts covering several thousand items. Most contracts provide for direct dealing between the member institution and the supplier. The institution orders directly from the supplier, under the terms, prices, and conditions negotiated by JPC.

The pressures on hospitals to adopt professional purchasing policies and procedures are well illustrated in the "prudent buyer" regulation on Medicare reimbursement issued by the U.S. Department of Health, Education, and Welfare:

> ". . . It is expected that a provider of service, like any prudent and cost-conscious buyer, will not only refuse to pay more than the going price for an item or service, but also will seek to economize by minimizing cost. Where a provider chooses to pay above the going price for an item or service, in the absence of clear evidence that the higher costs were unavoidable, the intermediary will exclude excess costs in determining allowable costs under Medicare.
>
> To determine whether the provider is paying more than the going price, intermediaries may employ various means for detecting and investigating situations in which costs seem excessive . . . such techniques as comparing the prices paid by providers with the prices paid for similar items or services by comparable purchasers, and spot checking and querying the provider about indirect as well as direct discounts. In addition, where a group of institutions has a joint purchasing arrangement which seems to result in participating members getting very favorable prices because of the advantages gained from bulk purchasing, any potentially eligible pro-

viders in the area that do not participate in the group should be required to justify any higher prices paid.[6]

SOME PERFORMANCE OBJECTIVES

After studying this chapter you should be able to

1. Trace the developments that led to a new awareness of the importance of purchasing in various nonprofit entities or organizations.
2. List the basic differences between governmental procurement and industrial purchasing.
3. Explain the alternatives to competitive sealed bidding offered in the American Bar Association's *Model Procurement Code.*
4. Review the basic purchasing policies and procedures of your local government, hospital, or educational institution.
5. Discuss the inconsistencies in the laws regulating procurement by federal agencies.
6. Suggest how the conflicting interests of scientific and technical personnel and those of their purchasing departments might be reconciled to the best interests of an institution.

To this point, we have been concerned primarily with the administrative and economic aspects of procurement. Increasingly, however, business in general is realizing—or has been made to realize—that it must operate within certain legal and ethical bounds as well as within its own policies. How some of these constraints affect purchasing is the subject of the next section, which begins with a chapter on the legal aspects of purchasing.

[6]*Intermediary Manual,* Audits-Reimbursement—Administration, U.S. Department of Health, Education and Welfare, Section 2130.1.

Section V

PUBLIC LAW AND PRIVATE POLICY IN PURCHASING

The Legal
Aspects
Of Purchasing

20

A purchasing manager's decisions must be legally as well as economically sound. Sales agreements of doubtful legality can lead to ill will among buyers and sellers, to confusions about the rights and obligations of the parties involved, and to expensive and time-consuming litigation. And unfavorable decisions in such litigation can mean substantial economic loss to the losing parties.

An old adage says that the layman who tries to be his or her own lawyer has a fool for a client. This is particularly true today in the highly complicated and ever-changing environment of modern industry, particularly in view of the increasing intervention of government in business. The discussion in this capter should therefore not be considered a substitute for professional legal advice. Its only purpose is to familiarize purchasing practitioners and students of purchasing with the basic principles of modern business law and to suggest ways in which these principles affect everyday purchasing decisions and operations. In any situation in which the legality of a sales agreement, contract, or business practice seems doubtful or controversial, legal counsel should be consulted.

THE LAW OF AGENCY

A purchasing manager, or purchasing agent, as the name implies, is an agent for the company. The word agent is common enough in everyday speech—there are insurance agents, real estate agents, and manufacturers' agents. In purchasing law, however, the words agent and agency have a more limited meaning.

Simply stated, an agent is someone who has been given the power to act on behalf of some other person or some institution. The person or institution for whom the agent carries out a task is called the principal. The extent of an agent's power to act on behalf of the principal is called the agent's authority. Finally, those persons or companies with whom an agent deals as a representative of his or her principal are called third parties.

There are many different kinds of agents, and they differ in the scope of their authority. Some have a very limited scope of authority— they are given the power to perform one specific task, and only that task, on behalf of the principal. Other agents have the authority to make many kinds of decisions on behalf of their principals. Agents may also differ in the kind of relationship that they have with a principal—an agent may or may not be an employee of the principal, for example. Special agents are those who have a very limited authority to perform a specific task. That is, a special agent does not have much discretion in determining how to carry out his or her duties. General agents, on the other hand, have much broader powers and have more latitude in using their own judgment to carry out duties assigned to them by their principals.

Purchasing managers are, for the most part, general agents, and more often than not they are also employees of their principals. A purchasing manager's status as a general agent is important because it gives a vendor the right to rely on the purchasing manager's written and oral statements. Furthermore, the purchaser's status as a general agent gives him or her wide authority to bind his or her principal to legally enforceable agreements. (The special agent's power to obligate his or her principal is narrower, and a seller does not have the right to assume that a special agent has a wide range of powers.)

Purchasing managers should keep in mind the fact that salespersons are themselves agents—agents for the vendor. Thus a sales representative, too, may have either a wide or narrow range of powers, depending on whether or not he or she is a general or special sales agent. In most cases, salespersons are special agents. That is, they may solicit orders, but they are not given very wide powers to change prices, to make promises about delivery dates, or to set the terms of a contract.

In dealing with a vendor representative, it is therefore always a good idea for one to have a clear sense of the scope of his or her authority—the extent to which he or she may create an obligation enforceable against his or her own principal—the supplying company.

Agency relationships can be created in several ways. The first and most obvious way is by direct authorization: a principal may directly authorize an agent to perform certain kinds of duties. For example, the purchasing director of a manufacturing concern may authorize a purchasing agent to issue all purchase orders for all lubricants needed by the firm. Such an authorization, which may be either written or oral, is called an *express authority.*

Authority may also be created by what is called the custom of the marketplace. For example, if it were customary for purchasing agents in this type of manufacturing concern to have the authority to purchase lubricants, then a seller should have the right to believe that the purchasing agent had such authority. Such authority is called customary authority, and a seller must be aware of what is "reasonable" and the "custom of the marketplace," locality, or profession.

An agent may also have what is called incidental authority: the authority to do whatever is necessary for him or her to carry out the duties that have been delegated or assigned—either expressly or through the custom of the marketplace. For instance, the purchasing agent who had the authority to buy lubricants for his or her principal but was not furnished with the cash to do so should have the authority to buy the lubricants on credit.

Finally, agency can be established by any act or acts that can reasonably be construed as creating an agency. Consider again the purchasing agent whose job it was to purchase lubricants for a factory. Suppose that the director of purchasing for the factory strictly limited this agent's purchasing authority to no more than $10,000 per month and that in one month the agent signed a purchase order for $16,000 worth of lubricants. The agent had in this case exceeded the actual authority given by the director of purchasing for the firm. However, the vendor (the third party, in this case) would have had no way of knowing that the agent's authority was limited to purchases of less than $10,000. The purchasing agent, in this case, had the apparent authority to sign a purchase order for $16,000 worth of lubricants. Thus, the principal is legally obligated by any such agreement made by the agent, as long as the third party might reasonably be expected to suppose that such authority existed.

The important thing to remember here is that all agreements reached by an agent with proper authority—be it express, customary, incidental, or apparent—do create a legally enforceable contract between the principal and the third party.

CONTRACT LAW

A contract can be most simply defined as a legally enforceable agreement. In their work, purchasing managers often must deal with contracts between their principals (the buying companies) and third parties (the vendors). If any purchase order is to have the status of a legally enforceable agreement, it must fulfill the requirements of a contract. The four conditions generally required to make an agreement an enforceable contract are

1. mutual assent
2. consideration
3. legality
4. competence

Each of these requirements is discussed at some length in the paragraphs that follow.

First, a contract must result from the mutual assent of the parties to the contract. Mutual consent consists of an offer made by one party and the unconditional acceptance of that offer by another party. A purchasing manager and a vendor may have long discussions or exchanges of correspondence about a particular sale, and they may discuss the quality, quantity, and price of the goods or services being offered. Such discussions and correspondence, however, do *not* create a contract. They are merely preliminary to the creation of a contract. Price quotations and invitations to trade (such as advertisements) fall within this "preliminary" category. They do not, in and of themselves, create a legally enforceable agreement.

The issuance of a purchase order might very well be the next step afte the "preliminary" discussion or correspondence that precedes a sale. A purchasing manager should keep in mind the fact that the issuance of such an order does not necessarily create a contract—an issued purchase order is really no more than an offer. The purchase order becomes a contract only after it has been accepted by an authorized agent of the vendor. This is the reason for acknowledgment copies, one of which is generally sent along with the purchase order, to be signed and returned by the vendor. It is considered good practice, therefore, to include in the acknowledgment copy the phrase, "We acknowledge and accept this offer." Such an explicit statement of acceptance will leave no question that an enforceable contract is being proposed by the buyer.

Suppliers, however, often acknowledge and accept orders on their own forms. Until the adoption of the Uniform Commercial Code by every state in the nation (except Louisiana), any such acceptance that differed in any way from the buyer's purchase order constituted a counteroffer. There would be no contract, because a counteroffer would terminate the original offer and propose in turn a new and different offer. Theoretically, the legal process of offer and acceptance could begin all over again and continue ad infinitum. In practice, that rarely happened, however, and the seller would generally provide what the buyer wanted. But the potential for conflict and litigation was there, and the "battle of the forms" was liable to break out at any time, until the Uniform Commercial Code was almost universally accepted. The UCC maintains that

> [I]f parties deal as though they have a contract, then they are deemed to have one. . . . A definite expression of acceptance or a written confirmation—sent within a reasonable time—operates as an acceptance. This is true even though it states terms additional to or different from those offered or agreed upon—unless acceptance is expressly made conditional on assent to the additional or different terms.

If the seller wants an agreement based on his or her terms and conditions, the seller must say so in his or her acknowledgment in these words:

> Acceptance of your order is expressly made conditional on your assent to the terms and conditions stated below and on the reverse side hereof, and we agree to furnish the material described herein only upon these terms and conditions.

If the supplier does not make the acceptance conditional on the buyer's assent, a contract will generally be formed on the buyer's terms.

Prior to UCC, if a purchasing manager accepted a shipment and there was a dispute concerning the terms and conditions, the courts generally ruled that the seller's terms and conditions automatically prevailed. Acceptance of the shipment by the purchasing manager was considered agreement with the supplier's "last shot," that is, the shipment, which constituted a counteroffer. Under the UCC, the supplier who ships an order—even when his or her terms and conditions differ from the buyer's—is often legally bound by the buyer's terms and conditions. If the supplier insists, in writing, on his or her terms, the buyer still has the choice of accepting the contract or calling it off.

Second, a legally enforceable contract must contain the element of consideration. Basically, *consideration* means that each of the parties to the contract makes a sacrifice and each receives a benefit. A one-way, or unilateral, contract, in which one of the parties does not receive a benefit and make a sacrifice, is not legally enforceable. In an ordinary contract of purchase or sale, the vendor agrees to sell and deliver and the buyer agrees to purchase certain goods or services. Default by either party creates a breach of contract and gives the other party the right to sue for damages. Any promise that is made *without* consideration is called a *gratuitous* promise and is unenforceable.

Each party's obligations in terms of quantity should be stated as clearly as possible in a purchase order. If the buyer's quantity requirements are not definitely known, the best approximation should be stated, along with a note explaining that the quantity listed is in fact an estimate. In other words, both buyer and seller may create a legally enforceable "estimated" contract by acknowledging, in the contract itself, that exact quantities were not predictable at the time that the contract was created. Purchase orders with such ambiguities often state a minimum quantity that shall be bought by the purchaser and a maximum quantity for which delivery can be demanded from the vendor. Thus, the ambiguity of the contract can be limited, and the parties to it can share equally in the risk of entering into such an agreement.

Indefinite contracts for future delivery must also fulfill the requirements of mutuality. If either the buyer or seller has no obligation, the contract is not enforceable. For example, if the buyer's need for certain goods is only hypothetical or conditional, and no consideration for this fact is given to the vendor, the contract is not enforceable. Furthermore, if the time of delivery depends solely on the whim of one of the parties, the agreement is not enforceable.

The buyer's obligation under a contract is also measured by the quantity specified on the order. A court action involving this point of law brought out the following facts.[1] The buyer in this instance, a building contractor, ordered a specified quantity of roofing tile to be specially manufactured, the order amounting to $2,526, for completing certain of his projects. The vendor's quotation, on which the order was based, was good for thirty days, but with the stipulation that the order was to be "subject to the approval of our Executive Office at Chicago." The vendor acknowledged the order, saying, "We are passing this to our Executive Department for consideration and attention"; no formal acceptance, however, was issued. Nevertheless, the vendor started manufacturing the tile and made several partial shipments, which were accepted and paid for by the buyer. During the course of the contract, after $1,431.56 worth of tile had been delivered and paid for, it became evident to the buyer that he had overestimated his requirements, and he refused to accept further shipments, whereupon the vendor filed suit to collect for the full amount of the order. The buyer contended that no valid contract existed because of the vendor's failure to make a formal acceptance of the order, and the lower court ruled in his favor. The case was carried to a higher court, however, and this decision was reversed. In holding the buyer liable for payment, the court cited the principle that the shipment itself indicated

[1] *Ludowici-Celadon Company* v. *McKinley,* 11 N. W. (2d) 839.

acceptance, and that shipment of part of the order is acceptance of the whole, "In the instant case," said the court, "plaintiff [seller] manufactured the tile, delivered a part therof, and tendered the remainder. Had the seller refused to deliver the remainder, the buyer could have recovered damages for the breach of the contract. It must follow, therefore, that the seller is likewise entitled to recover damages because of the buyer's refusal to accept the remainder of the tile." In other words, the obligation is a mutual one. A reasonable variation from the specified quantity, plus or minus, due to manufacturing conditions, is recognized as coming within the meaning of the contract and satisfying its obligations, but this allowable variation is generally limited to a fixed percentage of the specified amount. Trade customs in the various producing industries are usually clear on this point and are accepted as governing in the legal interpretation of a contract.

The purchase order should be quite specific as to the price as well as the quantity of goods or services to be delivered. It is not, for example, a good idea to issue an unpriced purchase order unless it is absolutely necessary to do so (as in industries in which the prices of certain commodities fluctuate very rapidly). A purchasing manager who feels that he or she must issue purchase orders without a specific price should give the vendor certain guidelines in notifying the buyer should the price rise above a certain level.

The time of delivery should also be clearly indicated on the purchase order and thus become one of the clauses of the contract. Such a schedule becomes part of the vendor's contractual obligation, and, if the vendor fails to meet the schedule, he or she may be held in default of the contract. The purchaser may even want to insert in the order, in certain cases, a clause stating that "time is of the essence." Such a clause may relieve a buyer of any and all obligations for that portion of the delivery that was not made during the specified time period.

The principle of consideration has been modified in recent years through changes in the law brought about by court decisions and the wide acceptance of the UCC. For example, in some states a party to a contract can be bound to a contract even without receiving consideration by merely stating that it holds itself legally obligated. More important, a party to a contract may, after the contract has been signed, agree to make an additional sacrifice without asking for an additional benefit in the terms of the contract. For example, a purchasing manager who has contracted for a shipment of steel in thirty days may suddenly find that his or her company desperately needs the steel in fifteen days. The purchaser may at that point call the vendor and ask that the shipment be "hurried up." The vendor is under no contractual obligation to expedite the shipment of steel. However, if the vendor does agree to the advanced delivery date and then fails to meet it, causing a loss to the purchaser's company, the vendor may be held liable for losses that the purchaser incurred. The legal principle involved here is that the purchaser relied on the vendor's promise to expedite delivery, and in so relying on the vendor failed to get his or her shipment on time. In other words, the purchaser relied on the vendor's freely given promise to his or her own detriment.

In general, however, the principle of consideration is still a basic requirement of all contracts. Without it, a purchase order is not likely to achieve the status of an enforceable contract.

Third, a valid contract shall not be in conflict with existing federal or local laws and regulations, so that performance of the contract would in itself be an unlawful act. Examples of this would involve agreements embodying discrimination in violation of the Robinson–Patman Act, agreements based on production under conditions in violation of wage and hour laws, assumption of tax charges by either party in violation of Internal Revenue Service rulings on tax liabilities, and many others.

Fourth, in a valid contract no fraud shall be practiced by either the buyer or seller in arriving at the agreement.

LAW OF WARRANTY

Warranties are of two sorts: express and implied. If, in the absence of express warranties of quality, fitness, or performance of a product given by the seller, the buyer makes known to the seller the particular purposes for which the goods or equipment are required, relying on the seller's judgment and skill, there is an implied warranty that the goods shall be reasonably fit for that purpose. The inclusion of an expressed warranty covering any of these points renders the implied warranty void, because the latter cannot exist when the seller expressly guarantees his or her merchandise.

Statements made by salespersons are not enforceable as guarantees. Courts have repeatedly recognized the natural tendency of sales representatives to "puff" the virtues of their products for the purposes of making a sale, without imputing to such enthusiastic claims the status of a formal guarantee. An employer is not bound by salespersons' guarantees unless (1) the guarantee is confirmed by the employer or someone in his or her organization authorized to do so, (2) the employer has notified the purchaser that he or she will be bound by guarantees made by the sales representative, (3) the employer has in the past, without such notification, accepted responsibility for such guarantees, thereby implying that the sales representative, has this authority, or (4) the guarantee constitutes actual fraud, in which case the employer is responsible for the action of his or her employee even though the employer did not authorize the salesperson to make the fraudulent statement or guarantee, either expressly or by implication.

In invoking the warranty clauses of a contract, the purchaser is under obligation to take action as soon as the deficiency of the goods or the breach of warranty is determined. Many claims based on inferior quality of merchandise delivered under contract have been thrown out of court because of unreasonable delay in ascertaining that such a condition does exist. Many sales contracts, for goods that are capable of inspection on receipt, place a limit on the time within which such claims may be made—usually thirty days—and these limiting clauses have been adjudged valid. There are other types of defects or deficiencies that are not ascertainable until goods have been put into use or until equipment has been installed and started in operation. In such cases, "reasonable" promptness is a matter of interpretation, and the buyer must be in a position to prove his or her alertness and promptness in discovering the alleged breach of warranty and taking action to recover. Furthermore, the buyer is not entitled to retain merchandise or to continue to use equipment at the same time that he or she refuses to make payment because of alleged breach of warranty.

THE UCC AND WARRANTIES

The Uniform Commercial Code (Article 2, Section 2-313) states that express warranties by the seller are created as follows:

> (a) Any affirmation of fact or promise made by the seller to the buyer which relates to the goods and becomes part of the basis of the bargain creates an express warranty that the goods shall conform to the affirmation or promise.
> (b) Any description of the goods which is made part of the basis of the bargain creates an express warranty that goods shall conform to the description.
> (c) Any sample or model which is made part of the basis of the bargain creates an express warranty that the whole of the goods shall conform to the sample or model.

Under the UCC, the buyer also has the protection of implied warranties established by law. A warranty of "merchantability" is implied in a contract if the seller is in fact a merchant of the goods involved in a sale.

Additionally, there is an implied warranty of "fitness for particular purpose or sale" when the seller at the time of contracting "has reason to know any particular purpose for which the goods are required and that the buyer is relying on the seller's skill or judgment to select or furnish suitable goods."

If a seller wishes to deny an implied warranty of merchantability or fitness, the seller must do so "conspicuously, in language that appraises the buyer of the fact." This requirement of conspicuousness is intended to invalidate the disclaimers of warranty that often appear on the reverse side of sales agreements or vendor acknowledgments in tiny, almost illegible, type—known popularly as "boiler plate."

The significance of the UCC to purchasing managers was summed up a short time after it had gone into force in every state (except Louisiana) by a well-known corporate counsel.[2] He pointed out that the UCC helps the buyer four ways: (1) If a seller makes an offer in writing, the seller has to live up to it for the period of time stated, (2) verbal agreements, if confirmed in writing and no objection made, are valid, (3) the conflict between a buyer's purchase order terms and a seller's acknowledgment terms has been generally resolved in favor of the buyer, and (4) as far as warranties are concerned, the purchasing manager can legally rely on the vendor to supply the item needed to do the job. The net effect of Article 2 of the UCC, he concluded, is to strengthen the buyer's hand in his or her dealings with suppliers:

> He can now count on added legal protection against trickery. He can more readily believe the express and implied warranties contained in a contract. But, most important, he can be secure in the knowledge that, in matters involving the four key points in Article 2, the courts will be more sympathetic to the buyer.

TITLE TO PURCHASED GOODS

Making a purchase involves a transfer of title to the merchandise from the seller to the buyer. It must be assumed—or ascertained, if any doubt exists—that the seller has a clear title to the goods in the first place. The time and place of the actual transfer of title are important, for ownership entails responsibilities and risks, and this point is the source of frequent legal controversy. Thus, the designation of an F.O.B. (free on board) point has a much more far-reaching effect than indicating whether the seller or the buyer is responsible for paying the transportation charges.

If goods are sold and shipped F.O.B. the seller's location, the pur-

[2] John D. Jackson, "Uniform Commercial Code: It's a Bonus for Buyers," *Purchasing Magazine*, February 6, 1969, p. 54.

chaser automatically takes legal title to the goods at the moment the shipment is delivered to the carrier. By doing so, the purchaser assumes full responsibility for all accidents, contingencies, damage, loss, delays, and the like, occasioned by the carrier. The purchaser is responsible for seeing to it that suitable insurance is carried on the goods while in transit and for recovering from the carrier any damages for which the latter may be liable through its negligence or other reason. (It has been ruled contrary to public interest for a shipper to agree to relieve the carrier from liability for loss or destruction of goods through negligence of the carrier, and such contracts have been held invalid.) The buyer or consignee is responsible for payment of the transportation charges to the carrier and for payment for the merchandise to the shipper, even though the shipment is lost or destroyed in transit.

In shipping F.O.B. seller's location, the title having passed, the seller cannot regain possession of the goods during transit even though the seller receives definite information that the buyer is insolvent before the goods have reached their destination. On the other hand, the seller is obliged to exercise ordinary prudence and good judgment in protection of the purchaser. In one leading case a buyer was adjudged to be not liable for payment for a shipment lost in transit, even though the terms of the contract were F.O.B. seller's city, because the seller had used poor judgment in making a nominal declaration of value ($50) to the carrier, when for a few cents additional the seller could have listed the true value ($500) of the merchandise.[3] Similarly, a seller defaults and assumes liability if he or she fails to follow the buyer's shipping instructions regarding the route, the carrier, packing equipment, date of shipment, or other reasonable instructions issued by the buyer. This law is applicable regardless of the usual law pertaining to shipments ordered F.O.B. the seller's location. When the testimony shows that a seller breached any competent clause or element in a valid contract, the buyer is relieved of his or her responsibilities, including those arising under F.O.B. shipment rules of law.

If goods are sold and shipped F.O.B. buyer's location, title passes to the buyer at the time when goods are delivered to the buyer by the carrier. Under these circumstances, the buyer does not assume the responsibilities outlined above, but they are for the account of the seller so long as the latter retains title to the merchandise.

FRAUD

Legal fraud has been defined as any act, deed, or statement, made by either a buyer or a seller *before* the purchase contract is signed or com-

---

[3] *Semler v. Schmicker,* 38 Atl. (2d) 831.

pleted, that is likely to deceive the other party. A seller is not liable for fraud if the evidence proves (1) that the seller or his or her sales representative made a false statement *after* the contract was signed, (2) that the seller or his or her sales representative actually did not know that the quality of the merchandise was not as claimed in the sales contract but merely expressed an opinion that he believed the quality to be as represented, or (3) that the purchaser did not believe or rely upon the statements made by the seller or his or her agent. If a purchaser inspects merchandise before entering into the contract, that purchaser is put upon guard and is expected by the law to use his or her own good judgment in respect to the quality and characteristics of the goods; if a purchaser is not sufficiently experienced to judge the quality of the merchandise that he or she inspects and relies upon a fraudulent statement made by the seller, however, the latter is liable.

LAW OF PATENTS

A U.S. patent is a monopoly created by law. There are five classifications or bases for patents: mechanical, process, composition, articles of manufacture, and design. The rights of the patentee are summed up as follows:

> The patentee has the sole right of making, using, and selling the patented articles, and he may prevent anybody from dealing with them at all. Inasmuch as he has the right to prevent people from using them, or dealing in them at all, he has the right to do the lesser thing, that is to say, to impose his own conditions. It does not matter how unreasonable or how absurd the conditions are.[4]

A patent can be extended by improvements on the original device, but, after the expiration of a patent (and an expired patent cannot be renewed), the patentee loses all former rights in the patent. Then anyone can make, sell, purchase, or use the invention without any chance of liability. A patentee may obtain another, new patent on some improvement of the original patent when the latter has expired, but this protection covers only the improvement; the original invention is unprotected after the patent period of seventeen years (or a maximum of fourteen years in the case of a design patent).

A person or a company may be liable for infringement of a patent (1) if he or she uses it, (2) if he or she makes it for his or her own use, (3) if he

[4] Cantelo, 12 Pat. Law R262.

or she purchases a part and combines it with other parts, comprising an infringing device, (4) if he or she conspires purposely or unintentionally with another and contributes in any manner to an infringement, or (5) if he or she purchases and resells an infringing device, although the purchase is made in the belief that the seller had a license from the patentee to sell or use the device.

CONTRACT CANCELLATIONS

The confidence and orderliness needed to do business satisfactorily depends on the sanctity of the contractual relationship, backed up with legal force. A good contract protects the interests and rights of both the buyer and seller, and its obligations are equally binding upon both parties to the contract. Cancellations and defaults in respect to contract agreements cannot be made arbitrarily by either party to the detriment of the other. Therefore, a fair and orderly procedure must be provided to meet the situation involving contract cancellations. Although it is probably true that no contract is actually "noncancellable," this statement does not mean that the existence of the contract in question can be ignored or that the obligation to hold the other party harmless from the consequences of such cancellation can be avoided.

In general, cancellations come within three classifications: for default by the seller, for the convenience of the buyer, or by mutual consent. It should be noted also that, as a general rule, contracts that are indefinite as to quantity or duration can be terminated at will by either party, unilaterally, without penalty, upon due notice to the other party. The very indefiniteness of the terms, in such a case, is construed in law as evidence of mutual consent for termination.

Cancellation for default.   The simplest case is that of a default by the vendor in failing to perform as agreed in the contract, in making deliveries that do not come up to specifications, or in failing to meet the specified delivery dates. All the essential factors should be so clearly and definitely incorporated in the terms of the contract as to become a part of the seller's obligation. Then any failure on the seller's part to fulfill the terms is a default on the contract, giving the buyer a cause for redress.

Cancellation for convenience of the buyer.   It may become necessary for the buyer to cancel a contract even though the seller is able and willing to perform his or her part of the agreement. In such cases of contract cancellation for the convenience of the buyer, the similar principle holds that the seller should not be called upon to incur any loss through the buyer's default.

Cancellation by mutual consent. Cancellation of a contract is not necessarily a cause for legal action. Just as the making of a contract represents a meeting of minds resulting in an agreement between the buyer and the seller to undertake certain mutual responsibilities, so there may be a meeting of minds in respect to the termination of that agreement without invoking a penalty on either side. There are many instances in the course of business when requirements change, so that a contract or open order is no longer appropriate to the buyer's need. A cancellation is indicated, for the convenience of the buyer. But, if no particular hardship to the seller is involved, for example, if the item concerned is so standard that another outlet can be found, or if it is of such a nature that materials and work in process can be diverted without loss to the orders of some other buyer, the seller may be quite willing to accept a cancellation in good faith as a normal risk of doing business. If an adjustment is in order because of special materials purchased or work done on the contract, a reasonable agreement can be reached through negotiation rather than litigation, based on the equity of the situation.

In each of these types of cancellations, there may be complex ramifications, so that the simple principles mentioned may be subject to different interpretations by the courts. In any event, if there is any considerable liability involved, or if there is any shadow of a doubt as to the liability that may be incurred, it is best to secure competent legal advice in advance of issuing a cancellation.

WAIVER OF RIGHT

A contract is a binding legal document designed to protect both parties, and the legal rights inherent in the contract agreement should be meticulously safeguarded, for they can easily be forfeited by careless action. For example, time of delivery or performance is an integral part of the contract if it is stated, as it should be, in the purchase order or contract. Yet it is a point upon which many buyers are inclined to be lenient, within reasonable limits, so long as systematic expediting is successful in getting deliveries made before the absolute deadline. Now suppose that a certain vendor is chronically tardy with his or her shipments on a continuing contract, requiring an undue amount of expediting effort, until the patient buyer eventually decides to terminate the agreement. The buyer claims breach of contract and has an imposing lot of evidence in the form of late shipments to support this claim. But, if the buyer has consistently condoned the lateness of deliveries in the past and has continued to accept overdue shipments, that buyer may find that he or she has waived his or her rights for legal action upon this point. The buyer can still cancel the contract, but his or her claim for any redress on the basis of the vendor's default has been forfeited.

Cancellation Clauses

Some purchasing departments include a special clause in their purchase orders and contracts, on the subject of cancellation. For the most part, such general clauses add nothing whatever to the rights or protection afforded by the contractual relationship itself. In fact, they may actually destroy the force of the entire contract by making the contract obligations or promises "illusory" in the eyes of the law. For example, the following clause appears in one purchase order, ostensibly to relieve the purchaser of continuing responsibility under a contractual agreement and to reserve the privilege of rescinding or canceling any portion of the order without liability:

> The buyer reserves the right to cancel any unshipped portion of this order.

The broad effect, in court, of such a general disclaimer of responsibility for carrying out his or her part of the agreement, however, would probably be a decision that the document is unilateral and that no contract legally exists under such a condition.

On the other hand, some practical advantage may be obtained by specifically stressing a particular phase of delinquency that is to be interpreted by mutual consent as cause for cancellation of an order by the buyer, without penalty. In most cases, clauses of this nature are based on the fact that time of delivery is "of the essence" of the contract and that failure to make delivery as promised relieves the buyer of his or her responsibility to accept and pay for goods furnished tardily under the contract. An example of such a clause is the following:

> Should any portion of this order be unfilled at the expiration of 60 days from its date, we reserve the right (notifying you) to cancel said unfilled portion without liability other than to make payments for that portion of the order that has been delivered.

Although it may be argued that this gives the buyer no rights that could not be equally accomplished by specifying a definite delivery date among the terms on the face of the order, it could be invoked in cases in which previous leniency in accepting delinquent deliveries (which would be a normal policy for occasional infractions and if the urgency of the requirement did not require rigid enforcement) was cited as precedent to diminish the force of a delivery agreement. It does serve notice on the seller that the time element is an essential part of the agreement and will be so interpreted. At the same time, it provides the means for clearing open-order files with reasonable promptness and for avoiding the accumulation of miscellaneous outstanding commitments.

Termination Agreements

It may be accepted as a basic thesis that a contract is made with the expectation of carrying it through to completion on both sides. But under certain circumstances there may be a strong probability that the buyer may wish to cancel at some stage prior to completion because of contingencies that can be foreseen in principle but not in detail. If ordinary forms of conditional contracts are not appropriate to cover these circumstances, it is highly desirable to have an understanding with the seller as to the prodecure to be followed in the event of such cancellation. This agreement may be embodied in a termination clause that is made a part of the contract. Sellers are naturally reluctant to accept termination clauses, and there is no obligation on their part to do so; they are fully entitled to stand on their contractual rights under the principles of cancellation for the convenience of the buyer, as outlined. But, if a good, continuing relationship has been established between the contracting companies, and if the contract is an advantageous one so far as it goes, the agreement may frequently be worked out as a part of the negotiation in such a way as to relieve the buyer of the extreme penalties or obligations involved in an ordinary cancellation, without calling upon the seller to sustain any loss by reason of the cancellation.

THE BUYER'S RESPONSIBILITY

There are many more aspects of law that have a bearing on purchase transactions and purchasing practice. This chapter has merely summarized the points that are most commonly encountered and that should be observed to keep free of litigation or to enhance the prospect of a favorable verdict when litigation cannot be avoided. The cardinal rule of law should be remembered: that no one should come into a court of law "with unclean hands," that is, without being sure that his or her own action and intent are lawful and that the breach of legal obligation is not on his or her own part. When the controversy concerns interpretation of an agreement, the court will endeavor to determine the real intent of the parties in making that agreement. But, on the whole, the legal principles and requirements are clear and well established, although their interpretation may be modified by the particular circumstances of their application in a given case.

It is important for the purchaser to read carefully and to know what he or she is signing, for this is the evidence of the agreement. Although the courts have in some cases ruled in favor of a buyer who failed to notice some contract clause that was inconspicuously placed or printed in excessively fine type or faint ink, or when the buyer had definitely been led to believe that no such condition was incorporated in the agreement, these are the rare exceptions to the general rule of responsibility for knowing what the contract contains.

Finally, by mutual consent, arbitration can be substituted for litigation. Contract clauses are valid by which contracting parties agree not to enter suit but, rather, to abide by a decision rendered by a disinterested arbitrator. Under such an agreement, the decision of the arbitrator is final and conclusive (unless in making the decision the arbitrator himself or herself is guilty of fraud, misconduct, or such gross mistake as would imply bad faith or failure to exercise honest judgment). Arbitration of contract disputes is encouraged in business practice and is supported by modern higher-court decisions; its legal effect is the practical elimination of litigations.

SOME PERFORMANCE OBJECTIVES

After studying this chapter you should be able to

1. Explain the law of agency.
2. Distinguish between expressed and implied authority.
3. Name the basic elements of a contract.
4. Differentiate between an expressed warranty and an implied warranty.
5. Discuss the ways in which the Uniform Commercial Code has helped the buyer.
6. Review the major types of contract cancellations.

Purchasing, like any management function, should have clearly defined policies, preferably in written form. In the following chapter, we discuss various approaches to developing and disseminating purchasing policy.

Purchasing Policies

Every purchasing department has policies, whether or not they are put into writing. They are one of the administrative tools of departmental management. The advantages of establishing specific policies, and recording them, are threefold:

1. An established policy eliminates the necessity for making a new decision every time a comparable situation arises.
2. A written policy assures understanding; it assures that decisions and actions will be consistent and in accordance with the judgment of the responsible department head.
3. An approved policy gives authority to the indicated course of action.

INTERNAL RELATIONSHIPS

The establishment of centralized purchasing is in itself a policy of company management. It immediately entails a whole series of internal, interdepartmental policies relating to lines of authority, channels of procedure, and departmental relationships in general. These policies should be promptly clarified and made a matter of record, for they define the scope and responsibilities of the purchasing function in any particular organization and determine to a considerable extent the effectiveness of the purchasing operation. The principles underlying these relationships have already been set forth in Chapter 2, but they cannot be assumed. Neither can they be set by the purchasing manager alone, because they affect the responsibilities and actions of other departments as well. The purchasing manager can suggest and try to persuade, but, to have valid force, such decisions must have management approval.

Policies in this category include such matters as the authorizations required on requisitions to purchase, permissions for vendors' sales representatives to contact plant personnel, the final responsibility for specifications, the procedures to be followed in standardization and value analysis recommendations involving engineering changes, and similar points on which conflicts of function and authority may arise.

To be effective, a policy must be clear and definitive, but it need not be arbitrary. Consequently, many policies set up criteria for decisions, or methods of handling situations, or conditions of action. For example, it is obviously undesirable to grant free access to plant personnel for all vendors' sales personnel, either at their own initiative or at the request of plant managers, for such a policy would negate the principles of centralized purchasing. Yet there are many situations in which such a contact is mutually desirable and is, in fact, an aid to intelligent procurement. A sensible and commonly accepted policy on this point is to require that such contacts be made through the purchasing department and that in such interviews no commitments are to be made by plant personnel as to preference for products or sources, which might weaken the position of the purchasing department in subsequent negotiations.

VENDOR RELATIONSHIPS

Relationships with vendors and their representatives, too, are subject to policy control. Should the purchasing manager's door be open to every business caller, and is every salesperson entitled to the chance to tell his or her story? Perhaps so, on the first visit; after that it is for the buyer to decide whether the proposal is pertinent and timely from the viewpoint of the company's needs and whether the interview time is warranted. Should specific, limited hours be set for interviewing sales representatives? That question can be argued endlessly. Departmental policy often compromises by "suggesting" fixed calling hours and making provision for exceptions in the case of the out-of-town caller and special appointments.

Should price information be kept confidential? In industrial purchasing, yes. (The governmental buyer, with a mandatory system of sealed bids and a public bid opening, has no such option. That is another policy, characteristic of a particular field.) Should vendors be permitted to revise their bids? Only in case of obvious error, or in a subsequent negotiating stage if terms, quantities, or specifications are modified so as to warrant a price adjustment. If the stated requirement is changed, should all bidders be given a chance to make a new quotation? Not necessarily. If it becomes a new proposal on the buyer's part, a new request for bids may be in order. But, if the vendor had been selected on merit, on the basis of the original proposal, and the terms are altered in negotiation, he or she will probably stand on the original choice. If the cost-saving changes come at the vendor's suggestion, fair purchasing policy demands that the vendor retain the patronage, with the status of a preferred supplier on succeeding orders. Should unsuccessful bidders be notified? Yes, and with the reasons for the adverse decision, if feasible.

Policies in this category have their roots in ethical considerations as well as in economics and "good business." The ethical aspects are discussed in greater detail in Chapter 22.

Should orders ever be issued on the vendor's contract form rather than on a standard purchase order? This is a point on which purchasing policy and sales policy frequently come into conflict. Ordinarily, purchasing policy favors the use of the buyer's standard order form and terms in all cases. But sometimes, when installations and special warranties are involved, the vendor's form that is specifically designed for these situations is more appropriate and obviates the need for writing in a lot of special clauses and conditions on the buyer's form. For such cases, purchasing policy can set up certain criteria for the acceptability of a seller's form—criteria that will safeguard the rights of the buyer and avoid conflict with other basic company and purchasing policies. The policy may include getting approval of the contract by the company's legal department.

To what extent should personal contacts with vendors be cultivated, including visits to vendors' plants? It may be good policy to put this on a systematic basis and to extend it with a policy of inviting vendors periodically, individually or as a group, to acquire a personal knowledge of the buyer's plant operations.

An example of a company policy on supplier relationships is shown in Figure 21-1.

POLICIES ON SUPPLY SOURCE

Another group of purchasing decisions that lend themselves to the guidance of a consistent and considered policy concerns the selection of supply sources. The policy of maintaining multiple or alternative sources is almost universal. But this does not answer the question of what kind of sources should be chosen.

Should any preference be given to local suppliers? In theory, the local supplier offers natural advantages of convenience, faster deliveries, and lower transportation expense. There are factors that weigh in his or her favor in any source consideration. However, the objective appraisal of supply sources may show others to be equally or more desirable, and a more distant competitor may underbid the local bidder sufficiently to offset his or her initial advantage. At this point another set of factors comes into play. How much is it worth to foster good community relations by patronizing local sources, to help maintain local prosperity by keeping business in the local area, to develop and maintain strong supply sources nearby? These factors have enough validity and importance to make some companies go so far as to establish a small percentage cost differential that is considered acceptable in dealing with local sources, all other things being equal. Such a policy is usually permissive rather than mandatory.

POLICIES ON SOURCE SELECTION

Assuming that facilities are adequate and that prices are competitive, should any preference be given, as a matter of policy, to dealing with either large or small companies as such? The case for the small company as a supplier usually hinges upon the mathematical fact that an order or account of given size looms proportionately larger in the operations of a small supplier, and it is logical to expect that he or she will give it closer individual attention and service than it might receive in the larger organization, where it is of relatively minor importance. Another argument cited in favor of the small company is the rather paradoxical one that the buyer's patronage helps the small company to grow larger; the inference in this case is that the buyer will get greater loyalty and cooperation from the small supplier. Both arguments are probably unfair to the many efficient and conscientious large supplier companies that have attained their present stature through high standards of service. Be that as it may, many large companies take pains to point out in their annual reports and public relations releases that a considerable part of their material needs is supplied by companies in the category of small business. This condition may be merely a reflection of the interdependence of all elements in the total economy, in which both big business and small business have a place.

Should an effort be made, as a matter of policy, to deal, so far as possible, directly with primary manufacturing sources rather than through distributors and other middlemen? If quantity warrants, there may be some price advantage on direct mill shipments. If the distribution

SUBJECT		NUMBER	
MATERIALS MANUAL		REVISION NO.	
CEMENTING SUPPLIER RELATIONS		EFFECTIVE	

MAJOR FUNCTION AFFECTED		PREPARED BY	APPROVED BY
SUPPLY		G. J. P.	G. J. P.
		PAGE 1	OF 4 PAGES

I.   CEMENTING SUPPLIER RELATIONS

The business health and prosperity of Rheem Manufacturing Company are supported on a tripod made up of:

A.   Customers.
B.   Employees.
C.   Suppliers.

Each leg of this tripod is equally important and the three grow and prosper together through the individual contribution of each member.

The only worthwhile and enduring relationship between buyer and seller is one that is mutually profitable and one in which there is respect and appreciation for the contribution of each member.

It costs time, effort and money to develop good suppliers. We must view our suppliers as valuable investments, important to our growth and progress in the future.

II.   THE ADVANTAGES OF CORDIAL RELATIONS

Some of the benefits of strong suppliers relationships are:

A.   Material Availability

The supplier who respects Rheem and finds our business attractive will make Material Availability for Rheem a MUST. He will protect our interests at all times and will give us the advantages of his advice and counsel during periods of difficult supply.

B.   Engineering and R & D Assistance

We will have first call on the engineering know-how and the R. & D. developments of our satisfied suppliers.

Figure 21-1. Detailed policy statement on supplier relations from a company manual. Courtesy, Rheem Manufacturing Corporation.

SUBJECT		
	MATERIALS MANUAL	NUMBER
		REV. NO.
	CEMENTING SUPPLIER RELATIONS	PAGE

C. Price Stability and Protection

The supplier who values our business will do all in his power to achieve price stability and to protect our interests during periods of rising prices.

D. Manufacturing Assistance

Often suppliers can suggest ways of improving our production methods and techniques. To obtain maximum assistance in this vital area, we must strive for a positive attitude toward new methods so that our suppliers regard us as open-minded to change and not content with "status quo."

E. Mutual Respect and Harmony

Do not attempt a climate of "one upmanship" with suppliers. Respect their position and the contribution they can make. Strive for a climate of mutual respect and harmony.

III. THE CEMENTING PROCESS

To achieve long-lasting mutually beneficial relations, consider utilizing these aids:

A. Constantly stress to the supplier that we are primarily interested in long-term relationships. We are not seeking temporary relationships of convenience.

B. Be commercially honest. The practice of playing suppliers off against each other is short-term and self-defeating.

C. Stress that our company believes in the private enterprise system. The foundation of this system is profits. We recognize that suppliers must make profits in order to remain strong and vigorous. A poor supplier can serve no one well.

D. We must consider the Materials Department as the supplier's representative in our company's councils. We must protect his interests accordingly.

system and price structure are such that there is no saving on direct purchases, as is often the case, there may be advantages in the distributor's services. The reputable manufacturer will support his or her product and warranties and will usually provide essential technical services in either case.

Purchasing From Minority Suppliers

A major shift in purchasing policy, particularly in larger companies, occurred in the late 1960s. The American business community involved itself more deeply than ever before in socioeconomic problems that came into sharp focus during and following the social unrest of that decade. A major part of the effort was directed toward bringing minorities into the mainstream of American economic life, particularly through the support of minority-owned businesses.

Purchasing executives have been among the most active participants in the minority business program since then. The National Association of Purchasing Management adopted a formal policy supporting the concept. N.A.P.M. and its local associations have worked closely with the Department of Commerce's Office of Minority Business Enterprise and the National Minority Purchasing Council, the latter representing a volunteer effort on the part of the private sector to address itself to helping minority businesses.

Industry in general has adopted definite policies on buying from minority companies, and the purchasing department almost always played a key role in implementing such policies. A typical policy statement distributed throughout the company by a major manufacturing company reads in part:

> It is the policy of the company to award an optimum portion of its purchase orders and subcontracts to qualified minority business enterprise (MBE) firms consistent with efficient and economic performance of its prime contracts.
>
> In carrying out this policy, purchasing personnel will actively seek new MBE sources for development into qualified suppliers. As practicable, technical and/or management assistance will be furnished to MBE firms not currently qualified to meet our procurement standards, but which have significant potential for doing so.
>
> In no event, however, will any award be made to an MBE firm when doing so would conflict with other contractual provisions, regulations or established company or material policies.

As discussed in Chapter 13, justifying support of often inexperienced minority companies has posed a challenge to purchasing personnel accustomed to selecting suppliers on a purely economic basis. But it is a challenge that has been met successfully by thousands of purchasing departments without harmful effect on basic purchasing policies or relationships and with favorable effect on American society as a whole.

Reciprocal Purchasing Policy

One of the most troublesome and controversial policy questions that purchasing executives have faced is that of reciprocity. The urge to select suppliers on the basis of how much they buy—or may buy—from one's company is both common and understandable. But it generally does not come from those purchasing managers who take scientific purchasing seriously. Most of the effort to promote reciprocal buying comes either from suppliers or from within the buyer's own organization—usually from top management or the sales department.

Under any form of reciprocal buying policy, purchasing becomes less selective because freedom of choice from among several suppliers is limited. It negates the critical criteria that scientific purchasing calls for in the selection of sources, and it discourages competition among other suppliers, who quickly become aware of its existence. In short, the purchasing manager is stripped of negotiating and buying power.

In recent years the Federal government has taken an increasingly dim view of reciprocity as a business practice. It has charged a number of companies with violating various antitrust provisions of the Sherman and Clayton acts by coercing or attempting to coerce suppliers to purchase their products, or products of subsidiaries, under threat of withdrawing their business from suppliers. Various edicts of the Federal Trade Commission have indicated that any pattern of purchases is suspect if it derives from a patronage agreement between companies and not from considerations of quality, price, and service. The FTC attitude has been that reciprocity does not necessarily have to be coercive to be considered in violation of Section 5 of the Federal Trade Commission Act; that is, it would be illegal in cases of (1) systematic use by a sales department of purchasing data in communicating with suppliers or (2) a discernible pattern of dealing between supplier and purchaser notwithstanding better price, quality, or service available from competitors.

POLICY MANUALS

At the beginning of this chapter, emphasis was placed on putting policies into written form. For policies that affect only the internal activities of the purchasing department, this may be in the form of standard-practice instructions. When policies affect activities outside the department, as in the case of interdepartmental relations and vendor relations, a more formal statement is desirable for purposes both of record and of communication. The most comprehensive and effective means of presentation is a purchasing department policy manual. The very act of compiling such a manual and committing it to writing is a useful project in itself, because it frequently clarifies ambiguities and points of issue; it may also reveal discrepancies or shortcomings in current policy, thus serving to improve departmental standards.

Because departmental policy reflects and is a part of general company policy, the manual must be approved by management authority. To secure that approval, the stated policies must be developed and agreed upon in consultation with those in charge of other phases of company operations who are affected by the rulings. Arrival at this stage of agreement is the most important part of the compilation of a policy statement and is essential to the workability and effectiveness of the policy. These consultations are on the plane of the best interests of the company as a whole, and they involve the whole management philosophy of centralized purchasing. They may call for a high degree of "selling" on the part of the purchasing officer in presenting his or her views on points at issue, as well as the art of compromise and adaptability to meet particular conditions.

The scope of the policy manual depends largely on the distribution that is contemplated and the ways in which it is to be used. Some companies have found it advantageous to supply copies to their entire list of vendors, and it has proved to be a potent means of developing good business relationships and cooperation. One representative manual designed for such widespread distribution consists of the following sections:

I. Foreword by the company president, giving authority to the manual as a statement of company policy.

II. Objectives of the purchasing department.

III. Scope and responsibilities of the purchasing department.

IV. Organization charts, showing the position of the purchasing department in the complete company organization and the detailed setup of the department itself.

V. Limitations (requirements of authorization to purchase; final determination of quality reserved to manufacturing and sales departments; certain classifications of purchases exempted, for example, food, insurance, rentals, advertising art and media, style and design sketches).

VI. Policies of selecting sources of supply (dealing only with reliable vendors, requirements of competitive bids, criteria used in evaluating sources, reciprocity).

VII. Policies on making commitments, placing purchase orders and contracts (all negotiations to be conducted and concluded by the purchasing department; no commitments to be made as to preference for products or sources by anyone outside the purchasing department; no commitments to be valid except as authorized by the purchasing department; conditions for acceptance of vendors' own sales contract forms).

VIII. Policies on vendor contacts (prompt reception of business callers; opportunity for complete sales presentation on initial call; arrangements for interviews with other departments to be made through purchasing; all correspondence, requests for catalogs and samples, and so on, to be cleared through the purchasing department; acceptance, trial, and report on free samples; price quotations held confidential; gifts and excessive entertainment forbidden; handling of complaints and adjustments).

IX. Policy on conflicts of interest (see Figure 21-2).

X. Relations of purchasing with other divisions and departments (reference to VI and VII; buyers to be alert in passing on to interested personnel in other departments all potentially useful information gained through sales contacts; purchasing department authorized to ask reconsideration of specifications or quantities, in the best interests of the company; purchasing department to consult with traffic, legal, tax, insurance, and credit departments on all pertinent problems; purchasing records to be available to the controller, treasurer, president, or any auditor delegated by them).

XI. Policy on centralized versus decentralized buying (director of purchases has authority to allocate responsibility for specific purchases or types of purchases in the best interests of the company, criteria used).

XII. Policy on buying for employees (limited to tools used in company activities that are customarily supplied at employee's expense).

The statements of policy are supported by an explanation of the principles upon which they are based and of the objectives toward which they are aimed. In addressing the manual to other departments and to suppliers, it becomes more effective when such reasons are briefly given as a background for the policies stated, which seem less arbitrary when thus presented.

For intradepartmental use, in training work, for indoctrination, and as an administrative guide, this is equally valid. Instructions are better received and better observed when the "why," as well as the "what" and "how," is included. Representative short-form manuals customarily include sections on customer and interdepartmental relationships, ethical considerations, and the like, emphasizing teamwork and cooperation in practical terms. Some of the more extensive manuals contain chapters discussing the principles of proper quality, quantity, price, and value, with applicable criteria, the use of specifications, and the fundamentals of purchase law, contracts, and patent rights.

A·B·DICK®

PURCHASING MANUAL

SUBJECT	NO.
CONFLICT OF INTEREST	C-4

I N S T R U C T I O N

I.   PURPOSE

This instruction acknowledges the right of Company employees
to engage in activities other than Company employment which
are private in nature, are conducted outside the normal
working hours for the employee and do not conflict with
or reflect unfavorably upon other employees or the Company.

II.   DEFINITION

A conflict of interest is any action taken in private or
under auspicious of Company assigned responsibility by
an employee which can be construed as causing doubt about
the employee's ability to make decisions in the best
interest of the Company and/or restrict or inhibit the
rights of other Company employees to perform their responsibilities in such a manner that serve the best interest of
the Company.

III. CRITERIA

This instruction is issued as a supplement to standing
Company policy described in Supervisors' Policy Manual,
Section F, titled "General Personnel Administration",
Page 22A dated June 12, 1962 and/or revisions and
amendments thereto that may be made from time to time.

Employees should avoid any action, position or situation
which could be considered, in fact or by implication, to
involve a conflict between their personal interest and
the Company's interest. Employees should not use their
position of trust and confidence within the Company to
further their private interest.

Employees shall be especially mindful of this policy if
their position with the Company is such that they may
influence decisions concerning firms or individuals with
whom the Company may have business relationships. For
example, Company employees or members of their families
should not own a significant interest in a supplier or
any other business entity if the employee is in a position
to influence orders placed or other decisions involving
A. B. Dick Company's interest.

ISSUED BY: *Clifton L. Smith*	DATE ISSUED	SUPERSEDES ISSUE DATED
Clifton L. Smith		
MANAGER - PROCUREMENT	11/7/74	PAGE 1 OF 4

Figure 21-2. First page of section on conflict of interest from a company purchasing manual. Courtesy, A. B. Dick Company.

378

Of particular importance in any policy manual is a statement from top management that establishes departmental policy as company policy and thus gives the entire code an authority that would otherwise be lacking.

SOME PERFORMANCE OBJECTIVES

After studying this chapter you should be able to

1. Review some of the policy questions to be settled (and the results recorded) before a purchasing department can be assured of operating efficiently.
2. Name at least six aspects of buyer–seller relationships that should be subject to control by policy.
3. Discuss the significance of the minority purchasing program covered in this chapter as it relates to the principles of supplier selection outlined in Chapter 13.
4. Differentiate between policy manuals and procedure manuals in purchasing.
5. Comment on the dangers to efficient purchasing inherent in a reciprocal purchasing policy (disregarding the question of the legality or illegality of reciprocity).
6. Discuss the importance of written top-management endorsement of policies and procedures presented in purchasing manuals.

A study of any function, including purchasing, must necessarily involve a variety of practices, procedures, and policy, and we have endeavored to examine these in depth in this and previous chapters. All these aspects are developed and carried out by people, however, and the ethical conduct of people has an important bearing on how well or how poorly a department meets its responsibilities and objectives. We turn to this question in the following chapter, the position of which in the book has no relation to its importance in the study of purchasing.

Ethical
Standards
in Purchasing

22

Although purchasing has developed the methods of a science, its decisions remain largely a matter of personal judgment and it is necessarily carried on, to a great extent, through personal contacts and relationships. The purchasing manager is the custodian of company funds, responsible for their conservation and wise expenditure. Moreover, through his or her contacts and dealings with vendors, the purchasing manager is a custodian of the company's reputation for courtesy and fair dealing. The ultimate act of selecting a vendor and awarding the order is essentially a matter of patronage. For all these reasons, a high ethical standard of conduct is essential. The purchasing manager not only must act ethically but should be above the suspicion of unethical behavior. Just as standard principles and patterns of procedure have evolved in the development of this function, so a code of conduct has also been formulated. The best statement of this code is embodied in the "Principles and Standards of Purchasing Practice" advocated by the National Association of Purchasing Management:

1. To consider, first, the interests of his company in all transactions and to carry out and believe in its established policies.
2. To be receptive to competent counsel from his colleagues and to be guided by such counsel without impairing the dignity and responsibility to his office.
3. To buy without prejudice, seeking to obtain the maximum ultimate value for each dollar of expenditure.

4. To strive consistently for knowledge of the materials and processes of manufacture and to establish practical methods for the conduct of his office.

5. To subscribe to and work for honesty and truth in buying and selling and to denounce all forms and manifestations of commercial bribery.

6. To accord a prompt and courteous reception, so far as conditions will permit, to all who call on a legitimate business mission.

7. To respect his obligations and to require that obligations to him and to his concern be respected, consistent with good business practice.

8. To avoid sharp practice.

9. To counsel and assist fellow purchasing agents in the performance of their duties, whenever occasion permits.

10. To cooperate with all organizations and individuals engaged in activites designed to enhance the development and standing of purchasing.

ETHICAL OBLIGATIONS

The above code is necessarily of a general nature and requires some further elaboration or interpretation as to its application to specific circumstances. As a generalization, it is an exceedingly practical code, like a great deal of our folk wisdom on the theme that "Honesty is the best policy." Hard-headed business moralizing is not predicated on the principle that virtue is its own reward; it recognizes much more tangible dividends. It is certainly true in purchasing that courtesy and fair dealing begets confidence and co-operation on the part of the supplier—assets that frequently spell the difference between a merely adequate purchasing performance and a major contribution to operating efficiency and sound profits. Without these, ordinary purchasing problems can readily become serious supply emergencies, particularly in times of economic change or stress. There are opportunists and "sharpshooters" in purchasing as in every other field, but they are rarely successful over any extended period of time. Any going concern that expects to be in business a year or ten years hence will do well to insist upon and to support high ethical standards in its procurement policies and practices.

OBLIGATIONS TO THE COMPANY

The purchasing manager's obligations to his or her own company, covered by the first four points of the code, and in part by the seventh, essentially consist of the responsibility for doing a complete and conscientious job in the function to which he or she has been assigned. Such terms as "the interests of his company" and "maximum ultimate value" are basic and self-explanatory; they summarize, in effect, the objectives of this entire study and discussion of the procurement function. "Knowledge of materials" and "practical methods for the conduct of his office" are the means of implementing these aims.

The code wisely goes beyond this, however, in emphasizing the obligation to buy without prejudice, which implies the obligation to maintain an open mind on purchasing matters. Prejudice is usually interpreted as discrimination against particular suppliers, their representatives, or their product, usually on personal or irrelevant grounds. Basically, however, prejudice concerns an attitude of mind on the purchasing manager's part that has implications far beyond this relatively simple and elementary example. Prejudice is not altogether a negative concept. A good part of all sales effort consists of the attempt to prejudice a buyer in favor of a product or supplier. There is nothing remotely unethical about this. Often it succeeds only too well. There are probably more orders placed because of the inertia that comes from habit, reinforced by relatively trouble-free experience with an established source of supply, than are withheld because of annoyance with a salesperson's mannerisms or dislike for his or her taste in shoes.

Freedom from prejudice implies a thoroughly objective approach to the purchasing problem. It means that propositions are not to be prejudged, or decisions predetermined, because the purchasing manager has closed his or her mind to facts and considerations that might modify or change previously held opinions. It means that irrelevant and superficial details, including personalities, should not be permitted to influence the just evaluation of a product or source in the light of its value to the company. It means that prejudices on the part of technical or operating personnel are to be combated just as consistently as those of vendors, with the same objective of maximum ultimate value.

The open mind, receptive to new ideas and capable of clear and objective judgment, is one of the outstanding characteristics of the successful buyer. Frequently it represents the difference between a merely competent job of buying and truly constructive and profitable procurement.

The purchasing manager has an ethical responsibility to his or her company not to place himself or herself under special obligation to any supplier by the acceptance of excessive entertainment or by permitting sales representatives consistently to buy his or her lunches, even though this may be done in the spirit of ordinary business courtesy and with the truthful and persuasive argument that it is a legitimate use of the salesperson's expense account. It is highly desirable that such relationships be kept on a thoroughly equitable basis, with the purchasing manager contributing his or her full share of the expense over a period of time. For this reason, progressive companies recognize the legitimacy and desirability of a purchasing expense account.

THE PROBLEM OF GIFTS

A special case arises in connection with the subject of Christmas remembrances. It is a fairly common business practice for a company to distribute some sort of gift to its customers at the Christmas season, and, frequently, through the natural sales contact, this may be addressed to some member of the purchasing staff. In the great majority of cases, this practice has no ulterior motive; it is general in its application, a genuine expression of appreciation and goodwill, and often prompted by personal friendship that has developed naturally in the course of mutual dealings and relationships over a period of time. But, because of the possible implication of commercial bribery, and on the grounds that such extra "sales expense" must eventually be reflected in some small way in the cost of goods sold and purchased, many purchasing departments have established a definite policy and regulation against the acceptance of such favors. Some weeks before the holiday season, vendors are apprised or reminded of this policy by means of a printed card or form letter and any gifts that are received contrary to this policy are returned with an explanation. Items of small value or distinctly of an advertising nature may be exceptions to such a rule, but there is danger in the haphazard interpretation that "two cigars are acceptable, but a box of cigars must be returned."

The Effects of Example

There are many cases in which the meticulous observation of such a rule may verge on the ridiculous, but it is one of the penalities of this particular function that standards cannot be relaxed. There is a further point in this regard. The practice can extend down the line to persons in subordinate purchasing positions, where the possibilities of insidious effect are greater. A department head, concerned with prestige and efficiency and freedom of choice in the buying operation, will avoid placing himself or herself or his or her department under any obligation to a supplier, as a matter of ordinary good business sense, but buyers farther down the line in the organization scale may not be so strongly motivated by such considerations and may be in an economic position in which favors of this nature seem more attractive. Therefore the overall policy is in the best interests of the company. It may be pertinent here to call attention to the tremendous responsibility of even a junior buyer in the allocation and disbursement of large sums in the form of purchase orders and to suggest that a most effective incentive or implementation of high ethical standards is a salary scale commensurate with that responsibility.

Finally, as was suggested in the introduction to this chapter, the purchasing manager has an ethical responsibility to his or her company to see that the company not only deserves, but actually enjoys in the trade, a reputation for scrupulously fair dealing. As the point of contact in dealing with vendors, he or she holds the company's reputation in this respect largely in his or her own hands. The purchasing manager may be very sure that his or her actions and conduct are critically judged and that this judgment, for better or worse, is quickly and widely disseminated among the sales fraternity at large. Frequently these impressions are based on incomplete knowledge or understanding of the facts, as seen from the outside, and they may be colored by disappointment and pique on the part of individuals. But, whether or not the criticism is justified, the purchasing manager cannot afford to ignore it.

VENDOR RELATIONS

It should be clear that the purchasing manager is under no moral obligation to see every salesperson, putting his or her time absolutely and indiscriminately at the disposal of any and all comers, however frequently or at whatever time or on whatever mission they may be calling. To do so would effectively destroy the possibility of organizing his or her work schedule efficiently and of accomplishing the work of his or her office, in which sales interviews are but one of many activities. To accept this statement is not contradictory to the policy of receptiveness and open-mindedness stressed in the preceding section. Some matters are patently not appropriate to the company's needs or are not timely for consideration at the particular moment that the sales representative elects to present or press them. Some salespersons are inconsiderate in making frequent calls with nothing new to contribute regarding their product and its application to the buyer's needs. The purchasing manager and not the salesperson, is the proper judge of when the calls become too frequent, but this does not relieve the buyer of his or her obligation of courtesy—a prompt acknowledgment of the call and a reason for not granting an interview. Every salesperson, should be be seen on his or her first call and be given an opportunity to tell his or her story; subsequent policy will depend on the particular circumstances. There is no justification for keeping any caller waiting for a protracted period if the interview is to be denied. And in any event, waiting time should be kept at a minimum.

Accomplishing this may be primarily a matter of organizing the reception procedure. Callers should be announced to the buyer on arrival. If there is an immediate answer, it can be given at that time. If there is to be any appreciable delay before the interview can be granted, for any reason, the sales representative should be apprised of the approximate waiting time that will be necessary, so that he or she can utilize that time to other advantage if desired, making a definite future appointment. If the waiting time exceeds the estimate, the receptionist should make it a point to remind the buyer and give an explanation to the caller.

Similar courtesy should prompt the purchasing manager to inform unsuccessful bidders when a proposition has been closed, as well as to inform the one who receives the order. Small companies, particularly, cannot afford to have a number of proposals outstanding, which would overtax their capacity should all bids be successful. They should therefore be relieved of these tentative commitments of capacity promptly. Furthermore, if the notification indicates in what respect the proposal fell short of the buyer's requirements, it will help the vendor in future negotiations and may lead to the development of a useful source of supply for the buyer. At the same time, it will temper the disappointment of an unsuccessful bidder to know that there was a real reason for the adverse decision.

When a sample is accepted for test, it entails an obligation on the buyer's part to make a fair trial, and it is a courteous gesture to inform the vendor of the outcome of that test, at least in general terms. Some buyers find it easy to terminate an interview by accepting a sample, even if they have no serious intention of giving it a trial. Such practice verges on misrepresentation and in the long run undermines the confidence that is essential to sound business relationships. It is avoided in many companies by a policy requiring that all sample lots for trial be bought and paid for by the buyer's company. This procedure works both ways: it incurs no obligation to the vendor, express or implied, beyond the transaction itself, and it gives the company a definite interest in completing the trial and making a fair evaluation of the product or material thus acquired.

Well-considered policies of this nature build confidence and respect and strengthen the personal relationships between buyer and vendor.

OBLIGATIONS TO VENDORS

In the large sense of obligations incurred in the course of doing business, the law is rather explicit, but there are many cases of interpretation and procedure that involve ethical concepts of this relationship, beyond the strict letter of the law. For example, if business is to be awarded on the basis of bids, the buyer should insist on receiving firm bids within a stated time. If the buyer permits or encourages revisions, particularly at the last moment, the way is opened for sharp dealing on the part of vendors, and the buyer is not free from suspicion of the same fault on his or her own side. If revisions are to be permitted, the same opportunity should be frankly offered to all bidders, and, if the specifications are changed because of an alternative product offered by one of the bidders, all should be invited to bid on the new specification.

The purchasing manager is not responsible for a vendor's error in calculating a bid. But, if one of the proposals seems excessively low, indicating that an error may be responsible for the discrepancy, it is good practice to ask for a recalculation. If it happens that some item has been omitted from the estimate or that a mathematical error has been made, the purchasing manager is not in the position of taking advantage of such an inadvertent slip to the detriment of the seller. On the other hand, it frequently happens that such a recalculation results in an even lower bid, although this possibility may have been far from the buyer's mind. Naturally, if the bid is accompanied by a detailed breakdown of costs and the error is patent, it would be unethical to hold the vendor to such a proposal, which obviously does not represent the vendor's real intention.

Once an order or contract has been placed on the basis of a legitimate bid, the buyer is not responsible for assuring the bidder a profit on the transaction. Sellers occasionally appeal for relief from a contract that turns out contrary to their expectations, but the buyer is under no obligation to surrender or modify his or her own contractual rights if the agreement has been made in good faith. The buyer has an ethical responsibility to his or her own company and to competitive bidders in cases of this sort. If an adjustment can be made, or an alternative source found, without sacrifice of the buyer's position, it may be wise to take such action on the grounds that service and satisfaction will be greater under the new arrangement. But the whole purpose of the contractual agreement is to provide for carrying out the transaction as planned, with a definite allocation of responsibility to both parties, including the risk of unforeseen developments. As a general rule, sellers respect the buyer who stands firmly on his or her rights and prefer to do business on this basis, having the corresponding assurance that the buyer will observe his or her responsibilities under the contract just as conscientiously.

CONFIDENTIAL INFORMATION

The buyer is under no ethical compulsion to answer questions other than those that relate directly to the proposal. Competitive price information is regarded as confidential and should not be disclosed under any circumstances. And, although it is generally true that full and frank discussion leads to a better mutual understanding and perhaps to a better purchase, there are circumstances in which factors other than price are also of a confidential nature.

For example, some sellers decline to bid unless they know the use to which their product is to be put. They argue that unsatisfactory performance on a job for which the product was never intended might react unfavorably and unfairly against the reputation of the product and the producer, and they prefer to forego a sale rather than risk this unjustified demerit. They point out, quite logically, that with knowledge of what is to be required, they can recommend or prescribe the best materials for the purpose. But sometimes, also, they have a sliding price scale according to the application of identical material, a marketing practice that can be plausibly explained on the basis of special concessions to capture new markets or applications, but for which the logic of purchasing value is somewhat more obscure when one ingot or roll is exactly the same as the other.

However, we are here concerned with buying reasons and policy. Although trade secrets are much less a factor in industry today than they were a generation ago, there are still a number of things that a company may wish to keep strictly "within the family"—little kinks of manufacture that make for the individuality of their product or short cuts that give them a slight advantage in competitive costs. All buyers are well aware that suppliers rarely know the full extent of the uses that their product serves. They have no desire to broadcast the direction of their experimental program or to have the vendor's sales representatives scurry around to their competitors with the "new idea." The buyer who is reticent about the proposed uses of the things that he or she purchases need not be concerned over the implication that his or her reticence is unethical. On the other hand, the buyer must recognize that under such circumstances he or she waives the benefits of any implied warranty on the seller's part and has no basis for later expressing dissatisfaction or pressing a claim for unsuitability in his or her purchase. The seller who is not informed as to the intended use is bound only to the extent of conformance with any specifications that may be set forth in the order.

ENGINEERING SERVICES

One question of ethics that is frequently raised is the proprietary interest of a supplier in business earned through valuable and extensive preliminary engineering services that produced a design or product adapted to the buyer's need. Is the buyer justified in sending out blueprints of such designs, product samples, or formula specifications for competitive bids, or does the supplier who originated them have a continuing claim upon the business? It is obvious that the seller must recoup these expenses and is legitimately entitled to do so. In the typical case, the service is not of a sort that can be protected by a basic or design patent. It is not a cost that he or she can pass along as a special charge, for the seller is not in the business of consulting engineering except as a means of making sales for his or her production facilities. It is a cost that will normally be reflected in his or her quotation, preferably spread over a reasonable manufacturing quantity, lest the original lot cost be excessively high for the buyer's purpose. Consequently, the distribution and absorption of this cost item frequently contemplate repeat orders to justify the quoted price, and the price is calculated in the expectation or hope of continuing business.

However thoroughly the buyer may recognize the implications of such a position and sympathize with the claims of the seller, the prospect of accepting and maintaining a monopolistic supply situation is contrary to the principles of good purchasing. The buyer cannot conscientiously agree to this solution. There will probably always be controversy as to the fairness of any compromise, but the logical answer, and the one in most common usage, is usually worked out in the form of a liberal term contract: the vendor originating the design or product supplies the buying company's requirements for a year, or more or less, depending on the quantities invoved, during which time the vendor is expected to recoup his or her experimental and development costs in addition to normal production profits. At the end of this period, the business is opened to more general competition, and it is expected that cost to the buyer will be reduced, for he or she cannot reasonably be expected to accept these development costs as a permanent factor of price. The original supplier, having already profited from his or her superior skill and from being a step ahead of the field, is still in a preferred position and has a substantial competitive advantage in a year's manufacturing experience as well as, perhaps, in patterns, dies, and tooling, which have been totally depreciated as a cost factor. Except in some very unusual cases, such an arrangement satisfies the buyer's ethical obligation to the vendor.

SHARP PRACTICE

The term "sharp practice," as condemned in the buyer's code, is best defined by some typical illustrations of evasion and indirect misrepresentation just short of actual fraud. They belong to the old school of unscrupulous shrewdness, when buying was concerned with the immediate transaction rather than the long-range program. These examples would have been commonplace among an older generation of buyers, and sellers in that period were habitually on their guard against such possibilities. In modern procurement and marketing, which are based on mutual confidence and integrity, such practices are frowned upon just as severely by the buyers themselves as by the sales organizations with which they deal.

It is sharp practice for a buyer to talk in terms of large quantities, encouraging the seller to expect a large volume of business and to quote on a quantity basis, when in fact the actual requirement and order are to be in relatively small volume that would not legitimately earn the quantity consideration.

It is sharp practice to call for a large number of bids merely in the hope that some supplier will make an error in his or her estimate, of which the buyer can take advantage.

It is sharp practice to invite bids from suppliers whom the buyer will not patronize in any case, using these quotations only for the purpose of playing them against the proposals of those who are really acceptable sources of supply. It costs money, time, and effort to prepare estimates and bids. Sellers are glad to undertake the expense in the hope of securing a contract, but the buyer has no right to impose these costs on a seller when the buyer has no intention of giving the seller an opportunity to get the business.

It is sharp practice to misrepresent a market by placing the price of job lots, seconds, or other distress merchandise in ostensible competition with real market prices.

It is sharp practice to leave copies of competitors' bids or other confidential correspondence in open view on the desk while negotiating with a seller, in the knowledge that the latter can scarcely fail to notice them.

It is sharp practice to deal only with "hungry" suppliers and to try and keep them hungry so as to force concessions. More generally stated, this applies to any abuse of purchasing power to the detriment of the seller. Although it is legitimately expected of a purchasing manager to make full use of his or her company's purchasing power, this factor should normally operate to mutual benefit, with the buyer's position strengthened by virtue of being a more desirable customer, offering greater volume, steadier flow of orders, more prompt payment, or similar considerations of value to the seller.

COMBATING UNETHICAL PRACTICES

The subject of business ethics is not one-sided. Purchasing managers and buyers are faced from time to time with unethical sales practices, although these are no more representative of selling policy in general than are the occasional instances of unethical buying. There is sharp practice in selling: collusive bidding, restrictive conditions in specifications, artificial stimulation of demand and prejudice among shop operatives, sabotage of competitive products, padding of orders and shipments, use of unfamiliar trade terms and measurements, supposedly sample orders that are magnified into excessive quantities, obscure contract clauses buried in small type, and many others. In most cases these can be avoided by proper selection of vendors, but perhaps only after unfortunate experience has indicated the disreputable sources of supply. In dealing with some of the practices, such as collusive bidding, more direct and aggressive action is called for as a corrective measure.

The best defense is competent, objective buying, supported by the necessary follow-through in insistence on contract performance, acceptance testing, and the like. The purchase order or contract in itself constitutes a legally enforceable document. All supplementary agreements, specifications, and special terms should likewise be reduced to writing, using care to see that no ambiguity exists in respect to what is expected of the seller. Reputable sellers respect the buyer who is alert, thorough, and conscientious in the conduct of his or her office, and they respond in kind.

Confidence in a supplier is an essential of any sound purchasing department, but confidence need not be blind. It must be earned and the reputable supplier welcomes the opportunity to show that he or she is worthy of confidence. The purchasing manager is grossly neglectful of his or her own responsibility who unquestioningly accepts the oft-heard advice, "Select a reliable vendor, then trust that vendor to supply the right material and to charge a fair price." The classic admonition, *"Caveat emptor*—Let the buyer beware!" was coined for that individual. No honest buyer apologizes for checking a delivery, making an acceptance test, or analyzing a quotation. These precautions are a test of his or her own judgment and performance as well as of the supplier, and the responsibility cannot be delegated.

SOME PERFORMANCE OBJECTIVES

After studying this chapter you should be able to

1. Give and defend an opinion as to whether or not it is ethical for a buyer to accept from a supplier (a) an occasional luncheon, (b) tickets for the theater or for a sporting event, (3) weekends at the supplying company's hunting lodge or similar facility, and (c) gifts of such items as TV sets and appliances.
2. Discuss the question of whether ethical conduct in purchasing is a matter of morality, good business, or both.
3. Describe top managment's role in ensuring ethical conduct in their individual businesses.
4. Discuss the notion that buyers are morally obliged to see that a supplier makes a "fair profit" on a sale.
5. Describe the most widely adopted solution to the problem of compensating suppliers for development and engineering costs incurred in preparing quotations.
6. Define sharp practice as it relates to purchasing and offer hypothetical examples. Describe actual situations involving such practice that you may have observed.

The foregoing chapters have presented a set of broad guidelines for understanding the purchasing function and for operating and managing that function. But the ultimate test of purchasing performance is not in how much a manager knows, it is in how successfullly he or she applies what they do know. As the logical culmination of this study, the next and concluding chapter deals with the difficult problem of evaluating just how well purchasing personnel are meeting their responsibilities.

Section VI

MANAGEMENT EVALUATION OF PURCHASING

Measuring Purchasing Performance

23

Purchasing and management executives alike would welcome some reliable yardstick for the measurement of efficiency in purchasing. Consequently, a great deal of serious thought has been given to the problem. It has been the subject of continuing study for several years by the National Association of Purchasing Management. At one stage of the study, cooperation of the National Association of Cost Accountants was enlisted, with liberal cash awards offered for the best papers submitted. Although such research has not resulted in any formula or method capable of general application, it has developed a number of principles that are helpful in approaching the problem.

SOME COMMON FALLACIES

It is easy to oversimplify when trying to measure purchasing performance. Probably the most common fallacy is to set a standard of efficiency by expressing departmental operating cost as a percentage of total purchase expenditures. This percentage is necessarily an average figure, for it is obvious that there is a wide disparity between the purchasing cost for orders of relatively small value, for hard-to-find items, and for those that are required only occasionally and the cost of procuring standard and familiar materials from established sources in substantial volume. Examples can be found of purchasing costs ranging all the way from 0.75 percent of expenditures to 2.0 percent or more, each of which could conscientiously be described as efficient performance for the particular company and conditions concerned. Independent purchasing services operate on percentages ranging from 2.5 percent to 5.0 percent and are able to demonstrate savings as compared with unorganized and inexpert purchasing. A reasonable average figure would be in the neighborhood of 1.5 percent to 2.0 percent, but this is the broadest sort of generalization and has little meaning for the individual company; a variation of 0.5 percent on any substantial purchasing program runs into significant dollar figures.

The fallacy of such a standard of measurement is readily demonstrable on a simple mathematical basis, for the percentage can be reduced to any desired level by the expedient of paying more for the materials purchased, which would represent highly expensive and inefficient purchasing.

The difficulty in generalizing about purchasing costs as a measurement of efficiency is indicated in some of the results obtained from a continuing survey on the subject (see Figure 23-1). In reporting on the survey, Albert J. D'Arcy of Union Carbide Corporation said

> We have been collecting data on costs over the years . . . . We have found that there is very little consistency in cost figures from various companies. It appears there is no simple, ready-made formula to tell you what purchasing cost should be in a given company or industry.[1]

Mr. D'Arcy went on to point out that company organization, accounting methods, objectives, definitions of costs, and company and departmental objectives vary widely. Straight cost analysis in respect to purchasing may not always give the right answer, as the purchasing department may be producing other benefits for the company—balanced inventories, innovative ideas, and so forth.

"Purchasing operating costs should be tracked," he concluded, "but it is important that management evaluate cost performance in the proper perspective."

Another method sometimes advocated is the measurement of cost per order. This has the virture of being tied to actual operations performed rather than to the incidental (though highly important) factor of funds expended. It is subject to the same sort of criticism, however, because cost per order can be reduced by issuing more orders for smaller quantities, whereas real purchasing efficiency may lie in the other direction.

---

[1] Albert J. D'Arcy, "Facts and Figures on the Cost of Purchasing," *National Purchasing Review,* Vol. May 1978, pp. 2–5.

ANALYSIS OF PURCHASING COST SURVEY MADE IN JUNE 1977

Worldwide Purchasing	Annual Data			Unit Purchasing Cost		
	Sales Million Dollars	Purchases Million Dollars	Purchasing Cost In Thousand Dollars	Cents Per Dollar of Purchases	Percent Deviation From Average	Cents Per Dollar Of Sales
Company A	307	125	1,100	.88	+ 52	.36
Company F	1,309	540	1,500	.28	− 52	.11
Company G	8,725	4,962	7,500	.15	− 74	.09
Company I	793	448	2,800	.62	+ 7	.35
Company L	28,000	1,700	17,500	1.03	+ 78	.06
Company R	12,507	1,900	10,300	.54	− 7	.08
Average				.58		
United States Purchasing						
Company E	2,052	1,028	2,425	.24	− 45	.12
Company H	2,255	1,089	4,986	.46	+ 5	.22
Company J	1,250	875	1,000	.11	− 75	.08
Company K	3,458	2,062	8,500	.41	− 7	.25
Company N	1,346	617	3,786	.61	+ 39	.28
Company Q	710	440	1,241	.28	− 36	.18
Company S	657	330	1,673	.51	+ 16	.25
Company T	1,920	1,200	2,250	.19	− 57	.12
Company W	355	126	1,500	1.19	+170	.42
Average				.44		
Headquarters Purchasing Only						
Company B	323	76	519	.68	+ 74	.16
Company C	1,054	400	1,118	.28	− 28	.11
Company D	1,069	118	914	.77	+ 97	.09
Company M	753	250	732	.29	− 28	.10
Company O	2,500	1,200	3,000	.25	− 36	.12
Company P	2,600	1,300	4,247	.33	− 15	.16
Company V	2,900	1,400	1,545	.11	− 72	.05
Average				.39		

Figure 23-1. Regular surveys made in recent years have shown that costs of purchasing vary widely from company to company. Courtesy, *National Purchasing Review.*

The positive principle to be deduced from these analyses is that there is a dual job of measurement to be done—efficiency in departmental administration and efficiency in procurement. There is the cost of operation and the cost of materials to be considered before performance can be truly evaluated. The first factor, administrative cost, presents a relatively simple problem; management science has developed standards and measures for such performance that can readily be applied. The second factor is more difficult; the approach has been suggested in the type of information included in purchasing department reports to management—inventory ratios, material costs related to current market levels, savings effected through good purchasing practice, adherence to material budgets, and the like, all tending to demonstrate specific accomplishments or performance in the actual procurement function.

The most satisfactory measurements are those in which the two phases are separately considered. For convenience, they may be designated as *efficiency* and *proficiency*, both of which are important to the company. Of the two, the second is the more characteristically related to specific professional skill in procurement, which is the functional purpose of the department. Furthermore, it is the phase that embraces total expenditures and product costs, whereas departmental administration represents only a small percentage of total cost. No really useful purpose is served by trying to force a relationship between the two, much less by trying to measure the greater and more fundamental performance in terms of the minor factor.

VARIABLES IN PURCHASE STANDARDS

One of the basic difficulties in devising a standard method of measuring purchasing performance is that so many variables are involved. This fact is apparent in the widely differing scope and character of requirements in various types of operations in which the value of purchased materials may range all the way from 20 percent to 80 percent of total expenditures, with a corresponding variation in the relative importance of the purchasing function. Thus the first principle of evaluation is that it must be done on an individual company basis. Comparisons are significant only to the extent that the type of industry and the size of the unit are comparable.

There is a further variation in the functional organization of individual companies and the responsibilities assigned to the purchasing department, which may range all the way from simple clerical detail to complete materials management, in companies of similar size within the same industry.

Purchasing itself deals in variables. Price is a variable. Price alone is not a proper measure of performance, because it is frequently subordinated to other considerations, so that better procurement may be effected by paying more for materials. It is, however, an important factor. In evaluating price performance, it must be considered against the variable standard of changing market levels or against adjustable standard costs as established in cost accounting procedure. Purchasing problems and effort vary with market conditions. Costs rise rapidly when intensive expediting is required to assure delivery or when constant research is needed to develop satisfactory sources of supply.

Inventory ratios and turnover are widely and understandably accepted as an indication of the efficiency of the purchasing policy and program. Here again, standards will vary according to conditions, as noted in the discussion of proper purchase quantities, for good purchasing policy calls for the accumulation of greater material reserves and greater advance coverage in times of advancing prices, which would result in less favorable turnover for the time being. In using such a yardstick, therefore, the condition at any given time could be seriously misleading, but the average of a month-to-month record over the period of a year would give a reasonably fair measure of accomplishment.

THE FUNCTIONAL APPROACH

No attempt will be made here to propose a formula capable of application in every case to measure the efficiency and proficiency of purchasing. But an approach to such a solution can be outlined. Throughout this study, emphasis has been placed upon the functional considerations of procurement. That is also a sound basis upon which to measure purchasing performance.

The functional responsibility of a purchasing department is to provide a steady flow of materials as needed, at lowest ultimate cost. This involves many factors—the right material, the right quantity, the right time, the right source, and the right price—that interact with one another so that each decision of what is "right" in a given case depends upon what is "right" in respect to some or all the other factors. A compromise or balance must be achieved to arrive at the best end result. In the same way, the measure of accomplishment is to be found in terms of the end result, in which these various measurable factors are contributory elements, to be reconciled in the final accounting.

The system of measurement should focus attention and effort upon performance rather than upon the details of rating, and the department head should have confidence that it will fairly reflect his or her accomplishments.

The system should conscientiously segregate the factors for which each department is directly responsible, so that the credits and demerits may be equitably applied. It should never be permitted to set up the type of interdepartmental competition that might discourage fullest cooperation toward the common aim of the most economical and profitable overall operation.

PRODUCT COST AS A BASIS OF MEASUREMENT

The end result of purchasing is product cost, and the measurement of purchasing performance can logically be based on that consideration. The direct responsibility of the purchasing department is the net cost of product materials up to the point of use, excluding the cost of maintenance and operating supplies. The standard of measurement is standard cost, arrived at by careful and detailed analysis of the complete bill of materials, with normal margins for waste and spoilage, corresponding to the standard costs used in accounting and in sales price estimates, and adjusted monthly to market fluctuations with the assistance of the purchasing executive. These costs will take into account the quality specifications representing the grade of material required to satisfy the company's standards of product and operation. The standard cost is expressed as one overall figure, either cost of purchased materials per unit of product or a percentage of total product cost, although the figure is made up of carefully itemized elements. This is done partly to simplify accounting and evaluation, but even more as recognition of the facts that flexibility is essential in working out the purchasing program and that attention should be focused on the end result rather than on the details. And the end result is total product cost.

Besides being adjusted periodically to market conditions, the standard cost is revised for any changes in product design, bills of material, or manufacturing policies at the time at which these changes are made. For example, if it is decided to purchase a component part in fabricated form rather than to manufacture it in the plant, in the interest of greater ultimate economy or for better utilization of facilities, a cost adjustment is in order. In this case purchase cost will necessarily be higher, because outside manufacturing services are now being purchased while the company's own manufacturing operations are being reduced. The same principle would apply if the decision were reversed. The object at all times is to reflect fairly the specific cost responsibility of both departments.

Such standard costs, which are in effect a purchase budget for product materials, provide a practical and significant basis for the measurement of purchasing performance in respect to the largest and most important phase of the procurement function. Adherence to the standard cost may be taken as 100. If the purchasing department succeeds in bettering this figure, the rating of performance is raised by a percentage corresponding to the saving; if costs are higher, the rating is proportionately reduced. In other words, performance is rated on a percentage basis, inversely to the costs actually incurred, as compared with total standard cost.

MODIFYING FACTORS

In many cases, this basic rating will be sufficient for the purpose. There are, however, a number of other factors involved in the complete operation and responsibility of purchasing, affecting full evaluation of performance. These can be considered separately and the results, properly weighted, applied as a credit or demerit to the rating just noted. The more important of these are as follows:

1. *Inventory performance.* Continuity of operation, to the extent of having materials on hand when needed, is a purchasing responsibility. It is recognized that this requires the maintenance of working inventory, entailing certain carrying charges that are a legitimate cost of business as production insurance. The size of this inventory, in relation to current operating rates, is a matter of company policy. If the approved policy is to carry a sixty-day supply, the inventory should amount to one sixth of the amount of annual expenditures; if it is a ninety day supply, the inventory would be one fourth of annual expenditures. This variable standard should be adjusted according to prevailing policy, and it should be measured in total dollar value. The cost of carrying inventory which is calculated upon experience by standard cost accounting methods ranges from 20 to 35 percent in most industrial companies (see Chapter 9).

If, by efficient planning, scheduling of purchases, and stores management, continuity of operation is maintained with a turnover of inventory every forty-five days instead of every sixty days, average inventory is reduced by 25 percent, and purchasing performance should be credited with the carrying cost of 10 percent on that amount. If the inventory runs high because of overbuying or inefficient materials control, resulting in a slower turnover, a corresponding debit should be applied.

Turnover is not the only measure of inventory performance. Losses due to obsolescence (unless due to change in design or other causes outside purchasing's jurisdiction and control), production delays due to lack of standard materials that should have been in stock when needed, and unnecessary extra transportation charges incurred for faster and more expensive means of delivery indicate poor performance. Obsolescence losses may be offset by credit for salvage operations and sales of scrap and surplus items. This group of factors does not lend itself to evaluation on a strictly quantitative or percentage basis and may call for a prorating with other departments, because the delays and emergency shipments may be caused by rush requisitions, changes in specifications, or abnormal and unforeseen demand. They should be noted, however, and a point rating assigned to fit the circumstances. It should be kept in mind that such demerits are not a serious reflection on purchasing performance unless they occur too frequently and run into large amounts.

2. *Quality factors.* The purchasing department is responsible for procuring materials of adequate quality, in accordance with approved specifications. Failure to do so is an indication either of faulty buying or of selection of the wrong supplier. In respect to most fabricated products, a

certain percentage of rejects is recognized in trade practice and in purchase transactions as allowable. In evaluating purchasing performance, demerits are in order for rejects in excess of the allowable margin and for the cost of working substandard items to make them usuable and up to specification.

3. *Maintenance and factory supplies.* This part of the purchase program is segregated from product materials because it is an indirect cost, allocable to the operating expense of other departments. For example, the quantity of supplies and expendable tools used for a given volume of production primarily reflects the efficiency of production departments, the quantity of fuel used reflects the efficiency of the power plant department and so on. It would be illogical to attribute excesses or economies to the purchasing division, even though purchases in these classifications make up a substantial part of the purchasing program. In companies that exercise a specific control over the purchase and use of supply items, the usual procedure is to budget such requirements as an amount or percentage based on current rates of operation or volume of production, as indicated by past experience, but without a detailed breakdown by individual items; adherence to the budget then becomes a measure of the efficiency of using departments.

4. *Savings other than price.* Savings due to buying at favorable prices, whether on product or maintenance and supply items, are taken into account in the basic evaluation of purchasing performance. Consequently, they are not considered separately. But savings from other sources—by substitution, standardization, specification changes, packing and transportation costs, and the like—are listed separately and totaled and are then credited on a point scale. Credit given for such developments should be liberal rather than strictly quantitative or percentage based, for not only are they repetitive in nature, but they represent the qualities of initiative that are the foundation of both efficiency and proficiency in purchasing.

5. *Administrative cost.* Administrative cost cannot logically be used as the measure of effectiveness, and it does not necessarily bear any fixed ratio to the amount of purchase expenditures. Another point to be kept in mind is that, although the effort should be made to keep department expenses at the practical minimum, this attitude should not be emphasized to a degree that would suggest or encourage doing without such departmental activities as research, training, cost analysis, and fieldwork by buyers at the company's plants and those of suppliers. During periods of economic turmoil (e.g., in 1973–1974 when shortages placed enormous burdens on purchasing departments), administrative costs may skyrocket. In the 1973–1974 period the real measure of purchasing perfor-

mance was its ability to get the material needed to keep production lines operating.

The measure of departmental costs should, therefore, be made against a budgeted standard cost developed by an analysis of activities, the volume of specific operations such as the number of requisitions handled and purchase orders issued, an allowance for incidental functions and special projects, recommendations and budget requests of the department head, and a proportionate share of general administrative overhead. This budget should be liberal enough to include personnel and facilities for carrying on a complete and progressive program of procurement—"spending money to save money." It should be close enough to represent prudent management, efficient work production on clerical and other processing operations, and good administrative control. In short, it should be a realistic appraisal of the job to be done. It should be adjusted from time to time as conditions change and as the department head can demonstrate the need for such adjustment. Evaluation of this phase is based on adherence to budget, with proportionate credit for keeping expenses below the estimate and proportionate debit for expenses above this figure.

In weighing this factor as it affects the general rating, a fair proportion would be the ratio that general company overhead bears to total manufacturing cost, because this is essentially what the figure represents.

USING THE RATINGS

Under such a plan, the total evaluation of purchasing department performance consists of a basic rating on product cost, which is the real test of the department's performance, and modifying factors representing various phases of departmental responsibility and accomplishment. Three of these factors—inventory ratios, cost of maintenance and supply items, and administrative cost—are measurable on a scale comparable to the basic rating and can be applied directly to that figure by giving them weight commensurate with their importance on a logical mathematical basis. The other two—errors in quality of purchased items and savings due to causes other than price—require a somewhat arbitrary point evaluation in applying them to the scale. The whole calculation can, however, be put in mathematical terms, arriving at a figure that may be either more or less than 100.

What does this figure mean? In the first place, although the 100-point standard in the various sections of the measurement and in the total rating represents an objective to be attained, it does not necessarily follow that it is attainable under all conditions or that a lower rating is the indication of incompetence, any more than it is true that a baseball player's batting average is expected to be perfect or that a sales department is expected at all times to provide orders equal to the company's total production capacity. Rather, it is an index of performance that can be interpreted as showing the department is falling short of expectations and not making its fair contribution to profitable company operation. On the other hand, it might show the department is coming close to the standards of performance that the company can reasonably expect in this phase of its business and is, thus, doing a competent job.

In the second place, it must be recognized that the standards in each case are based on judgment that may or may not be accurate and realistic in its expectations. An index of this sort measures both the performance and the standards against which it is rated. A record that is consistently above or below the stated standards may show that management is expecting too much or too little of its purchasing division. This discovery in itself is highly important; it may suggest and demonstrate that the estimates of material costs, or administrative costs, or policies of procurement should be revised to conform more closely with actual performance, but the competitive and profit factors of doing business must be based on actual performance. And, for purposes of the rating itself, the standards and the expectation must be reasonable in relation to the conditions, both internal and external, under which purchasing is done.

Third, the ultimate rating provides a comparison of performance not only in relation to the stated standards, but also in relation to performance in previous periods. This ratio is important for management to know. However, the rating is not a measure of comparison with purchasing performance in other companies or a definitive percentage measurement of excellence. There are too many variables in the type of materials purchased, the volume of purchases, and the specific organization responsibility, as well as variables of judgment in setting standards, to permit any such general interpretation.

These qualifications do not imply that the measurement and rating are inaccurate or of little value. Rather, they constitute a warning against a too superficial or arbitrary acceptance of the numerical result as the significant figure, and especially against the psychological inference of "100 percent" performance. Systematic measurement of performance is a highly desirable guide to intelligent management and to intelligent functional and administrative policy; the method outlined here covers the essentials so far as purchasing activities are concerned and is believed to provide as accurate an evaluation as possible in this field in which judgment and adjustment to changing conditions play such an important part—in which so much depends on what is not done as well as on positive decisions and on timing.

It is recommended that, in using this scale, all the several factors and their respective ratings be shown, as well as the composite figure. This is because each phase has a significance of its own as an indicator of efficiency and proficiency, and the breakdown is the surest guide as to where attention and effort should be concentrated for improved performance. In particular, the basic rating on cost of product materials should be shown both before and after the modifying factors have been applied, because this is the figure that reflects the functional accomplishment of purchasing. A good record on this one essential point justifies the purchasing operation. Also, it is an important factor—sometimes the determining factor—in respect to policies of design, pricing, and marketing; it may well be the key to the company's competitive and profit position. In companies for which it is impracticable to undertake a complete and detailed measurement of departmental performance, this analysis of the materials factor of product cost may in itself serve the purpose.

JOB ANALYSIS AND EVALUATION

Many experienced purchasing executives who are convinced that no practicable performance-rating system can be applied to purchasing have turned to job analysis and evaluation. The method sets forth specific responsibilities of the function and the minimum qualifications of education, training, experience, personality, and ability to fulfill the requirements of the position. On this basis, with suitable relative weights assigned to the various items, a rating of individual competence and performance can be made. It is a workable method, and it can be applied to all grades of personnel in a purchasing department, as in other departments.

The method has serious limitations, however, in that its significance depends entirely on the adequacy of the basic definitions. These definitions are necessarily couched in terms of minimum requirements, and there is a real danger that these minimum requirements may tend not only to become the maximum opportunities permitted to purchasing department personnel, especially in the higher grades, but also to limit the scope of what management expects of its purchasing department, thereby limiting the potential achievement. The greatest values of good purchasing performance as a contributing factor to efficient company operation and profits lie in the superior field of performance that is broadly indicated by the term "proficiency," involving those attributes of imagination and resourcefulness that are outside of any definition. The desirable objective viewpoint implied by such a system of analysis may also be a limiting factor to truly proficient performance. This is so because the able purchasing officer himself or herself is not only the best qualified, but he or she may be the only person in the organization qualified to recognize the full potential of his or her function and its service to the company.

A somewhat similar approach involves the use of a series of check points for evaluating performance. Included would be such inquiries as

1. What are the personal characteristics, ability, and organizing skill of the department head that have a particular bearing upon his or her competence in the performance of his or her function and his or her value in serving the overall company interests? This question recognizes the principle that departmental efficiency largely reflects the competence of the department head. The evaluation would necessarily be made by a superior management executive or by a professional management engineer.

2. Does the purchasing department have a broad statement of policy, preferably in written form? Is it a good policy? Is the policy observed in practice? Has the policy been brought to the attention of all suppliers?

3. Does the purchasing department have a standard procedure, preferably in the form of a written manual? It is a good procedure? Is it efficiently carried out in practice? What checkpoints are used to determine adherence?

4. Is the performance of the purchasing department satisfactory in securing the delivery of quality material at the time needed?

5. Are materials secured at the right price? Measurement of this factor may be against the standard of market price for buyers in a comparable industrial position and for a comparable volume of purchases, or against "standard cost" prices as established in the accounting procedure of the company. The most practicable method of determining this point is by a systematic spot check or audit of the more substantial purchases, including an examination of the method of inquiry and choice of supplier as supporting evidence of whether or not the right prices are being obtained.

6. What is the cost of operating the department? It may be judged in relation to the departmental administrative budget or measured by the cost of placing an order or by what it costs to spend a dollar in purchasing.

7. To what extent does the purchasing department create or dissipate goodwill for the company? The general reputation of the purchasing department in the trade and among its suppliers has a bearing on this point.

An analysis of this sort, giving proper weight to the relative importance of the various points checked, will not provide a numerical rating of efficiency, but it should establish with a reasonable degree of certainty whether or not the purchasing department is operating satisfactorily in respect to its major responsibilities. This sort of information is valuable both to the purchasing executive and to the company management.

In one phase of its purchasing performance appraisal program, NCR Corporation uses the standards shown in Figure 23-2. Other measures are also used to evaluate buyer performance, including how well they meet predetermined targets for cost reduction on specific company end products. The latter method involves determining the material content of the end product (e.g., an accounting machine), identifying those items that make up 75 percent of that material cost, giving the buyers of the various commodities specific cost-reduction targets, and measuring them against those targets.[2]

NATIONAL SCIENCE FOUNDATION AND PURCHASING PERFORMANCE

The widespread interest in—and significance of—measurement of purchasing performance received special recognition in 1976 when the National Science Foundation provided a substantial grant for a nationwide study of the subject.

In an executive summary of the study submitted to NSF, Robert M. Monczka and Phillip L. Carter of the Graduate School of Business Administration, Michigan State University, noted the following:[3]

1.　Eighteen leading U.S.-based organizations participated in the study, and more than 200 managers and buyers were interviewed. *More than 200 purchasing performance measures* were identified (italics added).

2.　The key measures in purchasing appeared to be price effectiveness, work load, cost savings, administration and control, vendor quality and delivery, and material flow control. The survey showed however, that there are important differences in the ways in which the companies measure performance in each of the areas named.

3.　Several important principles related both to systems and to people were suggested by the research:

[2] Somerby Dowst, "Job Evaluation Takes More Than Numbers," *Purchasing Magazine,* July 26, 1977, p. 26.

[3] Robert M. Monczka and Phillip L. Carter, "Purchasing Performance: Measurement and Control—Executive Summary," Unpublished study, School of Business Administration, Michigan State University, East Lansing, Mich., January 1978.

PURCHASING PERFORMANCE APPRAISAL PART II

X-1174-107A 3/76

NAME	POSITION		DATE	APPRAISAL PERIOD TO

PERFORMANCE RATING POINT SCALE

7 = VERY HIGH 6 = HIGH 5 = HIGH AVERAGE 4 = AVERAGE 3 = LOW AVERAGE 2 = LOW 1 = NOT ACCEPTABLE

CATEGORY	PERFORMANCE ELEMENT BEING MEASURED	POINTS
I. **ADMINISTRATIVE** **SKILLS** Those skills that reflect the Buyer's ability to perform this function efficiently and effectively.	A. ORGANIZATION The Buyer is organized in a manner that permits maximum utilization of time and effort.	
	B. PLANNING The Buyer arranges his work to ensure priority matters are achieved while remaining details are pursued to fulfill objectives and targets.	
	C. DOCUMENTATION The Buyer maintains records that show adequate details of all transactions.	
	D. FOLLOW-UP The Buyer will continue to initiate action toward results in order to fulfill his commodity responsibilities.	
	I. Sub-Total Points	
II. **INTERPERSONAL** **TRAITS** Those traits which identify the Buyers' personal attributes and qualities.	A. HUMAN RELATIONS The Buyer is sensitive to the needs and wants of others and takes these into consideration in his actions.	
	B. VENDOR RELATIONS The Buyer develops a relationship with vendors that fosters an atmosphere of trust and understanding.	
	C. COMPETITIVE AGGRESSIVENESS The Buyer pursues his task by being aggressive and persuasive in his dealings with others.	
	D. COMMUNICATION SKILLS The Buyer is able to present a message, verbal or written, in a manner that is clearly understood by his recipient.	
	II. Sub-Total Points	
III. **JOB** **COMMITMENT AND** **EFFORT** Those skills which express the Buyers' desire and willingness to become involved in work goals.	A. PERSONAL/SELF DEVELOPMENT The Buyer keeps abreast of the latest purchasing and business concepts to aid him in the performance of his job.	
	B. FLEXIBILITY The Buyer adjusts to frequent changes in job demands without disrupting business routines or the attainment of stated goals.	
	C. INDEPENDENCE The Buyer performs his work independently and does not require the constant guidance of a supervisor.	
	D. INITIATIVE The Buyer is a self-starter and often gives suggestions for improvements.	
	III. Sub-Total Points	

Figure 23-2. Form used in one phase of a corporate program of rating purchasing performance. Courtesy of NCR Corporation.

CATEGORY	PERFORMANCE ELEMENT BEING MEASURED	POINTS
IV. TECHNICAL SKILLS	A. NEGOTIATION ABILITY The Buyer applies good negotiation principles to purchasing transactions.	
Those skills that represent specific purchasing techniques which are developed through job experience and training programs.	B. COMMODITY/PRODUCT KNOWLEDGE The Buyer seeks knowledge about the use and function of the commodities he buys and their application to NCR products.	
	C. SUPPLIER PERFORMANCE The Buyer monitors supplier performance and maintains contact with key personnel to ensure delivery, quality and price meet the needs of NCR.	
	D. CREATIVITY The Buyer is alert to various ideas and recommendations. Through value analysis, he translates these to tangible benefits-	
	IV. Sub-Total Points	

S U M M A R Y

RATING DESCRIPTION	TOTAL POINTS	CODE
Significantly exceeded position requirements consistently	97/112 = Very High 81/96 = High	3
Met position requirements and exceeded at times	65/80 = High Average 49/64 = Average	2
Met basic position requirements	33/48 = Low Average 17/32 = Low	1
Not Acceptable	0/16 = Not Acceptable	0

CATEGORY	POINTS
I. ADMINISTRATIVE SKILLS	
II. INTERPERSONAL TRAITS	
III. JOB COMMITMENT & EFFORT	
IV. TECHNICAL SKILLS	
TOTAL PERFORMANCE RATING POINTS	
PERFORMANCE CODE	

Comments: _____

_____

_____

_____

_____

_____

_____

_____

_____

REVIEWED BY	DATE	APPROVED BY	DATE

409

A few narrowly defined measures are more effective than several loosely defined and partially understood ones.

Every measure must be based on a valid and comprehensive data base used by all individuals in the purchasing organization.

There is no one best way of measuring purchasing performance; each organization must tailor its own.

Standards for purchasing performance cannot be fixed but must be adapted to changing conditions.

One overall measure of purchasing performance is not feasible.

The performance measures and data base must be reviewed periodically.

The cost of purchasing performance measurement must be weighed against the benefits.

Purchasing performance measurement is not a substitute for good management.

Communication is of paramount importance in creating an effective measurement system; expected performance levels and the use of measures must be clearly understood by all.

The measures should be used to motivate and direct behavior, not to punish individuals.

SOME PERFORMANCE OBJECTIVES

After studying this chapter you should be able to

1. Identify the inconsistencies in the argument that purchasing performance can be judged by purely quantitative standards, for example, by departmental operating costs.
2. Discuss the difference between measuring purchasing efficiency and purchasing proficiency, and give an opinion on how the results of each measurement should be interpreted.
3. Name five other factors that can be considered in evaluating purchasing performance.
4. Describe the concept of standard costs and its use in determining the effectiveness of the purchasing department.
5. Make your personal evaluation of the system for gauging the performance of a purchasing department described on page 406.
6. List the key measures in evaluating purchasing performance as determined by the study funded by the National Science Foundation.

Appendix
CASE
STUDIES

Chapter 1

Bergman's Sons Furniture Company

Harold Bergman was the owner of a relatively small but thriving furniture manufacturing business. The basic products were various types of wooden garden furniture. To supplement this business, which was somewhat seasonal, Bergman took contracts or subcontracts for such items as home workbenches and hotel and institutional furniture. As a matter of policy (Mr. Bergman's personal decision), the market was limited to a rather small geographical area. He felt that this enhanced the company's local business relationships and to some extent relieved him from the pressures of strong outside competition.

The company's profit position was good. The principal raw material was lumber, for which several reliable supply sources had been developed over the years. This item represented about 40 percent of product cost. Other materials and supplies represented an additional 15 percent. Because sales and administrative costs were low, Bergman was able to add a comfortable 40 percent markup on the standard lines. One of his business axioms was that, so long as lumber was bought right, the company had no cause for worry. On contract business, generally more competitive, the margin was not so great, but it was still satisfactory because he was highly selective in the type of contracts he accepted.

411

Eventually, Mr. Bergman decided to retire and turn the business over to his two sons, then in their thirties. Both had worked for him for a number of years.

When George and Edward Bergman assumed full control over the business from their father, they found it in excellent shape. The cash balance was large and materials inventories high in asset value. Plant and office were staffed with experienced older employees. The vogue for "outdoor living" continued to bring more orders for garden furniture. Also, the growing popularity of "do-it-yourself" projects was creating a steady and promising market for home workbenches. The brothers decided to add these items to the regular line, and their hardware and department store customers showed good interest in the new numbers. This gave better diversification and balance to the company's operations. The younger Bergmans gradually went a little farther afield to extend their market. At the same time, they continued the policy of seeking some contract work to keep manufacturing volume at a high level.

As the business grew, they leaned heavily on Fred Wilt, who had been general manager under their father. They left all procurement and production responsibilities to Wilt, while George took charge of sales and Edward concentrated on finance and personnel. Wilt was a competent, conservative executive, as the older Mr. Bergman had been, and was completely loyal. He was considered an expert in all types of lumber and woodworking processes. He took pride in quality of product and in high standards of service. To maintain these principles, he believed in dealing only with established suppliers whom he considered loyal, and in having "plenty of materials" on hand at all times. And he tolerated no slipshod methods of workmanship in the plant.

In his search for contract business, George Bergman took a small order to do some laminating of plywood and plastic panels for a specialty packaging company. The project was experimental for both companies, but it turned out very satisfactorily. Within a year additional orders came in steadily, and this phase of the business boomed until it accounted for nearly 25 percent of all Bergman sales. This meant a rapid increase in plant personnel, a buildup in inventories, and an expansion in purchasing, both in dollar volume and in the number and diversity of items purchased. Plastics, adhesives, and metal trim were a few of the new items added to the buying list.

With expanding business, the Bergmans realized that a larger executive staff was needed. Among other things, they saw the need for a purchasing manager to relieve Wilt of the growing burden of procurement details. Wilt felt that this could be accomplished more simply by adding one or two persons to his own staff. The brothers, however, aware that manufacturing problems, too, were becoming more complex and demanding, and looking ahead to further growth, decided to follow out their plan for a separate purchasing department. Temporarily, at least, the new purchasing manager would double as office manager, a responsibility heretofore carried by Edward Bergman. For this position, they settled on Frank Parvis—like themselves, in his thirties. Parvis was currently employed as purchasing manager for a book publishing concern. He knew the Bergmans only slightly, but he came to their company highly recommended by close mutual friends.

In a general way, the Bergmans looked upon Parvis as one of a small group of "comers" who could help build the company into a substantial enterprise. He was given a good salary and assurances that he would receive generous bonuses based on annual profits. He was told that he had a free rein in organizing and running a complete purchasing department—except that "for the time being" Fred Wilt would continue to purchase the major raw material, lumber.

Parvis set up the new department and procedures on the basis of his experience in his previous purchasing position. He took on two young men from within the company as buyers. One had been a clerk under Mr. Wilt and had handled the routine buying of shop supplies. The other had served in various positions in the plant, with a consistent record of promotions in recognition of his capacity to accept additional responsibility. Both men had been with the company for upwards of five years. Both had two years of college education, and the first one was attending evening classes to complete his work for a degree in business administration.

Except for the normal problems encountered in building any organization from scratch, Parvis had no great difficulties. Mr. Wilt seemed quite cooperative, even to the point of expressing relief that the detail of buying had been lifted from his shoulders and gratification that two of "his boys" were to be in the buying positions. At the same time, he made it clear that he considered lumber buying to be his prerogative and had no intention of surrendering it, for two reasons: his expert knowledge of the material and his continuing responsibility for quality of product. Although, nominally, he turned over the rest of the buying to Parvis, he continued to see most of the regular suppliers who called at the plant, and occasionally he would call Parvis or send him a memo requesting favorable treatment for a certain supplier. Early in his experience at Bergman's, Parvis learned the expediency of tending toward liberal margins of safety in ordering and inventory, merely to forestall Wilt's outspoken anxiety over possible shortages of "minor" nonlumber materials, and he took pains to see that no actual shortages developed. The implied criticism, he felt, was of policy rather than of fact.

The situation was not intolerable for Parvis, but he did feel frustrated by having to share a divided buying responsibility. He felt that neither his personal nor his departmental performance could be fairly evaluated on the basis of a partial purchasing program, especially because the material excluded from his control was, in terms of dollar expenditure, the largest single factor of total purchases. Personally, he got along well enough with Wilt and had no desire to raise the issue of organization on personal or theoretical grounds. Objectively, he considered Wilt's position to be a roadblock to good, professional purchasing. He realized, too, that he had his own position to establish and prove before he could effectively challenge management's organization plan. The Bergman brothers, with complete confidence in Wilt, were not aware of any shortcoming or conflict. Meanwhile, Parvis was so occupied with other details, both of purchasing and of office management, that he tried to live with the situation until he could have his own organization fully developed and could talk with the Bergmans about centralizing all purchasing in his department.

In preparation for such a proposal, Parvis made an intensive study of the entire materials and procurement situation, documented so far as possible by actual purchase records and specifically related to the criteria of product cost and overall company interest. Among the points he noted were the following:

1. With extended markets and the introduction of new products, the company is meeting with harder competition, so that the markup and profit margin are narrowed. To date, increased volume has maintained total profits and has enabled Wilt to effect some manufacturing economies. The materials factor of product cost has not changed significantly. The profit squeeze is intensifying, and the point of breakeven volume is steadily rising.

2. With diversification of product beyond the simple garden furniture line, lumber is no longer the unique and dominant item of purchased material cost in the same degree that it had previously been. The company is buying more lumber than before, but, instead of the previous 40:15 ratio, it is now just about equal in dollar expenditure to the sum of other materials.

3. In view of both the above-mentioned factors, the theory that "right buying" of lumber is the answer to all materials cost problems must be discarded. Query: What is "right buying" of lumber?

4. Prices paid for lumber have risen sharply over the past year, corresponding to the general advance in the lumber market. On new materials purchased since product diversification, there is no basis for comparison, but contracts now in force assure that the present level will hold for another six months. On materials previously used, and

now bought by the purchasing department, a modest saving of 3 percent overall can be shown, despite rising markets. There are a variety of reasons in respect to individual items; in general, the saving can be attributed to the closer attention given to these so-called "minor" items. Query: Is it reasonable to assume that similar savings could be made on lumber through specialized purchasing attention?

5. On nonlumber items, economical order quantities, scientifically calculated, average 45-days' supply; inventory quantities average three-weeks' supply. On lumber, order quantities are usually dictated by the carload unit, and inventories are maintained at 60-days' supply. This adds a substantial carrying cost at time of use. Query: Could scientific methods of determining order quantities, closer scheduling of deliveries, and inventory control be applied to reduce carrying cost by half? Could broadening the base of supply provide the assurance of ample material now provided by reserve stocks?

6. Concede Wilt's expert knowledge of lumber and Parvis's lack of experience with this material. Buyer No. 2, with excellent experience in working with lumber in varied shop operations, is (or can become) well qualified for lumber procurement. Standards set by Wilt or with his approval, and observed in purchasing, can give the needed assurances of quality.

7. The company now has no consistent purchasing policy. It has two policies, independently developed and administered. There should be a single policy, with the authority of executive approval.

Before Parvis had the opportunity of presenting this brief and argument to his management, the Bergmans announced plans to acquire a small electronics company in a nearby city. This concern produced control mechanisms in small lots. Its annual sales volume was about half as great as the Bergmans'. The company was highly engineering oriented. It had two buyers, both graduate engineers, working under a vice president responsible for product development as well as for procurement.

They called in Parvis, explained the new venture, and asked him to submit a report covering three points:

1. *What kind of purchasing organization do you recommend for the company, including the furniture, laminating, and electronics divisions? How should present personnel be assigned? Will more people be needed?*

2. *Write a statement of purchasing policy applicable to the entire organization.*

3. *How would you evaluate purchasing performance for all divisions, and how can we, as owners and managers, be kept informed?*

Chapter 2

Ayers Company

The Ayers Company fabricates metal parts and uses considerable quantities of abrasive compounds in its finishing operations. For a number of years, brand A compound had been purchased and used exclusively for one stage of the process, because that was the product the finishing department foreman had insisted on having. Price of the product was $1.92 a pound, but there were several competitive brands available in a price range from $1.60 a pound and up, which the purchasing manager considered suitable for the operation. The specification calling for brand A had the usual modifying phrase, "or equal," but the words were practically meaningless as the foreman declared that the other brands were not equal. The production manager supported the foreman on the grounds that he knew the operation and was responsible for results in his department: brand A was known to be dependable, and a substitute material might slow operations or affect the quality of the finished product, offsetting the small saving on price. The purchasing manager argued that 16 percent was not a small saving. The production manager was not impressed. "On 6,000 pounds it comes out less than $2,000 at best—and I think that's a small price to pay for assurance of quality—and a satisfied foreman." The purchasing manager also concluded that the amount did not warrant making an issue of the matter, so he let it drop.

Some months later the production manager moved on to another company and was replaced by a man accustomed to conferring with the purchasing department on material specifications and buying practices. The purchasing manager eventually brought the matter of abrasive compounds to his attention and he responded by suggesting tests of the lower-cost compounds.

Several brands were tested on the basis of one shift's operations. "The foreman was right," the new production manager said. "Nothing you've shown us does the job as well as brand A. Here are the brands that come closest. Brand B turns out almost as many pieces per pound, but it slows down the process so that we get fewer pieces per machine-hour. Brand C keeps the machines up to speed, but they eat up about 10 percent more compound. However, you have a point, too. We can save some money. Here's what the cost comparisons show, figuring machine time at $14.00 an hour":

Brand A—$1.92 lb, 120 pieces produced

8 hr machine time	$112.00	per piece	.933
10 lb compound	19.20	per piece	.160

Cost of operation per piece			1.093

Brand B—$1.80 lb, 115 pieces produced			
8 hr machine time	$112.00	per piece	.974
10 lb compound	18.00	per piece	.156
Cost of operation per piece			1.130

Brand C—$1.60 lb, 120 pieces produced			
8 hr machine time	$112.00	per piece	.933
10 lb compound	17.60	per piece	.147
Cost of operation per piece			1.080

"Machine time is the big factor," he continued. "Frankly, even if brand B had shown a cost saving, I'd have turned it down because we need full output to keep our production lines in balance. I'd be interested in anything that would speed production—even at a higher cost. Brand C does the job. The real savings comes out to about half of what you estimated, but on about 60,000 pieces a year I'm not knocking them. Let's try C."

After using brand C for a few weeks, the foreman complained that he was able to turn out only 110 pieces each shift and he was using up to 15 lb of compound to do it. His costs were up nearly 15 percent. Switching back to brand A didn't help much. Less compound was used—about 12.5 lb per shift—and production remained at the lower rate.

Analysis of the problem revealed that, although the same type of steel was being used for the part, one of the changes instituted by the new production manager was in the heat treating prior to finishing, which resulted in greater surface hardness, thereby slowing down the finishing process.

The purchasing manager resumed his search for a suitable compound, but concentrated on those that offered faster cutting properties. He bought a trial lot of a premium-priced compound—brand D at $2.21 a pound. This made it possible to bring production up to the required 120 pieces per shift, using 15 lb of brand D. Unit finishing cost was still up about 11 percent compared with the original operation. But, on the hard-surfaced steel, unit cost was less than with either of the other compounds, despite the face that brand D was substantially more expensive than either. The important thing was that the production rate had been restored.

The purchasing manager was still not convinced that the best solution had been found. As he now saw the problem, there were still three alternatives that would satisfy the requirement:

1. Use brand D on the surface hardened steel, 120 pieces per shift. Estimated unit finishing cost: $1.21.
2. Finish the parts before hardening, using brand C as before, and heat treat after the finishing operation. Estimated unit finishing cost: $1.08.
3. Assuming that brand D, used on the parts before hardening, could step up output to 125 or more pieces per shift, use brand D and heat treat after the finishing operation. Estimated unit finishing cost: $1.16. This cost is lower than one and higher than the other of the above, but it does assure a higher production rate, which is one of the production manager's objectives.

Should the production department in this case have been required to justify its reason for certain product preferences? Which department should have the final decision on what should be purchased? Is purchasing justified in questioning, by implication, manufacturing policy in presenting alternative solutions (2) and (3)? How can purchasing judge the factor of production rates when no monetary valuation has been put on them?

Chapter 3

Blesting Company

As part of a planned program of acquisition and diversification, Futura, Inc., a Chicago-based publishing company, bought out the Blesting Company, manufacturers of heavy duty lift tables used primarily at loading and receiving docks and in metalworking operations. Blesting, located near San Diego, had annual sales of about $80 million. Previous Futura acquisitions included a bookbinding company in New York City, and a small chain of hardware stores on the west coast.

Viola Dopple, Futura's director of purchasing, had visited Blesting shortly after the company was acquired. She met with Hayward Blesting III, vice-president of operations, and Sheila Yardavis, a longtime employee was both secretary of the company, and its manager of purchasing and services. They explained the division of purchasing responsibility in the company: Mr. Blesting was responsible for negotiating most of the major purchases, such as machinery, steel plate, castings, fittings and hose, and motors; Ms. Yardavis, with a clerical assistant, handled the paperwork on those purchases and also bought all other items, primarily maintenance, repair and operating (MRO) supplies.

Annual expenditures for purchases averaged about $35 million and between 300 and 400 purchase orders were issued each month. They had no specific figures on the cost of operating the purchasing function. Both were of the opinion that some additional help was needed in purchasing, but said they were so busy with their assorted duties that they "just hadn't had time to get around to doing anything about it."

Ms. Dopple, shorthanded and pressed for time herself, suggested no great changes in the Blesting purchasing system, but did ask that one copy of each purchase order issued be sent to her office Mr. Blesting and Ms. Yardavis agreed to that arrangement. They told Ms. Dopple they would cooperate in any way and looked forward to working with her to improve their own purchasing.

Blesting's purchasing system was conventional: a six-part purchase order was typed for every requisition received in purchasing: the original and an acknowledgment copy went to the vendor; one copy went to the receiving department; another went to the requisitioner; and two remained in the purchasing department, to be filed alphabetically by vendor and by item. (Mrs. Yardavis saw no problem in having one of purchasing's two copies go to Futura's purchasing department as requested by Ms. Dopple).

When orders were delivered, the Blesting receiving and stores clerk, prepared a three-part receiving notice—one copy for purchasing, one for accounting, and one to remain in receiving. All vendor invoices came to purchasing for checking, and were then sent to accounting for payment.

Several months after Ms. Dopple's visit to Blesting, a Futura management trainee with a B.S. in business administration, was assigned to her department for a four-month period. The trainee, Angelo Tobias, had spent time in the marketing and financial departments. During his original interview, he had expressed interest in a career in finance or purchasing and materials management.

In his first two months in purchasing, Mr. Tobias showed considerable aptitude and the director decided to send him on temporary assignment to the Blesting plant. "I have talked to Hay Blesting and Sheila Yardavis about you," she told him. "We have agreed that you should get some actual buying experience there, but we also want you to study their procedures and possible personnel requirements, and get your opinion about what, if anything, might be done to improve their efficiency. They are cooperative people, both executives, and open-minded to new ideas. When you're ready with your recommendations, report to me first then we'll sit down with the Blesting people to discuss them."

Shortly after his arrival at Blesting, Mr. Tobias undertook a thorough study of the company's complete purchasing cycle. He began with an analysis of all purchase orders for the previous year. Concurrently he reviewed order-related activities with requisitioners, receiving personnel, accounting personnel, and several suppliers of MRO and office equipment items. On occasion he sat in on sales calls with Ms. Yardavis, and was an observer during two major negotiation sessions conducted by Mr. Blesting.

In his procedure analysis he found that almost three quarters of all purchase orders had a value of less than $500, and of those just over half were for less than $200. He concluded that on the average Ms. Yardavis and her clerk spent as much or more time placing and handling the less-then-$500 orders as they did on larger orders. The amount of paperwork required in issuing, receiving and paying for the smaller orders was the same as for the larger ones.

Mr. Tobias concluded the major problem facing the Blesting purchasing department at the time was the disproportionate burden of the relatively small and less important orders that Mrs. Yardavis, with limited help, had to handle, as well as the cost of processing the paperwork on those orders at every stage of the purchasing cycle. Although he had three weeks to go in his assignment, he felt it was time to make his recommendations to Ms. Dopple.

Assume you are Mr. Tobias. What recommendations would you make in regard to purchasing procedures and personnel requirements? Be specific about changes or innovations you feel are necessary, and explain in detail how they should be implemented and what results can be expected from them.

Chapter 4

Bardolph & Whitbread

Bardolph & Whitbread, Inc. is a manufacturer of metal-cutting saws and related equipment. About 25 percent of the company's output is in the form of standard machines used in metal service centers and in metalworking plants. The balance is made up of custom-made units for both types of businesses. Although there is a 3:1 ratio of special to standard machines in the manufacturing mix, approximately 60 percent of the parts used in both types are interchangeable. The company does some fabricating of parts for its machines, but it purchases the great majority of materials and components. Purchased items, in fact, account for about 75 percent of the cost of producing each machine.

B&W had recognized the value of the computer several years ago but had approached the automation of administrative operations on a step-by-step basis, beginning with accounting operations such as payrolls, billing, and so forth. When Burton Hill came to the company as purchasing manager, no direct procurement operations had been computerized. However, inventory control, which is a responsibility of the production control department, had been programmed into the computer.

Sales forecasts at B&W are issued quarterly for the following five quarters, with the approval of top management. Machines scheduled for production are "exploded" into units by analysts, who forward the information to the computer for checking against the stock status file or inventory record. This computer file shows the exact status of all parts, both those manufactured by B&W and those purchased on the otuside, as well as the number of pieces in finished stores, in process or on order from suppliers.

The file is updated daily by various transactions, including shipment of repair parts, withdrawals for use in manufacturing, and receipts from suppliers. Detailed computer printouts on stock status are the basis for requisitions to the purchasing department for those items that are to be bought rather than manufactured in-house.

Encouraged by the success that the company had with the gradual approach to computerization, B&W management decided to study the feasibility of bringing every major function of the company, including purchasing, into the program. The company president asked representatives of the systems and accounting departments—who had had the most experience with the computer—to serve as a committee to handle the study project and to make recommendations. The two committee members were as enthusiastic as they were knowledgeable about computers. They called in purchasing and manufacturing representatives as part of a regular consultation program to determine how the capabilities of the computer could serve the interests of both departments and management.

Mr. Hill, believing that the introduction of purchasing operations into the computer was of critical importance, designated himself as the purchasing representative for these meetings.

Assuming that you are Mr. Hill, outline your ideas on computerizing various phases of purchasing. Indicate what types of information you want from the computer, why it is of importance to you as a department manager, and what its contribution to overall company objectives would be.

Chapter 5

Nearfrank Roller Company

Nearfrank Roller Company manufactures a wide variety of steel rolls used on industrial machinery, ranging from small printing presses to large food-processing equipment. Its purchasing department buys a relatively small number of items—quality steels, several types of components, and maintenance supplies—but the critical nature of the materials requires a high degree of skill in the buying staff.

Harry Fenlon, the director of purchases, had reorganized his department two or three times in the fifteen years that he had held the position. In the last reorganization, eight years ago, he had settled on an arrangement that paired a buyer and a clerk-typist in a "buying team." The clerk-typist's responsibilities under this arrangement were quite broad. In addition to typing orders, he acted as the buyer's secretary. He handled all routine follow-up of orders, answered requests for delivery information from operating departments, and occasionally handled the purchase of nontechnical, noncritical items such as office supplies, janitorial equipment, and so forth. Several of the more competent clerk-typists were recognized unofficially as "assistant buyers" and were considered capable of handling many of the buyer's responsibilities in his absence. There were six buyer-clerk-typist teams in the department, one receptionist-file clerk, an accounts payable clerk, and a part-time clerk who helped check invoices and handle overload work.

Mr. Fenlon was quite satisfied with the arrangement and had no reason to believe that his department's performance was considered anything but good by the company's management. When the president called in a management consulting firm to study the operations of major departments of the company, he cooperated wholeheartedly in the project. He instructed his departmental personnel to provide the consultants with information on their jobs, work habits, allocation of time, and so forth. He discussed the activity of the department and its individual members with the consultants.

To Mr. Fenlon's surprise, the management consulting firm's final report included a strong criticism of the purchasing department organization and recommended a drastic change. Excerpts from the section dealing with the purchasing department follow:

> The team basis for buying is not acceptable, as within my knowledge no other company of comparable size is using it . . . In the team arrangement, the clerk-typist acts as a crutch for the buyer, thus weakening him to a point where he delivers less in the way of productive effort rather than more.

Many purchasing departments are handling your ratio of orders per buyer without the use of a buying team.

Under the team setup, each clerical member of a team reports to the director of purchases, but organizationally they are well removed from his or her direct supervision. As a consequence, each member sets his or her own pace.

The entire clerical group is a functional one, as distinct from the line group of buyers. Their function is to handle all paperwork and recordkeeping. This function should be handled separately from the line group in a centralized arrangement.

Labor is a commodity. You are paying too high a price for it in the purchasing department. There is not enough awareness of the productive capacity that a dollar will buy.

We recommend that the department be reorganized, with all clerical help grouped together under a clerical supervisor who should be appointed immediately. At least two and possibly three members of the clerical force could then be let go or moved to other departments, because work loads would be more evenly distributed and more efficiently handled.

The president called Mr. Fenlon in and handed him a copy of the section of the management consulting firm's report that dealt with the purchasing department. "They're pretty outspoken in their comments, Harry," he said "and I want you to be the same in your answer—which I'd like to have right away."

Mr. Fenlon dictated a point-by-point reply to the criticisms listed. Then he wrote the following general memorandum and sent both documents to the president:

The consultants support the concept of a strictly functional approach. I still support a combination functional line approach.

Every company designs it own purchasing facility to fit its own needs, with the objective of developing a strong, well-trained profit-making group. Therefore, broad statements about what should be done about reduction of clerical costs or changes in organization must be considered along with their effect on our ability to carry out major objectives.

The consultants are well qualified to determine practical clerical work loads. But they seem unwilling to give our buyers the assistance that they need to perform their functions—that is, to give good service to the shop, save the company's money, and continually increase their knowledge of the products that they buy. Buyers have to have time to review requirements, get the most out of sales interviews, and make visits to suppliers' plants. They have to be free to attend conferences away from their desks and to take on another buyer's responsibilities in case of sickness or absence for some other reason. And above all they must have plenty of time for the preparation and conduct of negotiations.

We must not reduce our clerical personnel until we are able to reduce the clerical work accordingly. We are adopting some changes, considering others, and expect to effect other improvements as we go along. Some of these will require the cooperation of other departments.

Our present organization and clerical procedure were adopted owing to the shortcomings of the functional-type operation previously followed. I believe that we have made good progress and would resist any backward steps in this respect. We have no intention of making any changes that would hinder the buyer or his or her ability to perform his or her proper function.

Write a point-by-point answer to the management consultants' criticisms and recommendations based on your understanding of the nature and scope of the purchasing function. List specific changes and improvements that could be carried out to improve the efficiency of the purchasing department. Describe and explain the need for each.

Chapter 6

Lund Stagelite Corp.

Bart Dawson was the intelligent, ambitious, and highly articulate purchasing manager for Lund Stagelite Corp., manufacturer of theatrical lighting equipment for commercial and institutional use. Sales of the company's products, about two thirds of which were made to order, and about one third produced for stock, averaged $18 million annually.

Approximately 55 percent of that figure was spent every year on purchased material and supplies.

Before coming into purchasing ten years ago, Mr. Dawson had spent close to eight years in various positions in the manufacturing and production control departments of the company. He was well known in the company, respected for the competence he displayed in every job he had held, but was considered by many to be motivated solely by a desire for personal advancement. In the course of his career, he developed an immunity to what others thought of him and concentrated on certain goals that he believed were in his own and his company's interest.

One of these goals was the establishment of a materials management system for the Stagelite Company. Mr. Dawson had developed a strong and very efficient purchasing department in the company. But his own experience and his regular study of other industrial purchasing departments had convinced him that a broader type of organization was needed to handle the materials cycle in his company. He made no secret of his view that there should be a materials department with jurisdiction over all activities involved with the acquisition, handling, and storage of raw materials. The department would, of course, be headed by a materials manager.

"Put your proposals down on paper," his executive vice president said one day following a conversation on the subject. "I'm interested, but I'd like something a little more concrete on which to base my judgment."

Mr. Dawson immediately prepared a memorandum to the executive vice president. Following a general description of the materials management concept, he outlined the objectives of such a program, using a list adapted from a definitive article on materials management he had read in a trade magazine. The list of objectives was as follows:

1. To provide materials at the lowest possible overall cost.
2. To keep investment in raw material inventories at the lowest level consistent with sales and production objectives.
3. To maintain lowest storage and carrying costs and develop optimum turnover rates.
4. To improve interdepartmental communication and thereby reduce administrative costs.
5. To develop and maintain favorable relations with suppliers.
6. To maintain continuity of supply.
7. To keep down acquisition and possession costs and minimize obsolescence and deterioration of inventories.
8. To improve techniques of purchasing and inventory control.

Specifically, he suggested that these objectives could be achieved by the Stagelite Company if the purchasing, inventory and material control, and traffic functions were combined into one department. The three groups would balance one another, he said: purchasing would buy materials against a planned program; inventory control and material control would maintain stocks at desired inventory levels (against known production requirements) and establish proper turnover rates; traffic would certify receipt of materials and be responsible for storing and disbursing them to the production department. Buyers and material control planners would act as teams in determining timing and amount of raw material purchases.

Mr. Dawson listed these advantages as accruing to the company under a materials management organization:

Responsibility for materials would be centralized and clearly defined.

Fewer people would be needed than in individual departments. Duplication of files would be eliminated; fewer copies of purchase orders and receiving reports would be needed.

Buyers could schedule deliveries from vendors on a much more rational basis when they had up-to-date knowledge of present inventory levels and anticipated production requirements. The time lag involved in getting this information would be eliminated. Therefore "peak-and-valley" ordering, frequent rescheduling of open orders, and short-lead-time ordering would be reduced and relations with vendors greatly improved. Close cooperation with vendors to match production requirements with their capabilities would help prevent emergencies.

There would be less repackaging and material handling, because packaging would be specified to meet production requirements.

More opportunities for advancement would be offered to personnel in all affected departments. The experience that inventory and material control personnel would receive would make them natural candidates for promotion to buying positions.

The executive vice president passed a copy of the purchasing manager's memorandum to Sid Scofield, production manager of the company and asked for his comments. Part of Mr. Scofield's reply was as follows:

The materials management organization suggested is more to the advantage of the purchasing department than to that of the Stagelite Company. It would eliminate the material control function and build up the purchasing function, but without the benefits claimed. Material planners would be dominated by higher-paid buyers, who would buy when and as much as they pleased without reference to others.

Responsibility is clearly defined now. Production control has responsibility for inventories. Purchasing has responsibility for getting material in on time. Material control has responsibility for maintaining stocks of raw materials at optimum levels. That's the way it should be.

Inventory turnover would not be any better than it is now. Turnover depends on amounts purchased and amounts used. Sales, then schedules, determine usage, and variations in these two elements are great. A combined buyer–specifier team would not improve the situation.

The alleged improvement in vendor relations is more of a device to improve purchasing's position. A buyer's success is measured by the relations that he or she builds up with the vendors and the job that his or her vendor does. The more the buyer can claim "better vendor relations," the more the buyer inflates his or her own importance.

Promotion opportunities exist for everyone in the Stagelite Company through our regular merit system. The material planner would be dependent on the buyer for advancement—again strengthening the purchasing department at others' expense.

The executive vice president studied the two memorandums and a week later prepared his own answer to Mr. Dawson and Mr. Scofield.

Write a memorandum analyzing Mr. Dawson's and Mr. Scofield's positions. Make and explain in detail your decision as to whether Lund Stagelite Company will consider establishing a materials management organization.

Chapter 7

Jackson Corporation

The Jackson Corporation, producers of electronic communications equipment, was founded primarily to supply the U.S. Air Force with certain highly specialized items. The company has, however, steadily sought to develop some less complex commercial business as a hedge against technological change or a sharp cutback in defense spending.

Jackson Corporation's purchasing department had grown along with the company, adapting itself to expansion and changing conditions. At the beginning, purchasing decisions were made by the engineer-owners, and the adminsitrative operations of ordering were carried out by clerks. Gradually, a full-scale purchasing organization developed to handle the rapidly increasing material requirements resulting from military orders during the defense buildup of the early 1960s. Production was limited to a few important items, and the four buyers brought into the purchasing department soon became familiar with the relatively complex parts and materials that they were buying. With only slight assistance from the engineering department, they were able to handle all procurement efficiently.

The company's business picked up during the space exploration program. Purchasing Manager Archer Dix continued to expand his department, to the point at which he had eight buyers working for him. Four of the buyers were college graduates, of whom three had business administration degrees. One had an undergraduate engineering degree and a master's degree in business administration. Four of the buyers had been with the company from the start and had been brought into purchasing from the manufacturing and stores departments. Two trainees, both with B.S. degrees in electrical engineering, joined the department a couple of years later and were used as expediters and general backup for the buyers.

Space-age production and procurement problems were more complex than those associated with production of relatively standardized military equipment, however, and the Jackson Corporation purchasing department felt the difference. Most of the products ordered for use in spacecraft were custom built for a particular mission, and output was in terms of one to five units, in contrast to the hundreds and thousands turned out during the war. Technological change was much more rapid. Components and materials satisfactory for one satellite were obsolete a few months later. Designers increasingly called for patented or proprietary items or highly specialized products available from single sources.

Under these complex, swiftly changing conditions, the buyers were not so quick to learn as previously, and their dependence on the components engineering department was much greater. The components engineers had responsibility for analyzing customer requirements, acting as liaison between customers and the design engineering department, and testing. They set the specifications for all purchased products that went into Jackson products. Increasingly, vendors with new ideas or suggestions for changing specifications would find themselves referred to the components engineering department after pleasant but unproductive visits with purchasing department personnel.

When the contradictions in the organization became apparent, General Manager Walter Walsh asked his operations manager to make a careful analysis of the situation. It showed that the components engineers were making more and more actual buying decisions although they had no clearly defined authority to purchase. They were also providing special services—testing, collecting technical data, and making recommendations on design—yet they had no direct responsibility for cost reduction. Further, they were spending as much time with vendors as the buyers were, with the result that sales personnel were obligingly making two calls—one to the buyer and one to the engineer—and wasting everyone's time.

Mr. Walsh decided that a revamping of the whole procurement operation was needed. He was able to get Sam Harmin, manager of materials of a recently acquired Jackson Corporation subsidiary, temporarily attached to his staff to undertake the job. Mr. Harmin was a brilliant young executive with broad experience in manufacturing and cost accounting and a master's degree in business administration. He was considered one of the bright lights of the Jackson organization.

After six weeks' study, Mr. Harmin came up with the following recommendations: The entire components engineering group should be moved into purchasing, because they are in effect already selecting vendors as well as specifying components. They should be called *procurement engineers,* or *materials engineers,* to indicate that they have buying authority as well as responsibility.

One of the present buyers (with the engineering degree) should be retained as a procurement engineer. One buyer should be given a special assignment as a packaging specialist, working with packaging vendors and with components suppliers on packaging of Jackson purchases. Two buyers should be assigned to buying other nontechnical, nonproduction items.

The four younger buyers should be grouped into an inventory control–buying group with responsibility for determining inventory levels and order quantities, handling all administrative details of ordering and expediting. The trainees should be transferred to another department, preferably manufacturing. The clerical help should be absorbed elswhere in the company.

He made no recommendation concerning Mr. Dix.

Do Mr. Harmin's recommendations offer a solution to the basic procurement problems of Jackson Corporation? Explain your answer. As manufactured products grow more complex, should there be a corresponding increase in the technical knowledge required of buyers? Is there a risk of wasting or misapplying engineering talent by giving technically trained people buying responsibilities? Conversely, would sound purchasing experience not be wasted under the organization suggested by Mr. Harmin? What effect, if any, does the difference between defense-oriented purchasing and standard commercial purchasing have on a situation such as the one that existed at Jackson Corporation? If you were Mr. Dix, what would you reply to Mr. Harmin's recommendation?

Chapter 8

Temple Drug Company

Temple Drug Company is a relatively small manufacturer of a number of proprietary items that enjoy good reputations. Temple Toothpaste, for example, has had good sales for many years at a premium price. Much of its success has been due to a distinctive flavor that appeals to many people and to an agressive merchandising campaign among dentists.

About two years ago, Purchasing Manager Arthur Kaplan had worked out a highly successful program for improving the quality performance of suppliers of packaging materials. The Temple Company buys several hundred different packaging items, including over a dozen varieties of collapsible tubes for its toothpaste and other extrudable products. The production department had complained that it was having trouble with various shipments of tubes: off sizes would cause machinery breakdowns, spillage, and general disruption on the packaging line. There were also other complaints of faulty packaging, but the problem of the tubes was the most troublesome one. Mr. Kaplan decided that a complete review of the company's procurement and use of packaging materials was needed.

He sought the cooperation of the company's package development section, representatives from the production department, and quality control engineers. Together they reviewed the company's packaging requirements, its packaging specifications, and the performance of packaging suppliers. At Mr. Kaplan's suggestion, they invited supplier representatives to a number of their meetings and frankly discussed their problems with them. Several of the committee members just as frankly expressed their suspicions that the suppliers were completely at fault for the quality problems that the company was facing.

Ultimately the facts came to light and, as usual, indicated that blame for poor quality performance could be shared by both sides. In its growth from a two-man manufacturing operation in one corner of a warehouse to a good-sized manufacturing company, the Temple Company had been satisfied with an informal approach to a number of functions. Its packaging department, for example, was a relatively recent development. Over the years, the company had relied on suppliers' suggestions and drawings in buying its packaging materials instead of developing its own.

In the case of collapsible tubes, existing suppliers had changed manufacturing methods, and new suppliers had taken their own approach to design. As a result, little "gimmicks" or variations in size or shape had gradually crept into the designs of the tubes. Instead of buying a standard tube from a number of suppliers, the company was in effect purchasing a large number of specials. Eventually these variations began causing trouble on the highly automated packaging line, which requires a high degree of standardization.

With the help of its suppliers, the company's package development group worked out a program for supplying its own drawings and setting acceptable quality levels for all major items. An interesting phase of the cooperative effort between buyer and suppliers was the program of reciprocal visits to permit representatives from the Temple Company and its packaging suppliers to see each other's manufacturing plants in operation. In one of the first visits arranged under the plan, the production manager of a bottle manufacturer was able to suggest a change that immediately cleared up a problem that had existed on the Temple Company bottling line.

A year later, Mr. Kaplan decided to try a slightly different approach to the problem posed by the rising number of complaints from the processing department about the quality of raw materials. He thought he would do some of the basic research himself in advance, rather than take the valuable time of a whole group of executives. He bagan by calling in vendors, discussing complaints about the quality of their products, and asking their advice. Several of the suppliers indicated that the problems were caused by the casual approach taken to specifications by Temple Company operating and procurement personnel. They pointed out that the company assumed too much knowledge on their part as to what was required, that specifications were often vague or incomplete. As a result, the suppliers would occasionally take advantage (consciously or unconsciously) of the general specifications to ship off-quality material.

On the basis of his own findings, and the comments and recommendations of major raw materials vendors, Mr. Kaplan drew up a memorandum to Fred Schulte, superintendent of the processing plant, and Morton Dunn, the chief chemist. In it he suggested that his chemical buyer, a chemical engineer, be named coordinator of a program to review and organize the company's raw materials specifications. The buyer could work with the laboratory and the using departments, as well as with suppliers in this project. As a start, he suggested taking USP (United States Pharmacopeia) minimum requirements as the basic Temple Company specifications.

"Up to now," he wrote, "different suppliers have practically been using the trial-and-error method to meet our requirements. I think we'll all agree that it's time to change this situation." He asked Mr. Schulte and Mr. Dunn to call him.

Instead of a call, he received an answering memorandum from Mr. Dunn the following day, indicating that a carbon copy had also gone to the president, Mr. Baker. In summary, it read

> Any program of this type will only lead to further deterioration of quality. Vendors will try to get us to lower our standards, so that they can sell us standard or lower-quality items that they are making in volume for other suppliers, at greater profit to themselves. We must force them to meet our specifications, or we run grave danger of losing the small but loyal market for such products as our toothpaste, one of the big features of which is its distinctive flavor.
>
> USP standards are inadequate for us, as they specify chemical purity. We make no compromise with purity, of course, but we do have special processes and special ingredients that differentiate our products from others—in color, taste, and texture. I believe we need more crackdowns and less cooperation with suppliers in this mater.

A short while later Mr. Kaplan had a call from Mr. Baker asking him to come into his office to discuss the situation.

Assess Mr. Kaplan's handling of the raw materials quality problem. Was his failure to get immediate cooperation from Mr. Dunn the result of a fundamental mistake on his part? Or was it merely a matter of timing and handling? Outline an approach that might have produced a more favorable reaction from Mr. Dunn. If Mr. Kaplan's plan is essentially sound, how should he attempt to salvage it? How can he get Mr. Baker's support for it?

Chapter 9

Williston Mills

Williston Mills is a family-owned woodworking and specialty shop. The company normally employs about eighty men. Mr. Williston, the present principal owner and manager, came up through the mill. Long firsthand familiarity with materials and with every phase of plant operations has given him an intuitive knowledge of quantities and costs; he prides himself on his ability to estimate jobs quickly and accurately. The business has grown in volume and profits under his leadership. He is impatient with details and paperwork, and has developed numerous rules of thumb to guide his decisions and action. "Practical results"—his only measure of performance—have been generally satisfactory. In addition to his general management and supervisory activities, he had done most of the purchasing. With increasing shop demands on his time, he decided to break in an assistant to take over the buying.

His choice for this assignment was Mr. Jarvis, a young man presently in charge of the stockroom, who had shown considerable aptitude and interest in the business. Jarvis was not altogether inexperienced in buying, for he had the responsibility of keeping the supply inventory replenished. The system was a very simple one. Arbitrary minimum stock limits had been placed on each item, based on experience as to average usage and on Mr. Williston's judgment. When the supply was down to this minimum quantity, restocking orders were placed in the quantity of the convenient commercial unit—nails by the keg, glue by the barrel, jig-saw blades by the gross, and so forth. Sometimes this entailed reordering every week. On the rare occasions when an item came uncomfortably close to running out of stock, the minimum-quantity limit was revised upward to forestall a recurrence of this condition.

Mr. Williston was a firm believer in "learning by doing." Consequently, Jarvis was introduced to his new duties by being handed a copy of the latest job order. It called for 12,000 instrument carrying cases, 12 x

6 x 6 inches in size, to be made and delivered at the rate of 1,000 per month, with the option of continuing the contract for a longer period. There were eight items of purchased material: plywood for the body of the case, vinyl covering, cloth lining, locks, handles, name plates, brass corner reinforcements, and carrying straps. Nails and adhesive would be furnished from general supply stock. Mr. Williston estimated that the material bill would amount to about $25,000.

"I want you to buy the materials for this job and keep them coming in as we need them," he said. "On the plywood and yard goods, allow 10 percent for waste in cutting; the rest is all counted out for you. We figure on keeping two weeks ahead at all times; that's for insurance. Anything you can buy in carload lots, do so; that's the cheapest way. On everything else, find out how long it takes to get the stuff delivered, and how much we would be using in that length of time. Buying in those quantities will get the shipments coming in just about when the old shipment is used up. We don't want a lot of stock hanging around here waiting until we're ready to use it; that ties up money for no good purpose—we want to keep our money working, too. You can stretch an order a little to bring it to even quantities, but don't do it just to get a quantity discount; that's a sales trick to pad the order."

Jarvis calculated total requirements on the job, checked the files to see where Mr. Williston bought the various items, and phoned the suppliers to get prices and delivery time. He then made a preliminary analysis (Exhibit 1) to set up the buying schedule according to the manager's instruction.

Jarvis respected Mr. Williston's judgment and was generally in agreement with the policy of maintaining a flow of materials to correspond with the rate of use. However, he questioned the efficiency of a buying schedule that involved issuing upwards of 200 purchase orders a year on such relatively simple requirements. He noted that more than half these orders would be for amounts of less than $100, which seemed uneconomical in view of the total amount to be spent. Despite Mr. Williston's warning on quantity discounts, it disturbed him to see that, except for the single instance of plywood, which could be purchased in carload quantity, the discount privilege on five other items was sacrificed even though total requirements were large enough to come into the quantity discount brackets if ordering quantities were increased beyond the stipulated two weeks' supply. He felt that there was a serious discrepancy in this policy, too, for his experience in storeskeeping made him conscious that plywood, the one item to be purchased in quantity, was by far the bulkiest and most difficult to store, and the heaviest to handle in and out of stock.

Jarvis was anxious to make a good record on his first major purchas-

Exhibit 1

	Annual Usage	Price	Annual Cost	Weekly Usage	Delivery Time	Order Quantity
Plywood	1,100 sheets 4' x 8'	15 cents sq ft, less 5% in carloads of 400 sheets	$ 5,026	22 sheets	1 wk	Carload (18 wk supply)
Vinyl	4,000 yd 36″ wide in 50-yd rolls	70 cents yd, less 5% in lots of 25 rolls	2,800	80 yds	3 wk	5 rolls
Lining	3,000 yds 42″ wide in 50-yd rolls	44 cents yd, less 5% in lots of 25 rolls	1,320	60 yds	1 wk	2 rolls
Locks	12,000	60 cents each, less 5% in lots of 1 M; less 10% in lots of 5M	7,200	240	3 wk	750
Name plates	12,000	12 cents each, less 3% in lots of 1 M	1,440	240	2 wk	500
Handles	12,000	14 cents each	1,680	240	2 wk	500
Straps	12,000	22 cents each	2,640	240	1 wk	240
Corner pieces	96,000	3 cents each, less 5% in lots of 10 M	2,880	1,920	2 wk	4,000
			$24,986			

ing assignment. At the same time he realized that his own conclusions, like Mr. Williston's buying policies, were only a matter of judgment and that he had no comparable background of experience to support his judgment. Before making an issue of the matter, or making a recommendation to change the buying schedule, he needed more tangible reasons. He had done some reading on the principles of storeskeeping and had in his possession a copy of the Westinghouse best-order-quantity table (see page 157. Such procedures had not seemed particularly important in a relatively small stores operation like that at Williston Mills, but he decided to make a second calculation on that basis to see whether it would confirm his own thinking.

Using the figure of annual usage on the various items, and assuming the lowest rate of inventory-carrying cost, he checked the indicated best order quantities and made a second tabulation (Exhibit 2).

Exhibit 2

| | Annual Usage | Weeks Supply to Order | | |
		Williston Policy	Best Order Quantity	
Plywood	$5,026	18 (weeks)	5.6 (weeks)	125 sheets
Vinyl	2,800	3	7.2	12 rolls
Lining	1,320	1	11.1	14 rolls
Locks	7,200	3	4.8	1,200*
Name Plates	1,440	2	10.6	2,500*
Handles	1,680	2	9.7	2,400
Straps	2,640	1	8.0	1,920
Corner pieces	2,880	2	7.2	14,000*

* On these three items, best order quantity automatically brings purchases into the quantity discount bracket and reduces annual cost by $360, $43, and $144, respectively.

This entire purchasing program could be carried out with only about one fourth as many purchase orders, receiving operations, and invoice payments as under Mr. Williston's proposal. As to material cost itself, the quantity discount savings of $547 were offset nearly half by failure to take a $254 discount on the plywood by buying in smaller quantities. Before presenting any recommendation to Mr. Williston, he made a further calculation to appraise the real effect of this in relation to the purchase investment in plywood and the potential effect in respect to purchases of vinyl and lining cloth. He tabulated these figures in Exhibit 3.

Exhibit 3

Plywood	
Net savings on 4,000 sheets bought in one lot	$ 96.00
Extra initial investment required	1,224.00
Return on extra investment—7.8% in 18 weeks	

Vinyl	
Net saving on 25 rolls bought in one lot	41.87
Extra initial investment required	410.13
Return on extra investment—10.2% in 15½ weeks	

Lining Cloth	
Net saving on 25 rolls bought in one lot	27.50
Extra initial investment required	214.50
Return on extra investment—12.8% in 21 weeks	

From this standpoint, Mr. Williston's instructions to buy plywood in carload lots seemed well justified, for the best-order-quantity table did not take variable prices into consideration. The advantage was even more pronounced on the other two items. By the same reasoning, therefore, the indicated buying policy was to increase the order quantity on vinyl and lining cloth to 25 rolls of each, at the quantity discount price. Jarvis revised the order quantities noted in Exhibit 2 accordingly.

Mr. Williston examined Jarvis figures with interest. He was skeptical of Exhibit 2 but could take no exception to Exhibit 3 even though it was in conflict with his theory of quantity discounts.

"We can afford to tie up $600 to save $70 twice a year," he said, "but remember, you're asking me to triple the investment, as you call it, on the rest of the materials as well. If we did that all along the line, I might have trouble meeting the payroll every Friday, or in keeping our suppliers happy so that they will continue to send along the smaller quantities we need to keep the plant running."

Mr. Williston's quantity buying policies logically consider many important factors—lead time, rapid turnover, and minimum idle investment. The discrepancy between his conslusions and those of the scientifically derived table suggest that other factors have been overlooked. What are some of the hidden factors? What additional cost information must he have to calculate best order quantity more effectively?

Is the Westinghouse order quantity table necessarily applicable in a business like Williston Mills? Is Jarvis right in accepting this as a standard? To what extent should he use it? Can he verify it for his own purposes?

Jarvis stresses the smaller number of orders to be written. Because these are routine and repetitive, just how important is this factor? Because suppliers' prices take quantity brackets into account, should Jarvis be concerned about quantity per order?

Williston links order quantity policy with problems of working capital. Would he do better to borrow for working capital, if necessary, to take advantage of the purchase savings and maintain his credit rating with suppliers? Is investment in materials actually idle, as he assumes?

Assuming that Jarvis takes over all purchasing for Williston Mills, what steps should he take toward formulating an order quantity policy? How would it affect the present system on supply items? What circumstances and what specific characteristics of materials should he recognize as limiting or modifying application of a general policy?

Chapter 10

Trigson & Howell

Trigson & Howell specializes in the production of processing equipment for the petroleum, food, and pharmaceutical industries. The company does most of its own work in the fabrication of equipment sections requiring piping and metal sheet or plate. Accessories, such as meters, controls, and other components, are purchased from outside suppliers. Units vary greatly in size, and short-run demand from the company's customers is unpredictable. Of twenty orders in the shop at one time, more than half may be for petroleum plants. When these are complete, there may be a period of six months or more in which no orders are received from that industry, and most of the company's production is scheduled for the food industry. As a result, there is unevenness in the use of raw materials, and management is particularly concerned that there be a reasonable supply of all major items on hand to meet the varying demands of customers.

The materials cycle on a given project begins when a bill of materials goes to the stores department, which is under purchasing jurisdiction. The storeskeeper checks off all items that are available in stock and allocates the necessary quantities to the job on his record, subtracting this amount from the balance-of-stock figures. The bill of material then goes to the purchasing manager, who places orders for the unchecked items. He also issues orders for special parts not ordinarily carried in stock. In ordering stock items—materials and components used regularly in most T&H products—the purchasing agent uses a table of economic ordering quantities based on annual usage. Orders are placed in these quantities or multiples thereof, and any excess over the amount of the immediate need is added to the reserve stock to be applied against the next requirement.

By this system, the supply of unallocated stock is constantly, though unevenly, replenished. Also, because the allocation is made on the records but physical stocks are not assigned until they are issued from stores against an order, there is a further cushion for immediate shop demands. The presumption is that materials on order, which cover the total needs for work in process, will be delivered in ample time to replace quantities that have been "borrowed" from preceding deliveries. On materials that are in current demand, there may be from two to half a dozen purchase orders outstanding or in transit. Thus, although orders are placed on what amounts to individual job requisitions, materials are actually received and put into production on a flow basis, with rapid turnover.

The purchasing manager does not see the bill of materials until engineering drawings and calculations have been completed. Manufacturing time ranges from three to four weeks on simpler jobs to four months on more complex units. Ordinarily, this provides enough lead time for procurement of purchased parts such as meters. But there are times when the shop wishes to take advantage of open time and begin work on the assemblies that T&H fabricates itself. When this happens, as it has with increasing frequency, the pressure on purchasing mounts.

The company bid on a number of pieces of equipment for a large food concern in late August and received the orders during the first week of October. Requirements of ½″ stainless steel tubing for the orders totaled 1,200 feet, and the normal order quantity was 500 feet. As the work orders were received, three purchase orders for that quantity were issued. Normal delivery time per order is about 2½ weeks. Two shipments of 500 feet each were expected by the end of the month, and 500 feet by the tenth of November.

Two weeks after the orders were in the house, the production manager stopped the purchasing manager in a hall. "Look," he said, "I have people sitting around out there in the shop twiddling their thumbs. I want to get to work on these Consolidated Food orders right now, then hold the units for final assembly. But we're all held up because you haven't gotten us enough stainless tubing. What kind of a deal is this?" The purchasing manager answered that his figures indicated that there was enough reserve stock on hand. They checked the situation together.

They found that on the first of October there were 1,100 feet of tubing on hand, but all of it was allocated to other orders. In fact, total allocation amounted to 1,550 feet; but, against this additional requirement, two orders of 500 feet each had been placed in September for early October delivery. Total supply on hand and on order was, therefore, 2,100, or 550 feet more than was needed at that time. The average unit of demand, or quantity called for on a single work order, was 450 feet. On the basis of annual usage of 10,000 feet, usage during the lead time of 2½ weeks would amount to 500 feet. Looking at it either way, the purchasing manager said, there was ample safety stock on hand.

He pointed out that the orders for the October jobs would add another 300 feet to the reserve, making it 850 feet in all. This, he said, was almost equal to a full month's normal usage, 70 percent over average usage during a lead-time period, and almost two average unit demands.

The production manager wanted tubing, not explanations. The fact remained that there was not enough in stock for his immediate need, despite the theoretical reserve. He rejected the purchasing manager's reasoning that the safety factor had been appreciably increased by the three latest orders. A reserve equal to "almost two" unit demands still covers only one demand adequately, he argued, so the situation was really no better than before.

He held that stock policy must be set in the stores department and not as a corollary to purchasing policy, that it must be measured in terms of actual physical, unallocated stock, not in purchase commitments, and that the predetermined minimum stock quantity should have as much force in initiating a purchase for replenishment as a work order or a requisition for actual use.

"The trouble with your system," he said, "is that you really make no provision at all for safety stock. When these new deliveries come in, you will claim to show a reserve of 850 feet of tubing, but it will actually be working inventory, not reserve. Your stock clerk will allocate it against the next order. You won't know about it, and won't buy again until he has too little on hand to fill an order. In other words, there is no safety factor at all—only a succession of stockout failures, which you may or may not be lucky enough to cover up before they become production failures."

The purchasing manager defended his policy on the ground that the determination of best ordering quantities necessarily took inventory needs and costs into consideration; that minimum stock quantities would have to be calculated as a function of lead time and usage, which were inherent in the purchasing formula; and that any scientific method (that is, formula) must be based on averages, particularly average usage, and not on exceptional rates of usage such as those experienced in the October orders.

The production manager disagreed on two basic points. In his opinion, lead time was wholly irrelevant to the size of safety stock, being of concern only as a matter of procurement in the timing and size of purchase orders. Second, he said, average usage broken down to anything less than the full-year period was mathematically bound to be wrong as often as it was right; the only dependable criterion for safety in stock was maximum demand or usage within the shorter period.

Is the production manager justified in his emphasis on the importance of having inventory in advance of need? What would be the effect of his proposals on the size and cost of inventory? What could he do specifically to help purchasing provide better service on materials?

Does the purchasing manager give enough importance to a safety factor in inventory? Does the reserve stock that he cites actually constitute a safety stock, or is it working inventory, as the production manager charges? Stock items are consistently purchased in quantities greater than the immediate need; is this a good policy? How could it be improved? Because the purchasing manager is in charge of inventory and stores, what factors other than stockouts must he consider?

Does the purchasing agent place too much reliance on order quantity tables as a means of solving inventory problems? Is he making proper use of the order quantity formula? What elements in the T&H operation tend to limit the effectiveness of this method?

Does purchasing lead time have any significance in respect to safety stocks? Can purchasing and inventory policies be separately determined? Is average usage an adequate guide to the amount of protective stock needed?

Chapter 11

Joseph's Colorants, Inc.

Polysil represents a substantial part of the end product cost of an item made by Joseph's Colorants, Inc. and sold to the tobacco, packaging, and toy industries. Polysil is a specialty raw material with high research and development and technical service costs and a high profit margin. It is a trade-name item, generically no different from the product sold by other producers and is a member of a broad family of products that have FDA approval.

Joseph's, using about a million pounds a year, is one of the three or four large buyers of Polysil. Joseph's prime concerns in respect to its end product are color stability, gloss, and resistance to abrasion. Sacrifice of any of these characteristics for a saving in the cost of Polysil, or any other intermediate advantage, would endanger the company's market position.

The price of Polysil is firm at 25 cents per pound, delivered in 30,000-pound truckload lots in nonreturnable polyethylene lined drums (550 pounds net per drum). Historically, the material, which is very hydroscopic, has been delivered in sealed, vacuum-packed, open-head drums, rather than in bulk.

Joseph's plant is in South Chicago and is supplied by two vendors: Alpha Chemical in St. Louis and Gamma Chemical in Cincinnati. Joseph's has excellent transportation facilities, including a rail siding, and it ships to its own customers by common carrier. Both suppliers have warehouses in the Chicago area.

Senior Buyer Jim Sands and Chief Engineer Tolley Nettles were discussing raw material requirements one day.

"It's tough making projections on a multifunctional product like Polysil," said Sands, "but obviously our sales volume looks as though it's going to increase rapidly and we're going to need a lot of that stuff. But that sales increase will be based on our ability to stay competitive. Sunrise Chemicals for one is going to give us a real run for our money from now on. So that means we've got to get better value on our Polysil buys."

Nettles agreed. "But where do we get it?" he asked. "Any real price reduction is out—that's a high-risk item, and both Alpha and Gamma have got to cover their investments. We've run cost estimates on them a number of times, as you know, and they don't have much room to maneuver. And we don't want to fool with quality, although we might be able to ease up somewhat on specifications. Packaging might be an area in which we could do something, but I don't know. We're probably paying well for those drums—yet we can't afford to have that stuff kicked around by some of the help we've got to live with these days. Let some of that material get contaminated, and we're in trouble."

"I think we ought to call Gamma's people in and talk to them," said Sands. "They've been cooperative in the past, and they should be able to come up with some ideas. There are a number of possibilities for better value—in specs, packaging, transportation, receiving, storing—all kinds of things. Why don't we ask them in and go over some of these points? Tell them we want ideas—real ideas—that we can really dollarize."

Four producers share a total market of approximately 40 million pounds as follows:

Alpha—50 percent
Gamma—25 percent
Beta—15 percent
Delta—10 percent

Joseph's business (a million pounds annually) is split two ways:

Alpha—60 percent
Gamma—40 percent

Engineering studies have shown that bulk delivery of Polysil is practical, with a 10 percent reduction in price as a feasible goal. However, the initial investment in a receiving and handling facility would be about $200,000, preferably borne by the supplier.

Joseph's long-range goal is a 15 percent increase in net sales. Their colorants are presently attractively priced at $8.00 per gallon and are still finding new uses.

Sands knows that Gamma is capable of handling all his company's requirements for Polysil with the same high standards of quality and service that they are now providing. He is willing to switch a substantial part of his business to either supplier on the basis of an attractive reduction in total cost. He decides to approach Gamma first.

Assuming that you are Sands, discuss the strategy and tactics you will use to achieve your company's objectives. Describe in detail your approach to getting "better value on your Polysil buys."

Chapter 12

Hawley & Brothers

After several years of pleasant but in many ways frustrating experience as purchasing manager for Hawley & Brothers, Dan Dinnock was getting restless. He had no complaints about his personal treatment from the company, an old, conservative manufacturer of toys and games. But the management was strictly engineering oriented and gave other departments, including purchasing, very little chance to use initiative, to innovate, or to depart very far from established ways of doing things. Mr. Dinnock, who made it a point to stay abreast of the latest procurement techniques through reading in trade magazines and attending educational sessions of his local purchasing association, felt stifled every time one of his suggestions for improvement was politely rebuffed.

He took a new lease on life, however, when Hawley & Brothers bought out a small firm, in the same city, that made baby furniture, wagons, and bicycles. His department was given a bigger buying job (the smaller firm's purchasing had been done by the two partners), and he gladly accepted the challenge of increased responsibility. The very fact that Hawley & Brothers was expanding, he reasoned, indicated that management might be more receptive to new ideas than they had been in the past.

One of the new concepts in purchasing that intrigued Mr. Dinnock was value analysis. Here, he thought, was a technique that could help make purchasing a scientific, profit-producing function. Still a little gun shy from previous resistance to his suggestions by management, he determined to build a strong case for value analysis—prove its worth beyond doubt—before proposing the idea of a formal value analysis program to his superiors.

Without mentioning it outside his department, he set up a small, informal value analysis program with his buyers. They met once every week, for two hours on Friday afternoon, to review components that they purchased for both divisions of the company. They submitted each of the parts selected for analysis to the "Ten Tests for Value" made famous by the General Electric Company. When a promising project appeared to be developing, one person was given the job of accumulating cost data on the part, estimating savings through substitution, capabilities of various vendors of the part, projected savings over a given period, and similar data. This extra activity was burdensome in terms of time and effort, but the entire group was enthusiastic about its possibilities.

After half a dozen inconclusive meetings, the group finally came up with a project that showed promise. Studying the function of four threaded rods used on a line of express wagons, they questioned the special design of the rod and the fact that the thread was cut on a screw machine. Buyer Jack Bolton, follow-up man on this project, ultimately came up with the following information:

> The holding function of the rod was not critical, could just as easily be performed if the thread were rolled (a much cheaper process than screw machining). The special bend in the rod had been designed in during the manufacture of an earlier-model wagon, was no longer necessary in the current streamlined design. A standard rod widely used in the automotive industry would do the job just as well. A specialty supplier, now making similar parts, could supply the rolled-thread, standard rods to Hawley & Brothers for approximately eight cents each. The company was currently paying forty cents each for the specially designed part.

In his enthusiasm over coming up with a substantial potential saving, Mr. Dinnock lost some of his caution. He went directly to the president. "T.J.," he said, "just look at this. An 80 percent reduction in part cost on just this one item. And we use thousands of them. Our group came up with this almost in their spare time. Think what we could do with a real value analysis program—with a full-time value analyst." He went on to explain the basic principles of the technique.

The president listened attentively and complimented the purchasing manager on an excellent "cost-reduction suggestion." But he seemed unimpressed by Mr. Dinnock's proposal to establish a formal value analysis program. "Our engineers will get around to these things eventually," he said, apparently assuming that the products of the toy and game division were already so well engineered that value analysis of them was unnecessary. "You can be a good stimulus to them by this approach—which is really only good buying to begin with, isn't it? Go and talk to the engineers about what you're doing, and the two of you can probably work out a good cost-reduction program."

Mr. Dinnock quickly realized that he had made a mistake. "Should have value-analyzed my own approach to value analysis," he ruefully told his buyers at their next meeting. They took him literally and began to suggest alternative approaches. Among their suggestions were these:

> Develop and document more than one value analysis project and present them as a "package" to the president, detailing in dollar figures the total savings to be achieved in one year.
> Present savings on a given product—the express wagon, for example—in

cumulative form and show, if possible, their effects on the profit margin on that product. Or, if the product is a highly competitive one, show how value analysis savings would make more competitive pricing possible.

Using the kind of figures developed above, make a formal presentation to the president, asking for an organized value analysis program in the plant. Show the potential "payoff" on value analysis as compared with the cost of setting up a value analysis organization.

Alternatively, suggest that purchasing be allowed to "borrow" an engineer from design engineering for a few half-days a week to work on value analysis projects developed in conjunction with buyers and vendors.

Go around management for the time being, and try to expand the informal program by bringing the production and engineering departments into it. Later, with concrete results obtained by this method, present a united front to management and ask for a formal value analysis program.

Was Mr. Dinnock's initial "secret" approach to value analysis sound? How else might he have run his campaign to get a value analysis program going? Wouldn't engineers consider purchasing's efforts at value analysis interference in their affairs? Do you agree with Mr. Dinnock's own estimate that he had "made a mistake" in taking his first value analysis project to the president? Explain.

Would you agree that the president's reaction is fairly common in industry? How much justification is there for it? Which of the alternative approaches suggested would you support? Discuss.

Chapter 13

Dubin Corporation

After many successful years in the electrical contracting field, the Dubin Corporation decided to go into the business of manufacturing and installing air diffusers in commercial and industrial buildings. The move was logical in view of the company's long experience in the fabrication and installation of electrical systems. Production problems would be few because of the relative simplicity of the product. Procurement could be handled by an expansion of the present buying department, which already had considerable experience with many components similar to those used in the ventilating system—sheet metal, ducting, fasteners, and so forth. Art Berlin, who had been Dubin's purchasing manager, was named director of purchases and given responsibility for getting the new division's purchasing program under way immediately.

Dubin Corporation's shop force was also expanded to handle assembly and installation of the diffusers. Several experienced machine operators and an additional foreman were added, all under the supervision of Ed Anderson, general superintendent.

Because of its early establishment in the industrial area in which it was operated, the high quality of its work, and its record of on-time performance, Dubin Corporation had had little effective competition in the electrical field. As a result, the purchasing department, although not indifferent to price, had concentrated on quality and assurance of prompt delivery in dealing with vendors. Prospects for competition in the air distribution field were different, however, both from equipment manufacturers and from contractors already well established.

Berlin took personal charge of establishing new supply sources for major items that the company had not previously bought. The most important of these were the production stampings used in the diffusion unit placed in the ceilings of buildings. Special requirements called for in specifications for stampings included smoothness and cleanliness to expedite further finishing in the Dubin plant, and close adherence to tolerances to permit tight fit in installation. Berlin had had no buying experience with stampings of this type and determined to make a careful study of suppliers before making any major commitment.

Berlin also had a number of disucssions with Anderson, with whom he had had an excellent relationship for a number of years. Both were aware of their limited experience with the special type of stampings to be bought for the new line, and agreed that they would, at least initially, depend heavily on vendors for advice and assistance.

After a concentrated study of the technical aspects of stamping (including an analysis of the components of a competitor's unit), Berlin began calling in suppliers. Several of them were helpful in offering suggestions when Berlin frankly told them of his lack of experience. Berlin reviewed the quotations of about six of the suppliers, considered their willingness to offer technical advice and service, and decided to narrow the field to three. The bids were not far apart, and all were within reasonable competitive range.

Following his custom with major suppliers to the electrical division, Berlin decided to visit each of the three stamping plants, in company with the superintendent and the new foreman. Because he wished to see the plants in normal operation, Berlin made arrangements for his visits by telephone, only one day in advance. This, he felt, would give the suppliers little or no time to cover up major deficiencies in their facilities. None of the three companies seemed to resent this tactic, however, and all welcomed his visits.

Berlin was somewhat surprised on his visit to company A, acknowledged as one of the leaders in the field, to find a rather old building and a number of old presses among the many new machines. Building and machines were, however, clean and well kept and, despite obvious high production, there were no signs of sloppiness, poor maintenance, or slowdowns because of inefficient equipment. During the tour of the plant, the company's sales engineer was joined by two men from the technical staff. They pointed out new deep-drawing equipment that produced better finishes on the stampings and an elaborate inspection setup for controlling quality. Throughout, they demonstrated an alert, progressive attitude and an interest in helping Dubin with its technical and procurement problems. Company A's bid was slightly higher than those of the other two suppliers.

Company B was in a brand-new plant, laid out for straight-line production. It was clean, well lighted, and almost completely equipped with new presses and other machinery. Berlin noticed that it apparently was not operating at full capacity. He was impressed by the skill of the machine operators and foremen and their willingness and ability to answer his and the superintendent's technical questions promptly. Company B's purchasing manager was in the executive group that welcomed Berlin. He showed them the equipment that would be used on Dubin's order if the business were placed with his company. Just before the entire party was ready to leave for lunch at a nearby restaurant, the purchasing manager asked Berlin and the superintendent to examine the raw material stockroom. It was spacious, well stocked, and well equipped with a variety of materials-handling devices. A carload of steel sheet was being unloaded at the time, and he showed them the receiving procedure, which included sampling for standard acceptance tests applied to each lot.

Company C was the low bidder. It had a mixture of both old and new equipment, all of which appeared to be working at top speed. Both men and materials seemed to be moving at a very rapid pace, and the foreman who took the party through was polite but preoccupied. Several times he was called away to answer telephone calls or to discuss various matters with machine operators. He did, however, spend a good deal of time explaining the company's inspection and quality control procedure, a feature of which was 100 percent inspection of all parts. At the end of the tour, he turned Berlin and the superintendent over to the general manager, who invited them out to lunch.

Do you think Berlin's approach to selection of suppliers was adequate, considering the nature of Dubin Corporation's problem? What other steps might he have taken before visiting the three stamping plants? What do you think of his technique of visiting plants with only short notice?

Based on the plant inspections, which company would seem to be the most desirable supplier in the long run, bearing in mind the price differentials?

Would the director of purchases and the superintendent agree in their judgments of the supplying companies? What factors would most strongly influence the decision of each? Would you have added anyone else in the Dubin Corporation to the inspecting team?

Chapter 14

Bristol Motors Corporation

Bristol Motors Corporation is a relatively small but well-known auto manufacturer that specializes in the production of taxicabs, airport limousines, ambulances, and light commercial vehicles. It has also managed to sell several thousand passenger automobiles annually, despite the formidable competition of the Big Three and other auto makers.

In the small but enthusiastic market for Bristol cars, the company has a reputation for making a high-quality product.

Bristol buys a higher percentage of auto parts than its bigger, more integrated competitors. To stay competitive in respect both to quality and price, it has leaned heavily on suppliers for technical assistance and competitive prices. To attract vendors to the Bristol business, in turn, the company has standardized on many engine and chassis parts (and to a lesser degree on body parts because of the number of styles it produces). This enables it to combine requirements into sizable orders that will command a volume discount.

Bristol's purchasing department enjoys an excellent reputation among auto parts suppliers. Although purchasing alone selects vendors, their representatives are given every opportunity to visit and consult with engineering and production personnel. This policy works to the advantage of Bristol as well, because it is so dependent on suppliers for new ideas and technical advice. Suppliers, in fact, provide much of the engineering talent that Bristol, unlike its big competitors, simply cannot afford.

The director of purchases and his staff have always prided themselves on being fair with suppliers—respecting their right to make a "fair" profit; giving sales personnel explanations of why they didn't get, or lost, Bristol business; refusing to play one supplier against another by requesting vendors to quote a second time after competitive bids have been received.

Purchasing had relied largely on the competitive bid system in getting prices on standard parts for a number of years. Its buyers were veterans in the automotive industry and had a good basic knowledge of markets and a general idea of what other auto makers were paying for the same or similar parts. Both they and the director of purchases felt that if they were generally in the same price area as their large competitors they were doing well. In recent years, however, the purchasing group had cause to doubt the wisdom of relying so extensively on the competitive bid system.

"Even though the auto market is booming," the director of purchases, Steve Brown, told his buyers at a weekly meeting, "we're under tougher competitive fire than ever before. The big boys have held the price line, so we have to also. Yet our costs keep climbing and climbing. We can't be sure any more that we're getting the lowest possible prices through competitive quotations."

Vendors' bids were creeping higher and the number of requests for price increases on current contracts was growing, he pointed out. He added that this was the classic reaction to a rising market, particularly from vendors who had a good backlog of orders.

"We've got to learn to say 'no'," the director of purchases told his buyers, and he called for less reliance on competitive quotes and more on negotiation, coupled with cost analysis. His new policy was put to the test shortly thereafter, when Bristol's main supplier of camshafts came in with a request for a 5 percent increase, based on increased material and labor costs. The vendor, Global Parts Company, had obtained the business six months earlier on a low bid, winning out over two other suppliers.

The director of purchases and the buyer, Ned Dillon, agreed to resist the requested increase by calling for negotiation. They invited the local representative and the regional sales manager in for a discussion. Before the meeting took place, Dillon called on Bristol's cost estimating group for help in analyzing Global's costs and possible justification for a 5 percent increase. The cost estimators studied the raw material content of the camshaft Global supplied, the machining operations and amount of labor they required, the probable overhead, and general and administrative costs. The director of purchases and the buyer applied Bristol's usual "fair profit" formula and concluded that the supplier was entitled to no more than a 4 percent increase, and possibly less.

In preparation for the negotiation, the buyer and the director of purchases agreed to ask a cost estimator to sit in on the session and briefed him on the overall strategy. "I think we can hold this guy to 2 or 3 percent," the director of purchases said, "although if we can send him away with nothing, so much the better. We might be able to get our requirements from the Crown Company at the current price, but you know the delivery problems we had with them a couple of years ago. Global has been doing a good job for us, and I think we need him as much as he needs us, so we've got to be flexible."

"Maybe so," replied Dillon, "but I have a hunch Global doesn't have all the business it would like to have in the shop right now. Even though it's trying to raise the price, I think it's a little hungry. Anyway, we ought to try to find out. We can do a little probing as we go along."

The negotiating team of Brown, Dillon, and the cost estimator went through a "dry run" an hour before the supplier's team arrived, concentrating on their estimates of the vendor's costs. Brown instructed Dillon to lead the discussion and call on him only when larger matters of policy came up. He urged both the buyer and the estimator to take every opportunity to put the supplier's representatives on the defensive.

After a detailed discussion on raw material, manufacturing and tooling costs, labor rates, overhead, and so forth, the supplier admitted that the price increase he was asking may have been "rounded out to about 5 percent." He agreed that any new price for the camshafts should include only added metal costs, added labor costs, and the profit related to these costs—but should not include additional profit on tooling, overhead, and administrative costs.

Global's regional sales manager said that he would be willing to go along with a 3 percent increase on the basis of the more precise costing carried out by Bristol's estimators. At that point, one of the estimators turned to Dillon and said, unexpectedly, "One of your other suppliers was ready to come in lower than that, wasn't he?" The buyer, aware that the statement was based more on conjecture than on fact, looked embarrassed, hesitated and then said, "Yes, but we've got to go over his costs again." He then returned to the discussion of Global's costs.

At this point, the supplier's representative asked for a recess. After consulting with the other members of his team, he opened the second session with a proposal that Global be relieved of responsibility for quality control. Under a plan developed a few years before, Global inspected Bristol's parts before they were shipped, then certified that they met quality standards. Its quality report showed the quantity of the lot shipped, date of inspection, size of sample, acceptable quality level, number of rejects, and related information. "If you can take this job off our shoulders," Global's sales manager said, "we can hold the increase to 2 percent."

The proposal obviously caught the Bristol group short, and the

Global sales manager quickly followed up with the statement that he could give the group an accurate figure on inspection costs then and there. So there would be no reason, he added, to recess. "It's a good deal all around," he said, "inspection costs run a little less than 1 percent of the price of each unit. Shall we go ahead?"

Was the Bristol purchasing department's planning for this negotiation adequate? Why?

Was Brown acting correctly in having the buyer lead the negotiation session? Evaluate his instructions to the buyer and estimator on tactics to use. Do you think the instructions reflect Bristol's traditional attitudes toward vendors? Why?

Was the estimator being ethical when he made the remark about another supplier being "ready to come in" at a lower price? What do you think of Brown's handling of that part of the discussion?

What do you think Brown's next move should be? Give your reasons.

Chapter 15

Auxiliary Coating Company

The Auxiliary Coating Company uses Solvosol, a flammable water-soluble commodity chemical, in several of its products. The primary use is in a trade specialty called Stripeeze, a paint, varnish, and lacquer remover.

There are five producers of Solvosol, but three of them share in about 85 percent of the market. These three also share equally in Auxiliary Coating's annual requirement of 3.6 million pounds. The producers are The Finesse Company, Continental Reactants, Inc. and the Specialty Commodity Corp. Finesse is located in Baton Rouge, La.; Continental in Bayonne, N.J.; and Specialty in Chicago, Ill.

Auxiliary Coating has three plant locations: Washington, D.C.; Cleveland, O.; and Pensacola, Fla.

Solvosol is currently priced at 15 cents per pound, freight allowed.

Expansion plans of the three dominant producers and an announced joint venture that will result in a new producer, Bi-Products Company, with a capability of producing 100 million pounds in two years, interested Auxiliary's purchasing manager, Colin Pearson.

"The current market in this stuff is balanced with an overall demand of about 450–500 million pounds," he said to his senior buyer, Raymond Paul. "I think when this new facility comes on stream, we'll see the price coming down. That should be within the next two years."

Auxiliary Coating buys Solvosol in 10,000-gallon tank cars and 5,000-gallon tank trucks. Auxiliary Coating presently purchases its requirement by plant location as follows:

	Washington, D.C.	Cleveland, Ohio	Pensacola, Florida
Finesse Co.	300,000	300,000	600,000
Continental	600,000	300,000	300,000
Specialty	300,000	600,000	300,000

"We've had no specific offer from Bi-Products," Pearson told Paul. "But they are talking about prices in the range of 12 cents a pound within 18 to 24 months. We've been getting mixed reports about them, some good, some bad. Our technical department for example is on the pessimistic side—they have some real doubts about the feasibility of Bi-Products' new process for producing Solvosol."

"We're under a lot of pressure," he continued. "More competitors have entered the market with products like our Stripeeze, and our marketing department is thinking of lowering the price on it. I don't think it's such a good idea—after all, Stripeeze is still the leader and still the best product on the market.

"But we'll go along, and try to get the raw material costs down this year. I'd even be willing to switch as much as two thirds of our requirements to one supplier if it could come up with a suitable incentive for us."

Auxiliary Coating's forecasts for the coming year indicate a usage of 4.0 million pounds of Solvosol; for the following year, 4.4 million pounds; the year after that 5.0 million pounds; and the following year, 5.4 million pounds.

All three suppliers of the product have been fairly equal in product quality, service, and price. Auxiliary Coating has split its business at each location to accommodate the suppliers' wishes of the largest share closest to their producing point.

The company, which has been producing Stripeeze, among other products, at all three locations, has been considering building a fourth plant in the Southwest or Far West. The market in that area has been growing steadily and presently accounts for about 15 percent of Stripeeze production. Most of this is supplied from the Pensacola and Cleveland plant.

Assume that you are the senior buyer, Raymond Paul. The purchasing manager has given you the job of analyzing your company's requirements for

Solvosol, current supply and price trends in the commodity, and the chances of negotiating more favorable contracts with one or more of your present suppliers. Draw up a set of recommendations covering a purchase plan for Solvosol for the next three years, including the negotiating strategy you suggest be used with the suppliers.

Chapter 16

Albree Motor Parts

The vice president of Albree Motor Parts was much impressed by the conveyor system in a new plant erected by one of its customers. The installation, he learned, had cost $110,000. It had been specially designed for that plant and was an integral part of the operating plan. The customer was well pleased with it. He had no breakdown of operating costs specifically applicable to this equipment but considered it the key to overall plant efficiency.

Materials handling was a major expense in Albree's own operation, amounting to nearly 30 percent of total manufacturing cost, or about $3 million a year. This included the movement of raw materials in and out of stores to the machines, and through several fabricating processes and delivery of fabricated parts to the production assembly line and then to finished stores. The plant was well laid out for sequence of operations and had been extensively mechanized; but, because the handling equipment had been acquired piecemeal as the company expanded and new needs arose, it was not completely coordinated. Considerable rehandling was required at and between work stations. By means of power-lift trucks, manual handling was kept at a minimum. Total investment in materials-handling equipment was carried on the company's books at the depreciated value of $130,000. Replacement cost at current prices was estimated at $300,000. There was $90,000 available in the capital equipment reserve account, accumulated on depreciation schedules.

The vice president sent the chief engineer and the general superintendent to inspect the installation at the customer's plant. At the same time, he asked Northeastern Equipment Company, makers of that equipment, to survey Albree's situation and make recommendations. Northeastern's proposal, after this study, was to retain about half the present equipment, with minor changes, replacing the rest with an overhead conveyor installation similar to the one that had appealed to the vice president in the first place, but tailored to Albree's special requirements. The cost was estimated at $140,000. It seemed probable that savings of double that amount would be effected in materials-handling costs each year. The superintendent felt that certain modifications and additions to this plan would be necessary to obtain maximum benefit. With these changes, $8,500 was added to the bid.

A conference was called, including the president, treasurer, and director of purchases, to consider the proposal. The discussion centered largely around the extra charge. The president and treasurer held the view that Northeastern, a specialist in the field, was best qualified to tell what was needed; they felt that only the original proposal should be considered. The superintendent contended that the problem at this point was to find the best possible solution to the materials-handling needs, and that those who were to use the equipment could make a practical contribution to that decision. It would still be possible to make any necessary compromise, for cost or any other reason, but it seemed more logical to him to have an optimum goal as the starting point. In the present instance, the indicated saving was more than ample to provide the complete installation.

The engineer agreed that the suggested changes were desirable, if not absolutely necessary, but recommended that cost studies be made to see whether the added investment would be justified economically. As a matter of fact, he pointed out, their cost information on the whole project was not only meager but hypothetical. It seemed fairly certain that substantial savings could be made, but he felt that these should be verified and calculated more accurately before the money was invested.

The director of purchases had two suggestions. He proposed, first, that Newell Company, which had installed most of the present conveyor equipment, should be asked for advice and costs of modernizing the existing installation, if possible, to achieve the same result. Second, he believed that competition should be invited to bid on systems comparable to Northeastern's so, that results and costs could be better evaluated. The engineer supported this view. The vice president was cool to both suggestions. As to the first, plant efficiency was already suffering from a patchwork policy on materials handling. As for alternative sources for new equipment, he had great confidence in Northeastern due to the installation he had inspected, and he felt under some obligation to that company on account of the survey they had made. The director of puchases felt no such obligation to Northeastern. He did feel a responsibility to his own company to explore the alternative posibilities. He could at least secure descriptive literature from a number of manufacturers, without committing the company in any way; if any of these products seemed appropriate, the group could then decide which manufacturers, if any, should be invited to make a proposal.

The chief engineer mentioned that he was planning to attend the annual Materials Handling Show in Cleveland some weeks hence. He suggested that the others also attend this exhibit to see at first hand what types of equipment were being shown and to judge how they might fit Albree's needs. The vice president, superintendent, and director of purchases also made the trip. They found several systems that were interesting, ranging all the way to full automation, and noted some new developments that could be incorporated to advantage in their own specification. By process of elimination, their preference was narrowed to two firms, Fitch Corporation and Merritt Conveyors, whose product was basically similar to Northeastern's. Bids were invited from each of these companies.

When these quotations were received, Albree had four proposals to consider:

Newell Company offered supplementary equipment amounting to $22,000, expanding the present installation to take care of increased volume, without any significant change in present methods or flow.

Northeastern, as previously noted, proposed to replace half the present equipment with a new overhead system that was considerably faster and more efficient. The cost was $148,500. The director of purchases believed that he would be able to dispose of the replaced equipment, within a reasonable time, for about $45,000, or 70 percent of its current book value.

Fitch's proposal was substantially the same as Northeastern's on a bid of $144,000.

Merritt bid on a completely new system, costing $275,000. Certain features of their equipment, they believed, were so far superior to the present installation that a fully integrated system would show much greater efficiency. In this case, the disposal of old equipment would bring up to $75,000.

In tabulating these several proposals, the director of purchases found it very difficult to evaluate relative performance and efficiency, because there was no direct factor of productivity that could be measured and applied against cost as in the case of production machinery. In consultation with the manufacturing and cost accounting departments, he listed three factors that might serve as useful indicators.

1. Direct maintenance charges of 5 percent annually on total cost of equipment.

2. Estimated savings in labor for materials-handling operations. With Newell's additional equipment, four of the present employees could be dispensed with or transferred to other duties. Northeastern's and Fitch's installations could be operated with nine fewer employees. Merritt's system, more completely mechanized and coordinated, would require fourteen fewer men than the present system.

3. As a measure of improvement in overall manufacturing efficiency and cost saving, a cost study was projected as accurately as possible for each of the proposed systems. Under present conditions, materials handling represented 30 percent of total manufacturing cost. With the additional Newell equipment, this would be reduced to 28 percent. With the Northeastern or Fitch equipment, it would be further reduced to 25 percent. With the completely new Merritt system, it would be only 22 percent.

The cost department further applied standard overhead and depreciation schedules for the new investment.

Technically, the engineer believed that any one of the four proposed systems would be adequate. In order of excellence of the completed installations planned, he rated them (1) Merritt, (2) Northeastern, (3) Fitch and (4) Newell. He stressed that this did not include any economic factors. It did give some weight to the newness of the equipment. This gave the edge to Merritt in the immediate evaluation, an advantage that might be modified if all bids contemplated a wholly new installation.

As a matter of personal preference, the vice president and superintendent were still favorably disposed toward Northeastern, largely on the basis of the successful installation they had inspected.

Evaluate the four proposals on the basis of information gathered and judgments expressed. Which factors should prevail in the final decision—management's concern with capital expenditure, the superintendent's preference as user of the equipment, the engineer's technical appraisal, or the purchasing director's economic analysis? How, and by whom, should the final decision be made?

Could the problem be solved more expeditiously, and just as competently, without the conference method? Should the director of purchases have been called into conference at an earlier stage of the project, that is, before Northeastern's original proposal was invited and received? The vice president and superintendent retained their original preference for Northeastern's equipment in spite of the elaborate studies; what are the advantages, if any, in making this additional investigation?

Chapter 17

Customcraft Associates

Customcraft Associates, designers and manufacturers of expensive, custom-built office furniture—desks, chairs, tables, cabinets, and the like—has an annual volume of about $21 million, and sales are increasing an average of 10 percent yearly. The company's products are sold and bought strictly as luxury items, so that the question of cost is secondary to the skill and reputation of its internationally known designers. The furniture is sold throughout the United States and Canada, but it goes primarily to such large cities as San Francisco, New York, Denver, Chicago, Pittsburgh, Toronto, Montreal, and Atlanta.

The company is located in a small town about 40 miles north of San Francisco, where Junius Dolp, founder, president, and major stockholder, first established himself as a cabinetmaker. Ambitious and acquisitive, as well as artistic, Dolp started the business about a dozen years ago with the help of some private investors, who now own about one third of the company's stock.

Buying for the company is under the general supervision of Chris McTiernan, manager of manufacturing and purchasing. Dolp, however, does most of the buying of the major raw material, hardwoods. He negotiates annual contracts with brokers for domestic birch and cherry, imported teak, and walnut and mahogany. Releases against these contracts are issued by McTiernan. Dolp also insists, almost obsessively, on getting involved in the purchase of packaging and protective materials used on outbound shipments of Customcraft furniture. McTiernan, who had had wide experience in general industry before joining Customcraft, respected Dolp's expertise in lumber purchasing but felt that he was unnecessarily extravagant in his selection of packaging materials. "Looking at some of that material, Junius," he once remarked, "people would think you were shipping the Mona Lisa back to the Louvre." "Well," Dolp replied, "at times I have been referred to as the Da Vinci of furniture designers."

Requisitioning and buying of components was done somewhat informally. Requests for purchase were initiated by both McTiernan and the chief designer, Maurice Ratelle. Theoretically, all requisitions should have been approved by McTiernan, but he did not object to Ratelle's sending an occasional one directly to Michael Todd, who was responsible for preparing and placing all purchase orders.

Todd, a young college graduate with a degree in business administration, was actually hired for a position in the accounting department but had picked up a grab bag of duties in his two years with Customcraft. In addition to his accounting tasks, he was responsible for processing purchase orders, as mentioned, and for handling all administrative details of Customcraft's shipments to customers. Because of his heavy work load, Todd's effort in the last two areas were primarily clerical; he had little time to negotiate with suppliers, much less to analyze and evaluate freight rates and charges, transportation modes, or specific carriers.

McTiernan's instincts and experience led him to feel that purchasing— of both materials and transportation — could be put on a more businesslike basis. He decided to broach the subject to Dolp but to do so somewhat indirectly by focusing first on transportation rather than the more sensitive area of purchasing.

Outbound shipments were almost exclusively handled by the San Francisco office of a coast-to-coast trucking company, with occasional orders picked up by local carriers for transport to San Francisco for transshipment either by rail or air.

Customcraft placed a relatively large number of small purchase orders, mainly with specialty vendors in the Chicago area, for customized laminations, quality hardware, trim, fasteners, drawer slides, and so on. Because of rush orders from customers, numerous design changes during the manufacturing process, and the generally erratic demand for components of custom-built products, a steady stream of small shipments—some times two or three a week from individual suppliers— arrived at the Customcraft plant. Because shipping instructions were generally limited to "ship best way" or " ship as soon as possible" (sometimes a combination of the two was used), the shipments came in by a variety of ways: via bus, truck, United Parcel Service, or U.S. mail and frequently by air freight.

McTiernan approached Dolp with the idea that an assistant, with purchasing and transportation responsibilities exclusively, be assigned. "We could get a little bit more organization in our buying," he said, "but I think the big advantage would be to give us a better handle on transportation costs."

Dolp demurred. "You have good control over purchasing now, Chris," he said, "and I don't see any great problems staring us in the face. As for transportation, it seems to me that we can't do much better than we're doing now. As I understand it, our suppliers ship F.O.B. the buyer's headquarters. It's easier all around. SpanAmerica Transit has been doing a good job for us for years, and I'm sure the price is right. Anyway, freight rates on the kind of luxury stuff we make are built right into prices. Our customers are not the kind that quibble over freight costs when they're spending a couple of thousand dollars on a desk. Why should we go to the trouble and expense of adding overhead when we are doing OK now?"

Dolp then reminded McTiernan that he and his wife were leaving on a long-planned around-the-world trip the following week. "Maybe I'll feel differently about it after I see how much it costs to move the two of us around the world," he said with a smile. "Let's talk about it when I get back."

During Dolp's absence McTiernan discussed his ideas with Todd, carefully avoiding any implication that Todd might be given the job if Dolp agreed that he should have an assistant. Todd said that he shared McTiernan's conviction that more clearly defined policies and procedures on purchasing and transportation would be in the company's best interests. Privately, he speculated that the change might be in his best interests, inasmuch as he had been handling many of the purchasing and shipping procedures up to now.

Assume that you are McTiernan and describe and explain the strategy you would use in an effort to convince Dolp of the soundness of your suggestions.

Chapter 18

Truetest, Inc.

Truetest, Inc., a manufacturer of sophisticated testing equipment, was founded in the mid-1970s by five former employees of a much larger California company that made similar products. The Truetest owners— two engineers, two marketing executives, and a production manager— established their business in Texas, where they felt that the oil, aircraft, and space industries—as well as industry in general—presented them with an unusual opportunity to prosper and grow.

They were correct and business moved ahead smartly in their first few years. But, along with increased sales came increased difficulties, in the form of service and quality problems with the suppliers of precision parts—particularly precision castings, which Truetest bought by the thousands. Parts suppliers in the area, most of them relatively new enterprises set up from five to ten years before Truetest, were hard put to keep up with demand in the rapidly expanding economy of the Southwest. They tended to favor their well-established customers in regard to service and technical assistance. Because of the critical nature and high prices of the parts that Truetest bought, Tom Whitnow, the owner who had overall supervision of manufacturing and purchasing, was uneasy over the relative indifference of local suppliers to quality problems that seemed to be arising more frequently.

Whitnow decided to discuss the situation with Mike Baumrose, whom the owners had hired away from the California company (where he had been a senior buyer) to become Truetest's purchasing manager. In the discussion Whitnow stressed the need for the company to develop more and better sources. Baumrose said that he had been in contact with a number of suppliers in other parts of the country but had not gotten much satisfaction. Prices were generally higher than what Truetest was paying, shipping costs could be considerable, and there was a surprising lack of interest in taking on a new account.

"I don't think we should stop there," he told Whitnow. "As soon as I get my desk cleared of some of this detail, I'm going to try to get a line on some foreign suppliers. I've heard that a representative of several Yugoslavian companies, including a couple that make the kinds of parts we need, has been very actively looking for business in this area. And he's apparently getting it. I thought I might call him in and talk with him."

Whitnow's eyes popped a bit. "Yugoslavia?" he said skeptically. "That's kind of way out, isn't it? I mean the idea of buying from some company we have never heard of—and a communist one at that. Do they really know anything about precision casting, for example? What would some of our customers around here think about our buying components in a place like Yugoslavia? And how would we pay people like that—in rubles or something?"

"Whoa," said Baumrose. "I haven't decided to buy anything. I just want to know how you feel about looking into the matter of buying overseas. We're actually in the middle of a world market, and we should be seeing what it has to offer us. In fact, we may be trying to *sell* in some of these countries before long if we keep growing the way we have up to now."

"Okay," said Whitnow, who was a reasonable, astute businessman despite his blustery manner. "Talk to the guy if you can locate him. But don't even hint at committing us to anything. Meanwhile, I'll discuss the idea with the others at our management meeting on Monday."

Baumrose called in the Yugoslav representative, Peter Pavelic, discussed Truetest's requirements with him in a general way, and asked for sales literature and some particulars on the two companies that Pavelic represented—Bosniatec and Kosovo Specialties. Baumrose was impressed by the sales literature and their list of European customers—including Saab of Sweden and Rolls-Royce of England.

Their discussion on prices was inconclusive; Pavelic was reluctant to be specific about them until sample parts could be sent back to Yugoslavia for study. He was most emphatic, however, that the companies that he represented could not only meet U.S. prices for many parts, but could also come in lower on some.

Baumrose declined to give him any sample parts, thanked him for the information he provided, and said he would get back to him after discussing their conversation with Truetest's top management some time during the next few weeks.

A couple of days later, Whitnow met Baumrose in the hallway and said, "The other fellows showed some interest in the idea of buying overseas. They'd like you to fill them in on things, including your talk with that guy from Yugoslavia. We'd like to get together with you in a day or two and get the whole picture. Can you meet with us in the conference room at ten-thirty on Friday?"

Although he hadn't expected to be asked to report so soon, Baumrose agreed to be there. His interview with Pavelic had further stimulated his interest in the possible use of foreign sources, and he had intended to do a more extended study of the subject. He felt, however, that he should not muff the present opportunity to (1) let the owners know that he was actively trying to help solve one of their pressing problems and (2) provide them with information that they would need to judge—if not make decisions on—various aspects of buying internationally, as it applied to Truetest.

Presumably, Baumrose would have about 10 or 15 minutes to give an informal report of the type that he had presented on similar occasions. If you were in his position, what points would you cover? Which, if any would you treat more extensively than the others? Describe how you would go about getting pertinent information in the limited time available to you. What suggestions or recommendations would you make to the owners at this time?

Chapter 19

Heights General Hospital

Rose Silver was for several years purchasing manager for a medium-sized electric cooking utensil company in New Jersey. In that position she was responsible for buying raw materials and components as well as maintenance, repair, and operating (MRO) supplies. She worked closely and harmoniously with engineering and production personnel and was respected for her competence and her ability to get along with people.

Although she did not make final decisions on prices and suppliers when machinery and equipment was being bought, Silver sat in on negotiations for such purchases. The negotiating teams in those instances usually comprised the manufacturing vice president (team leader), the engineering manager, the production manager, and herself. Although primarily an observer during the actual negotiations, she played a valuable role in the collection and coordination of data in the prenegotiation planning phase.

When her father died, Rose Silver felt compelled to return to her native Georgia to care for her mother. In her search for a position in the Atlanta area, she responded to an advertisement in the executive employment section of a local newspaper. Heights General Hospital, a 600-bed institution, the ad read, had an opening for a purchasing director with broad experience, not necessarily in the health care field, who had the potential to move up to the position of materials manager as the hospital implemented its plans for a major expansion of its facilities. The salary mentioned was in line with those offered for comparable industrial positions for shich she had been interviewed. Sensing the interesting career opportunities in the growing health care field, and attracted by the idea of being able to participate in a form of social service while earning a living, she applied for the job.

Ms. Silver had interviews at several levels of the hospital organization, including one with the purchasing manager, who was retiring after having served for many years in the receiving department, the stockroom, and finally the purchasing department. She had a particularly extensive discussion with Warrington Ranson, the hospital administrator, who seemed impressed by both her personal and professional qualifications. "We've got a lot of work ahead of us," he told her. "We need an aggressive, yet cooperative, purchasing executive who can bring a lot of expertise into this hospital. Our medical and technical people are tops in their professions. I want our administrative people to be equally good in their specialties."

One day, when she had been on the job for about six months, Rose Silver received an interoffice call from Dr. Earl Spiller, head of the radiology department. Dr. Spiller was a long-time member of the hospital's medical staff and had one of the highest incomes. In turn, his department generated substantial revenues for the hospital. The hospital, which owned the equipment that he used, paid him a minimum salary and a third of the gross earnings of the department. "Rosie" he said cheerily, "come up here right away, will you? And bring your order pad with you, please. " A bit stunned at first, Rose Silver attended to a couple of details and then went to Spiller's office.

He got right to the point. "I want you to order a Model L-971 high-intensity X-ray processor from New Age Radiology, Inc.," he said, glancing at papers on his desk. "The price is $21,700. I dealt with Elmer Jarvis, the New Age regional manager on this, so if you have any questions, take them up with him. OK?"

"Well, it's not really quite OK yet, Doctor," Silver replied. "There are a number of things about this purchase that I'd like to discuss with you. It just isn't good business to buy an expensive piece of equipment of this size without . . . ".

"Look, Rose," Spiller interrupted," in this department we're dealing with people's health—their lives, even—and we can't afford to go shopping around for the lowest bid. It's my responsibility to get the best thing for the job, and I want that machine. New Age is the only company capable of supplying the kind of equipment I need."

"I'm not questioning your judgment or your authority, Doctor," she said. "At this point, I'm not questioning the price you mentioned or even suggesting that we put the requirement out to bid. All I'm saying is that there are a number of aspects about a purchase like that where I can be helpful—and protect the interests of the hospital. There's shipping, contract terms . . .".

Spiller broke in again: "Rosie, Mr. Jarvis assured me that all those details will be taken care of. Look, I've got to get out of here in a few minutes to catch the plane to the Bahamas. Be a good girl and get that order moving immediately, please." With that he left the room.

Is there any justification for Dr. Spiller's circumventing normal purchasing procedures, selecting the supplier, and approving the price of the L-971 machine? Explain. What aspects of the purchase would come within Rose Silver's scope of responsibility in any case? What other hospital departments would be of assistance to her in ensuring that there would be no problems in ordering, receiving, and installing the machine? Beyond these details, how should Rose Silver proceed if she wants to meet the expectations of the administrator that she would bring "business expertise" to the job of buying for Heights General Hospital?

Chapter 20

Rumford Machine Company

After careful investigation of competing types of equipment, a committee that included representatives of purchasing, engineering, and production decided to buy a new multipurpose machine tool for the Rumford Machine Company. It was the latest model of a numerically controlled unit that could perform drilling, milling, and boring operations on a single piece in any sequence. The machine was manufactured by Bradley-Donald Machine Tool Company, a leader in the field and a supplier to Rumford on numerous occasions in the past.

During the negotiations for the equipment, in which all committee members participated, Rumford Company engineers had asked for several modifications on the machine to meet their particular problems. The supplier's technical representatives agreed that the changes could be made. The price finally agreed upon was $93,000, and the Bradley-Donald representatives were told they would receive a purchase order by mail.

The Rumford Company's purchasing manager asked his engineers to send him a detailed listing of the changes that they wanted made on Bradley-Donald's standard model of the machine. From this he had a set of specifications transcribed to the purchase order; then he issued the order carrying the price of $93,000 agreed on previously.

Within a few days, the Bradley-Donald Company acknowledged the order, but not on the copy of the Rumford Company purchase order designated for this purpose. Instead of his own acknowledgment form, the purchasing manager received Bradley-Donald Company's contract form. He examined the form closely and reviewed the clauses carefully with the company's legal department. They agreed that there was nothing inimical to Rumford's interests in the "fine print" on the contract order. The purchasing manager, however, was not satisfied with the simple statement that the contract called for "one Brad-O-Matic, Model 64, installed . . . $93,000." No mention of changes previously agreed to appeared on the form. He called Bradley-Donald's district sales manager in to discuss the matter.

The supplier's representative pointed out that is was customary for the company to acknowledge orders on that form—and, in fact, it had done so previously on orders from the Rumford Company.

When the purchasing manager objected to the fact that his original specifications were not included in the contract, the sales representative replied that he did not have authority to change the contract. But, he added, he would insert the words "Changes to come" beneath the model description and notify his home office that the order would be followed by a letter from the purchasing manager detailing the modifications to be made on the standard machine.

The purchasing manager agreed, and after the words had been inserted in the contract, both men initialed both copies. Before the day was out, the purchasing manager had sent a letter to the Bradley-Donald Company's home office specifying the changes to be made on the machine and mentioning the contract he had initialed.

In the final stages of the installation of the machine, the Rumford Company received an invoice for $101,500, covering "one Brad-O-Matic, Model 64" at $93,000 and additional charges of $8,500 for "modifications as per your letter." Just before he planned to call Bradley-Donald's sales office, the purchasing manager received an urgent call from the shop. The test runs on the machine were not up to expectations, and it was obvious that it could not meet the performance standards that the Rumford Company's engineers expected of it. They could get no satisfaction from the supplier's technical representatives, who said that there must have been some understanding as to the capabilities of the machine. They suggested that the matter be taken up with their district sales office and perhaps the company's home office.

The purchasing manager called the district office and protested to the manager. He asked for an immediate change in the invoice and adjustment of the machine to meet the Rumford Company's requirements. Following his call, he dictated a letter to the Bradley-Donald Company home office outlining the situation and making the demands.

The Bradley-Donald Company answered that the extra charge was justified because it covered instructions given after the contract had been signed for a standard machine. It claimed that the words "Changes to come" merely indicated that such instructions would follow but were not a part of the contract and were not included in the contract price. As to the performance of the equipment, they would be glad to continue giving technical assistance and advice at no cost, but would not be held to any warranties in the contract. The machine to which the warranties applied, they claimed, had been altered at the customer's instructions and to the customer's specification.

The Rumford Company refused to accept the machine, and the Bradley-Donald Company sued for the full amount of the invoice.

Who comes into court with the strongest case? Why? Analyze the mistakes in the Rumford Company's conduct of negotiation and contract procedure, pointing out how the company could have protected itself by alternative approaches.

Chapter 21

Dalton-Frankel Corporation

Dalton-Frankel Corporation is a large producer and marketer of building materials. Its products include asphalt tile, roofing paper and composition shingles, caulking compounds, wallboard, and insulation. The company is organized according to product divisions, with a strongly centralized administration, including finance and accounting, sales and advertising, and purchasing.

The company's policy has been to conduct its manufacturing operations in relatively small plants devoted to a single product, located individually in small and medium-sized companies throughout the territory that it serves. There are fourteen such plants in four adjoining middle western states. None of the product divisions or plans are dominant in their respective fields, but collectively they form a large and influential organization in the building materials sector. Similarly, the combined purchasing power is substantial, and centralized purchasing capitalizes on this fact. Despite the diversity of materials purchased, the company is able to deal to advantage with the larger companies among its supplier industries; it has, in fact, the status of a national account.

The reasons for decentralizing manufacturing operations in smaller cities are chiefly concerned with labor relations—a more stable labor supply, generally lower wage rates, better environment, and smaller employee groups. But there are also sales advantages. The scattered plants provide an opportunity to maintain good warehouse stocks of the entire line at strategic points throughout the company's marketing area. This in turn promotes the feeling among the building trades that Dalton-Frankel is essentially a local industry, even though a specific product of the company may be manufactured several hundred miles from the point of use.

With both these objectives in mind, Dalton-Frankel's management has developed an active program of local public relations, stressing community pride and service and participation in community affairs wherever its plants are located.

The director of public relations suggested to the purchasing manager that the company's purchasing policy was not consistent with the overall company program. He said that purchasing might be able to contribute a great deal to the effectiveness of the public relations efforts without compromising purchasing principles. Because the company was interested in the economic prosperity of the areas in which its plants were located, he pointed out, buying more from local sources would tend to create and stimulate markets for Dalton-Frankel products. While recognizing that a strict "buy at home" policy was probably impractical in respect to the various plants, he contended that diversified suppliers— including minority suppliers—could be found within the area as a whole, of a size and character to constitute satisfactory sources. This situation, he added, could be capitalized on to promote the public relations program.

Was the public relations director's suggestion sound and feasible? As a purchasing manager, how would you respond to such a proposal? What steps, if any, would you take before making a decision on the proposal?

Chapter 22

Beston Food Products Company

Carl Hopkins was in his second year as director of purchasing for Beston Foods, He had come to the company after eight years as purchasing manager of a division of a major steel company to succeed a man retiring from the post after thirty years' service. In his first year with the company, he had concentrated on improving his understanding of those areas of food industry purchasing for which his experience in heavy metals had not prepared him—primarily, the technical and commodity market phases. When he felt sufficiently grounded in the basics of these specialized areas, he began turning his attention to some of the broader phases of procurement common to all industries—including such aspects as administrative procedures, purchasing policies, vendor relations, and buyer training. He had had no other mandate from the food company management other than to see that the department was kept "up to date" and at a high level of efficiency.

In the process of reviewing procedures and policies in the Beston Company's purchasing manual, which had not been revised in several years, Hopkins came across a section that read:

> We believe that our vendors carry out their responsibilities to us when they provide us with good service and high quality at lowest possible cost. Any effort on their part to go further than this through the giving of gifts or gratuities is unnecessary and should be courteously but firmly discouraged.

The policy on gifts and gratuities in Hopkins' former company had been written at company headquarters and was much more precise and stronger. It had specifically forbidden any employee to accept gifts of any kind, other than advertising items, or to accept entertainment or lunches from suppliers. It pointed out that any employee accepting gifts was, at worst, involving himself or herself in commercial bribery and, at best, violating company policy. Mr. Hopkins had personally endorsed the policy, and he and his buyers scrupulously followed it.

Mr. Hopkins had no desire to try to force this stricter code on his new company, or even on the purchasing department. Yet he felt that there was an obvious contradiction between the Beston Company's policy and the practice of his department. During his first Christmas season with the company, he had seen a few gifts—a bottle of liquor, a box of cigars, and similar items—on his buyers' desks. He knew also that at least two buyers had attended Sunday World Series' games as guests of one of the Beston Company's best and most respected suppliers.

Mr. Hopkins decided to bring some consistency into the situation. He called his supervisory buyers together for a frank talk about this phase of vendor relations. To his surprise and gratification, they were not only glad to discuss the matter but indicated that they would welcome a more specific prohibition of gifts and entertainment. "They're more bother than they're worth" was the consensus; such gifts were accepted only to avoid embarrassing reputable vendors of standing. Several pointed out that they were aware of the statement in the manual but had never heard of anyone trying to implement it.

They agreed that a letter should go out over Mr. Hopkins' name to the Beston Company's entire vendor list, carefully explaining a new purchasing policy on gifts and gratuities and asking the recipients to refrain from offering them to members of the purchasing department. The following letter was prepared for mailing right after Thanksgiving:

> In recent years employees in our department have received Christmas gifts from some of our suppliers. They generally have been modest tokens of the esteem and friendship we know exist between our organization and those with whom we do business. We feel, however, that it would be in the best interests of all if we kept our relationships on a strictly business basis.
>
> We have therefore decided on a policy of not permitting any member of this department to accept personal gifts from any firm or individual doing business with our company. We sincerely hope you appreciate our position that quality, service, and price should be the only considerations in our buying.

Meanwhile, the Beston sales department was aggressively merchandising a new line of canned luxury foods—pate de foie gras, vichysoisse, smoked oysters, and similar delicacies. Pictures of the foods were displayed by the company's reception room and mentioned in a new "welcome booklet" for visiting sales representatives. A small selection of several items had even been mailed as a gift to all Beston Company stockholders at the end of the last fiscal year with a note encouraging them to recommend the delicacies to their friends.

During the fall season, the sales manager had what he considered a brilliant idea. Among the many reports run off on the company computer that were available to his office was one listing every supplier with whom the Beston Company was doing business, together with their addresses. Here, he reasoned, was a captive audience on which he could try a first-rate merchandising idea. Without informing the purchasing department, he sent a letter addressed to the sales manager of every Beston supplier during the first week of December. It read in part:

> During the coming holiday season, what better way could you find to express your gratitude to customers for their business during the past year

than with a gift of fine food? And what finer food is there than Beston's Gourmet Specialties . . . . Remember your special business friends with a boxed selection of Gourmet Specialties . . . Available beautifully gift wrapped in $10, $25, and $50 sizes . . . .

It did not take long for Mr. Hopkins to discover what had happened. Within a few days he had one mildly sarcastic letter from a supplier, containing copies of the letter on prohibiting Christmas gifts and the one promoting Beston products as gifts. Which one, he said in effect, am I supposed to believe? Mr. Hopkins, furious, went directly to the executive vice president and complained of the embarrassing situation he and the company had been put in. The executive vice president called in the sales manager, who seemed only slightly amused by the whole affair.

Was the director of purchasing justified in complaining? Had his approach to the problem of gifts been too arbitrary? Too naive? What other methods might he have used in establishing a no-gift policy that would have avoided the situation described above?

What do you think of the sales manager's tactics — were they businesslike, ethical? Do you think he should have had free access to the purchasing department's vendor lists? Why? Assuming that you were the executive vice-president, what actions would you take to solve the problem?

Chapter 23

Gunther Stove Company

The executive committee of Gunther Stove Company had designated Franklin Associates, a management consulting firm, to make a thorough study of the company's organization and procedures and to recommend any changes that might be made to improve efficiency. This was prompted not by any serious dissatisfaction with present performance, but to get the benefit of an expert, objective evaluation. The study was made in great detail, covering every department, using checklists and standards that the Franklin organization had developed for the purpose. When the data had been assembled and analyzed, Mr. Franklin presented his report to the committee. It was generally favorable, with a number of suggestions regarding each department designed to simplify or expedite the work. His recommendations concerning purchasing were to bring traffic control under the jurisdiction of this department; to add one buyer, preferably with engineering training; to set up a special fund that would permit the handling of small local orders on a petty cash basis, eliminating considerable paperwork on these dealings; and to transfer the checking of invoices to the accounting department, because he felt that no department should audit its own transactions.

"By the way," said Mr. Gunther, the company president, "how is our purchasing department doing? I've been in the management of this company forty years and I've never had a satisfactory answer to that question."

Mr. Franklin said that, in his judgment, the department was doing very well.

"How well?" Mr. Gunther persisted. "Would you rate it as 95 percent, 90 percent, 85 percent, or what?"

Mr. Franklin said that it was impossible to set objective standards of performance that would permit a rating of this sort. There were too many variables and intangibles involved. A rating depended, first, on what you expected and second, on whether that expectation was reasonable.

"But you must have some basis for saying that our buyers are doing a good job, and that's what I'm trying to get at. After all, purchasing is a pretty tangible business. We spend X number of dollars, and we buy X tons or carloads of iron and nickel and bolts and coal and shipping cases. What I want to know is whether we're getting full value for our dollars and whether it's costing us more than it should to buy those materials. I'm not interested in how many purchase orders we issue or how much we deduct in cash discounts. I'm interested in the quality of our buying performance and in results. What I'd like to see is a simple report, maybe six or eight really significant figures, that would give me the picture."

"I think we can get the figures for you," said Mr. Franklin. "You'd have to make your own evaluation, as we do. At the start I doubt that you could rate them any closer than *excellent, good,* or *fair.* After the first few months, when you have a chance to make comparisons, you may be able to apply some sort of scale—if you still think it's worthwhile."

Mr. Franklin went back to the purchasing manager, and together they worked out a report to give Mr. Gunther the information he wanted. Their first step was to define the areas of purchasing activity to be considered in an evaluation; the second step was to select measurable factors in each of these areas that were known or available from existing records and that would indicate to a significant extent the quality of performance and results obtained. The areas they decided on were:

1. Effectiveness of procurement as a service of supply
2. Price performance in buying

3. Cost reductions; specific savings
4. Inventory performance
5. Administrative performance, efficiency, cost of purchasing
6. Miscellaneous and intangibles

Under each of these headings they jotted down everything that came to mind pertinent to that area of activity and responsibility. Despite Mr. Gunther's aversion to statistical information, they found that much of the information was basically of this nature. However, the figures acquired more than statistical significance when they were related to other figures in the form of a ratio or as a proportion of the total; one of the problems was to find the appropriate standards of comparison and methods of presentation. Some of the factors were of a negative nature, inverse to the quality of purchasing performance; nevertheless, they were important in any complete evaluation. "We'll have to differentiate," said Mr. Franklin, "between those that are rated on a low score, as in golf, and those that are rated on a high score, as in bowling. If we get to the point of making a numerical rating, there are simple mathematical means to take care of this, but we'll run into the even tougher problem of assigning weights to the various factors."

The list of suggested possible indicators grew much longer than the half-dozen criteria that Mr. Gunther had requested, but this was a necessary preliminary to the process of selection. When they had finished, the following factors were noted on their worksheet:

1. *Service of Supply*

Number of delinquent deliveries

Machine downtime due to lack of material

Schedule revisions necessary due to lack of material

Successful substitutions made by purchasing department to avoid downtime or schedule revisions

Number of rush orders handled (proportion of total orders? of dollar volume?)

Number of change orders issued

Follow-up action (number of orders? cost of follow-up?)

Number and amount of premium transportation charges paid to get deliveries on time

Number of deliveries rejected by inspection department

Cost of reworking substandard materials

Number of overdue orders in open-order file

Commodities for which alternate supply sources have been established and used

2. *Price Performance*

Number of price changes, up or down, from previous prices paid

Number of orders placed on competitive bidding

Number of orders placed by negotiation

Commodities covered by term contracts (how long a term?)

Actual prices paid compared with published market (market at time of purchase or at time of use? should this be shown for individual key commodities, as currently kept in chart form in purchasing office, or could it be put in the form of comparative price indices?)

Inventory valuation, actual cost versus replacement cost

Variances from standard costs

Direct material cost per unit of product

Average cost of selected commodities, year to date and projected to annual average on the basis of current price

3. *Cost Savings*

Specific instances, savings projected on basis of annual usage, cumulative totals

Savings through change of source

Savings through change in method of buying

Savings by substitution

Savings by change in specification

Savings by standardization

Savings in transportation costs

Savings in manner of packaging

4. *Inventory Performance*

Ratio of dollar inventory to sales volume

Inventory increase or decrease during month

Extent of forward coverage (weeks)

Inventory turnover (by commodity classifications)

Number of items under maximum–minimum stock control

Number of stockouts

Quantity discounts earned by revision of stock limits

5. *Efficiency of Operation*

Total cost of purchasing related to dollar volume

Number of buyers

Number of nonbuying personnel (breakdown by functions)

Number of requisitions unprocessed within 24 hours

    Number of small orders ($50 and under)
    Cash discounts earned and forfeited
    Average waiting time for salesmen

6. *Miscellaneous*

    Sales of scrap and waste
    Hours spent in staff training courses
    Number of vendors' plants visited
    Business and professional meetings attended

"I have evaluated your department on a number of other intangible factors," Mr. Franklin said, "such things as morale, public relations, organization, supervision, and the like, as well as on adequacy of records and procedures. You'll hear about these when the general manager discusses my report with you and other department heads. There's no doubt that they have a distinct bearing on performance, and they are reflected in many of the items we have set down here. They are measurable, too, but not in the same sense as your specific activities. They are factors that you, as department head, should be evaluating for yourself, and on which top management will evaluate you. I have recommended a simple plan for doing this systematically and confidentially throughout all departments of the company."

Consider, first, the general areas selected for evaluation. Are they all pertinent? Are they all necessary for this purpose? What changes, if any, would you suggest in this approach? Should the various areas be weighted according to their relative importance? How? Should an effort be made to include the intangibles that Mr. Franklin has reserved for separate rating? Assuming that his proposal for a general evaluation system is adopted, would this obviate the need for, or reduce the usefulness of, the detailed evaluation of performance, which was not included in his original recommendation?

Consider the measurements suggested under each heading. Which of these are most significant? How should they be presented? Prepare an outline for a monthly performance report based on the selected factors.

Is Mr. Gunther unreasonable or impractical in asking for a mathematical rating of purchasing performance?

What advantages, if any, would accrue to the purchasing department from systematic evaluation?

Bibliography

GENERAL

Aljian, G.W., ed., *Purchasing Handbook* (3rd ed.). New York: Mc-Graw Hill Book Co., Inc., 1973.

Baily, Peter, and David Farmer, *Purchasing Principles and Technique* (3rd ed.). London: Pitman Publishing Limited, 1977.

Corey, E.R., *Procurement Management: Strategy, Organization and Decision Making.* Boston: CBI Publishing Co., 1978.

Dowst, S.R., *More Basics for Buyers,* Boston, C.B.I. Publishing Co. 1980.

England, Wilbur B. and Michiel R. Leenders, *Purchasing and Materials Management* (7th ed). Homewood, Ill., Richard D. Irwin, Inc., 1979.

Lee, Lamar Jr., and Donald W. Dobler, *Purchasing and Materials Management,* (3rd ed.). New York; McGraw-Hill Book Co., 1975.

Pooler, Victor H. Jr., *The Purchasing Man and His Job,* New York: American Management Associations, 1964.

Westing, J.H., I.V. Fine and G.J. Zenz, *Purchasing Management: Materials in Motion* (4th ed.). New York, John Wiley and Sons, 1976.

CHAPTERS 3-7

Ammer, Dean S., *Materials Management* (4th ed.). Homewood, Ill.: Richard D. Irwin, Inc., 1979.

Baker, J.R., et al, *Purchasing Factomatic.* Englewood Cliffs, NJ: Prentice-Hall, Inc., 1977.

Bierman, E.J., ed., *NAPM Certification Handbook.* New York: National Association of Purchasing Management, 1979.

Dowst, S.R., *Basics for Buyers: Principles and Procedures.* Boston: Cahners Books, 1971.

473

International Business Machines Corp., *Communications Oriented Production Information and Control Systems, Vols. 1-8.* New York, 1972.

Kudrna, D.A., *Purchasing Managers' Decision Handbook.* Boston: Cahners Books, 1975.

National Association of Purchasing Management, *Guide to Purchasing,* New York, 196 , plus periodic supplements.

Peckham, H.H., *Effective Materials Management.* Englewood Clifts, NJ: Prentice-Hall, Inc. 1972.

Willets, W.E., *Fundamantals of Purchasing.* New York: Appleton-Century-Crofts. 1969.

CHAPTERS 8-15

DeRose, L.J. *How to Negotiate Purchase Prices.* Cambridge, MA: Management Center of Cambridge, 1970.

Grant, E.L. and R.S. Leavenworth, *Statistical Quality Control* (4th ed.) New York: McGraw Hill Book Co. 1972.

McDonald, Paul R., *Government Contracts and Subcontracts.* Glendora, CA: Procurement Associates, published annually.

Miles, Lawrence D., *Techniques of Value Analysis and Engineering,* New York: McGraw-Hill Book Co., 1972.

Orlicky, Joseph, *Materials Requirements Planning: The New Way of Life in Production and Inventory Management.* New York: McGraw-Hill Book Co., 1975.

Procurement Quality Assurance, Handbook H57, U.S. Department of Defense. Washington, D.C.: U.S. Superintendent of Documents, 1969.

Tersine, R.J., *Materials Management and Inventory Systems.* New York: Elsevier, North Holland, Inc., 1976.

CHAPTERS 16-19

Ammer, Dean. S., *Purchasing and Materials Management for Health Care Institutions.* Lexington, MA: Lexington Books, 1975.

Armed Services Procurement Regulations (ASPR). Washington, DC: Superintendent of Documents, published annually.

Combs, P.H., *Handbook of International Purchasing* (2nd ed.). Boston: Cahners Books, 1976.

Holmgren, J.H., *Purchasing for the Health Care Facility.* Minneapolis: Charles C. Thomas, 1975.

Housley, C.E., *Hospital Materials Management.* Germantown, MD: Aspen Systems Corp., 1978.

National Motor Freight Classification. Washington, DC: American Trucking Associations, published annually.

Report of the Commission on Government Procurement, Vols. 1-4, Washington, DC: Superintendent of Documents, 1972.

Ritterskamp, J.J., F.L. Abbott and Bert C. Ahrens, *Purchasing for Educational Institutions.* New York: Columbia University, Bureau of Publications, 1961.

Uniform Freight Classification. Chicago: Tariff Publishing Office, published periodically.

CHAPTERS 20-23

Garrett, T.M., *Business Ethics*. New York: Meredith Publishing Co., 1966.

Monczka, R., P. Carter and J. Hoagland, *Purchasing Performance: Measurements and Control*. East Lansing, MI: Michigan State University Business Studies, 1979.

Murray, J.E., *Murray on Contracts*. Pittsburgh: Purchasing Management Association of Pittsburgh, 1978.

Murray, J.E., *Purchasing and the Law*. Pittsburgh: Purchasing Management Association of Pittsburgh, 1973.

Index